STUDIES IN VICTORIAN LIFE
AND LITERATURE

GEORGE ELIOT'S SERIAL FICTION

Carol A. Martin

OHIO STATE UNIVERSITY PRESS
Columbus

Portions of chapter 5 appeared in different form as "Revising
Middlemarch," *Victorian Periodicals Review* 25 (1992): 72–78.

Library of Congress Cataloging-in-Publication Data
Martin, Carol A., 1941–
   George Eliot's serial fiction / Carol A. Martin.
      p.   cm. — (Studies in Victorian life and literature)
   Includes bibliographical references and index.
   ISBN 0–8142–0625–5
   1. Eliot, George, 1819–1880—Criticism and interpretation. 2. Serialized fiction—
England—History and criticism. I. Title. II. Series.
PR4688.M38   1994
823'.8—dc20
                                                                      93–34631
                                                                          CIP

Text and jacket design by Nighthawk Design.
Type set in Sabon and Galliard by Connell-Zeko Type & Graphics, Kansas City, MO.
Printed by Cushing-Malloy, Inc., Ann Arbor, MI.

9   8   7   6   5   4   3   2   1

To Lonnie Willis,
Anne Marie Mullaney,
and Matthew Mullaney

CONTENTS

ACKNOWLEDGMENTS

ACKNOWLEDGMENTS TO THOSE who made research for this book possible go to the National Endowment for the Humanities for the role its grants and programs have played in providing me opportunities for research and intellectual exchange with others fascinated by George Eliot and Victorian serialization. In particular I am grateful to Professor Jerome Beaty of Emory University, whose 1980 NEH seminar on George Eliot and the Victorian novel helped set me on the path toward this book. With many detours, the way led through two National Endowment for the Humanities Seminars for School Teachers, which I directed in 1987 and 1989. The participants in these seminars read with me the serial fiction of George Eliot and others and encouraged me by their lively discussion and enthusiasm. An NEH Institute at the Yale Center for British Art in 1991 enabled me to complete my research in the extensive collection of George Eliot–George Henry Lewes manuscript materials in the Beinecke Library; for this I thank British Art Center director Duncan Robinson and particularly institute professors Patrick Brantlinger and Anthony Wohl, whose formal presentations and informal conversation on matters Victorian provided stimulating advice and support.

I also thank Boise State University and the Office of Research Administration for grants that helped finance my research travel and provided funds for a research assistant for a year when administrative tasks threatened to postpone indefinitely the completion of this book. ORA associate director Larry Irvin has again and again given me help and advice on these grants.

I also owe a tremendous debt of gratitude to librarians at the British Museum, the Colindale Newspaper Library, the National Library of Scotland in Edinburgh, the Pierpont Morgan Library in New York City, and the Beinecke Library at Yale University for the gracious help I received during my visits, and to librarians and archivists at Harvard

University and the University of Texas for their patient long-distance help.

Among many supportive friends and colleagues in the BSU English department, I owe special thanks to my research assistant, Pam Peterson, and to Mike Markel, who both made invaluable suggestions on style and content. Pam's knowledge of Victorian fiction, her research skills, her sharp editing eye, and her unwillingness to let any fact go unverified or any possible error undetected cannot be acknowledged sufficiently. BSU librarians also provided invaluable assistance, particularly the interlibrary loan staff, Gwen Pittam, Carol Johnston, and Beverly Miller; Adrien Taylor, coordinator of reference services; and Gloria Ostrander-Dykstra, assistant director for technical services. I am also grateful to my former undergraduate and graduate student Heather Garonzik, now a doctoral candidate at Indiana University, who took time from her research and writing to read proofs of this work.

And most of all, I thank my family, to whom I dedicate this book—my husband, Lonnie Willis, and my children, Anne Marie Mullaney and Matthew Mullaney.

LIST OF ABBREVIATIONS

George Eliot's Novels:

AB	*Adam Bede*
DD	*Daniel Deronda*
FH	*Felix Holt*
M	*Middlemarch*
MF	*The Mill on the Floss*
SCL	*Scenes of Clerical Life*
SM	*Silas Marner*

Other Abbreviations:

BL	British Library
GE	George Eliot
GHL	George Henry Lewes
Maga	*Blackwood's Magazine*
NLS	National Library of Scotland

PRINCIPAL ARCHIVAL RESOURCES

British Library	Manuscripts for all of George Eliot's novels except for *Scenes of Clerical Life*
British Newspaper Library	Original newspapers from the nineteenth century
Beinecke Library, Yale	George Eliot and George Henry Lewes journals and diaries
National Library of Scotland	Manuscript letters in the Blackwood collection
Pierpoint Morgan Library	Manuscript of *Scenes of Clerical Life*

INTRODUCTION

G<small>EORGE</small> E<small>LIOT</small>'s is not the first name that Victorian scholars think of to head a list of serial novelists, and many general readers in the twentieth century are not even aware that she wrote installment fiction. Charles Dickens is more famous as a serializer and as the "inventor"—for the Victorians, at least—of publication in parts; he is known for writing up to his deadlines and paying close attention to public taste. Many readers are aware that he altered his ending for *Great Expectations* to anticipate audience response, and that the publication of *Pickwick Papers* and *Oliver Twist* was interrupted because he was too afflicted to write in the month following the death of Mary Hogarth. Thackeray and Trollope might come next on the general reader's list of installment writers, and some might also think of Wilkie Collins and Elizabeth Gaskell, perhaps for their contributions to Dickens's *Household Words* and *All the Year Round*. Collins's sensation novels and mysteries seem especially suited to the Victorian equivalent of the soap opera. Thomas Hardy's serial writing has received attention of a different kind, focusing on the differences between the volume editions of his later novels and the expurgated versions that appeared in late Victorian "family" periodicals. But George Eliot's slowly developing plots and strong emphasis on characterization make her seem an unlikely writer to have elected the serial route.

Even to her contemporaries George Eliot was different. She was the "philosophical novelist," the portrayer of character rather than plot, the author whose works contained numerous wise sayings. Simultaneously with the appearance of *Middlemarch*, Alexander Main compiled Eliot's sayings as *The Wise, Witty, and Tender Sayings of George Eliot*.[1] Yet, as her contemporaries also knew, George Eliot did write installment fiction. One-half of her full-length works were first published serially, including her first work and her two longest novels, *Middlemarch* and *Daniel Deronda*.

Like many Victorian fiction writers, Eliot got her start by serializing her first work in a popular, well-established periodical. "The Sad Fortunes of the Reverend Amos Barton" appeared in two installments of *Blackwood's Magazine* in January and February 1857. Magazine publication gave her the chance to "start small," and it also provided the anonymity Eliot needed, given two facts from her personal life likely to cause reviewers to prejudge her work: her gender and her status as an unmarried woman living with a married man, George Henry Lewes. This brief first story was greeted enthusiastically by her publisher, John Blackwood, and by other readers as the work of a new and original writer. "Mr Gilfil's Love-Story" followed immediately, from March through June 1857, with "Janet's Repentance" closing the series, from July to November. From the start these stories had been advertised as part of a single work, *Scenes of Clerical Life*, which Eliot had expected to continue in a fourth story. However, Blackwood's difficulties with the third story's frank treatment of alcoholism and abuse prompted her to turn instead to *Adam Bede*. Despite reservations, she planned this too as a serial, but disagreements with Blackwood and the challenges involved in writing to deadlines led Eliot to choose instead the traditional three-volume format for *Adam Bede* and for *The Mill on the Floss*. Consequently, her next serial work did not appear until July 1862, when she began *Romola* in the *Cornhill* magazine. By then, Eliot had had the experience of serializing *Scenes of Clerical Life,* with constant feedback from publisher and public, and of designing her next two novels with serialization in mind, even though they were not, finally, published in parts. This apprenticeship meant that by *Romola,* Eliot had acquired many of the devices and techniques essential to successful serialization. Nevertheless, *Romola* was not an unequivocal success as a serial; while serialization gave Eliot's public the leisure to "read slowly and deliberately," as Lewes told friends (*Letters* 8: 304), perhaps nothing in the way of technique could have made it entirely suited for division into small parts. Even reviewers who regarded it as her best work to date were not enthusiastic about the format in which it first appeared.

For her next novel, *Felix Holt,* she returned to the prevailing non-serial, three-volume format. This format, however, did not suit either of her last two works, and for them, Lewes proposed eight half-volume installments. *Middlemarch* was published in five bimonthly and then three monthly installments from December 1871 to December 1872, and *Daniel Deronda* in monthly installments from February to September 1876.

Of her eight full-length works of fiction, one-half were published in installments—two in periodicals and two in separately issued parts. This is a far smaller proportion than the ratio of serial to non-serial for writers like Dickens or Trollope. The former issued only a few full-length works in volumes without serializing them first; the most famous of these is probably *A Christmas Carol,* and it is barely "full-length" compared to his twenty-part novels or even those serialized in periodicals. Trollope experimented with several modes of serialization in thirty-four different novels from *Framley Parsonage,* in the *Cornhill* in 1860–61,[2] to the posthumously published *Landleaguers,* in *Life* from November 1882 to October 1883.[3]

But, as contemporary reviewers often noted, George Eliot was another kind of novelist. In their view, she was a writer who refused to pander to the press or public. Yet her journals and correspondence show that, while she did often adhere to her artistic vision despite pressure from Blackwood and others, she also made numerous alterations and adjustments to fit the demands of serialization. Eliot was aware of these special demands and wrote to produce the most effective installments she could. Reviewers, who from the start distinguished her from the "ordinary run of novelists," still assumed that her four serial works would read like good serial fiction. They commented on her serial technique and expected her to follow the established conventions to keep them and other readers returning for the next part.

This study of George Eliot's serial novels begins with a chapter on serialization: its history, its conventions, and its benefits and drawbacks for writers and for readers. I then examine the four serialized works of George Eliot as well as her temptations to engage in what she called "the nightmare" of the serial for *Adam Bede* and *The Mill on the Floss.* I discuss her reasons for choosing serialization, her use of serial techniques, the context in which she wrote, and the responses of her contemporaries, particularly those who represent the ordinary readers of the daily and weekly newspapers. These newspapers published hundreds of unindexed reviews, particularly of Eliot's last two novels. Many reviews are quoted here to establish the popular context for, expectations from, and responses to her serial fiction. George Eliot, like Dickens, Trollope, Thackeray, and others, was influenced by the commercial publishing climate that helped the Victorian novel become a preeminent form of entertainment in an era in which popular and intellectual fiction were two faces of the same thing.

[3]

I

"Vulgar, and below the Dignity of Literature": Part Publication in the Eighteenth and Nineteenth Centuries

IN THE FIRST CHAPTER of Elizabeth Gaskell's *Cranford*, Captain Brown, a devoted reader of Dickens's Mr. Pickwick, and Miss Jenkyns, a disciple of Dr. Johnson, debate the merits of their favorite authors. After some initial skirmishing, Miss Jenkyns thinks to administer the final blow to Captain Brown's favorite:

> "I consider it vulgar, and below the dignity of literature, to publish in numbers."
> "How was the Rambler published, ma'am?" asked Captain Brown in a low voice. (48)

Captain Brown's response reminded Victorian readers[1] that the experiment in serial publication, either in independent parts or in magazine installments, was not new in the mid-nineteenth century. In fact, serialization of literature began two generations before Dr. Johnson wrote his essays for the *Rambler* in 1750. As R. M. Wiles observes in his study of serial publication before 1750, books were published in installments during the last part of the seventeenth century, "but it was not until a few works advertised in the *Tatler* (1709–1711) had proved successful that the possibilities of developing the piecemeal publishing of books into a thriving business began to be recognized" (4).

Although nineteenth-century serial publication is especially identified with fiction, eighteenth-century publishers first used part publication for other kinds of works. One of these was the continuing series, i.e., individual works published separately but as part of a larger generic grouping, such as a series of playbooks published before 1700. Wiles points out that people very early must have accepted "the principle of the continuing series" because there are extant "composite volumes made up of separate quarto editions of individual plays" by Otway, Shadwell, and Dryden, all from the 1690s (15–16). These early serials appeared at irregular intervals, but by the 1730s, regularity became key to the successful serial as plays "began to appear at *regular* intervals, once a month or once a week" (Wiles 16). Robert Walker, who published "more number books than any other single bookseller before 1750" (19), regarded regular publication as important enough to be stressed in his advertisements: "'One Play compleat, stitch'd in blue Paper, shall be delivered every Monday at the Subscribers Houses, or any Place they shall appoint'" and "'The first Play will be published and delivered on Monday next, being the 27th of this Instant January, and on every Monday following till the whole is compleated'" (20).

Complete individual plays to be bound later in volumes were not the only type of serial publication popular before 1750. Newgate pamphlets appeared in series intended for binding in volume form. The *Grub-Street Journal* for March 12, 1730, advertising *A Compleat History of Executions,* announced that the parts "would 'at the Year's end . . . make a handsome Volume; for which Purpose a compleat Index will be given with the concluding Number'" (Wiles 22). Other less sensational series publications included sermons, political works, and grammar treatises. These early experiments in part publication encouraged readers to form a "habit of purchasing successive units of the series at regular intervals, much as they were becoming used to receiving successive issues of newspapers and periodicals" (25). Once the pattern of regularity was established, prompt delivery to subscribers "was of the greatest importance. . . . When delays were unavoidable, as when an intervening holiday made it impossible to keep to the regular day of publication, the proprietors— at least after 1732—usually were careful to insert a notice in the newspapers" (221).

Early in the eighteenth century, newspapers and periodicals also began to include serial essays and stories; however, tracing the history of newspaper serials is more difficult than examining series books because the former are less likely to have been bound and consequently preserved. The very nature of newspaper items (daily occurrences, advertisements soon to be obsolete) meant that much of the content would quickly be useless; any "continued" work that a subscriber might wish to keep by having it bound could not be separated from the ephemeral. Nonetheless, some readers did have their serials bound and thereby ensured their survival in libraries. Thus, "the two most extensive surviving runs of the *Original London Post; or, Heathcote's Intelligence* have been preserved precisely because on the first two pages Heathcote printed consecutive installments of lengthy works evidently of sufficient interest to be kept and bound as volumes" (Wiles 26). One of these works, appearing thrice weekly, was a description of English counties, of which someone wanted the Kent parts bound. The other was a reprinting of the first two parts of *Robinson Crusoe*.

The earliest eighteenth-century novels to be printed in parts in newspapers were works that had already appeared in volume form, such as *Robinson Crusoe*, which continued to be a popular serial and volume re-issue into the nineteenth century. In the 1860s, for example, in one year "new *Robinson Crusoes* came in book form from Routledge . . . and Beeton . . . , and in penny numbers . . . from Cassell's . . . [and] Henry Lea" (Nowell-Smith 80–81). Other works were disguised by being given new titles. Heathcote printed an alleged translation from "the French" called "The surprising and fatal Effects of rash and violent Love. Illustrated in the following faithful History of two Noble, but Unfortunate Lovers" from July to September 1724; it was actually a reprinting of a novel by Eliza Haywood, published in May 1724 (Wiles 27–28). Obviously publishers were not always very scrupulous about copyrights.

Pirating of books was widespread. Newspapers and magazines could evade the copyright laws by making even slight abridgments of novels, a practice protected by a parliamentary act of 1710 "so long as they published less than the whole" (Mayo 160). Further complicating the publishing situation were the variations in the stamp acts themselves and in their interpretations. One early loophole in the stamp tax legislation encouraged newspaper publication of fiction to supplement the news and to fill out a number of sheets not specified as taxable by the law:

When the Stamp Tax was first laid on newspapers in 1712, the amount of the tax on a half-sheet (one folio leaf) and on a whole sheet (two folio leaves) was duly set out; but no provision was made for the amount of tax payable on a sheet and a half, because there had been no papers of such a size published before that time. It soon occurred to some ingenious mind that this was equivalent to a bounty of a penny per copy (the amount of the tax) on any paper that came out in three folio leaves: but in times when news of "occurrences, foreign and domestic" was always scarce and expensive to procure, it was a considerable problem to find sufficient matter to fill the paper out to its full three leaves. . . . Among other expedients was the reprinting of a work of fiction in instalments. (Pollard 254–55)

Mayo also credits the stamp act of 1712, which distinguished between the single sheet newspaper and the larger pamphlet, with the rise of the six-page weekly journal. "From this time the weekly journals became in effect both news-sheets and miscellanies for the amusement and instruction of the newspaper-reading audience" (49). When the loophole was closed, newspaper fiction continued, suggesting that installment fiction itself helped sell newspapers. History, biography, memoirs, and letters were also popular subjects for newspaper serials.[2]

Another type of serial publication became popular in the eighteenth century, with a few examples extant as well from the last quarter of the seventeenth century. This was the custom of issuing whole books in fascicles, a practice akin to selling encyclopedias in modern supermarkets week by week to make works available inexpensively. Fascicle issue was the production, in unbound parts, of long, expensive works such as encyclopedias, dictionaries, and scientific and religious books. Parts were divided according to the number of pages to be included in each issue; suspense was not a factor, and a part might end mid-sentence. Fascicles were also distinct from magazine and newspaper serials in using continuous pagination throughout the volume. The earliest English example of this type of work is Joseph Moxon's *Mechanick Exercises, or, The Doctrine of Handy-Works*, which began January 1678 (Wiles 79).

Another early fascicle book closer in type to Victorian serials is the *London Spy*, published in eighteen parts beginning November 1698. The author, Edward Ward, "proposed to keep his readers both edified and diverted with his 'compleat Survey of the most remarkable Places, as well as the common Vanities and Follies of Mankind, both by Day and Night.'" Its first-person narrator concludes individual parts self-consciously in ways similar to *Pickwick Papers*, with which Wiles compares it, and *Great Expectations;* part V of the *Spy* ends: "' . . . an account of which, for want of Room, I shall defer till my next'" (Wiles 81). Similarly, *Great Expectations* concludes four of its thirty-six numbers with explicit reference to Pip's act of storytelling (Nelson 82). Installment 10 (Feb. 2, 1861) ends with "[my time] never did run out, however, but was brought to a premature end, as I proceed to relate" (160). At the end of installment 22 (April 20, 1861), Pip interrupts his story, "But, before I proceed to narrate it . . . I must give one chapter to Estella" (318), and at the end of installment 23 he returns his readers to the important event being held in abeyance.³ And in the penultimate installment (35; July 27, 1861), Pip acknowledges coming to the end: "After three days more of recovery, I went down to the old place, to put it in execution; and how I sped in it, is all I have left to tell" (482). Like *Pickwick Papers* and other Dickens works, the *London Spy* also frequently incorporated "within the narrative framework . . . several short stories . . . used for didactic and entertainment reasons" (Kay 19).

Despite occasional earlier examples, part publication did not begin to flourish until 1732, when its economic advantages became apparent. Publishers started to realize the profits to be made not only from monthly but, even more, from weekly serials, which meant the consumer could make a smaller individual outlay for—of course—a smaller part. Lively competition ensued, and rival publications of translated works or works on similar subjects began to crowd the booksellers' shops. That they were both publishing *A History of the Bible* did not prevent the Reverend Thomas Stackhouse and the publisher Thomas Edlin from engaging in a vituperative published exchange in which each attacked the "vile Trash" (Stackhouse's phrase) that the other was peddling. For the consumer, the battle over this pious work must have seemed indecorous. Too, it must have been confusing to ask a "bookseller for the current number of *The History of the Bible* and [get] the wrong one" (Wiles 113). The competition demonstrates the enormous profits that could be realized by publishing fascicles.

An advantage for eighteenth-century publishers of serial parts was that they began to receive profits immediately upon publication of the first part, so that sales from early parts could finance the printing of later ones—an attractive feature of Victorian serial publication as well. Robert Patten notes, for example, that with *Pickwick Papers* "each part had more or less financed the next, [so that] when the final part was published and sold, the book was virtually paid for. Thereafter, any sales were almost pure profit" (71). Eighteenth-century serials, like those of Dickens and his imitators, could add to their commercial appeal by including illustrations. Smollett's *Sir Launcelot Greaves*, in 1760, was "the first illustrated serial novel" (Price 199).

Fascicle issue also had advantages for eighteenth-century consumers.

Wealthy buyers who wanted their library bound uniformly with a particular color and type of leather and embossed with a family coat of arms could have the parts bound to order just as they did with individual, non-serial volumes issued in sheets or in wrappers or boards (Sadleir 12–13). Fascicle issue allowed less wealthy purchasers to buy in small units, and if they decided partway that they were not interested, they could save the rest of the purchase price. Furthermore, the total cost was sometimes less than the cost of the same work in volume form. This was true in the nineteenth century as well. A standard three-volume novel cost a guinea and a half (31s. 6d.), but readers could buy all twenty installments of *Vanity Fair* or *Nicholas Nickleby* for 20s.: eighteen numbers at 1s. each and the final installment, number 19–20, for which the consumer received forty-eight pages, for 2s. If serial buyers desired to have their installments bound, the cost for the cheapest binding was very small. The final issue of *Nickleby*, Sept. 30, 1839, listed in the advertising papers the price of various bindings, including a paper cover for 1s. 6d.[4] (Sept. 30, 1839; U of Pennsylvania P facsimile).

Among the non-monetary advantages of serial publication was another that eighteenth-century and Victorian readers shared: installment buyers received new works earlier than those who chose to await the complete volume publication. This was a mixed blessing. Reviewers of George Eliot's last two novels noted the impossibility of waiting for the complete volume, given the popular interest her novels aroused. A *Manchester Examiner and Times* review of *Daniel Deronda* complains that part 1 does not even take the reader to the chronological point at which it began. The reviewer would prefer to wait until the whole is published, but that is difficult:

> We might be told that no reader is compelled to read 'Daniel Deronda' before its completion; but is that really so? Let anyone who made a like experiment when 'Middlemarch' was in course of publication recall his experience. Was it possible to meet one's friends during that long winter without hearing the infatuation of Dorothy [*sic*], and her subsequent awakening, with its consequences, the subject of general conversation? (Jan. 29, 1876; 5)

Undoubtedly serial readers' ambivalent response—receiving a part before volume readers, but having to endure the suspense of waiting weeks and months for future installments—was greater for fiction than for dictionaries and encyclopedias. Eliot herself wanted readers to read the installments rather than wait for the entire volume, and not solely for economic reasons. After two installments of *Middlemarch*, she wrote John Blackwood: "You and other good readers have spoiled me and made me rather shudder at being read only once, and you may imagine how little satisfaction I get from people who mean to please me by saying that they shall wait till Middlemarch is finished and then sit up to read it 'at one go-off'" (*Letters* 5: 257). Her assumption that serialization meant that her book might be read more than once is also made in reviews of her novels, which pointed out that the first, serial reading often focused on suspense and the plot, while later readings allowed contemplation of the subtleties of the work as a whole.

Suspense was less significant in building a serial audience when the works published were classics that readers might already know, as was often the case in the eighteenth century. A list of the most distinguished pre-1750 authors to be published serially indicates that *Cranford*'s Miss Jenkyns herself might have regarded them as quite the opposite of "vulgar, and below the dignity of literature"—classics, in fact. Some of the fascicle books before 1750 were by "undistinguished" authors, but the list also included works by "Moses, St. Paul, Virgil, Horace, Josephus, John Foxe, Martin Luther, Shakespeare, Sir Walter Ralegh, Cervantes, John Milton, Archbishop Tillotson, several bishops, and a dozen Frenchmen with impressive names" (Wiles 256). Not only does Robert Mayo's "A Catalogue of Magazine Novels and Novelettes 1740–1815" (431–620) include anonymous works and unknown writers, but it lists fiction by Fielding, Richardson, and Smollett—often in reprints twenty to thirty years after the original volume publication. Thus, *Joseph Andrews* appeared in the *Novelist's Magazine* in 1780 [Mayo, "Catalogue" No. 644], thirty-eight years after its first appearance in volume form. Dr. Johnson's *Rasselas* is amply represented, appearing in various pirated abridgements and redactions as "The Adventures of Imlac" in the *Edinburgh* magazine (1759) [Mayo, "Catalogue" No. 48]; the "History of Rasselas" in *Novelist's* (1787), *Grand Magazine* (1759), *London* (1759), and *Universal* (1759) [Mayo, "Catalogue" Nos. 633–36]; and "A Young Prince's Search After Happiness, or No Fixing on Any Particular Condition of Life upon Incontestable Reasons of Preference" in *Weekly Amusement* (1765) [Mayo, "Catalogue" No. 1365].

Although I have singled out examples of serial fiction, much of what was published in parts in the eighteenth century was not fiction. Readers became accustomed to serialization through a wide variety of genres, not the least of which was the single essay periodical, like the *Tatler* and the *Spectator*, and later Johnson's *Rambler*. But all these works paved the way for an increasing number of serialized fictional works as the century drew to a close. The single-essay periodicals in fact published some of the earliest regular fiction: authors included brief tales within the essays to illustrate their points. The earliest long work of original fiction to be written serially and published in magazine installments is Smollett's *The Life and Adventures of Sir Launcelot Greaves*, which appeared monthly in *British Magazine* from January 1760 to December 1761.

Eighteenth-century publishers and authors sought wider circulation and a greater chance of profit through serialization; however, they had other reasons as well, not all of them economic. The nine booksellers who joined together to publish a translation of *The Compleat Herbal: or, the Botanical Institutes of Mr. Tournefort* in 1719 explained in their preface both economic and editorial reasons for monthly publication:

> first, 'the Expence . . . , which otherwise would have amounted to too Considerable a sum'; second, the ease with which the undertaking could be dropped with minimum loss, 'if it does not answer the Expectations, nor hit the Taste of the Curious'; third, the possibility of correcting errors, since 'in this Manner of publishing, all Mistakes may be with less Trouble rectified'; fourth, the possibility of including original contributions submitted either to the printer or to the publisher by those who 'wish the Propagation of useful Knowledge' and are inclined to 'communicate some new Observations.' (Wiles 91)

Each of these reasons has its parallel among Victorian publishers.

Part publication offered a way for the public to buy novels much more cheaply than in the 31s. 6d., three-volume format that dominated the publishing industry until the 1880s and 1890s; the latter, which at least initially benefited publishers and the circulating libraries, kept the price of books out of the reach of most ordinary readers (Griest 55–57). With the advent of part publication, publishers were more willing to take a chance on a new author because they could drop the work if it proved unsuccessful. A relative unknown in 1847, Thackeray had no guarantee that *Vanity Fair* would run to completion. In fact, his publishers almost terminated it with the third installment. The drama of Becky Sharp's "Oh, Sir—I—I'm *married already*" (142) at the conclusion of installment 4 undoubtedly helped to keep it going; but "even [a]s late as the fifteenth number it was uncertain whether *Vanity Fair* was to complete in eighteen or twenty instalments" (Sutherland, *Victorian Novelists* 101). The lengthy essay on society and politics in Pumpernickel in installment 18—which some might call "padding"—suggests that the author had almost reached the end of his plot. Thackeray's skills as satirical essayist kept the copy coming even when the Becky-Amelia story had nearly run itself out.

Some dozen years later, Dickens as an editor had to deal with a similar problem with *A Day's Ride, a Life's Romance* by Charles Lever. Following the tremendous success of Wilkie Collins's *The Woman in White*, Lever's novel caused such a fall in *All the Year Round* sales that Dickens saw his investment threatened and had to begin *Great Expectations* on December 1, 1860. Though he promised Lever he would continue his story, Dickens quickly gave it second billing and then reduced the number of installments. Lever obligingly accepted what his editor decreed. Whether Edgar Rosenberg's term for Lever—"self-flagellating"—is accurate (Rosenberg 315), Lever's deference to editors was apparently possible because of the way he wrote, as another story of his relationships with publishers demonstrates. Two years after his difficulties with *A Day's Ride*, Lever submitted a novel to John Blackwood on which he encouraged him to "'Use your knife'" and "'When not too late to amend, if anything reach you that you think ill of, do not hesitate to say so at once. I can change—in fact, it is the one compensation for all the inartistic demerits of my way of work, that I can change as easily as I can talk of changing'" (Porter 3: 229).[5] Not all writers were as pliable. Elizabeth Gaskell had a serious falling-out with Dickens when he refused her the space she thought she had been promised for *North and South* in *Household Words* in 1854–55.[6]

Another advantage to serialization was that an author could correct errors in the text before volume publication. "An 'affable' barrister" wrote to George Eliot on June 4, 1872, after the fourth installment of *Middlemarch* appeared, telling her that Mary Garth's apprehension that she had marred Fred's prospects was needless (*Letters* 9: 58–59). To correct the erroneous impression—without making it evident that she was doing so, Eliot incorporated the barrister's information in part 5 in a conversation between Mary and Mr. Farebrother, wherein the latter—speaking for Fred when he would rather be making love to Mary himself—decides first "to clear [Mary's] mind of any superstitions, such as women sometimes follow when they do a man the wrong of marrying him as an act of atonement." Accordingly, Mr. Farebrother tells her that legally, her "action made no real difference to Fred's lot" (505). Although any writer could revise later editions of a book, serialization allowed authors to incorporate new information smoothly and dramatically the first time the work appeared, as Eliot did here.

Conversely, serial publication could also conceal authorial errors, at least for a time. In the third edition of *The Woman in White,* Wilkie Collins corrected an error in the elaborate chronology of events at Blackwater Park after the *Times* review pointed out Collins's mistake about the dates on which the solution of the mystery depends. Apparently Collins's readers became so engrossed in his narrative that they failed to notice the error. The novel's serialization probably contributed to this lapse. With the important dates spread over weeks of installments, readers forgot what appeared at the time to be incidental details in the earlier parts. Only when the story appeared in volumes did the mistake become apparent—and then only to one reviewer.

In the "Postscript" to *Our Mutual Friend,* Dickens explains the effect of piecemeal reading on the readers' perception of details and interconnections. He had foreseen "the likelihood that a class of readers and commentators would suppose that I was at great pains to conceal exactly what I was at great pains to suggest: namely, that Mr. John Harmon was not slain, and that Mr. John Rokesmith was he," but he was flattered rather than "alarmed by the anticipation." However, Dickens *was* at pains to conceal "another purpose originating in that leading incident," the pretended hostility between Mr. Boffin and John Harmon. This was, for him,

> the most interesting and the most difficult part of my design. Its difficulty was much enhanced by the mode of publication; for it would be very unreasonable to expect that many readers, pursuing a story in portions from month to month through nineteen months, will, until they have it before them complete, perceive the relations of its finer threads to the whole pattern which is always before the eyes of the story-weaver at his loom.

Nonetheless, Dickens "hold[s] the advantages of the mode of publication to outweigh its disadvantages" (821).

Publishers with an altruistic turn of mind also saw part issue as a way to bring reading matter to the working classes. Others regarded the practice as a waste of time and resources, and even a dangerous encouragement to lower class unrest. A letter-writer in the *Grub-Street Journal*, September 19, 1734, complains that "so many Persons in the lowest Stations of Life, are more intent upon cultivating their Minds, than upon feeding and cloathing their Bodies," and that one might see a man buying portions of history books or the Bible "when perhaps his Wife and Children want a Bit of Bread, and himself a Pair of Breeches." The real nature of this writer's grievance is clear in the next sentence: "to take them off to read Books, was the Way to do them Harm, to make them, not wiser or better, but impertinent, troublesome, and factious" (qtd. in Wiles 236). Nearly one hundred years later, in 1826, the Society for the Diffusion of Useful Knowledge was founded. While the Society's success in achieving its goals has been disputed, Scott Bennett argues that "the S.D.U.K. played a critical role in the development of the [mass reading] market." Its most successful publication was the *Penny Magazine*, but it also issued

> two Libraries of Useful and of Entertaining Knowledge, offering dozens of treatises on the natural sciences, geography, mathematics, history, biography, on the collections at the British Museum, and on the life and manners of such places as Egypt, India, China, New Zealand, and Canada; . . . series of books for farmers and young readers; almanacs and companion publications; a famous series of maps; the landmark *Penny Cyclopedia* and *Biographical Dictionary;* a gallery of finely engraved portraits; and . . . the *Quarterly Journal of Education.* . . . This plethora of reading matter appeared at stated intervals in serial parts; in marketing terms there were few differences between the Society's "books" and its "periodicals." (Bennett 228–29)

The Society's success should be measured by the unprecedented sales of its mass market publications, Bennett argues, not in terms of its meetings, demonstrations, and petitions. Those who argue that the S.D.U.K. publications were dull need to ask "why the *Penny Magazine* was purchased more than ten million times in 1833" (250).

The success of this and other S.D.U.K. serial publications prepared the public for similar ventures in the Victorian era after the Society's decline in the 1840s. John Cassell aimed to provide "educational and recreational reading for the working man" by issuing works "in cheap weekly numbers or monthly parts, to be sold up and down the country, from house to house, by colporteurs" (Nowell-Smith 36). "Many of Cassell's publications were issued in five forms: *viz.*, weekly *numbers*, monthly *parts*, quarterly *sections*, half-yearly *divisions*, and annual *volumes*" (36n1). This gave the Victorian public the widest possible variety of forms for their reading matter. In addition, Cassell's magazine, the *Popular Educator*, provided not only occasional pieces, but a regular course of advanced study that would have carried working people through the University level except for matriculation requirements (47).

Victorian part publication can be divided into two main types: separate part publication and serialization within an existing periodical that includes stories, essays, or poems. Magazine and newspaper serials generally did not include the author's name, regardless of gender or notoriety. The periodicals were various—including Saturday editions of four-page provincial newspapers and literary monthlies like the *Cornhill* and *Blackwood's*, which reached subscribers in the farthest stations of the Empire. Dickens attempted his own weekly magazine in 1840, *Master Humphrey's Clock*, in which he planned to include miscellaneous essays and stories, but his readers anticipated a long work of his own fiction. "When the sales of the second and following issues of the weekly plummeted, apparently because readers realized that they were not being provided with an ongoing story, [Dickens] tentatively began in June 1840, as the twelfth number of *Master Humphrey*, a new novel, *The Old Curiosity Shop*" (Kaplan 117). *Barnaby Rudge* followed, and then *Master Humphrey's Clock* expired. However, in 1850 Dickens was more fortunate with *Household Words*. Together *Household Words* and its successor, *All the Year Round*, published not only his own *Hard Times*, *A Tale of Two Cities*, and *Great Expectations*, but also works by Gaskell (*Cranford*, *North and South*, *My Lady Ludlow*, *A Dark Night's Work*), Collins (*A Rogue's Life*, *The Woman in White*, *The Moonstone*), and Trollope (*Is He Popenjoy?*, *The Duke's Children*, and *Mr. Scarborough's Family*).[7]

Thackeray was the first editor as well as a contributor for the *Cornhill* magazine, established in 1860; his novels *Lovel the Widower*, *The Adventures of Philip*, and *Denis Duval* all appeared there. Other *Cornhill* contributors like Trollope, Eliot, and Gaskell preferred the more leisurely writing pace and longer installments this monthly publication provided in contrast to the weekly deadline pressure and brief installments of Dickens's two magazines. The problems of weekly versus monthly serialization were undoubtedly part of the reason George Eliot was unwilling to publish with Dickens, though he wrote her a flattering letter after the publication of *Adam Bede*, encouraging her to do so (Eliot, *Letters* 3: 114–15).

The other format for Victorian serialization, separate part publication, was not as common as is often believed, based on Dickens's example of the successful one-shilling installment of thirty-two pages plus advertisements. Dickens's phenomenal sales of works in this format, from *Pickwick* to *Our Mutual Friend*, have given the impression that it was the principal mode of Victorian publishing and was widely imitated. Robert L. Patten argues that the success of *Pickwick Papers* (April 1836 to November 1837) led to serialization's becoming "for thirty years a chief means of democratizing and enormously expanding the Victorian book-reading and book-buying public" (45). Of serialization generally, this is undoubtedly true. However, in an essay detailing the limitations as well as the imitations of the thirty-two-page serial after *Pickwick*, John Sutherland demonstrates that "the number of Victorian novels brought out in monthly numbers is tiny. Over the period 1837–70 an estimated 8[,000]-9,000 works of fiction were produced in England. At the beginning of this period (its boom time) there were at maximum some 15 part-issued shilling serials a year." In the 1840s there were only about five a year, and by "the end of the 1860s, it had dwindled to one or two" ("Chips" 97–98). Sutherland also points out that this was a format seldom employed by women authors (102). J. Don Vann provides substantiation for Sutherland's argument that serials in periodicals were more common than independent-part publications. In *Victorian Novels in Serial,* Vann includes sixteen major and minor Victorian authors, a total of 192 novels. Of the 188 appearing in more than one part, 158 were published in magazines or newspapers, 25 in individual parts, and 5 in both magazines and individual parts.

Among the successes in the twenty-part serial were *Vanity Fair* and other "*Punch*ified" novels issued by Bradbury and Evans, which were "democratic, good-natured, and tolerantly ironic of the foibles of life" and which "introduced a far wider range of unfettered pictorial talent than Dickens would ever have permitted" (Sutherland, "Chips" 109). Other shilling part novels include Trollope's *Orley Farm, Can You Forgive Her?*, and *The Way We Live Now.* By the time Gwendolen Harleth found objectionable "the quality of the shilling serial mistakenly written for her amusement" in *Daniel Deronda* (set in the 1860s [112]), the form had already declined. And by late 1874, when Gwendolen's creator was shaping the scene in which this offensive but unnamed serial novel appears, the thirty-two-page installment had given way entirely to magazine serialization or to the longer individual parts that George Eliot used for *Middlemarch* and *Daniel Deronda.*

Anthony Trollope tried many formats, while Wilkie Collins and Thomas Hardy, both prolific serial writers, avoided separate part publication outside the magazines, but published extensively within them. In addition to the twenty-part serial format, Trollope experimented with thirty-two weekly parts in *The Last Chronicle of Barset* and *He Knew He Was Right;* eleven monthly parts, *The Vicar of Bulhampton;* and the eight monthly parts that Eliot introduced, *The Prime Minister* (Vann, *Victorian Novels in Serial* 141–69). He also published in a dozen magazines, including *Whitehall Review, St. Paul's Magazine, Blackwood's, Macmillan's, Fortnightly Review, Good Words, Life,* and the *Manchester Weekly Times* supplement. Besides *Household Words* and *All the Year Round,* Collins published serials in the *Cornhill, Harper's Weekly, Cassell's Magazine, Temple Bar, Belgravia,* the *World, Canadian Monthly, Leigh Journal and Times, Illustrated London News,* and the *Graphic*—where Thomas Hardy's *The Mayor of Casterbridge* and *Tess of the d'Urbervilles* appeared later. These are just a sample of the periodicals in which the most prominent authors appeared; many now forgotten newspapers in England and Scotland included installment fiction, often on Saturdays.

Any new method of publication involved risks, especially if the author was new and unknown. In the eighteenth century, the Reverend Francis Bromefield, a Norfolk antiquarian, could not find a suitable publisher for his *Essay Towards a Topographical History of the County of Norfolk.* Consequently, he bought a London press and "proceeded to publish at a shilling each the successive folio numbers." His introduction (March 25, 1736) explains why:

> Several Reasons there are that induced me to publish in this Method, among which, these are the Chief, *viz.* the Improvements that may be made as I go on, by Gentlemens seeing in what Manner I proceed, and helping me, as I come to their Parts, to a sight of old Evidences, of Antiquities, or by Subscribing for Plates of their Seats, Monuments, Arms, Ruins, or other Things worth Observation, which Advantage I could not have had, if I had done it at once.

The question of price is an afterthought: "besides, I don't fear but I may hereafter meet with several Subscribers, who will willingly expend a Trifle every month, that would not have chose [*sic*] to lay down half the Price before-hand, (as is the common Way) . . ." (qtd. in Wiles 141). For Herbert Spencer more than a century later, money is not an afterthought, but the sole reason for publishing his *System of Philosophy* by subscription. In his *Autobiography*, he records his difficulty in finding "any official position which would give me sufficient means while affording me a share of leisure" to write. "Among plans despairingly thought over there occurred to me that of issuing by subscription." With the encouragement of friends, including Lewes and Eliot, he prepared a "programme [that] stated the method of issue," specifically, publishing "parts of from five to six sheets octavo . . . to be issued quarterly; or as nearly so as is found possible" at a cost of half-a-crown per part, or 10 shillings a year (51). The "plan succeeded fairly well," with a subscriber list of "over 440" in Britain, and through friends he also obtained "more than two hundred subscribers" in the United States (52–53). This "programme" committed him, at age forty, to a publication plan that would extend for the next twenty years, a formidable undertaking (56).

The risks for authors like Bromefield and Spencer were considerable, but the rewards could be great as well. Just as Thackeray became famous with *Vanity Fair* despite its coming close to cancellation, so Dickens a decade earlier survived and triumphed in an even more problematic situation—when Seymour's suicide exacerbated a crisis brought on by poor sales of the first parts of *Pickwick*:

> Here was a new firm [Chapman and Hall], lately returned to publishing . . .
> after weathering a severe depression in the book trade, faced with a losing
> serial from which the more important contributor had just violently re-
> signed. It is to their eternal credit and fame that, inspired by Dickens's
> runaway enthusiasm, they decided to continue, on an 'improved plan' of
> thirty-two pages of letterpress and two illustrations per month. (Patten 65)

That plan started Dickens on his way to a legendary career and inaugurated the vogue for serialization of new fiction that lasted through the century.

This story also points to another risk, serializing before authors and illustrators had completed their work. It was rare that a work was finished before installments began, and authors sometimes not only failed to leave sufficient time for revision and proofreading, but occasionally could not complete their week's or month's installment, causing a break in the regular appearance of the work. Problems resulting from deadline pressure were not new in the nineteenth century. The 1732 preface of Patrick Barclay, D.D., to *The Universal Traveller; or, a Complete Account of the*

Most Remarkable Voyages and Travels of Eminent Men of our own and other Nations, to the Present Time contains the author's apology for errors resulting from haste:

> I am very sensible that there are many defects in it. All that I can say for them is, that it had been better, if I had been allow'd more time: And however easy for readers, and the less rich purchasers of books, the modern way of publishing (at so many sheets a week or month) may be, I cannot but observe, that it is a great hardship upon an author, or compiler, to be hurried, to keep the press going. (Qtd. in Wiles 125)

The lament is echoed by many Victorian serial writers. Often writing to the deadline, they sometimes missed it. No June 1837 number appeared for *Pickwick Papers* and *Oliver Twist* because Mary Hogarth's death left Dickens too grief-stricken to work. Thackeray's illness in the fall of 1849 caused number 12 of *Pendennis* to be delayed from October 1849 to January 1850. Given their practice of beginning to publish serial works before they were completed, it is not surprising that Dickens, Thackeray, and Gaskell all left works unfinished when they died. Thackeray had barely begun *Denis Duval* when he died, but nonetheless it was published posthumously in four installments of the *Cornhill* from March to June 1864. The June issue included Frederick Greenwood's "Note by the Editor," which began "readers . . . have now read the last line written by William Makepeace Thackeray" (666), but Greenwood added quotations from letters and notebook entries to show how the story was intended to develop. Less than two years later, the *Cornhill* again lost a favorite contributor when Elizabeth Gaskell died suddenly on November 12, 1865. However, *Wives and Daughters* was so nearly finished that the loose ends could be tidied up by Greenwood in a final installment in January 1866.

When Dickens died in June 1870, readers lamented that *The Mystery of Edwin Drood* was only partly written. The resulting possibilities for reader speculation on "Whodunit?" that began immediately have continued into the 1980s, in both book and musical form. *The D. Case, The Truth about the Mystery of Edwin Drood* intermingles chapters from the novel with scenes from a conference of time-warped experts in detection, including Sherlock Holmes, Hercule Poirot, Father Brown, and Philip Marlowe—along with the editor of the *Dickensian*, all of whom are assembled to uncover the villain in Dickens's story.[8] A musical play based on the novel appealed to 1980s London and New York audiences to adopt a favorite role of Victorian readers—completing the story to their own satisfaction. "When Dickens's plot runs out in mid-Act II of the musical version, the audience 'solves, resolves and concludes the mystery' by voting by voice and hand to a series of multiple-choice propositions" (Rich C3). The composer improved on Dickens's double ending for *Great Expectations* by writing for *Edwin Drood* "a dozen variations, any of which the actors can nimbly put into service"; like many a Victorian author, the "host" of the show directed the audience's choices. "Though Jasper is the obvious culprit (even, apparently, to Dickens), [the host] Mr. Rose encourages us to select someone less suspicious" (Gussow H3). The complexities of reader and text interaction that Michael Lund explores ("Literary Pieces") in reference to *Edwin Drood* do not, however, seem to be motivating factors if *New York Times* reviewer Mel Gussow is correct in his assessment of the audience's reasons for selecting the culprit: "Last summer, the Princess Puffer, the flamboyant proprietress of an opium den, was often the winning candidate, at least partly because she was played by Cleo Laine. The audience wanted to hear her sing another song." Victorian responses were not always much more sophisticated, motivated as they often were by readers' desire for a happy ending.

Just a few months before Eliot's first work appeared in *Blackwood's*, Samuel Warren, a regular contributor, made amusing use of the delayed serial in his two-part "Tickler Among the Thieves!" This dog's-eye view of the world of dognappings toys with the convention of the suspenseful ending, breaking off just as the suddenly returned Tickler begins the tale of his absence: "But his adventures . . . were far too interesting and affecting for me to give them to the world at large, before affording him an opportunity of hearing me read them to him for his correction." The narrator promises to do this and "then let the reader form his own judgment—next month" (*Blackwood's* Feb. 1856: 208). Several months, however, intervened. The next part, in August, began "Apologies for Delay," and parodied serial readers' anticipation of the new installment of a favorite story: "March! April! May! June! July!—Yes, Tickler, I acknowledge that it is too bad, indeed. On the first of each of the aforesaid months, the sagacious little creature, who knew that the new Maga [a popular abbreviation for *Blackwood's*] made its appearance on those days with clock-work regularity, frisked about the room with the utmost glee for some time." Hearing the bad news that his adventures were not recorded there, (almost) like any disappointed reader, "all his vivacity disappeared, and he hid himself under the sofa, where he would lie as if asleep, but in reality vexed and melancholy" (198). As a result, the author has had to lay aside his projected *Essence of Everything* and finish the simple tale of Tickler among the dognappers. This satirical picture of serial reading hints that readers are more interested in tales of adventure than in comprehensive philosophical works. The spoof has particular poignancy for readers of George Eliot, the *Essence of Everything* looking ahead to the "Key to All Mythologies" in *Middlemarch*.[9]

Apart from actual breaks in the publishing schedule, the novelist met with constant struggle and tension to comply with the recurring deadlines of serial publication. Here, too, Smollett leads the way. Although Sir Walter Scott's description of Smollett writing his installments of *Sir Launcelot Greaves* only an hour or half an hour before post time has been partially discredited (Knapp, *Smollett, Doctor of Men and Manners* 228–29), Smollett complains to a friend on February 25, 1761—roughly halfway through the appearance of that novel—that he is "tied down to the stake by periodical Publications" (Knapp, *Letters* 96). Dickens jokes about the pressure of writing *Martin Chuzzlewit* in a letter declining a dinner invitation: "The Garrickers and the Aldermen are wonderful temptations; so are the Vintages, if not the Vintners. But I fear I must not go out to dinner next week. It is the week in every month in which I never go out to dinner, except on some tremendous provocation—such as a twin brother's coming home from China, and having appointed to return next Morning. Which does not often happen" (*Letters* 4: 63–64). Sometimes, accepting invitations left Dickens with no choice but to work, despite the discomforts caused by late hours of conviviality. Near the end of *The Old Curiosity Shop*, he writes to Forster: "I shall certainly not stir out today, for we were not home [from a party] until half-past five, and not up until half-past twelve. Unless I look very sharp, I shall not have done the No. [43] by tomorrow night—for I drank punch last evening in considerable quantities" (*Letters* 2: 179). Punch-drinking might not have been conducive to writing, but Dickens met his deadline for this installment, as he generally did despite the many distractions in his life.

Concerned like Dickens with earning a living, Thackeray committed to more than he could always manage, and he was often behind schedule. With *Vanity Fair* he agreed to furnish Bradbury and Evans with the text and illustrations for each installment by the fifteenth of each month . . . , but [we know] that he was still writing numbers five, seven, fifteen, and eighteen after that date, and that he completed work on numbers nine, eleven, thirteen, and fourteen, plus the final double installment close to publication date. . . . Shortly after finishing number fourteen, Thackeray himself commented: "At the end of the month I always have a life-&-death struggle to get out my number of Vanity Fair." (Harden 8)

Even the concluding installment of the novel meant that "for [the] past ten days, [I was] in such a state of work and excitement as have put me in a fever. Don't you see I am so nervous I can hardly write," he wrote to Mrs. B. W. Proctor. Nonetheless, Thackeray was able to joke about the pressure in a letter to his mother: "My dearest old Mammy. Vanity Fair is this instant done and I have been worked so hard that I can hardly hold a pen and say God bless my dearest old Mother" (Thackeray, *Letters* 2: 393, 392). Both letters are dated June 29, 1848, two days before the final installment of *Vanity Fair* appeared.

Lesser-known writers faced the same problems, sometimes with aggrieved frustration and sometimes with the wry humor that Dickens and Thackeray manifested. Samuel Phillips, whose *Caleb Stukely* appeared in *Blackwood's* fifteen years before *Scenes of Clerical Life*, wrote to the Blackwood brothers, "If the earthquake does not happen, or if it does and I am spared, I hope to send you the half of the 5th part on the 1st of April, and the other half on the 15th" (Oliphant, *Annals* 2: 302). No earthquake occurred, but illness forced him to ask for a month's postponement of part 5. He attempted to make the best of the situation by pointing out that "Half of the work is already published. Part 5 is the commencement of the second half. The break of a month in a way divides them." One month became two, a delay that, Margaret Oliphant notes, "must have been trying enough for the publisher as well as for the sick man" (303). Phillips's next appeal betrays a method of composition that allowed for no overview, backward glances, or correcting: "I propose to write on until the last day of the month, when I will send you all that I have been able to accomplish, and every following day the post shall carry to you a portion of the conclusion." Oliphant, a serial writer herself, empathizes:

> I do not know any good reason why it should be more interesting and
> pathetic to note a struggle like this than almost any other struggle which a

sick man can carry on with the obstacles of living; but it certainly strikes upon the chords of pity with a deeper stroke, perhaps because composition is a thing that can be done or attempted at any moment of possibility, the hour or half-hour of comparative ease which comes now and then even to the greatest sufferer, while the man whose work is out of doors, whether in the fields or amid the routine of an office, is not tantalised by any such possibility. Also the sharp and poignant contrast between such affecting labours and the fact that the result of the labour is to amuse and please an often indifferent reader . . . adds to the pathos of the situation. . . . (304)[10]

Wilkie Collins relates that during the serialization of *The Moonstone* "the bitterest affliction of my life and the severest illness from which I have ever suffered, fell on me together. At the time when my mother lay dying in her little cottage in the country, I was struck prostrate, in London . . . by the torture of rheumatic gout." Nevertheless, he knew his duty to the public. "My good readers in England and in America, whom I had never yet disappointed, were expecting their regular weekly instalments of the new story. I held to the story—for my own sake, as well as for theirs" (29). He recounts this real-life drama with adjectives and nouns that resemble those used to evoke pathos and drama in his fiction.

The mere possibility of illness caused anxiety. With over 600 subscribers to his *System of Philosophy*, Herbert Spencer "resolved to proceed," though he was a "nervous invalid":

when I look back on all the circumstances,—when I recall the fact that at my best I could work only three hours daily,—when I remember that besides having not unfrequently to cut short my mornings, I from time to time had a serious relapse; I am obliged to admit that to any unconcerned bystander my project must have seemed almost insane. (*Autobiography* 54)

Yet, he writes, "as the result has proved, the apparently unreasonable hope was entertained, if not wisely, still fortunately" (56). George Eliot, too, felt the pressure of deadlines and feared that her susceptibility to illness, especially nervous headache, would cause her to rush her work or not have it ready on time.

Weekly serialization produced greater pressure than monthly installments, not only because of the more frequent deadlines but because of the difficulty of shaping an installment in about one-quarter of the space that a writer had for a thirty-two-page monthly number. Preparing *Barnaby Rudge* for *Master Humphrey's Clock*, Dickens wrote Basil Hall on

March 16, 1841, that "I have great designs in store, but am sadly cramped at first for room" (2: 238), a complaint that echoes his letter to Forster nearly a year earlier regarding the weekly installments of *The Old Curiosity Shop*: "I was obliged to cramp most dreadfully what I thought a pretty idea in the last chapter. I hadn't room to turn" (2: 80). Years later the preparation of *Hard Times* for *Household Words* evoked an even stronger cry of despair from Dickens to Forster: "The difficulty of the space is CRUSHING. Nobody can have an idea of it who has not had an experience of patient fiction-writing with some elbow-room always, and open places in perspective. In this form, with any kind of regard to the current number, there is absolutely no such thing" (Letter to Forster, qtd. in Butt and Tillotson 203). His difficulties did not ease with time, and, as Butt and Tillotson note, Dickens finally had to increase his space allotment to 10 pages.

Pressures of space and deadlines led to other problems. Over the long period of writing a serial, authors working against the clock often had no chance to reread what they had written and were liable to forget the details of their own work. Geoffrey and Kathleen Tillotson point out that "after the fourth number [of *Vanity Fair*] there can have been little time for careful proofreading. The result may be seen in the large number of variants—about 120—between issues of the first edition." The errors they cite mostly concern the names of minor characters (Tillotsons xxiii, xxiiin. ll). Slips by other authors were sometimes more momentous, and humorous. John Blackwood once had to remind Charles Lever, whose *Tony Butler* was appearing in Maga, that "it spoils the *vraisemblance* of a story to begin to describe an interview in the winter and end it in summer" (Porter 3: 228). Elizabeth Gaskell had a similar problem with forgetfulness. On December 6, 1864, she wrote to George Smith, editor of the *Cornhill*, about requesting a copy of *Wives and Daughters* as far as it had been published: "I did not know I asked for any more copies of Wives & Daughters—and I think you must have misunderstood,—or I must have expressed myself badly when I said—or meant to say—I should like one more printed copy of all I had written, as I had not one either in MSS or print, and had forgotten all the names" (Letter 557). Whatever Smith sent was too late to correct that month's inconsistency in Miss Browning's given name, which began as "Sally" in chapter 1, published August 1864, but by December had become "Clarinda" (*Cornhill* 10: 704). And in October 1865, Gaskell rechristened her again as "Dorothy" (12: 396–397).[11]

Serial writing and publishing created a relationship between author and public different from the one established with volume publication. Dickens quotes Mackenzie in his preface to the first edition of *Nicholas Nickleby* to illustrate the special intimacy and sense of the present found in "periodical performance":

> "The author of a periodical performance," says Mackenzie, "has indeed a claim to the attention and regard of his readers, more interesting than that of any other writer. Other writers submit their sentiments to their readers, with the reserve and circumspection of him who has had time to prepare for a public appearance. He who has followed Horace's rule, of keeping his book nine years in his study, must have withdrawn many an idea which in the warmth of composition he had conceived, and altered many an expression which in the hurry of writing he had set down. But the periodical essayist commits to his readers the feelings of the day, in the language which those feelings have prompted. As he has delivered himself with the freedom of intimacy and the cordiality of friendship, he will naturally look for the indulgence which those relations may claim; and when he bids his readers adieu, will hope, as well as feel, the regrets of an acquaintance, and the tenderness of a friend." (Slater [Ed.] 46–47)

 This intimacy sometimes led the public to see themselves as coauthors, who had their own ideas about how a work should develop.

Those who reviewed individual installments of a serial work most explicitly adopted the coauthorial role. When Eliot did not end *Daniel Deronda* as the *Figaro* had prescribed, its reviewer was indignant:

> Although we feared from the incidents in the preceding part that the author would make the mistake of marrying Deronda to Mirah Lapidoth, we did not give up hope it might be otherwise. If no other way out of the difficulty could have been found, we thought an accident might happen by which Deronda's marriage with the young Jewess would have been rendered impossible. It is quite certain if he could not have married Mirah he would have been only too glad to have had Gwendolen. But George Eliot does not let him marry Gwendolen, and a book which had promised to be so satisfactory falls from our hands as we finish it with a sense of absolute annoyance. (Sept. 27, 1876; 12)

Eliot was not disposed to give Victorian readers the happy ending they craved, but other authors were sometimes more obliging.

A novelist who apparently saw himself as a coauthor was Edward

Bulwer Lytton. Dickens resisted public presssure in the case of *The Old Curiosity Shop*, but succumbed to Bulwer Lytton's advice regarding *Great Expectations*. Approaching the death of Little Nell in the former, Dickens writes Chapman and Hall, "I am inundated with imploring letters recommending poor little Nell to mercy.—Six yesterday, and four today (it's not 12 o'Clock yet) already!" (*Letters* 2: 153). The public's eagerness to know her fate is recorded by Edgar Johnson: "Waiting crowds at a New York pier shouted to an incoming vessel, 'Is Little Nell dead?'" (1: 304). Twenty years later Bulwer Lytton convinced Dickens to rewrite the ending for *Great Expectations*, arguing that the public would not stand for the origially planned conclusion in which Estella has remarried after the death of Bentley Drummle, and Pip encounters her only briefly in the final chapter. Readers have debated the merits of this alteration ever since.[12] In June 1872, after part 4 of *Middlemarch* appeared, Bulwer Lytton also suggested to George Eliot the desirable fate for Casaubon: "Mr. Casaubon is excellent, but as he is quite good enough to die, and too good to change for the better in this world, I hope for Dorothea's sake that it will please her creator to remove him to another world before the end of the book" (Eliot, *Letters* 9: 57). Mr. Casaubon does die in the next installment, but not because Bulwer Lytton proposed his death to Dorothea's "creator." Eliot had sent part 5 to the publisher on April 6, 1872, two months prior to Bulwer Lytton's correspondence (*Letters* 5: 264), and earlier installments had prepared the way for Mr. Casaubon's plausible demise.[13]

Trollope attributes the death of Mrs. Proudie in *The Last Chronicle of Barsetshire* to a conversation he overheard between two members of the Athenaeum Club, who were discussing his penchant for reintroducing his characters in new novels. They soon "fell foul of Mrs. Proudie. It was impossible for me not to hear their words, and almost impossible to hear them and be quiet. I got up, and standing between them, I acknowledged myself to be the culprit. 'As to Mrs. Proudie,' I said, 'I will go home and kill her before the week is over.' And so I did" (Trollope, *Autobiography* 230–31).

The public's eagerness to know a plot's outcome meant that publishers had to take care that those with early access to parts of a novel, i.e., compositors, did not share them with unauthorized persons. An author could, of course, send a friend an early copy of a part, as Dickens did for Angela Burdett Coutts:

> It has occurred to me—this is a kind of vanity to which the meekest of
> authors are occasionally liable—that when you came to read this week's

number of the Clock, you might possibly desire to know what the next one contained, without waiting seven days. I therefore make bold to send you, inclosed, the two numbers together, begging you not to be at the trouble of returning them, as I have always plenty by me. (*Letters* 2: 192)

Readers not so fortunate in their friendships had to resort to strategem to gain early access to the serial parts, as one Helen Walter of Milton, New York, did when William Dean Howells was publishing *Indian Summer* in 1885. Under the pseudonym Elizabeth C. Meader, Walter told Howells that she was an invalid who might die before the work was completed. Completely taken in, Howells wrote her on November 18, 1885 that he would ask the editor to send her the advance sheets, relying upon her to be the only reader and "to destroy them as soon as you have read them." He added that he was "sincerely and humbly grateful . . . to be the means of lightening the moments of sickness to you, and this book of mine will always have a peculiar interest to me because it has interested you at this time" (Howells, *Letters* 3: 134). Howells's editors were more skeptical and upon their demand for a physician's confirmation, the hoaxer confessed.

When Howells made use of this incident in *Fennel and Rue* in 1908, his character Verrian reveals some of the vulnerability Howells must have felt twenty-three years earlier.[14] His fictional account of the young woman's letter reflects not only the flattering appeal to the author's vanity, obviously part of the original incident, but the public's awareness of the conditions of serial writing. The woman in *Fennel and Rue* concludes her description of her "morbid foreboding that she should not live to read [the story] in the ordinary course" with an acknowledgment of her awareness of the circumstances of serial composition: "She had read that sometimes authors began to print their serial stories before they had written them to the end, and he might not be sure of the end himself; but if he had finished this story of his, and could let her see the last pages in print, she would owe him the gratitude she could never express" (3). Three years before Howells published *Fennel and Rue*, he had occasion to revert to the incident, because something similar had happened to Katherine Cecil Thurston, whose *The Masqueraders* was being serialized in *Harper's Bazar* in 1904. Thurston's invalid correspondent, whose letter was published in an advertisement for the novel in *Harper's Weekly*, was genuine; Howells felt constrained to postpone the appearance of *Fennel and Rue* to avoid charges of plagiarism and opportunism. (See his letter to Elizabeth Jordan, Jan. 6, 1905; Howells, *Letters* 5: 117.)

A major problem for serial writers was how to structure the parts. Each part had to be both a whole and part of the larger design. Each also needed a suspenseful ending to induce readers to purchase the next installment. Eighteenth-century writers seldom faced this demand. Cohesion and suspense were not issues with fascicles. Parts were divided without regard to internal coherence, breaks often being dictated by the number of pages allotted. With reprinted works of fiction, drama, theology, and history, suspense was not a motivating factor for buyers. Even in a work of original fiction like *Sir Launcelot Greaves*, Smollett tended toward episodic divisions rather than the cliff-hanger ending popular with Victorian writers. As Robert Donald Spector points out, Smollett's method produces little suspense, because he is writing

> in the picaresque tradition, and the episodic technique that composes its structure out of minor narratives is hardly conducive to arousing anticipation from one chapter to the next. . . . Out of its twenty-five chapters, less than half may be said to create the excitement that comes from the continuity of the narrative; and these occur chiefly at the beginning of his novel where he can depend for interest on the introduction of Greaves and on revelations of the details of his situation. (88)

Even at the beginning of the novel, however, the technique does not include the cliff-hanger ending, which requires that an event be interrupted midway, at a moment of great anxiety for the reader. Episodic breaks work the opposite way, the pause coming between events rather than interrupting a single event midway.

Tracing the complex connection between narrator and reader established in *Sir Launcelot Greaves*, John Vladimir Price notes that the end of chapter 1 invites the reader to await until next month an introduction to the man who is knocking on the inn door so tremendously—even though "most authors would probably prefer a little impatience from their readers" (qtd. in Bold 200). Price suggests that Smollett undercuts the suspense by the comic exaggeration of Sir Launcelot's knocking being forceful enough to bring down the house. Other comic elements that undercut the potential for dramatic tension include Tom Clarke's legalistic monologue with its bawdy puns, the incongruity between the preparations for battle and the narrator's comments,[15] and the hints of cowardice in Tom Clarke and Mr. Ferret's retreat. Finally, by advising the reader to wait "with patience for the next chapter, in which he will see the cause of this disturbance explained much to his comfort and edification" (45), the narrator soothes, rather than excites, his audience. The fact that Smollett's readers returned to buy further installments might be attributed to reader expectations. Eighteenth-century readers were accustomed to the essay serial; Smollett's conclusions, being perfectly in keeping with their expectations, posed no problems.[16]

In contrast, Thomas Hardy took the cliff-hanger ending to its logical conclusion: literalness. In *A Pair of Blue Eyes*, serialized monthly in *Tinsley's Magazine* from September 1872 to July 1873, the close of installment 6 has the hero hanging from a low "tuft of vegetation" (206) on a high and steep cliff on the west coast of Cornwall, whose steepness, with the sea and rocks below, has been fully described in the preceding paragraphs. For the heroine to run to the nearest dwelling and back will take three-quarters of an hour. But the dangling hero says, "'That won't do; my hands will not hold out ten minutes.'" The heroine looks about, but the "common was bare of everything but heather and grass," and after a minute more of hopeless contemplation, disappears (207). The hero is left hanging, as were the readers of *Tinsley's* until the next month (March 1872), to find out if and how Henry Knight would be rescued.

Dickens is more episodic than suspenseful in *Pickwick Papers* (not surprising given the essay style of *Sketches by Boz* and his youthful addiction to eighteenth-century fiction). In his later fiction and work as an editor, Dickens became expert at demonstrating and explaining the complex demands of the form. In a letter to Jane Brookfield, dated February 20, 1866, regarding a manuscript on which she had asked his advice, he outlines the expectations of an editor reviewing a work intended for serialization:

> If you will take a part of it and cut it up (in fancy) into the small portions into which it would have to be divided here for only a month's supply [of copy for *All the Year Round*], you will (I think) at once discover the impossibility of publishing it in weekly parts. The scheme of the chapters, the manner of introducing the people, the progress of the interest, the places in which the principal places fall [*sic;* he probably means principal breaks], are all hopelessly against it. It would seem as though the story were never coming, and hardly ever moving. There must be a special design to overcome that specially trying mode of publication.

Dickens recommends that Brookfield look at "any two weekly numbers" of his periodicals and "notice how patiently and expressly the thing has to be planned for presentation in these fragments, and yet for afterwards fusing together as an uninterrupted whole" (Paroissien, *Selected Letters* 318). These problems were acute for authors of weekly parts, which demanded a particular compression of the narrative and more frequent dramatic endings than did novels issued monthly.

George Eliot took her place in the well-established tradition of the serial novel almost by accident, when George Henry Lewes encouraged her to write her first work of fiction, *Scenes of Clerical Life*, and negotiated with his own publisher John Blackwood for its monthly appearance in *Blackwood's Edinburgh Magazine* from January to November 1857. Subsequent chapters in this book will examine how she came to adopt a serial format for this and her other three serial works (*Romola, Middlemarch*, and *Daniel Deronda*), the format's effect on her writing, and the response of her readers.

2

Striking Situations and Serial Endings:
Eliot's Apprenticeship in
Scenes of Clerical Life

"I LEARN FROM THE NEWSPAPERS that many remarkable novels, full of striking situations, thrilling incidents, and eloquent writing, have appeared only within the last season" (42), says the narrator in "The Sad Fortunes of the Reverend Amos Barton," the first story of *Scenes of Clerical Life*, published in two installments in *Blackwood's Magazine* in January and February 1857. Eliot, however, declines to follow the fashion by providing the "striking situation" that readers expected at the close of an installment to lure them back to buy the next weekly or monthly part. Instead, the January number introduces a dull, almost tedious hero and a quiet heroine. Even when the villagers of Shepperton see scandal in the relationship between Amos Barton and the Countess Czerlaski, readers are too thoroughly acquainted with Barton to share the titillation. The story's interest centers on the more mundane question of how long Milly Barton's health will endure under the extra work caused by a guest who possesses the ordinary, unsensational vices of selfishness and laziness.

Expressing an idea repeated in Eliot's later works, the narrator appeals to the reader to "learn with me to see some of the poetry and the pathos, the tragedy and the comedy" of ordinary human lives, whose very "insignificance" is part of that pathos (42). However, by the second and third stories in *Scenes*, "insignificance" no longer meant dullness, and the nature of her serial conclusions changes. She becomes adept in manipulating the serial breaks and attending simultaneously to the demands of both part and whole. Instead of length determining the break, later installments are arranged to conclude with dramatic or pathetic events, sometimes both. Each part is a microcosm with its own structure, while it is also integrated with the whole. Given the early revelation of the outcome in the second and third stories, Eliot's handling of suspense in each part is especially skillful. Her serial technique in the three stories of *Scenes* shows an increasing sophistication that prepared her for the complex demands of the three full-length serial novels that followed.

The story of Eliot's turn to fiction after a career as translator, reviewer, and essayist is well known. According to her journal entry on December 6, 1857, *Scenes of Clerical Life* began with a descriptive sketch, which Lewes encouraged her to continue. She put off doing so for some months, but one morning, "as I was lying in bed, thinking what should be the subject of my first story, my thoughts merged themselves into a dreamy doze, and I imagined myself writing a story of which the title was—'The Sad Fortunes of the Reverend Amos Barton'" (Eliot, *Letters* 2: 407). The general plan for a series of stories was formed, and Lewes "at once accepted the notion as a good one—fresh and striking" (408). This retrospective suggests that her intention was vague until September, but her journal for July 20, 1856, is definite. John Chapman had invited her to contribute to the *Westminster Review*. She was "anxious to begin my fiction writing," however, and "not inclined to undertake an article that will give me much trouble." She proposed to Chapman "an article on 'Silly Women's Novels' might be made the vehicle of some wholesome truth as well as of some amusement" (*Letters* 2: 258). Apparently she felt sufficiently informed about contemporary women novelists that the subject would not give her "much trouble."

Eliot next mentions her own fiction in a journal entry on August 18: "Walked in Kew Park and talked with G. of my novel." She began to write "Amos" in September, had written "to the end of the 2nd chapter" by October 13, "brought [her] story to the end of the 4th chapter and began the 5th" on October 25, and finished it November 5 (GE Journal). The next day Lewes wrote to Blackwood to "trouble you with a m.s. of 'Sketches of Clerical Life' which was submitted to me by a friend who desired my good offices with you. It goes by this post" (*Letters* 2: 269).

The decision to serialize was probably Lewes's. He was already a contributor to *Blackwood's*,[1] and he handled the initial negotiations for publication of "Amos Barton." His journal for January 7, 1857, calls his return to *Blackwood's* (as the author of "Seaside Studies") "the proximate cause of Marian's introduction to fiction" (GHL Journal). Given Eliot's diffidence about her powers to write fiction, the serial form was an ideal way for her to begin. It allowed her to test her abilities and get an immediate response to a short work, and even to parts of a work. An additional advantage was the anonymity then customary in magazine publication: "We had long discussed the desirability of her trying her powers, in that direction; and the temptation of appearing anonymously successfully in *Blackwood* [*sic*] induced her to begin a series of tales." (GHL Journal, Jan. 7, 1857). Like most articles in Maga, her stories were published without even her pseudonym, which she did not reveal to John Blackwood until February 4, 1857:

> Whatever may be the success of my stories, I shall be resolute in preserving my incognito, having observed that a nom de plume secures all the advantages without the disagreeables of reputation. Perhaps, therefore, it will be well to give you my prospective name, as a tub to throw to the whale in case of curious inquires, and accordingly I subscribe myself, best and most sympathizing of editors,
>
> Yours very truly,
George Eliot

(*Letters* 2: 292)

This letter is only her second to the publisher, and she and Lewes alone knew the extent of the "disagreeables" that would be attached to a revelation of her identity. When Lewes wrote on November 6, 1856, he used the masculine pronoun for his "friend" (2: 269–70). Blackwood was both flattering and subtly inquisitive in a letter Eliot refers to in her journal for December 19, 1856. She records "Another great satisfaction . . . a letter from Blackwood expressing more cordially than ere his admiration of 'Amos Barton,' and hoping that the 'Great Unknown' is laying the keel of other stories."[2] Lewes continued as intermediary until December 29, 1856, when Blackwood sent the first installment of "Amos," addressing the author as "My Dear Sir" (2: 283). Thanking him January 4, 1857, Eliot subscribed herself "The Author of Amos Barton" (2: 288), which Blackwood playfully turned into "My Dear Amos" on January 30, 1857 (2: 290). Perhaps this salutation led Eliot to realize the usefulness of having a name to attach to the stories to secure her anonymity more certainly.

Anonymity was especially necessary given Eliot and Lewes's extralegal relationship, but it also shielded her as a woman author, whose gender alone would have biased reviewers. Both were aware of reviewers and readers' expectations when the author of a new book was known to be a woman. On September 22, 1856, the day her journal records the beginning of "Amos Barton,"[3] Eliot wrote to Sara Hennell that "we should all of us pass very different judgments now and then, if the thing to be judged were anonymous" (*Letters* 2: 264). Three months later, Eliot transmitted Lewes's opinion about Sara's own book: that she should "by no means put *Sara*, but S. S. Hennell. He thinks that Sara would do harm" (2: 282). Knowing that his union with Eliot would complicate the reception of "Amos," Lewes requested that Blackwood conceal even *his* connection with the work. Correcting Blackwood's assumption that "your friend is a Clergyman" (2: 275), Lewes adds, "I am not at liberty to remove the veil of anonymity—even as regards social position. Be pleased therefore to keep the whole secret—and not even mention my negotiation or in any way lead guessers—(should any one trouble himself with such a guess—*not* very likely) to jump from me to my friend" (*Letters* 2: 277). Eliot and Lewes's concealment of her identity worked so well that reviewers shared Blackwood's misimpression. The *Daily News*, for instance, ventured that "Mr. Eliot writes as a man who has dined at country clerical clubs and taken tea and talked scandal with farmers' wives, and men mixed up in the tragic strifes and momentous squabbles of country towns" (Feb. 5, 1858; 2). Few readers—Dickens was one—even guessed that the author was a woman, much less a woman whose life would be the subject of farmers' wives' scandal. Recounting these early transactions between John Blackwood and the Eliot-Lewes household, Margaret Oliphant comments that "This surmise as to the writer's profession must have caused some amusement in a household so little clerical" as that of the two authors (*Annals* 2: 436).

The need for secrecy was validated two years afterward when speculation grew, and the Liggins controversy forced Marian Lewes to acknowledge her pseudonym. In June 1859, Barbara Leigh Smith Bodichon mentioned the accurate guesses of her acquaintances about the authorship of *Scenes* and *Adam Bede*: Mrs. Owen Jones claimed "that there is a reason for secrecy great enough to explain the obstinate mystery, for the book could not have succeeded if it had been known as hers; *every newspaper critic would have written against it* (!!!) Evidently they think when it is know[n] the book will be differently judged." Bodichon laments, "From their way of talking it was evident they thought you would do the book more harm than the book do you good in public opinion. . . . Oh Marian, Marian, what cowards people are!" (*Letters* 3: 103).[4] Although Lewes was quick to protest against people's thinking "there was any *fear* of the effect of the author's name" and to insist that "You may tell it openly to all who care to hear it that the object of anonymity was to get the book judged on its own merits, and not prejudged as the work of a woman," the final phrase of this last sentence belies his confidence: "or of a particular woman" (*Letters* 3: 106). Anonymous serial publication of *Scenes* in Maga followed by pseudonymous publication of *Adam Bede* allowed for an unbiased critical reception for Eliot's first two works.

Serial publication gave Eliot the chance to begin slowly, but it was accompanied by risks arising partly from her newness to publishing fiction and partly from circumstances common to established novelists as well. Blackwood could either demand the completed work in order to judge it before he began to issue it in Maga, or accept it in parts and hope that later parts would equal the early ones. At first he was cautious. Having read "Amos Barton," he asks Lewes, "If there is any more of the series written I should like to see it, as until I saw more I could not make any decided proposition for the publication of the Tales in whole or in part in the Magazine" (*Letters* 2: 272). Lewes replied that his "clerical friend, . . . though somewhat discouraged by [Blackwood's response], has taken my advice and will submit the second story"—but he cannot begin it for three weeks (2: 273–74). To this, Blackwood responded that he had not meant to disappoint "your friend" but "thought the Tale very good." He cites an editor's difficulty in committing to a serial that might turn out poorly: "I always think twice before I put the decisive mark 'In type for the Magazine' on any M.S. from a stranger. Fancy the intense annoyance (to say nothing of more serious considerations) of publishing month after month a series about which the conviction gradually forces itself on you that you have made a total blunder." Nevertheless, if the author

> cares much about a speedy appearance I have so high an opinion of this first Tale that I will waive my objections and publish it without seeing more; not, of course committing myself to go on with the other Tales of the series unless I approved of them. . . . If you think also that it would stimulate the author to go on with the other Tales with more spirit I will publish Amos at once. (*Letters* 2: 275)[5]

Blackwood's instincts told him he was dealing with an unusually talented author, and Lewes's support added weight to his own opinion. Another comment in the letter just quoted suggests both: "I am very sanguine that I will approve as in addition to the other merits of Amos I agree with you that there is great freshness of style."[6] Lewes's response assures Blackwood that he has said the right thing for this "sensitive" friend and asks him to "publish the general title of 'Scenes of Clerical Life'—and I think you may do this with perfect safety, since it is quite clear that the writer of Amos Barton is capable of writing at least one more story suitable to Maga, and two would suffice to justify the general title" (*Letters* 2: 276–77).

Blackwood's confidence in Lewes led him to accept this advice. This was beneficial for Eliot, but risky for the publisher. Not only did Eliot sometimes have trouble meeting deadlines, but Blackwood was committed—especially with "Janet's Repentance"—to details that, when he encountered them much later, he feared would offend Maga readers. Blackwood had had the whole of "Amos Barton" in hand before he agreed to publish it, but he began the serialization of "Mr Gilfil's Love-Story" and "Janet's Repentance" before Eliot had completed either one. Receiving them one or two parts at a time, Blackwood approached the installments as any reader would have, knowing nothing of the author and receiving little preparation or contextualization. In addition, he usually had little time to ponder them or seek the opinions of others. He thus gave Eliot her first experience of the serial readers who were to be her audience for four of her eight books of fiction; like them, he reacted to the partially revealed plot, anticipated what was to come, was sometimes disappointed, adjusted his expectations, and usually in the end—like most other readers—affirmed the author's judgment.

Meeting a monthly deadline for a work not yet completed was a problem Eliot shared with her contemporaries—Dickens, Thackeray, Gaskell, Trollope,[7] Collins, and others. Though her letters do not display the anguish of a Dickens or a Thackeray when they had fallen behind, Eliot too was sometimes writing up to and beyond the time that her publisher needed to have copy (and perhaps type) in hand. Though he hinted the fact discreetly, it is obvious that Blackwood worried about whether the copy would arrive on time. Part 2 of "Amos" had appeared February 1, and the next story was scheduled to begin March 1. On February 4, Eliot wrote that she "hope[d] to send you a second story in a few days, but I am rather behind-hand this time, having been prevented from setting to work for some weeks by other business; and having, since then, been retarded by a bilious attack—surely one of the worst among the 'calamities of authors'" (*Letters* 2: 292). This is the first of many instances in which illness retarded the progress of her serial fiction writing and caused considerable anxiety for author and publisher alike.

No story having arrived in a "few days," Blackwood responded on February 10 with a gracious but anxious reminder of the risks of publishing serially: "It would be a monstrous pity not to come to time with No. 2 of the series and I hope the M.S. is either on the way or will be dispatched in response to this." He does not want her to "hurry" herself "to the detriment of the story, . . . but it would be a serious disadvantage to baulk the public expectation now fairly raised." He concludes, "I am uncommonly anxious to see No. 2, and when I get it will not allow grass to grow at my heels until I read it and let you know what I think" (*Letters* 2: 293–94). Obviously, he couldn't allow much grass to grow with the publication date only two-and-a-half weeks away. Fortunately the first two parts were ready, and Eliot found his impatience a good sign; her journal for February 11 records: "Sent off to Edinburgh the first two parts of 'Mr. Gilfil's Love Story,' after having a delightful letter from Blackwood, impatient for more M.S." The next day Lewes posted the manuscript to Blackwood. Blackwood's next letter, February 13, asks Lewes to tell the author "that I read it all last night and am quite delighted. . . . I shall be able to write with [printer's] proof the day after tomorrow. Meanwhile I shall have no fear in starting poor Gilfil before I see the conclusion of the Story." His directions to the printer on the manuscript, "Maga quickly," indicate the imminent deadline (MS., Pierpont Morgan Library, New York City).

Blackwood's willingness to take this story on faith is especially notable in light of his comment in the same letter that he was "puzzled as to how the love part is going to be managed" (*Letters* 2: 296). Perhaps his comment is a sign of approbation. While readers await the next part and ponder the plot's possible directions, their interest intensifies for what is yet to come. However, three days later, Blackwood begins the first of his "debates" with George Eliot regarding her realism, which troubled his sense of propriety throughout the second and third clerical stories. He explains notations on the accompanying proofs:

> the last marks affect <rather seriously> the plot of the story but I think my objections may be obviated without any serious alteration of the plan. It is not a pleasant picture to see a good fellow loving on when the lady's heart is openly devoted to a Jackanapes, and I am a little puzzled as to how you are to bring the excellent Gilfil out <unless> without making him too

abjectly devoted a lover for a man of character. I think the objection would be readily met by making Caterina a little less openly devoted to Wybrow and giving a little more dignity to her character. (*Letters* 2: 297)

Blackwood knows his contemporary fiction. "Nice" Victorian heroines are not supposed to show their feelings—or even to have them—until a man proposed in due form. But perhaps recalling Lewes's advice on Eliot's sensitivity, he breaks off abruptly: "I hope she finally rejects the insufferable Wybrow—but I must not speculate upon your plot, and if I am wrong in my opinions about the demeanour of Caterina with Wybrow recollect that I write to some extent in the dark" (*Letters* 2: 297). Eliot responded by pointing out, as she was to do with "Janet's Repentance," that "my stories always grow out of my psychological conception of the dramatis personae. For example the behaviour of Caterina in the gallery is essential to my conception of her nature and to the development of that nature in the plot" (*Letters* 2: 299). Blackwood's fear that Caterina is too unladylike was probably exacerbated by his editor's knowledge that the gallery scene would receive special emphasis by being placed at the end of the first installment.

A notation next to chapter 3 in the manuscript, "Go on with this Leisurely," may explain why he has "not been able to get part 2 in type yet" to include its proofs with a letter expressing reservations about the part: "I do not recollect of any passage that moved my critical censorship unless it might be the allusion to dirt in common with your heroine and the cool proceeding of Wybrow at the close of the part" (2: 297–98). Again, the placement emphasizes Tina's unladylike behavior. Eliot may aim at "the presentation of mixed human beings," but Blackwood had to consider serial readers' reactions, especially to female characters.

By now Eliot was well ahead of deadlines. She finished part 3 on February 28 and sent it to Blackwood along with proofs for part 2. By April 8 she had completed the last part (GE Journal), although Lewes did not post it until April 16 (*Letters* 2: 316). Even so, Blackwood's direction to the typesetter, "Magazine quickly," seems unnecessary, with a month and a half remaining before publication. However, Blackwood may have been slow to get to the part, since he doesn't acknowledge it until April 28 or send proofs until April 30. Perhaps he delayed because he wasn't sure how to convey tactfully his impression that it "strikes rather too drearily upon the heart" (*Letters* 2: 322).

Her own poor health and concern for her sister and family, who were seriously ill in spring 1857, slowed Eliot's work on "Janet's Repentance." While she began her "third story—title not decided on" on April 18, she did not complete part 1 until May 30, a month before its scheduled publication (GE Journal). Blackwood's impatience is recorded in a letter to Lewes on May 28, concluding, "Hoping soon to hear from you and also from G.E. with the next Tale" (2: 335). When he read the first part, Blackwood's reservations led to an exchange of letters that no doubt added to Eliot's stress. Sending proofs of part 1 on June 8, Blackwood expressed misgivings and, on June 14, hinted cautiously that he would like to have more of the work in hand: "I wish much now that I had the rest of your M.S. as I feel sure that it would enable me to write and heartily congratulate you upon a new success" (*Letters* 2: 352).

Both letters contain such strong criticisms that they undercut his confident prediction that "Janet" will be a "new success." He is more candid in a letter to his brother William on June 8: "Our views of George Eliot's new story seem very similar. I have read it over again today and not being quite able to make up my mind what to say to him I have postponed writing to him until tomorrow. It is *very clever* indeed and I have no doubt a capital story is coming but it is confoundedly disagreeable" (National Library of Scotland). In fact, he wrote the same day, and Eliot responded: "I am not much surprized, and not at all hurt by your letter," adding ambiguously that "It is a great satisfaction—in fact my only satisfaction, that you should give me your judgment with perfect frankness" (*Letters* 2: 347). On June 16, she thanked him for his "kind letter. It shows that you have understood me, and will give me confidence in the future." But she cannot provide any more copy because "I have not enough in readiness for you, to make that worth while" (*Letters* 2: 353).

In a journal entry on June 22, her first in over three weeks, Eliot describes her mind as "too intensely agitated and occupied during the last three weeks, for me to have energy left to make entries in my journal." Her usual writing anxiety was exacerbated by correspondence with the family lawyer, Vincent Holbeche, "inquiring about my marriage" and by correspondence with the Brays and with her sisters. Nonetheless, she completed part 2 on June 27 (GE Journal) and sent it to Blackwood three days later with a letter whose puzzling content may have caused Haight originally to misdate it February 24, 1857 (see *Letters* 2: 300). The new date, June 30, given in *Letters* 9: 342, does not resolve the puzzle. Her story has "grow[n] longer than [she] expected" and therefore she can only send what she has ready "instead of waiting, as I had intended, until

I had wrought the story up to its climax." If Blackwood "feel[s] a reluctance to print until you have seen the whole, it will do no harm for you to
have read the first half a little beforehand" (*Letters* 2: 300; Addenda and
Corrigenda in *Letters* 9: 342 move the date and place of this letter to June
30, 1857, at Gorey). By June 30, it was impossible for Blackwood to wait
to print until he had seen the (still) unwritten whole. The July issue had
already been sent to Eliot (Blackwood's letter of June 30 begins, "I hope
you have got your copy of the Magazine and find Janet correctly printed
in all respects" [2: 359]), and was scheduled for public sale the next day.[8]
    In his own letter of June 30, Blackwood remains anxious about both
characterization and realism in "Janet." He has no doubts about "the
power, ability, and lifelike character" of part 1, but fears that the "harsher
elements . . . are painted without relief." However, he adds, "I feel
perfectly confident that the continuation of the Story will cause my objections to disappear altogether." Perfect confidence did not mask his considerable anxiety to receive that continuation: "The temptations to idleness in this hot weather in Jersey [where Eliot and Lewes were staying]
must be very great; nevertheless I hope to see a batch of M.S. very soon"
(*Letters* 2: 359). These two letters with their curious cross-purposes were
in the mail at the same time; given the remarkably good postal system,
Blackwood should have received part 2 within a couple of days. By July 7,
he was able to send proofs, along with a letter that makes no mention of
Eliot's mooted assumption that he could delay publication. Whatever his
views about its tone, the story would presumably continue as long as she
met her deadlines. On August 1, she records that she "finished Part 3. of
'Janet's Repentance,' and read it to G. in the evening" (GE Journal). He
mailed it the next day, and on August 9, she wrote Blackwood that the
story would end in two more installments (*Letters* 2: 373). While Lewes
was on the Continent visiting his sons, she worked on part 4, "put the
last stroke" to it on September 2, and read it to him on his return
September 3. Lewes mailed it to Blackwood the next day (GE Journal).
On September 5, Eliot reiterated her intention to conclude "Janet" with
part 5 and announced that she would end the series with this story,
explaining that she had a novel-length subject in mind (*Letters* 2: 381).[9]
Part 5 was completed on October 9; less than two weeks later, on October 22, her journal records, "*Began my new novel, 'Adam Bede.'*"
    Eliot had the option of serialization or volume publication for her
novel. Because of the brevity of the stories in *Scenes of Clerical Life*, she
had little choice—especially as a new author—but to begin with maga-

zine serialization. *Scenes* had the advantage of continuing the tradition of linked stories to which Victorian readers had become accustomed from *Pickwick Papers* to numerous successors, including *Cranford*. *Pickwick's* importance as a literary prototype for both *Scenes of Clerical Life* and *Cranford* is suggested by its place in early installments of both works. In installment 1 of *Cranford*, Captain Brown is "deeply engaged in the perusal of a number of *Pickwick*" when he is killed by the train (chapter 2). In the second number of "Amos Barton," the Reverend Archibald Duke "thinks the immense sale of the 'Pickwick Papers,' recently completed, one of the strongest proofs of original sin" (52).

In *Pickwick*, unity comes not so much from the story line as from the members of the Pickwick Club. In *Scenes of Clerical Life*, the unifying factor is place. Character and place together provide unity to the loosely structured narrative of *Cranford*, which Gaskell originally envisioned as one or two discrete sketches, "a couple of tales about Cranford" as she described them when they first appeared (Gaskell, *Letters* 174).[10] Gaskell made little attempt to use suspenseful endings in the early parts, whose discreteness is indicated by the spacing of their publication: parts 1 to 4 appeared December 13, 1851, January 3, March 13, and April 3, 1852. These installments are especially episodic, each being a self-contained unit that achieves its own closure. They are connected by a single setting, a recurring body of characters, and a consistent narrator. By installments 5 and 6 on the "Panic" (January 8 and 15, 1853), the plot links are stronger, and installments 7 through 9 are unified by the bank failure and its aftermath (April 2 and May 7 and 21, 1853).[11]

Cranford, Gaskell's three-part "Lizzie Leigh" (which began in *Household Words*, number 1, March 30, 1850), and other serial stories of the 1850s by popular writers like William Howitt and Harriet Martineau are full of domestic drama and pathos—the element Lewes felt sure Eliot could write after he read Milly Barton's death scene in chapter 8 (*Letters* 2: 408). There is no evidence that Eliot was thinking of *Cranford* when she began her clerical stories, though she probably had heard the general characteristics of this popular work and, perhaps more than coincidentally, chose to read it for the first time while she was writing "Mr. Gilfil."[12]

One part of the context in which Eliot's readers encountered her first work was, of course, *Blackwood's* itself. In her history of the firm, John Blackwood's daughter, Mrs. Gerald Porter, recalled that "A magazine with my father was a magazine, meaning a collection of everything, where authors, professional or non-professional, soldiers, politicians, clergy-men, travellers—all might exhibit their wares" (21). The other "wares" exhibited with George Eliot's first fiction illustrate Blackwood's and readers' tastes and expectations. In the first installment, Eliot's realism and humor contrast sharply with the standard Christmas ghost story, supplied by Margaret Oliphant's "A Christmas Tale," which mixes Gothic detail with anticipations of the sensation novels of the 1860s. Gothic elements include a mysterious gabled house; a solemn vow unbroken for 300 years; a ghostly, speechless family; and a haunted room at the *Witch*-erley Arms (emphasis added). Other details point to the familiar, contemporary setting and time of 1860s sensation fiction, especially the references to the railways (76). Gothic horrors, rather than safely distanced, are "In England, and in the nineteenth century!" (81).[13] Oliphant's story provides both titillation and reassurance to January's readers seated by their own firesides by resolving its mystery through the convention of the narrator's dream, from which he awakes to find "myself in my own crimson easy-chair, after dinner, with the fire glowing into the cosy twilight, and no dark avenue or lonely manor-house within a score of miles" (86).

This seasonal conjunction of content with publication date also looks back to *Pickwick*, whose January 1837 number includes Mr. Wardle's Christmas festivities and an interpolated ghost story with a moral. In the January 1857 *Blackwood's*, "Amos Barton" is the domestic contrast to Oliphant's ghost story. Its placid, domestic realism and quiet humor were well suited to the family readers and conservative image of Maga, and reviewers responded with enthusiasm. The *Leader*, on January 3, 1857, saw "Amos" as "the representation in fiction of direct and observant experience. The manner is quiet, the style concrete, humorous, and easy; the presentation very vivid, and the story evolved with dramatic skill." While noting the "striking contrast" with Oliphant's story, "which once more repeats the thousand times repeated trick of solving a mystery by making the whole story a dream," the review concludes ambiguously: "Nothing but consummate skill could justify so worn-out a device" (16).

John Bull and Britannia likewise called readers' attention to the "observant eye" of the author, whose "pages teem with keen touches on our social weaknesses, and gatherings from the homely realities of our country folks' sayings and doings." As a conservative "establishment" newspaper, *John Bull* liked "Amos" for its role in informing future generations about the past: "Long years hence, when the face of society will probably have altered in very many particulars—some, perhaps, for the better, many, no doubt, for the worse—we can quite imagine that it will be a matter of great curiosity with our descendants to trace the precise relation which the poor parson bore in our day to the social features around him" (Jan. 3, 1857; 12). This review did not, however, disdain the outworn device of "A Christmas Tale," but called the tale "one of those old-fashioned stories which used to be so plentiful in *Blackwood* years ago, and which we should like to see more abundant now." As a radical newspaper, perhaps, the *Leader* was less susceptible to "old-fashioned" qualities—the fake Gothicism of an ancient manor house setting—and more aware of the conventionalism of the dream resolution.

The *Illustrated Times* calls "Amos," part 1, "fresh, vigorous, and hearty." Its "author has a keen sense of humour of the Dickens' order, which he endeavours in vain to bridle, but which will be heard, and pushes its way into his dialogue and descriptions." The characters are "well drawn . . . all good class types, correctly imagined and successfully carried out." The story's authorship is puzzling; the writing is "apparently not that of a new hand, although it is difficult to decide which of the 'Blackwood' staff it belongs to," but it is "the freshest and healthiest novel writing which has adorned [that magazine's] pages since the days of 'Lady Lee's Widowhood.'"[14] The *Illustrated Times* did not apparently find "A Christmas Tale" worth mentioning (Jan. 17, 1857; 43).

In February, the *Illustrated Times* reviewer has almost decided that the new story does not fit anyone regularly writing for Maga:

> The editor and proprietors of "Blackwood" may well be proud of their new acquisition in the person of the writer of the "Scenes of Clerical Life." New? I think so, though there are times when I imagine that Colonel Bruce Hamley knows a good deal about it. There is a character in "Lady Lee's Widowhood"—a curate . . . very like poor Amos Barton. . . . Never mind; whoever it may be, writes with an ease and aptitude, and a delightful mixture of humour and pathos, that it is refreshing to meet with in these days of filtered, ladylike sentiment and forced buffoonery.

Lewes, had he seen this, would have been pleased at the confirmation of his own judgment that Eliot could write both humor and pathos. He and Eliot might also have been amused, and relieved, at the assumption of male authorship by a reviewer who asks readers to "agree with me at once that it is the writing of a man of the world, endowed withal with kindly feelings and a thorough insight into human nature." Giving the story an unusual amount of space in the month's "Magazines" column, the review prefaces a long quotation from Milly's pathetic death scene with "Mr. Dickens himself has never written a more touching bit than this" (Feb. 7, 1857; 91).

A second fictional companion to "Amos" in *Blackwood's* was Oliphant's *The Athelings*, begun in June 1856 and continuing through half the run of *Scenes of Clerical Life*, to June 1857. Neither ghostly nor realistic, the first installment begins slowly with a family not unlike Amos's, modestly genteel, with scant means. The tone, however, differs from the bleak realism of "Amos Barton," and the ordinary family quickly proves quite extraordinary. A daughter barely out of her teens has published a novel, which has reached "A Second Edition" by the third installment (Aug. 1856; 167). In the first few numbers, Oliphant lays her groundwork for events to come, but only hindsight makes this clear. Read serially, the first half must have seemed to lead only to blind alleys; the story changes direction again and again, and readers can hardly guess which family members are central, much less anticipate possible plot directions. The early installments end with non-cliff-hanger truisms [e.g., "What a pleasant night it was!" (July 1856; 45)] and Dickensian sentiment [When the Atheling daughters return from visiting a wealthy patron of writers, the narrator intones: "Not all the luxuries . . . of Mrs. Edgerly's drawing rooms . . . were a fit balance to this dearest little group, the mother and the children, who made beautiful beyond all telling the sombre face of home" (Oct. 1856; 402)]. Finally, the scene shifts from the Athelings' home in Islington to the country neighborhood of the wealthy, wicked Lord Winterbourne—where seduction, betrayal, and illegitimacy belatedly enliven the plot.

Founded in 1817, with its reputation well established by 1856, *Blackwood's* continued existence did not depend wholly on the excitement of a serial story. Yet neither could its publisher ignore this inducement to buyers, especially when new periodicals were flooding the market. The repeal of the last penny of the stamp tax on June 20, 1855, was one factor in a sudden increase in both newspapers and periodicals; growth also resulted from improvements in printing and manufacturing techniques, railway distribution, and the repeal of the paper duty in 1860 (Williams 194). Some new publications were begun to "accommodate the semiliterate millions," while others addressed the increasing demand for publications for middle-class readers "of superior education but relatively little spending money" (Altick, *Common Reader* 359). A serial story's ability to attract and hold readers was thus no negligible consideration for an editor—even at *Blackwood's*.

In part 1, "Amos Barton" examines a past time through realistic details observed by an outsider, a more "knowing" narrator sympathetic to the quirks and foibles of the characters that he wryly describes. The scenes are commonplace, unexciting, almost uneventful, and "Amos" declines to employ the conventional cliff-hanger ending that Oliphant exploits in the January number of *The Athelings*. Until part 7, December 1856, Oliphant's narrative had been at best a series of vignettes. Suddenly, however, the melodrama begins. The wicked Lord Winterbourne is inexplicably persecuting twins (boy and girl) believed to be his own illegitimate offspring. Installment 8 hints that they are the legitimate children of the previous Lord Winterbourne by a young Italian wife; hence, the boy is the true Lord Winterbourne in a drama of usurper versus rightful heir.

Despite the obviousness of the plot, Oliphant tries to create excitement by hurrying the Athelings' eldest son off to Italy to prove the heir's claim, but the absurdity of the characterization produces more humor than suspense, as Charlie Atheling asks: "'Is it Italy?—I don't know a word of Italian. . . . Never mind, I'll go tomorrow. I can learn it on the way'" (57). John Blackwood's love of miscellaneousness in Maga could hardly have been better served than by the contrast between Charlie's optimistic confidence that he will learn Italian "on the way" to uncover the truth, and Amos Barton's plodding lack of self-knowledge—a lack that guarantees he will never learn the perceptiveness and language of diplomacy needed to communicate with the workhouse inmates or the wealthy farmers in his parish.

If "Amos Barton" bears little resemblance in subject and serial structure to the tales of mystery, crime, and the supernatural that were popular with Blackwood, Dickens, and other editors at Christmastime, its setting at least fit the season. Subscribers to *Blackwood's* could gather around the fireside while one member of the family read aloud the descriptions of the sleet through which Amos trudges on his way to and from the "College," the snow that covers the ground when the Bartons walk to dinner at Mr. Bridmain's, and the cold against which Milly prepares her shawl for early morning darning.[15] But these homely details by themselves might not sustain long-term reader interest. The rather quiet conclusion to part 1 of "Amos Barton" may have prompted Blackwood to give a hint to his new author. Without referring explicitly to the serial convention of the cliff-hanger ending, his first letter to George Eliot (rather than Lewes), dated December 29, 1856, points to the importance of attracting readers to a new work, and, by implication, of keeping them. Enclosing the first installment of *Scenes*, he explains that he began "the number with Amos . . . because his merits will entitle him to it and also because it is a vital point to attract public attention to the *first* part of a Series, to which end being the first article of the first number of the year may contribute" (*Letters*, 2: 283). Already informed by Lewes of the author's sensitivity, Blackwood, by pointing to his own awareness of readers, may have hoped that Eliot would take his gentle hint and become similarly aware herself. In later correspondence, he praises her conclusions to those endings of "Mr Gilfil's Love-Story" and "Janet's Repentance" that seem most calculated to stimulate readers' curiosity and maintain suspense. With "Amos Barton," the story's one serial ending was already printed in the issue that accompanied Blackwood's letter; a cliff-hanger ending was, in any event, impossible. The only potentially sensational event, Milly's death, is quietly and soberly presented and occurs too far into the story to be a dividing point.

Eliot's readers loved the pathos of the death scene. Even the "luminaries of the Garrick," Blackwood told her, "generally seem to have mingled their tears with their tumblers over [her] death bed" (*Letters* 2: 293). He might have been thinking of what a good ending the death scene would have made when he wrote on January 30, just before the second and final installment, that "A good many people will be disappointed at finding his history so speedily wound up" and predicted that Milly's death would "go to the hearts of all readers. It is a most touching death bed scene" (*Letters* 2: 290). Only by writing more of the widower and his children could Eliot have exploited the death scene's pathos for serial purposes, and this she refused to do. Even when she became aware that others wished more had been done with "Amos," she held fast to her vision of the story. Three months later, she responded to Blackwood regarding his feeling that her stories were "huddled up" at the end. "There must be something wrong in the winding up of 'Amos,' for I have heard of two persons who were disappointed with the conclusion. But the story never presented itself to me as possible to be protracted after Milly's death. The drama ends there" (*Letters* 2: 324).

Instead of the death scene, Eliot needed a breaking point roughly midway. The serial stories in *Blackwood's* usually filled between eighteen and twenty-two pages, and a break was possible either before or after the short chapter 4. If the break occurred before chapter 4, part 1 would have been just over nineteen pages long, with part 2 almost twenty-two pages; if the break occurred after chapter 4, part 1 would have had twenty-one and one-half pages, and part 2, nineteen and one-half. Ending with chapter 5 would also have been possible, though it would have resulted in a first installment of twenty-six pages, with a much shorter one to follow. Internal evidence, in the style of the close of part 1 and the opening of part 2, suggests that Eliot planned the break to occur after chapter 4, although she did not mark it on her manuscript. Her failure to do so prompted a letter from John Blackwood suggesting a break different from the one Eliot chose. In a letter extant only in a Blackwood's letter book, John Blackwood proposes a break after chapter 3: "The explanation of the previous life of the Countess makes a capital wind up for a part, but probably it might be desirable to leave the readers [*sic*] curiosity excited as to her for a month."[16] Eliot, instead, elected to end part 1 after the explanation of the Countess's life in chapter 4.

This break gives each of the two parts an internal coherence that is remarkably finished for the work of a novice writer. In the first installment, chapter 1 examines the people of Shepperton and environs. The middle chapters, 2 and 3, acquaint readers with Mr. and Mrs. Barton. In chapter 2, Amos's "deficiency of small tact" (27) prevents his noticing that Mrs. Brick would like a bit of snuff, an apparently minor incident that anticipates Amos's more significant and damaging blindness to what is too clear to the "keen-sighted virtue of Milby and Shepperton" in installment 2 (47). In chapter 3, the focus is on Milly Barton, who is such a "hamable [amiable] woman" (34) that she makes no fuss about the gravy spilled on her worn but "best" gown. Likewise, in installment 2, she makes no fuss about the serious inconvenience of the Countess's six-month stay at the vicarage. The narrative commentary in chapters 1 and 4 frames these middle chapters on Amos and Milly.

The seeming paradox of open-ended closure typifies installment fiction. The ideal serial conclusion rounds out an installment by providing its own closure, but it also directs readers' thoughts toward the future. In part 1 of "Amos," this open-ended closure is achieved through self-conscious narration rather than dramatic action: "The thing we look forward to often comes to pass, but never precisely in the way we have imagined to ourselves. The Countess did actually leave Camp Villa before many months were past, but under circumstances which had not at all entered into her contemplation" (41). This final paragraph turns readers' attention toward the Countess's future with not-too-subtle hints of a mystery to come.

Such direct narrative prediction is not uncommon in nineteenth-century serial fiction. Dickens uses a similar phrase to conclude number 5 of *Nicholas Nickleby*: "Poor Kate! she little thought how weak her consolation was, and how soon she would be undeceived" (1: 160). Installment endings are sometimes more explicit in pointing to the narrative as such. Chapter 1 notes the similarities between self-referential endings in the *London Spy* and *Great Expectations*. Other instances abound. Installment 2 of *Nickleby*, for example, ends with the narrator's comment: "*It may be a very undignified circumstance to record,* but after he had folded this letter and placed it in his pocket-book, Nicholas Nickleby's eyes were dimmed with a moisture that might have been taken for tears" (1: 64; emphasis added). Installment 8 of *A Tale of Two Cities* concludes with a predictive address to the reader: "Perhaps. Perhaps, see the great crowd of people with its rush and roar, bearing down upon them, too" (book 2, chapter 6). Even *The Woman in White*, whose serial breaks are usually full of high drama, ends installment 27 dully with "The following particulars comprise all that Miss Halcombe was able to discover" (390).

These metafictional devices are not exclusive to serialized works. Some of the best-known Victorian examples are *Jane Eyre*'s apostrophes to "Dear Reader," and the narrator's explanation that other novels' lack of "proper confidence between the author and his readers" will not be found in *Barchester Towers* (chapter 15). Trollope's narrator later discusses readers' interest in the "sorrows of heroes and heroines" rather than in their joys (chapter 51), and he reappears to distribute the "sugarplums" that readers expect at a novel's end (chapter 53). These narrative intrusions provoked negative criticism in some contemporary critics. The *National Review*, October 1858, for instance, censured Trollope for "frequently and somewhat offensively coming forward as author to remind us that we are reading a fiction. Such intrusions are as objectionable in a novel as on the stage: the actor who indulges in extempore and extra-professional hints and winks to the audience, and the author who interrupts his characters to introduce himself to our notice, are alike guilty of a violation of good taste" (Greg 425).

Momentary violations of the realistic illusion have varying effects. In a serial work, the effect is likely to be diminution of dramatic excitement at the end of a part. By their very nature, as devices that call readers' attention to the fictive quality of the work, self-referential endings usually lack the requisites of cliff-hangers and suggest closure rather than open-endedness. The most dramatic serial breaks halt the action at a high point, forcing the reader to await, reluctantly, restively, for its resumption a week or a month later. As Wolfgang Iser observes, the best installment endings occur at the places where the reader would be least likely to create a break (*Act of Reading* 191).

Self-referential endings, on the other hand, often indicate a new narrative, a new development, a shift of subject to begin in the next part. Offering few clues to what is coming, they fail to exploit readers' sense of suspense, which depends on knowing enough to fear the worst and hope for the best. The ending of *Pickwick Papers* for October 1836 is a good example. Perker's clerk Lowten bids Mr. Pickwick to notice one Jack Bamber, who could talk about Gray's and other "old inns" of London "forever," whereupon the installment concludes, "This was the figure that now started forward and burst into an animated torrent of words. As this chapter has been a long one, however, and the old man was a remarkable personage, it will be more respectful to let him speak for himself in a fresh one" (313). Having no idea what the old man's story is to be and only the narrator's word that he is "remarkable," Dickens's readers could probably wait with considerable equanimity until the next month, to hear Jack Bamber's story. Similarly, in part 22 of *Great Expectations* (Apr. 27, 1860), Pip's story pauses: "A great event in my life, the turning point of my life, now opens on my view. But, before I proceed to narrate it, and before I pass on to all the changes it involved, I must give one chapter to Estella. It is not much to give to the theme that so long filled my heart" (318). Having given a number to that theme, the futility of his love, Pip tells readers at the end of the next number (May 4): "[N]ow that I have given the one chapter to the theme that so filled my heart, and so often made it ache and ache again" (330), he can proceed in the next installment to the "great event" alluded to the week before. These self-referential endings to installments 22 and 23 interrupt no action, but instead attempt closure for past events and, at best, mild anticipation of a coming new twist in the plot. This is the technique Eliot adopted in "Amos Barton." The stage has been set and the characters introduced. A story proper will begin in the next installment, but just what that story will be is hard to tell, and it is no wonder that some readers expected more to come after Milly Barton's death.

The ending Blackwood proposed after chapter 3 would not have made a more directive serial conclusion, and the final lines for the chapter are uninteresting. A break after chapter 5, on the other hand, would have been more dramatic, occurring *in medias res*, and it would have had the advantage of emphasizing Amos Barton, in contrast to the end of chapter 4, in which the central figure is the Countess. The final lines of chapter 5 refer to present problems and future complications: "With a like inky swiftness did gossip now blacken the reputation of the Rev. Amos Barton, causing the unfriendly to scorn and even the friendly to stand aloof, at a time when difficulties of another kind were fast thickening around him" (48). The diction ("inky swiftness," "blacken the reputation," "fast thickening") and contrast ("friendly"/"unfriendly"; "scorn"/"stand aloof") heightens the dramatic effect and even hints at the cliché "the plot thickens"—just as it should with a good serial break.

The actual ending fails to provide definite, limited directions for speculation in the month's interval between parts. Rather, it breaks the narrative at a point where guesses as to subsequent events were likely to be quite random and, therefore, to fall wide of the mark. Apart from the Bartons' growing debt, the first four chapters give no clue to the nature of the coming conflict or even to the crucial connection between the Bartons' lives and the Countess's. These chapters focus almost entirely on character, with a sop to plot thrown in at the end. In making this choice for a serial break, Eliot marks out the territory—careful psychological presentation of character, strong narrative control, and detailed contextualizing—that was to become central in all her fiction. In her later works, however, including the second and third stories of *Scenes*, Eliot became more attentive to the drama at the close of her installments.

The drawback of emphasizing the Countess at the end of part 1 may have occurred to Eliot; in chapter 5, *Blackwood's* February readers return to Amos instead of to the mystery of the Countess's future.[17] Opening a new installment at a place different from the story's close the month before is common in serial fiction. Sometimes readers are held in suspense while the narrative introduces important background matter before their curiosity is satisfied. Several installments of *Vanity Fair* open with events unconnected to the climax of the previous number. Installment 2 does not immediately tell impatient readers whether Jos Sedley did "pop the question at Vauxhall," but instead begins with the school days of Dobbin and Osborne. This digression undoubtedly seemed as strange to the original readers as it does to students who read serially now. But readers had, after all, bought the installment and would probably continue reading until they found out what Jos did.

Later in this multi-plot novel, shifting the scene not only tantalizes readers but allows for a return to a neglected plot. Installment 9 ends with George Osborne's "lying on his face, dead, with a bullet through his heart" (315); installment 10 begins in Miss Crawley's Brighton household, as James Crawley and Pitt the Younger battle over her money in a parody of the war theme. Readers hear nothing of the widowed Amelia until three chapters into the number. Part 14 ends with young George Osborne in the custody of his paternal grandfather, and his mother at the nadir of her story. There she remains out of sight for the whole of installment 15, which is devoted solely to Becky at the zenith of her aristocratic career. This device is especially effective in multi-plot novels where the narrator has several plot strands to keep before the readers and can return to any one to start a new number.[18]

While "Amos Barton" cannot be called a multi-plot novel, the first part has a dual-character focus, on the Bartons and the Countess. The narrator draws Amos and Milly into a dialogue to reengage readers with these central characters. Amos is, as "you perceive, in no respect an ideal or exceptional character." Three lengthy opening paragraphs "bespeak your sympathy" for ordinary unheroic characters and expound Eliot's doctrine of realism (41–42). Then the narrator leads readers back to the story: "Meanwhile, readers who have begun to feel an interest in the Rev. Amos Barton and his wife, will be glad to learn that Mr Oldinport lent the twenty pounds . . ." (42). The suspense is still rather slight, being confined principally to the Bartons' monetary difficulties, but the digression reestablishes the bond between narrator and reader in lieu of more dramatic ways of capturing serial readers' attention. This kind of bridge is also an established serial device. Gaskell, for example, employs it in *Cranford*. In opening part 3, the narrator's chatty discussion of everyone's "small economies" and description of reading letters by a single candle (Miss Matty's small economy) effects the transition from the story of Miss Matty and Thomas Holbrook, completed in installment 2, to a different past event, her brother Peter's disappearance. A narrator's lengthy digression at the head of a new installment also occurs in "Janet's Repentance" but not in Eliot's next clerical scene, "Mr Gilfil's Love-Story." Both stories, however, illustrate changes in her serial technique.

The four parts of "Mr Gilfil's Love-Story" were published from March to June 1857, and the five parts of "Janet's Repentance," from July to

November. In terms of plot, "Amos Barton" and "Mr Gilfil's Love-Story" fit comfortably within the bounds of Victorian fictional conventions, which welcomed pathetic tales of domestic poverty and quiet devotion as well as romantic love stories. In "Gilfil," with the love interest a generation's remove from the prosaic narrative frame, Caterina's violent, passionate acts are distanced for readers, although Blackwood still worried about the effect of her passionate responses to Anthony. "Janet's Repentance," however, pushed more emphatically against the boundaries of appropriate subject matter. The story's alcoholism and wife abuse anticipate the freer handling of social improprieties and vices, especially in women, in the sensation fiction of the 1860s. Blackwood's anxiety was not reduced by Eliot's skillful use of serial endings, which emphasize the drama in the stories and yet mitigate the sensational effect. While repeating the complex characterization, narrative control, and detailed re-creation of time and place found in "Amos," Eliot's next two stories pay more attention to the structure and cliff-hanger endings commonplace in serialization.

Like "Amos," both stories open slowly, with detailed introductions to characters and locale. In "Gilfil," however, the basic conflict has been defined by the end of installment 1: Anthony Wybrow has bowed to duty and the "inflexible will" of Sir Christopher (114) and will marry the daughter of Sir Christopher's "earliest love" (115). Nonetheless, his continued flirtation with Caterina allows readers to speculate on possible outcomes of the plot based on fictional love triangles encountered elsewhere.

Of the three stories, "Mr Gilfil's Love-Story" bears the greatest resemblance to other contemporary serial or volume fiction. In fact, readers of the first installment in *Blackwood's*, March 1857, did not have to look beyond its pages for a story with similar conventions and situations. In this number of Maga, Louisa Melville Fraser's single-installment tale, "Hester Benfield," offers two love triangles on which readers of *Scenes of Clerical Life* could base their speculations. In addition, Oliphant's continuing serial *The Athelings* has taken a direction, finally, and its central issues—inheritance, love, and revenge—are also those of "Gilfil."

"Hester Benfield"'s two-generational love complications feature several stereotypical Victorian characters and situations: a virtuous young seamstress (Hester); an aristocrat who rescues her from a drunken sailor; their clandestine marriage, undertaken by the aristocrat to punish the woman of his own class who has rejected him; the new husband's belated discovery that his beloved had rejected him only in a moment of pride, but that she does indeed love him; his (resisted) temptation to deny his marriage; his (not resisted) temptation to abandon his now pregnant wife; his wandering abroad for many years; her Providential rescue by two benevolent strangers; her later marriage with a kind and gentle man, after she is convinced—erroneously—that the clandestine marriage had been a sham; her first husband's reappearance; their agreement to conceal the fact of their marriage (she does not know her first husband's true identity and is devoted to her daughter from the bigamous marriage); and her deathbed confession. The daughter of the bigamous marriage conveniently dies, and the story concludes with Hester's son's being recognized as his father's legitimate heir; his aristocratic lineage uncovered, he marries the daughter of the woman his father had once loved, whom he met and fell in love with after rescuing her father (his commanding officer) when he was attacked on patrol in India. As this brief summary suggests, this single-installment story contains more incidents and complications than the four installments of "Gilfil." Although the two works may seem to have little in common, the essential ingredients of the two love triangles in "Hester Benfield" are nearly identical with those in the love triangles of Eliot's narrative. Both stories work from clichés—a wealthy man toying with the affections of a poor girl, pride going before a fall. In that sense, all of romantic literature provides a context for "Mr Gilfil's Love-Story." But as reader-response critics demonstrate, each individual reader's response to a text is conditioned by the prior reading he or she has done. With "Hester Benfield" in the same issue as part 1 of "Gilfil," the thematic connections—even if stereotypical—are reinforced.

The penniless, orphaned Caterina, the mature, worthy clergyman Gilfil, and the aristocratic, self-absorbed heir Wybrow form a triangle parallel to the orphaned seamstress Hester, the worthy lover (in "Hester Benfield," a doctor—"minister" to the body rather than the spirit), and the reckless aristocrat George Asleigh. A second triangle juxtaposes Caterina, Wybrow, and Beatrice Assher against Hester, Asleigh, and Lady Helen Maldon, Asleigh's cousin. In both stories, an older generation attempts to relive their thwarted loves through the younger. Sir Christopher attempts to replicate his early love for Lady Assher by promoting Anthony's marriage to Miss Assher; Asleigh and Lady Helen Maldon never marry, but her daughter and his son form a union in the second generation.[19] Both aristocratic heroes are reckless of the young, naive girls who come under their sway. In "Gilfil," Wybrow toys with Caterina from conceit and boredom. Even as he embraces her, he thinks, "'Poor little Tina! it would make her very happy to have me. But she is a mad little thing'" (98). The narrator expands on his motives: "There was little company kept at the Manor, and Captain Wybrow would have been much duller if Caterina had not been there. . . . What idle man can withstand the temptation of a woman to fascinate, and another man [Gilfil] to eclipse?—especially when it is quite clear to himself that he means no mischief, and shall leave everything to come right again by-and-by" (113–14). Idleness and the woman's reluctance also motivate Asleigh. He "frequently waylaid [Hester] in the evening, on her return to her solitary lodging. At first, curiosity and mere idleness induced him to seek her, then, piqued by the coldness of her manner and her resolute endeavors to avoid him, he became more earnest" (340).

Review columns in Victorian newspapers and journals demonstrate that readers encountered one story in a kind of mental juxtaposition with another.[20] With the whole of Fraser's story appearing in the March number of *Blackwood's*, its readers could not only observe the initial parallels between Anthony's behavior to Caterina and Asleigh's to Hester, but could see possibilities for plot developments in "Gilfil" in Hester's completed story. What plot expectations might readers of "Gilfil," part 1, have formed in the context of the two other stories published with it in March 1857?

Thematically, the two stories reenact the cliché "pride goes before a fall." The family pride of Asleigh and Lady Helen Maldon is matched by the pride of Sir Christopher Cheverel, who cuts off an entail that would have passed his property to the son of an elder sister with whom he has quarreled (113). Instead he designates as his heir Anthony Wybrow, son of his youngest sister. Beatrice Assher's pride is affronted when she thinks Anthony has made love to Caterina who, in her view, is inferior both socially and physically. Caterina's injured pride leads to confrontations with Anthony that increase his palpitations, and injured pride sends her flying to the Rookery, dagger in hand.[21] Both stories formulate a moral on the subject of pride. The final four lines of "Hester Benfield" are explicit: "and if there is a fault which grandmamma [Lady Helen], in her lectures to Alice's little daughters, particularly condemns, it is that of pride" (355). Eliot's moral is more smoothly integrated into the characterization. Sir Christopher confesses to Gilfil after Anthony's death: "I didn't think anything would unman me in this way; but I'd built everything on that lad. Perhaps I've been wrong in not forgiving my sister. She lost one of her sons a little while ago. I've been too proud and obstinate"

(169). Sir Christopher then endures another blow to his pride, when Gilfil announces Caterina's disappearance and affirms that Anthony had, "Before his marriage was talked of . . . behaved to her like a lover" (225).

The initial parallels in the characters' circumstances, in the love triangles, and in the shared theme of pride offered readers various channels for forming expectations as they anticipated new installments of "Gilfil." Enlarging these channels was *The Athelings*, whose March 1857 installment shares "Gilfil's" theme of uncertain heirship, love, and revenge. Oliphant's convoluted March installment includes the death of the false Lord Winterbourne's son and Charles Atheling's Italian search, instigated by the late Lord's daughter, avenging her lover's death at the usurper's hand. The love plot thickens as the younger Miss Atheling becomes attached to the half-Italian, rightful heir. Passion and melodrama characterize both stories.[22]

The focus of an installment's conclusion is crucial in shaping expectations for the next installment. "Gilfil," part 1, concludes with the narrator's comparing the night thoughts and attitudes of each of the principals in the triangle of Gilfil, Anthony, and Caterina. This description follows immediately a scene in which Anthony embraces Caterina in the Gallery. As Caterina responds warmly, one outcome must have occurred to Victorian readers: what "Hester Benfield" calls the "'old tale,' so often told" (342) of a woman seduced and abandoned; and Blackwood termed "the usual sad catastrophe" a year later, after he read what were to have been installments 1 to 3 of *Adam Bede* (*Letters* 2: 446). Though Anthony does not physically seduce Caterina, their relationship and his assumption that all will "come right" no matter how he behaves, anticipates the Arthur-Hetty relationship in *Adam Bede* (1859), in which the self-indulgent, idle young man always, of course, means no harm.[23] Eliot's dissection of the rationalizing conscience of the seducer is unique, but *Adam Bede*'s main action was common enough in Victorian life and literature.[24]

This "old tale" of a wealthy gentleman seducing and deserting a poor girl was foregrounded in Victorian readers' imaginative horizon by the *cause célèbre* of Gaskell's *Ruth*, which had treated the young seamstress-victim sympathetically only four years before (1853). The theme recurs in *The Athelings*, in the monitory tale of Mr. Atheling's sister, who dies of a broken heart when she learns the false Lord Winterbourne's true intentions. Apparently even an unsuccessful attempt to seduce a young woman, if her affections became engaged, could be fatal.[25] In early installments,

Mrs. Atheling had warned her daughters with a very general statement: "'Oh, take care!—you do not know how much harm might be done in a single day,'" a statement too oblique for Marian, the beautiful younger sister (Sept. 1856; 309). The elder sister, whose bluestocking, novelistic propensities apparently give her more insight, becomes responsible for looking after Marian to prevent a recurrence of Miss Bride Atheling's sad tale of thwarted love, decline, and death. In installment 6, Mrs. Atheling tells them their aunt's story, repeating it for her son Charles in installment 9, February 1857—one month before *Blackwood's* readers encountered Caterina's dilemma in "Gilfil."

With these and other literary examples before them, Eliot's readers could readily form expectations of a tragic fate for Caterina. Blackwood's request that Eliot make "Caterina a little less openly devoted to Wybrow" and give "a little more dignity to her character" (*Letters* 2: 297) reflects his awareness of the social and moral censure as well as the danger of seduction that could befall a too responsive woman. The first installment's revelation that Gilfil later married Tina does not render an earlier seduction impossible. The doctor marries Hester Benfield even though he believes her to have been seduced through the ruse of a pretended marriage; her son, whom the doctor adopts, is generally regarded as illegitimate and takes his mother's family name. Caterina's fate is more like Bride Atheling's; she survives the blow of Anthony's treachery and death only long enough for a brief marriage to Gilfil before she dies.

Installment 2 of "Gilfil" ends with a dramatic confrontation centered on the second love triangle, two women courted by the same man: Anthony proclaims "'Miss Assher be hanged!'" as his "fascination of old habit" returns, he embraces Caterina, and she rushes from the room (128). Though Anthony's lack of feeling and general indolence make the fulfillment of Caterina's wishes unlikely (even had the narrator not begun the story by telling the readers about Caterina's marriage and death), sentimental (and forgetful) readers nonetheless might still hope for a miracle for the next month. Readers—and even authors, as Dickens in *Great Expectations* and Hardy in *The Return of the Native*[26] demonstrate—sometimes allowed the hopes for a happy ending to take precedence over the probable. More astute, or more skeptical, readers might wonder whether Anthony's indiscretion will drive the haughty Miss Assher, like the proud Lady Helen, to reject her suitor, only to repent later. Although the unsensational tone and events of "Amos Barton" mitigate against expectations of a secret-marriage-and-bigamy plot in

"Gilfil," readers saw that its passionate, willful characters were different from the mild Amos. The violence in the emotions of thwarted lovers Asleigh and Caterina might even suggest another scenario, not necessarily excluding the first, in which despair drives Caterina, like Asleigh, to desperation. What will she do after rushing passionately from the room at the end of installment 2? Nothing very sensational—yet.

At the start of installment 3, the reader discovers Caterina seeking consolation of her old friend Bates the gardener, but his praise for Miss Assher's beauty moves her to leave him in despair. Caterina grows more desperate, Miss Assher more suspicious, and Anthony more callous as he proposes to Sir Christopher that Caterina marry Gilfil. The installment ends as Caterina, dagger in her hand and murder in her heart, rushes to the Rookery to find Anthony apparently dead. While John Blackwood praised the ending generally, the dagger was, for the editor of a family publication, a bit *too* sensational. Fearing negative reader response, he wrote Lewes of his "grave doubts about the dagger . . . I am pretty sure that [the] dear little heroine would be more sure of universal sympathy if she only dreamed or felt as if she could stab the cur to the heart" (*Letters* 2: 308). Blackwood preferred the dagger to remain abstract like the clichéd "dagger in my heart" in "Hester Benfield" (353). An imaginary dagger, he suggested, "would be more consistent with her character." But then, apprehensive about discouraging his diffident author, Blackwood backs away from his remarks: "I may be wrong however and I daresay many will prefer the dadger" (*sic; Letters* 2: 308). Eliot appreciated his "retain[ing] a doubt in favour of the 'dadger,'" and refused to acquiesce in any change: "it would be the death of my story to substitute a dream for the real scene. Dreams usually play an important part in fiction, but rarely, I think, in actual life" (*Letters* 2: 309). Blackwood later acknowledged that Eliot was "quite right in [her] plan," after explaining that he had not meant, in any case, "a dream that 'I dreamed in my bed' . . . but a passing dream or thought in the mind not carried the length of actually getting hold of the dagger" (*Letters* 2: 334). Perhaps second thoughts also recalled to him the clichéd dream explanation of Mrs. Oliphant's Christmas story, and he realized that George Eliot's work was of a different order.

By the end of installment 3, "Gilfil" contains the same dilemma as "Hester Benfield": a happy outcome for all the principals is impossible. Despite a satisfactory love match for the second generation in the latter, no *deus ex machina* can intervene to satisfy readers who wish for a happy ending for both generations of lovers. Likewise, Eliot's readers are at a loss about how to resolve "Gilfil" happily for all. John Blackwood's response is a measure of what other readers of Maga would have thought at this point, because he too read the story in installments. He praises the conclusion as "a fine climax to a part," but is "puzzled as to whether Capt. Wybrow is dead or not" (*Letters* 2: 308). The juxtaposition of these statements is curious. Was his puzzlement part of the excellence of the conclusion? Perhaps he saw increased potential for speculation if readers must contemplate for the next month whether Wybrow really is dead. The two options resulting from this ambiguity provide numerous dramatic possibilities for future plot directions. Sentimentalists might hope for a minor heart attack, a *memento mori* bringing remorse and reformation to the Captain—though how to satisfy both Caterina and Gilfil, to say nothing of Sir Christopher, remains a problem. (Miss Assher is so disagreeable that readers would have applauded her defeat and humiliation, as later readers wished for the deaths of Casaubon, Rosamond, and Grandcourt.) Realistic readers, alive to earlier hints about Wybrow's health, might assume his death and anticipate a pathetic closure showing Caterina's decline and death.

The March 1857 installment of *The Athelings*, two months before Anthony Wybrow is found dead, reinforces this latter expectation. Oliphant eliminates an inconvenient heir-apparent by the sudden death of the impostor Lord Winterbourne's son. Of course, unless readers had completely forgotten Eliot's first installment two months before, the potential for speculation and suspense was limited by the earlier revelation that Caterina eventually married Gilfil and died not long after her marriage. This worried Blackwood. On the eve of publishing part 3, he wrote to Lewes that he considered the early revelation of the ending unwise: "It is a dangerous thing to let the reader know the *upshot* of a Tale before he gets to the end of it, [but] no one could *in the circumstances* have kept up the interest more powerfully than George Eliot has done" (*Letters* 2: 322; emphasis added). Though two months have passed, Blackwood still regrets that the opening chapter of "Gilfil" reveals so much when the possibilities for pathetic denouements are so splendid.

Blackwood believed the pathos of the story to be one of its strengths. At the same time, he worried that it "strikes rather too drearily upon the heart" and "was glad to hear from George Eliot that his next story is to be on a brighter theme," the kind that Victorian readers, including Blackwood, liked (*Letters* 2: 322). "Hester Benfield" and *The Athelings*, though replete with examples of disappointed love, end with optimism. There is satisfaction for the new generation in "Hester Benfield," and in *The Athelings*, for old and young. Blackwood's view did not, however, find universal support. Some reviewers applauded "Gilfil" for avoiding the conventional happy ending of its Maga contemporaries. The *Atlas* could have been thinking of "A Christmas Tale," "Hester Benfield," or *The Athelings* in noting that Eliot's "characters are not the lifeless *silhouettes* that too often stalk through three volumes of twaddle, but are real flesh and blood creations. . . . His stories are entirely free from anything like exaggeration, rose-pink sentimentality, or spasmodic intensity." Though it is "difficult to say which [of the three tales] displays the greatest merit," the *Atlas* singles out "Gilfil" for "certain rare touches of pathos which it contains." Given the praise for Eliot's freedom from "spasmodic intensity," it is curious that the review does not share Blackwood's view of the dagger scene, which it quotes at length, prefaced by the remark that "We do not remember a more picturesque and vivid scene than this incident" of Caterina's rushing to the Gallery, taking the dagger, and hurrying to the Rookery (Feb. 6, 1858; 89). The *Morning Chronicle*, which finds "more than average merit in these doleful volumes," calls Eliot "essentially a tragic writer." Even though Gilfil marries Caterina, "our author, who, as a bare observer, will not allow us to be comfortable, kills her very shortly after marriage" (Jan. 15, 1858; 6).

For some reviewers, the exciting incidents of "Gilfil" made it more appealing than "Amos." The *Morning Advertiser*, for instance, notes the "graphic and powerful hand" that depicts the domestic events in the very ordinary life of Amos Barton. But the next story, "which is characterised by the same graphic descriptive power . . . has the additional excitement of a number of love incidents, including a gallant captain, who adores chiefly himself, but who has succeeded in gaining the affections of two ladies." Describing Wybrow as "gallant" even while acknowledging his self-centeredness suggests that this reviewer has derived romantic expectations from other literary examples, certainly not from Eliot's narrative. A second allusion to the "excitement" places the reviewer firmly in the romantic reading tradition: "The perplexities of the situation are finely worked out, and, in fact, the story affords an abundance of that excitement of which the habitual reader of fiction is so fond" (Jan. 8, 1858; 3). The *Times* reviewer also selected "Gilfil" as the favorite, but for its realism rather than its romantic qualities: "It has the peculiarity of being a retrospect commencing from Mr. Gilfil's death," with the "effect of the whole [being] to reconcile us to human nature." The reviewer differs from Blackwood regarding the early revelation. "The artificial elements of the story are thus kept within bounds, the tendency to sacrifice to their exigencies is compensated by a reference to the actual results of experience, and a closer resemblance than usual is thus established between the conceptions of fiction and the realities of the world" (*Critical Heritage* 62).

These reviews appeared after all three stories were published together in volume form. Serial reviews of *Scenes* were less extensive, being confined to occasional mentions of the work in newspapers such as the *Leader, John Bull and Britannia*, and the *Illustrated Times*, whose columns regularly reviewed the monthly magazines. Their reviewers were impressed by the exceptional talent of the unknown author, and from the start, praised the originality and freshness of these realistic pictures of life—the same qualities that had appealed to John Blackwood. Some of the earliest comments about "Amos Barton" in its serial format have already been quoted. When "Gilfil" began, reviewers in the *Leader* and *John Bull* became even more enthusiastic. The *Illustrated Times* found the story too conventional, at least in the first three installments. The story lacks "both the interest and the good writing, which characterised 'The Sad Fortunes of the Rev. Amos Barton,'" and its fictional companion in the March issue, *The Athelings*, is no better: it "drags its slow length along—a dull family story, with long-winded conversations and dreary platitudes" (Mar. 7, 1857; 155). In the second installment, the plot is "Gilfil's" principal weakness:

> though containing many happy descriptions both of character and scenery, [it] lacks interest, and is becoming rather wire-drawn. The same fault was shown by the author in his little history of Amos Barton. He is evidently a keen observer, and endowed with a great sense of the ridiculous; but he lacks the power of weaving a skilful and complicated plot, which, it is needless to say, is a great essential in such writing. (Apr. 4, 1857; 218)

Not until May does the complaint of conventionality become definite, when the writer argues that Gilfil has "scarcely any" of the good qualities, "the novelty of style, the quaint descriptive power, and eventually . . . the depth of pathos which was evinced" in "Amos Barton." If that story had little plot, this new story is written on the gold-beating principle of spreading a little matter over a large surface, and has not even originality for its recommendation. The characters of Caterina and Captain Wybrow, the two personages in whom the interest is supposed to be concentrated, have been painted a hundred times. The petulant, self-willed, jealous, impulsive girl, and the handsome heartless "swell," are just as much stock characters with the present as the rustic beauty and the vicious lord were with the past generation. Miss Assher, the haughty, cold, inanimate heiress, is equally conventional; while poor Mr. Maynard Gilfil, of whom we hear very little, is the very type of that patient, unloved-but-always-loving, large, athletic, honourable and good-natured Briton, of whom the virtuous English reader is particularly fond.

The reviewer does not mention specifically *The Athelings* or "Hester Benfield," but the character types he denigrates could have come from either. *The Athelings* contains a past generation's vicious lord and more than one rustic beauty.

This reviewer shares Blackwood's concern about the dagger (though for different reasons) and the premature revelation of the ending, and he may also have expected Caterina's seduction.

> There is not sufficient incident in the story to bear the wire-drawing process to which it has been submitted; and although, by the introduction of a clap-trap and rather "London-Journal"-like effect at the conclusion of the month's instalment, it would appear that the preconceived notion of the dénouement will be slightly altered, yet as we know that Caterina eventually married Mr. Gilfil, and died shortly after, there can be at least no mystery as to the fate of the heroine. (May 16, 1857; 310)

What the "preconceived notion" was is not explained here or in the *Illustrated Times*'s other serial notices, but seduction is certainly high on the list of possibilities. The review concludes by demanding that "an unknown tale-writer in the leading magazine should have a strong framework for his story, and at least put some novelty in his novel." The *Illustrated Times*'s final review of "Gilfil" is more positive, especially compared to its comments on *The Athelings*, which also concluded in June: the "concluding chapters [of "Gilfil"] are perhaps the best written of the series. The 'Athelings,' always a dull tale, is brought to a dull conclusion" (June 13, 1857; 375).

These are the most negative notices of "Gilfil." No other serial or volume reviews object to conventionality in general or to the dagger scene in particular. On the contrary, after the May installment, the *Leader* "express[es] our gratitude for 'Mr. Gilfil's Love Story,' which fills us with increasing admiration as it proceeds" (May 8; 448). The same month *John Bull* argues that "the author . . . has thrown a strong spell on us in the previous numbers of his tale, which becomes still more powerful as the story progresses. The writer is no stranger to the motives of the human heart, and he has the gift of bringing them vividly before his readers" (May 2; 284). In June, *John Bull* notes "Gilfil's" conclusion and hopes the series "will proceed with another of their interesting narratives next month" (363). The *Leader* assumes that *Scenes* is being replaced by Bulwer Lytton's *What Will He Do With It?*, which began in the same number, and is disappointed: "it is questionable whether the exchange will be much to our advantage. We shall miss the quiet power, delicate insight, and subtle truthfulness which gave the 'Scenes of Clerical Life' so peculiar a charm. . . . the loss will scarcely be supplied by the new story" (June 6; 544).

One hopes that these favorable reviews were a consolation to John Blackwood, because he was destined to be disappointed in his expectation of a "brighter theme" in Eliot's next story. This narrative, whose installments he continued to receive one at a time, was to test Blackwood's faith in his author. Not only was "Janet's Repentance" not the pleasant story he had anticipated to relieve the gloom of "Gilfil," but the subject matter was even more distasteful than Caterina, her passion, and her dagger. A young—and foreign[27]—woman with a thwarted passion might be permitted a dagger that she never uses, but an English housewife with a penchant for the brandy bottle was too much for Blackwood and, he feared, for his readers, especially when added to Dempster's brutality: "The first scene . . . is deuced good but rather a staggerer in an opening scene of a Story of Clerical Life. Dempster is rather too barefaced a brute and I am sorry that the poor wife's sufferings should have driven her to so unsentimental a resource as beer." He also objected to the abundance of characters and the harshness of their presentation. The first installment

is exceedingly clever and some of the hits and descriptions of character are first rate, but I should have liked a pleasanter picture. Surely the colours are rather harsh for a sketch of English County Town life only 25 years ago. The glimpse at the end of the part shows that a powerful and pathetic story is coming and I rather wish you had plunged sooner into it instead of expending so much humour in the delineation of characters who do not seem likely to assist materially in the movement of the Story and who are not in themselves interesting. (*Letters* 2: 344)

This is one of Blackwood's strongest negative statements to his sensitive author. While his first letter on Gilfil used some of the same words ("It is not a pleasant picture"), his role as serial reader allowed him to hedge: "if I am wrong in my opinions about the demeanour of Caterina and Wybrow recollect that I write to some extent in the dark" (2: 297). His resistance to "Janet's Repentance" is stronger and his closing apology patently a sop: "If my comments upon Janet disappoint you, consider that I am wrong and attribute my want of appreciation to a fortnight of hot weather and hotter dinners in London" (2: 345).

Blackwood's emphatic "Surely" indicates the extent of his concern that the story would disappoint readers who anticipated a continuation of the well-defined conflicts, romantic story and appealing characters, and the clear plot direction of "Gilfil," where even the satire had been more benevolent. Blackwood's next paragraph suggests shortening the opening scene, a suggestion he could perhaps feel confident in making because this part is as long as installment 1 of "Amos" (22 pages), whereas the most recent installments of "Gilfil" had run only 18 to 19 pages. Exactly what he wanted to effect by this condensation is uncertain. The sentence immediately following the suggestion is the one quoted above, referring to Dempster's "brutality" and Janet's beer drinking. However, the opening scene shows only Dempster and his male companions drinking in a public house. He is loud, but not brutal, and he is drinking brandy and water, his own and Janet's preferred alcoholic beverage. Probably Blackwood's numerous concerns became intermingled as he tried to state them tactfully to Eliot without unsettling her.

Blackwood's problem is complicated by the conflicting requirements of serialization and a family readership. The topics he objects to—the number of characters and the subject matter—make up nearly all of part 1. To eliminate both would have reduced the part to almost nothing. He knew that a serial with too many characters at the beginning might confuse readers, and that characters treated too satirically might fail to win their interest and affection. His worries about the "harsh" treatment of the people of Milby were not alleviated by Eliot's observation that the "real town was more vicious than my Milby" (*Letters* 2: 347). The numerous characters are offstage by the end of the installment, and the focus is on "the powerful and pathetic story," as Blackwood called it (*Letters* 2: 344), of the two main figures. But now the subject matter is questionable, as Janet and Dempster are drunk, and he is beating her. Furthermore, this objectionable subject matter is highlighted by coming at the end of an installment. Victorian readers would respond to the pathos in Janet's situation,[28] but Blackwood had also to beware of bringing "a blush into the cheek of the young person," as Dickens's narrator says in the well-known phrase from *Our Mutual Friend* (129). Would family readers be susceptible to the pathos or simply be offended by the realistic depiction of alcoholism and wife abuse?

The issue of what was appropriate to a Victorian reading audience was no small matter to a publisher. If Mudie's circulating library burked a book, the result could be financial disaster. Publishers also had to fear negative reviews that might impact sales, especially of female novelists. Monica Correa Fryckstedt cites Geraldine Jewsbury's reviews in the *Athenaeum*, particularly of Rhoda Broughton's novels, which were "Too 'wicked' to find favor with Mudie in the 1860s" and which Jewsbury would have reviewed even more sternly "Had she but known that the anonymous novelist was a woman" (22–23).[29] After the authorship of Eliot's works became known, James Craigie Robertson argued anonymously in the Tory Scottish *Quarterly Review* that once female authorship had been suggested, it was impossible "to read through [her] books without finding confirmation of it in almost every page." Among the signs to the contrary was "a good deal of coarseness, which it is unpleasant to think of as the work of a woman" (Oct. 1860; 471). For a magazine serial, Mudie's influence was not an immediate threat, but readers also had long-established expectations about their favorite periodicals; the publisher of a conservative Edinburgh magazine like *Blackwood's* had to be especially careful when breaking new ground.[30]

Until she received Blackwood's comments, Eliot does not seem to have realized that the subject matter could be objectionable, and her response was precisely what Blackwood had wished to avoid. She is willing, she says, to alter certain small matters, but cannot change her

> own conceptions of life and character. There is nothing to be done with the story, but either to let Dempster and Janet and the rest be as I *see* them, or to renounce it as too painful. I am keenly alive, at once to the scruples and alarms an editor may feel, and to my own utter inability to write under any cramping influence, and on this double ground I should like you to con-

sider whether it will not be better to close the series for the Magazine *now.* I daresay you will feel no difficulty about publishing a volume containing the story of Janet's Repentance, though you may not like to hazard its insertion in the Magazine. (*Letters* 2: 348)

Blackwood quickly reassured her, "I do not fall in with George Eliots every day and the idea of stopping the Series as suggested in your letter gave me 'quite a turn,'" adding that he was not "'afraid' to publish it" (*Letters* 2: 352). Nonetheless, he continued to have difficulty with Eliot's realism.[31] In part 2, the characterization of the bishop was especially troublesome. And although Blackwood no longer hoped that Eliot would make changes, he lamented to Lewes before the final installment was printed that he "wish[ed] I had pressed George Eliot more to curtail or to indicate more delicately the Delirium Tremens scene. It is too naked and the shudder with which one turns from the picture is too much akin to disgust. He does push his Theory of qualifying any description by its truth too far" (*Letters* 2: 394–95). With publication day almost at hand, Blackwood was particularly apprehensive. The copy was already set in type, proofed, and due to appear before the public on November 1.[32]

By then, Blackwood had seen the entire story and, therefore, could not resort to the disclaimer in which he played the role of a somewhat naive reader, giving an initial and, perforce, partial reaction to a piece of serial writing. Throughout their correspondence about *Scenes of Clerical Life,* Blackwood attempted to propose changes to the text while also placating his diffident author. He would pose criticisms, and then qualify what he had just written by playing the role of serial reader with only a part of the whole before him. A part is not entirely satisfactory, but he will withhold judgment because of its promise. For example, in his second letter about "Janet," after assuring Eliot that he is not "afraid" to publish "Janet" and that the "individual pictures" are full of "ability and truth," he adds that he "only wished to convey my fear that you are wasting power in sketching in so many figures who would not help on or add to the popularity of your story" (*Letters* 2: 352). The tension between truthful "individual pictures" and "the popularity of your story" remains unresolved.

In his next paragraph, his characteristic disclaimer repeats phrases he had used for "Gilfil" four months earlier:

> From the tone of this first part I do not think that it will be much liked, but you know what groundwork you require, and when I have not seen the whole of your M.S. you must always take my remarks as those of one

writing to some extent in the dark. I wish much now that I had the rest of your M.S. as I feel sure that it would enable me to write and heartily congratulate you upon a new success. (*Letters* 2: 352; emphasis added; cf. 2: 297)

Her reply suggests that Eliot happily accepted him in this role of naive reader: "The descriptions of character are not so alien to the drama as they possibly appear to you at present, and several other things that seem to have puzzled you will I dare say, become clear as the story proceeds." She will send him more copy as soon as it is ready: "now I have your cordial words to give me confidence it will go on more swimmingly" (*Letters* 2: 353). Nonetheless, her journal entry on her exchange of letters with Blackwood during June rather equivocally calls it "an interesting correspondence" (June 22), and her frequent term for his letters is "pleasant." While Lewes was admonishing Blackwood to temper disingenuously his reactions, Eliot was capable of some disingenuousness herself. She was gracious yet firm in her letters, and clearly made her own decisions about her future fiction. Eliot's feeling that she was misunderstood by her publisher grew, and, by summer's end, she had determined not to publish any further clerical scenes.

On the eve of "Janet"'s first number, Blackwood's doubts remained. On June 30, he repeats his fear that "too many of the harsher elements of character are painted without relief"; he does not yet know "how Janet is going to take with the public." Then he discounts his fears, resuming the role of the serial reader whose access to the text is limited to the installment in hand: "but I feel perfectly confident that the continuation of the Story will cause my objections to disappear altogether" (*Letters* 2: 359). His objections did *not* disappear altogether. In his first letter on part 1, he had asked, "When are you going to give us a really good active working clergyman, neither absurdly evangelical nor absurdly High Church?" (2: 345), prompting a spirited defence in which Eliot argued that "The collision in the drama is not at all between 'bigotted churchmanship' and evangelicalism, but between irreligion and religion" (2: 347). Blackwood is still sensitive to the religious delineation in part 2, and again repeats the pattern of criticism and disclaimer. He objects to the satirical treatment of the Bishop, which did not accord with Eliot's treatment of religion in "Gilfil," where he "liked the religious feeling . . . much" (*Letters* 2: 352). While the Bishop in "Janet" is "doubtless a true sketch," Blackwood "wish[es] he had been a better sample of the cloth." Even so, he anticipates that "the best of the Story is yet to come" (*Letters* 2: 359–60). His "doubtless" conveys considerable doubt whether it is desirable to present such a Bishop, even if one happens to exist.

Just as she had defended her portrayal of alcoholism and abuse in Dempster and Janet (*Letters* 2: 347), Eliot appeals to realism and to the individuality of a fictional portrait to justify her Bishop. She is certain that "readers will perceive . . . that I am not in the least occupying myself . . . with Bishops in general, but with . . . a particular Bishop." She then articulates her artistic principles:

> Art must be either real and concrete, or ideal and eclectic. Both are good and true in their way, but my stories are of the former kind. I undertake to exhibit nothing as it should be; I only try to exhibit some things as they have been or are, seen through such a medium as my own nature gives me. The moral effect of the stories of course depends on my power of seeing truly and feeling justly; and as I am not conscious of looking at things through the medium of cynicism or irreverence, I can't help hoping that there is no tendency in what I write to produce those miserable mental states. (2: 362)

In his concerns about this last story, Blackwood was obviously torn between his high regard for his new author and what he regarded as excesses of realism. Eliot, who had already refined her theory of art in reviewing for various periodicals earlier in the 1850s, held firmly to her beliefs. Blackwood had no choice but to accept them.

Reviewers of "Janet's Repentance" generally did not share Blackwood's negative reaction. The few comments in the first serial notice in *John Bull and Britannia* are tentative: of the July number, the reviewer says, "In Blackwood [*sic*], we turn at once to the 'Scenes of Clerical Life,' which will always be a welcome announcement to its legion of readers. The author begins a new story, 'Janet's Repentance,' which we can scarcely expect will rival the past beauty of 'Mr. Gilfil's Love Story.' Janet marries against the wish of her widowed mother, and the cruel husband shows a different phase of human life to the last tale of true love" (July 4, 1857; 427). The reviewer had no comment in August; by September, the "different phase" is more definite; the story is "continued with a powerful though painful interest" (Sept. 5; 572). By October, the "deep pathos" of the story makes its impression (Oct. 3; 636), and the concluding notice, despite sharing Blackwood's concern about the melancholy tone, wishes for more: "The concluding chapters of 'Janet's Repentance' are very mournful, but we hope the author will give us another of the beautiful stories he is so well able to narrate, although to our mind in this number he has a morbid inclination to dwell on scenes of suffering and sorrow" (Nov. 7; 715). Eliot's Wordsworthian subject matter had impressed the *John Bull* reviewer from "Amos Barton," part 2: if the story is

> penned by a hitherto unknown hand, we think we may venture to augur great things for its author. He has the rare faculty of winning our sympathies for the commonest sorrows of man, and extracting matter for thought from the commonest things. In fact, his preconceived purpose, like that of Wordsworth, is to insist on the interest which dwells in
> "The common growth of Mother Earth"
> (Feb. 7; 92)

The *Illustrated Times* argues that the third story "bids fair to be a good number," but "the interest not being so concentrated," it is inferior to "Amos," (July 4, 1857; 11). Apparently the reviewer shared Blackwood's reservations about the number of characters. In August the best of the story is still anticipated: "This number leads up to, rather than reaches, that part of the narrative which promises to be the most interesting, as giving scope for the force and pathos of the writer" (Aug. 15; 123). There was no September review; space was at a premium because of the Indian Mutiny. By October, "Janet" is the "cream" of this number of *Blackwood's*; if the author "fulfil his present promise [he] will assuredly at once take rank among our first novelists." The review praises the story's realism, about which Blackwood was so anxious: "Whether in the delineation of the strongest passion, or in the rendering of common countrytown gossip in provincial dialect, he is perfectly true to nature, and his power is at once apparent" (Oct. 10; 250).

Despite an analogy that undercuts its effect somewhat for the twentieth-century reader, the final review is effusive: "THIS month sees the conclusion of 'Janet's Repentance,' the best story that has been published for years in the pages of BLACKWOOD, being superior in its light and shade of humour and pathos to 'Lady Lee's Widowhood,' which is giving it high praise indeed." Both the alcoholism and the depiction of religion are realistic:

> In the delineation of the squabbles and intrigues of a small country town, the religious discord invariably to be found among the narrow-minded men and foolish old women, the petty interests and mean enjoyments which

form the basis of every thought, and action of the people whose whole world is contained in so small a compass, the author of "Janet's Repentance" is wonderfully accurate. Nor are the leading characters in his drama less powerfully drawn—the drunken savage lawyer, the patient half-erring wife, and the clergyman, comforting, not by words alone, but by the story of his own previous errors and his present humble atonement, are all masterpieces.

Like Blackwood and other readers, the reviewer assumes a clerical author, who "is said to be the Rev. James White, author of 'The King of the Commons,' &c," adding, "Whoever he be, he need no longer write anonymously, for this work is enough to place him in the first rank of modern novelists" (Nov. 14; 327).

The *Leader's* review of the monthly magazines also several times includes brief comments on Eliot's individual installments. Like the already-quoted notice of part 1, the February review praises "Amos Barton," for "a pathos so exquisite that we do not remember anything in fiction more touching or more lifelike" (Feb. 7, 1857; 134). By September, when most readers are on holiday and therefore "magazines naturally remain unread in deserted libraries and reading-rooms, and . . . generally justify such neglect," the *Leader* notes, this year is an exception. *Scenes* is preferred to Bulwer Lytton's new story, *What Will He Do With It?*, which is full of

affected writing and stilted sentiment. One cannot help feeling, indeed, that there is a covert satire in introducing these stories together, the inflated, superficial feeling and exaggerated style of the one being a striking foil to the serene depth of insight, the delicate handling and perfect naturalness of the other. It is difficult to give an adequate notion of these [latter] qualities by extract, as they pervade and give vital unity to the whole rather than special brilliancy to detached parts. (Sept. 5; 857)

The final notice in the *Leader* hopes that *Scenes* will continue, "as they have been from the first admirable pictures of English life, marked by rare delicacy and depth of moral insight." On January 9, 1858, the *Leader* published a brief, positive notice of the two-volume edition. The "quiet and original humour, the delicate insight into character displayed, the tender and subtle pathos of the several stories, have gained for Mr. Eliot a considerable and not a common reputation, which will of course be largely increased now that *Scenes of Clerical Life* have passed out of a magazine into the circulating libraries" (43).

Other reviews of the two-volume publication note the original humor, but they especially applaud the pathos in all three stories. Volume reviews also address the issue of propriety, the clerical character of the stories and their presumed clerical author, and their relationship to contemporary fiction. Several reviews cite "Janet's Repentance" as the best of the three stories.

The *Nonconformist* praised all three stories for their depth and originality, but "Janet's Repentance" especially. Eliot "opens up scenes, and depicts varieties of character, which have not yet been much employed by the novelist." The narrative does not "halt . . . for the exposition of a lesson," nor does it include "elaborate plots," "descriptions of scenery," or "mere pictures of manners, which in so many of our fiction-writers is their besetting sin." The reviewer applauds the psychological presentation and realism of the characters. The author "seems to have first studied *one* character from life, deeply, patiently, and exhaustively; then to have looked round on the persons of the group by which such a character may be surrounded, and to have thoroughly penetrated the individuality of these." The characters are so realistic "that you feel they *must* have lived, and have spoken and acted just as they are represented to have done. In short, the whole air of the story is that of conscientious truth to real life. But . . . one is struck with [the author's] great knowledge of the human heart—his penetration of its mystery of feeling and motive, his conversance with its rarer experiences and its unspoken struggles and sufferings."

The reviewer then cites "Janet's Repentance" as the prime instance of this psychological penetration. "The character of Janet Dempster, in the third tale, is very powerfully worked out;—it is Mr. Eliot's greatest success." The "inner process" of her repentance is "so deeply true as to have both a psychological and a moral interest of an unusual intensity." The other two stories are similarly knowledgeable about human nature, "though in a less degree." This Dissenting newspaper alludes obliquely to the subject matter in "Janet" in praising the story's moral tone: "generally healthy as is the tone of the novel now-a-days, Mr. Eliot's stories may still be named with especial approbation, for their warmth and purity of human feeling, and their manly reverence for everything great and sacred" (Feb. 10, 1858; 115–16). With its emphasis on moral tone and particular praise for "Janet," the *Nonconformist* obviously did not share Blackwood's reservations.

The *Saturday Review* also praised "Janet" as the "finest of these *Cleri-*

cal Scenes."³³ Its diction echoes Blackwood's expressions of uneasiness, but its conclusions are different. On October 15, two weeks before the final installment, Blackwood still feared that the pathos might not overcome objections to the subject matter:

> The pathetic interest is very great and gathers strongly round Janet in spite of the unpoetic nature of her weakness and temptation. It was *a bold choice of a plot* and some will object to such a feature in a heroine, but there is no more common agent of human misery and trial than drunkenness, and consequently there can be no more legitimate material for the writer of Fiction. There is an air of reality about the whole story and that is in itself about the greatest of all merits. (*Letters* 2: 386; emphasis added)

This letter suggests an editor convincing *himself* as well as placating a valued contributor. From the start, George Eliot had argued realism as the basis for her depictions in "Janet" and would hardly have needed a reminder of it. But the final installment, including Dempster's delirium tremens and Janet's temptation by the hidden brandy bottle, was only two weeks from publication, and Blackwood remained anxious.

For the *Saturday Review*, the "*boldness* of this writer" is laudable. "He calls upon us to accept as a heroine a woman driven by ill-treatment and misery to that unpoetical, but unhappily too real, refuge—wine! This tragic sin is dealt with at once delicately and *boldly*; and the story of her repentance and victory is one of the most pathetic scenes we know." Mr. Tryan's influence is "represented in a style so truthful that we seem to be reading an actual biography" (May 29, 1858; 566; emphasis added). This praise must have pleased Eliot by affirming her argument for truthful delineation, in contrast to Blackwood's wish to dilute the realism to accommodate family (read: female) reading. The *Saturday Review* also sounds a note that comes to be heard with increasing frequency in Eliot's twenty-year career. "To make a hero out of such a curate [as Amos] required steadfast faith in the power of truth, and disregard of conventions. The same disregard of circulating-library principles is seen in the portrait of the Rev. Mr. Gilfil" (566). Reviewers, more easily than publishers, can disdain the conventional characters and subjects favored by fastidious libraries.

This issue of suitability is raised by other reviewers, only one of whom shares Blackwood's misgivings. The *Atlas* sides with Eliot and even expects family readership for her stories. Their volume publication will preserve the tales for family reading. "All knowing readers of *Maga* will be rejoiced to welcome Mr. Eliot's charming triad of stories in an independent form." These stories "should not be left scattered in fragments through the back numbers of a magazine, to be referred to with difficulty, and to be read only by those who do not fear to brave the dust of those strange library nooks and corners where old serials are ignominiously cast." These volumes belong in the circulating libraries, "to eventually find their way into quiet families where there are charming girls, studious boys, sensible papas, and amiable mammas; families that never by any chance see the magazines, but which order all the new novels with religious punctuality" (Feb. 6, 1858; 89). The story of Janet's alcoholism cannot have offended a reviewer who so readily recommends it to families with a list of members beginning "charming girls."

On the other hand, James Craigie Robertson, reviewing the second edition of *Scenes*, the sixth of *Adam Bede*, and the recent publication of *The Mill on the Floss*, laments that "The idea that fiction should contain something to soothe, to elevate, to purify seems to be extinct." His argument, in the *Quarterly Review*, is shaped largely by the revelation of the author's gender. His conservative views about women are evident in offhand parenthetical remarks, such as a comment regarding Dinah Morris, about whom he is "sceptical . . . perhaps because she is utterly unlike such female Methodists as have fallen within our own (*happily, small*) experience" (478–79; emphasis added) and in diatribes against "new and abnormal modes of thought" exemplified by the Brontës:

What could be so new and so unlikely as that the young and irreproachable maiden daughter of a clergyman should have produced so extraordinary a work as 'Jane Eyre,'—a work of which we were compelled to express the opinion that the unknown and mysterious 'Currer Bell' held 'a heathenish doctrine of religion;' that the ignorance which the book displayed as to the proprieties of female dress was hardly compatible with the idea of its having been written by a woman; but that, if a woman at all, the writer must be 'one who had, for some sufficient reason, long forfeited the society of her own sex.' (469–70)[34] *See note*

Likewise, despite *Scenes*'s power, the stories are "unpleasant to think of as the work of a woman; and . . . the influence which these novels are likely to exercise over the public taste is not altogether such as a woman should aim at" (471). Not only is "the uniformly melancholy ending of the tales . . . an exaggerated representation of the proportion which sorrow bears to happiness in human life," but the author "delights in unpleasant subjects—in the representation of things which are repulsive, coarse, and degrading" (474–75). Robertson singles out two incidents: "Tina is only prevented from committing murder by the opportune death of her intended victim" and "a drunken husband beats his beautiful but drunken wife, turns her out of doors at midnight in her night-dress, and dies of '*delirium tremens* and *meningitis*.'" He objects that Janet is depicted "staggering about the streets" (an inaccuracy on his part) and being tempted by the hidden brandy bottle, a scene he quotes at length (475). Dismissing Tina as "an undisciplined, abnormal little creature, without good looks or any attractive quality except a talent for music," he seems alarmed that readers are asked to see "the handsome, amiable, and cultivated" Janet inebriated: "all these good properties are overwhelmed in our thoughts of her by the degrading vice of which she is to be cured" (476–77). Nothing much can be expected from a plain, "abnormal," "musical" woman (are these latter two adjectives code words for "foreign"?), but for a handsome and cultivated (British?) woman, expectations are higher.[35]

Most other reviewers celebrated the volume publication of *Scenes*, but one strong dissenting voice, the Church of England's weekly *Guardian*, attacks the clerical verisimilitude. The stories were sufficient for their original purpose, but don't deserve "the honour of a more permanent shape. There is some cleverness . . . [and] incident enough to carry you through a few chapters at a time with interest." Blackwood feared the stories were too real; the *Guardian* argues that they "have no probability, and the characters no truthfulness. It is all melodramatic and unreal." The case is clearly one of disappointed expectations: "the name is partly resented as a deception, when you discover that the 'scenes' are supposed to be enacted some fifty years ago. It probably amounts to a confession, that the author knows little of contemporary 'clerical life.'"

The "clerical" character of the stories was an issue that naturally interested other religious papers as well, including the *Church of England Monthly Review* and the *Nonconformist*. A *Church of England Monthly Review* article, titled "Clerical Novels," published in April 1860, does not mention "Gilfil" at all and treats "Amos Barton" with a sarcastic, tongue-in-cheek tone. Amos is "insupportable"; he "was picked up at some little hedge-side conventicle, . . . far away from the golden repose of Parson Irwine and his church [in *Adam Bede*, which the *Church of England Monthly Review* had reviewed a year earlier]." As for the meeting of the clergy in chapter 6, it is "very unlikely" that one would find only one clergyman among the convening seven who "in any degree satisfies the standard of pastoral excellence." It is also unlikely that clergymen are "so hard up for topics, that they must needs fall to gossiping after a manner scarce befitting the servants' hall" (275).

The *Monthly Review* prefers the "ideal" in fictional portraits of clergymen and objects to Tryan's confession in a work that is otherwise a "masterpiece . . . to praise which would be to paint the lily, for in places it reminds us of a harmony, and all through of a life-picture" (276). On Tryan's "statement of a foregoing fellowship in actual vice, the oneness of his sympathy and the success of his efforts on her behalf are somewhat exclusively made to turn." Preferring sinless confessors and intercessors, the reviewer points to the "sinless Saviour" and asks, "to whom, after our Lord, are the untaught yearnings of the penitents of half Christendom directed? It is not to Mary Magdalen, the love-anointed penitent; but to Mary the Virgin, snow-white as the lily" (277). Overall, however, the *Monthly Review* praises the moral tone, exemplified by Evangelicalism's influence on Milby parishioners' "idea of duty" (chapter 10), and the "pathetic simplicity" of Tryan's funeral (chapter 28).

The *Nonconformist* was less likely than the *Church of England Monthly Review* to object to Amos as a clerical representative of the Establishment or to fault Eliot for showing its clergy in backstairs gossip. Nor was it offended by the portrayal of Tryan's confession. Instead, the *Nonconformist* argues that "The conception of the Evangelical clergyman, Mr. Tryan, in its simple every-day truth, does honour to the author's heart, shaming Mr. Trollope, who represents Evangelicism by a vulgar, perspiring, scheming Mr. Slope [in *Barchester Towers*]." Mr. Jerome gives a positive image of the Dissenter and the author "knows something of Dissent," but it is "unfortunately, of Dissent under some of its worst aspects in small and obscure country towns. He quietly laughs at the Dissenting ministers; and we willingly let him, for he is never sneering and never malignant. . . . We part with him with vastly more pleasure and moral satisfaction than we ordinarily feel in closing a novel of contemporary life" (116). In all three religious papers' reviews,[36] when the reviewer objects, it is not to the aspects of "Janet's Repentance" that concerned Blackwood, but rather to the fine points of Eliot's delineation of clerical characters and events. The objections, even so, never focus on Eliot's Bishop, and Janet's weakness is seen as part of the story's moral purpose.

Among the secular press, the "clerical" of the title also provoked remark. The first serial notice of *Scenes* in the *Illustrated Times*, January 17, 1857, begins with a parody of novelistic addresses to the reader, and emphasizes its difference from the clerical tradition (even though the *Illustrated Times*'s final notice assumed the author to be a clergyman): "Be not alarmed, oh reader! at the title; the clergyman of 'Blackwood' has nothing in common with the 'snowy-banded, *dilettante*, delicate-handed priest' in long black coat and narrow necktie, who so perseveringly captivates all the nice girls in Mr. Parker's novels; but a quiet, plain-sailing curate" (43). The *Morning Chronicle*'s description of "Janet" as "the most clerical" of the stories (6), probably refers to the greater role that Mr. Tryan's religious function per se plays in this tale. The reviewer voices no reservations about alcoholism and abuse as subjects for fiction.

The *National Review* is more explicit in praising Janet's characterization in connection with the story's clerical function. "Eliot's strength lies in the conception of female character," each story being "but a framework for the setting of a woman's portrait." Only "Janet" has "any *interior* 'scene of clerical life,' with events really hinging upon its spring of character. In the first story it is the outward lot, not the inward personality, of the curate, that spreads the stage for the drama; and in the second, it is a mere accident that there is any clergyman at all" (Oct. 1858; 490). The *Literary Gazette, and Journal of Belles Lettres, Science, and Art* also commented on Tryan's clerical role. "Amos" is the "least successful" of the stories; "Gilfil" is favored for the humor of the title character, and "Janet" "is in a more serious and tragic vein." The *Gazette*'s only objection is to Tryan's love for Janet:

> This *dénouement* is perhaps to the taste of those young ladies who can never be content with a popular preacher unless they can have him to preach to them at all times and places; but to our mind it is disappointing. That a clergyman should not be able to hear the confession of a handsome penitent of the other sex, without straightway wishing to marry her, is not heroic. It is artistically a mistake to lower the reader's estimate of Mr. Tryan's moral greatness just at the end of the book. (83)

Eliot and Lewes were relieved to see the reviews and the responses of friends and acquaintances. Eliot's journal for December 8, 1858, records her satisfaction in the responses of two clergymen. "[Blackwood] reports that an elderly clergyman has written to him today that 'Janet's Repentance' is exquisite—another vote to register along with that of Mrs.

Nutt's rector, who 'cried over the story like a child.'"[37] On January 3, 1858, Lewes notes that the *Times*'s preference for "Gilfil" notwithstanding, "As far as opinions reach me Gilfil is thought the least good of the three stories, and Janet the best" (*Letters* 2: 417). James Anthony Froude's enthusiastic letter pleased Eliot so much that she recorded it in her journal:

> I do not often see Blackwood, but in accidental glances I had made acquaintance with "Janet's Repentance," and had found there something extremely different from general Magazine stories. When I read the advertisement of the republication, I intended fully at my leisure to look at the companions of the story which had so struck me, and now I find myself sought out by the person whose workmanship I had admired, for the special present of it. (Qtd. in GE Journal, Jan. 30, 1858)

Froude wrote again September 26, 1858, hoping to make her (or "his," as he thought then) acquaintance, and again on March 13, 1859: "Janet is the greatest character which you have drawn, and I should say the healthiest. . . . Janet abides with me, and will abide while I live—your other figures, admirable as they are, will in time fade away" (*Letters* 3: 35n3). By then Eliot seems to have forgotten the early enthusiasm for "Janet," for she told him his letter "has done me real good. . . . so far as I am aware, you are only the *second* person who has shared my own satisfaction in Janet. I think she is the least popular of my characters" (*Letters* 3: 35). Elizabeth Gaskell (*Letters* 3: 197) and Bessie Rayner Parkes (*Letters* 8: 241) also shared Froude's admiration for this story. Two years after publication, Eliot's retrospective opinion was "that I had done nothing better than the writing in many parts of 'Janet'" (*Letters* 3: 267), and she hopes the book has not been forgotten.

The moral impact of the book was thus affirmed by individual readers and by reviews in many different kinds of newspapers and periodicals. This should have quieted Blackwood's fears, though the responses came too late to resuscitate Eliot's discarded plan for a fourth serial story. Fears about the story's effect on his family readership blinded Blackwood to the skill with which the conclusion to each part diminishes the effect of Janet's vices, highlights the pathos of her situation, and emphasizes her place in the human fellowship achieved through suffering. Eliot's careful manipulation of the serial endings made Janet's suffering, rather than her weakness, the foremost image in readers' minds during the month between installments.

The first installment begins as "Gilfil" did, with a broad canvas, and moves gradually to a detailed picture of individuals in conflict at the close. The larger community is represented by Dempster's public role, his boisterous drinking, and his aggressiveness in leading the battle against the Tryanites, but by the end of part 1 the focus is on the Dempsters' private lives. Three main conflicts are posed for readers to ponder in speculating about the next installment: the battle between Tryanites and anti-Tryanites, the domestic strife between Janet and her husband, and Janet's personal struggle with alcoholism. At the close of the part, the second and third conflicts are primary. The satirical tone, which Blackwood feared would be offensive, is gone. The narrator is reticent about Janet's alcoholism and stresses instead her suffering, and her mother's. The drunken Dempster curses his wife as a "creeping idiot" and a "pale, staring fool"; these details merely hint at Janet's own inebriation. Pathos and horror are mingled as Dempster threatens to "beat [her] into [her] senses." With his hand in "a firm grip on her shoulder," he pushes her into the dining room (224–25), and Janet stands "stupidly unmoved in her great beauty, while the heavy arm is lifted to strike her. The blow falls—another—and another." Leaving the rest to readers' imaginations, the scene turns suddenly from both the physical abuse and the drunkenness to the portrait of Janet's mother hanging on the dining room wall— "Surely the mother hears that cry—'O Robert! pity! pity!'" (225)—and then to the actual mother sleepless at home "dread[ing] this may be a cruel night for her child."

This conclusion appeals to readers' love of pathos and conventional images of motherhood and religion. The portrait of the sleepless mother suffering because her daughter suffers and the associations with the suffering Christ soften the grim realities of abuse and alcoholism. *Blackwood's* readers were accustomed to pathetic appeals on these grounds, especially the first. The idealized Victorian mother had played an important role in "Hester Benfield" and in *The Athelings*, which concludes in the same issue of *Blackwood's* in which "Janet's Repentance" begins. Several times in its thirteen parts, gratuitous references to Mrs. Atheling's dead children appear to stimulate readers' sympathy and sentimentality. In "Janet" the suffering-mother image mediates the reader's response, giving Janet a favorable "maternal" context. The final paragraph's religious allusion adds to the effect. Mrs. Raynor "too has a picture over her mantelpiece, drawn in chalk by Janet long years ago. She looked at it before she went to bed. It is a head bowed beneath a cross, and wearing a crown of thorns" (225). This juxtaposition of undeserved, unresisted blows falling on Janet and the image of Christ scourged and suffering, with Mrs. Raynor, Mary-like, helpless to prevent her child's pain, anticipates the main theme of the story—sin and redemption. The ending controls readers' responses, directing them to the suffering and the redemption, rather than to the sin.

Part 2 opens with an abrupt shift. Realism demands a complex Janet, not simply a melodramatic victim-heroine, and various details depict her in her multiple relationships and roles. Religion resumes its mundane garb; the "Sunday garments" the ladies of Milby don for the confirmation service are more visible than the suffering Redeemer wearing his crown of thorns. After discussing these ladies in general, the narrator observes one "bright-looking woman walking with hasty step along Orchard Street so early," and asks, "Can it be Janet Dempster, on whom we looked with such deep pity, one sad midnight, hardly a fortnight ago?" (227). This question reminds readers of the story's interruption the month before and sets Janet in a new context, among ordinary Milby women. Her sufferings are intermittent, and her character is mixed. She helps prepare the placard against Tryan not only because she is "pleas[ed] at being appealed to by her husband," but because "she really did like to laugh at the Tryanites" (236). This complicity with her reprobate husband, which could easily have alienated readers, is balanced by Janet's association with more sympathetic anti-Tryanites, old Mr. and Mrs. Crewe. With her alcoholism already established, the installment refrains from depicting it. Instead, it shows Janet and her husband in affectionate harmony, and Dempster himself in a filial moment with his aged mother. Furthermore, Eliot carefully structures the installment so that the ending again emphasizes redemption rather than sin.

The close of part 2 repeats a device from "Amos Barton," in which the narrator reveals his superior knowledge about an unexpected event in the future. This time, though, in contrast to the vague speculation about Countess Czerlaski's future, the prediction is precise. As Tryan leads his congregation through the opposing forces, the narrator foresees "once more . . . a crowd assembled to witness his entrance through the church gates. That second time, Janet Dempster was not looking on in scorn and merriment; her eyes were worn with grief and watching, and she was following her beloved friend and pastor to the grave" (251). This ending again emphasizes pity for the suffering woman. Readers' sympathy in this part is elicited mostly for the Tryanites; this forward-looking final paragraph makes

Janet prospectively one of Tryan's party and concentrates readers' attention during the coming month on the pathos of Tryan's funeral and on Janet's future repentance rather than on the nature of her sins.

The installment endings for parts 3 and 4 substitute drama and excitement for the pathos of Janet's suffering and Tryan's funeral in parts 1 and 2. A stronger, more determined Janet begins to emerge. At the end of part 3, Dempster drunkenly thrusts her out of doors in the middle of a cold March night after she has defied him (chapter 14; 274). Part 4, in which Janet has fled both Dempster and drink, closes with Dempster being carried home—"No one knows whether . . . alive or dead"—after a driving accident (chapter 21; 300). Earlier plot developments and characterizations make both events credible; neither appears to pander to readers' tastes for a dramatic ending. Resumption of the narrative in parts 4 and 5 also demonstrates Eliot's sophisticated handling of transitions between serial parts.

The climax to part 3 builds slowly. In its opening chapter, the religious "wars" in Milby continue. As in *Barchester Towers*, the war image is unseemly in the clerical context. But unlike Mr. Slope and Mrs. Proudie, the Evangelicals are sympathetic figures, as the *Nonconformist* observed. In *Scenes* they get and deserve the upper hand: "at the end of a few months, the balance of substantial loss was on the side of the Anti-Tryanites" (252). Mr. Tryan exemplifies a central tenet in Eliot's philosophy of life: the necessity of fellow feeling with the rest of suffering humanity. As the narrator explains, "the only true knowledge of our fellow-man is that which enables us to feel with him" (257).

The serial endings are organized to create this strong fellow feeling for Janet in her readers. In chapter 12 the story moves from Milby generally to the heroine particularly. "[K]indness is my religion" (264), she tells her Tryanite friend Mrs. Pettifer, and her quiet deeds for the elderly and the poor lead to a meeting with Mr. Tryan while they are both on a charitable visit to a poor consumptive. Having heard so much against him, Janet is surprised by the image of Tryan as person rather than caricature. His humble words to Sally Martin and his appearance, "pale, weary, and depressed," identify him as a sharer in the "fellowship of suffering" (265). Their accidental meeting prepares Janet to seek his help later, when she recognizes her need—a need as yet more visible to the reader than to herself.

Alcoholism is central in the third installment. Yet the narrative again avoids too directly depicting Janet either drinking or drunk, even though

Dempster has been both from the first chapter. The focus is rather on Janet's misery and the aftermath of her drinking. Small details create credibility and sympathy. The "morning light" paradoxically reveals the "hideous blank of something unremembered, something that must have made that dark bruise on her shoulder, which aches as she dresses herself" (267). But it is not merely Dempster's abuse, it is also Janet's own determination that builds sympathy for her in this part. In contrast to her attempts to please and placate her husband in part 2, she begins to assert herself against her addiction and her abuser and to alter the dynamics of the marriage. As the *Saturday Review* pointed out, the story has the truthfulness of an "actual biography" (566). The climax of the installment delineates the guilt and shame of the alcoholic, abused woman, and Janet's instinct and training toward obedience. Hung over, despairing, guilt-ridden, Janet struggles with her addiction and her emotions. A "morning after" of bitter exclamation against her fate is succeeded by restored calm and self-control. Following Dempster's orders, she prepares dinner for his guests, and lays out his evening clothes, an action which he had often "scolded" her for failing to do (272). In a pattern common to abused women, she is cowed and struggles to please. But Dempster returns having "evidently drunk a great deal" and throws the clothes at her and into the drawing room. In an act of impulsive defiance, she refuses to pick them up, even though guests may arrive at any moment: "for the first time in her life her resentment overcame the long-cherished pride that made her hide her griefs from the world. There are moments when by some strange impulse we contradict our past selves—fatal moments, when a fit of passion, like a lava stream, lays low the work of half our lives" (273). The actions and characterization, however, subvert these narrative comments. The phrase "lays low the work of half our lives" carries a judgment on Janet and a sense of loss. Her (womanly?) work of submission and patience has been (unfortunately?) undone by her one impulsive, rebellious action. And yet it is this action that frees her from her past self. Refusing to pick up—i.e., hide—the clothes symbolizes her refusal to hide the shame of her life any longer, so that when Dempster throws her out the door late that night, as he had the clothes she had laid out, she does not behave as he expects.

Heretofore, Dempster has relied on intimidation and Janet's reticence to keep her under his control. Submissiveness and shame ensure her silence. (In the next installment he reflects on his drunken behavior the night before: "'She's as timid as a hare; and she'll never let anybody know about it. She'll be back again before night'" [283].) But the text under-cuts the narrator's statement that Janet's outburst "lays low the work of half" her life, by demonstrating that womanly submissiveness and vic-timization may be identical. In their silence, she and her society, which gossips and does nothing, have consented to her victimization. By refus-ing to remove the clothes from sight before the guests arrive, Janet repu-diates her identity as the victim habitually concealing her husband's vio-lence. Private act becomes public statement. Janet will face public censure rather than endure further abuse. In installment 4, defying Milby gossip, she remains away from home, seeks the counsel of Mr. Tryan, and at-tends his morning service.

At the climax of installment 3, these possibilities are only hinted. At first, Janet's instinctive defiance gives way to dread of the consequences of her unusual action. Dempster's "devilish glance of concentrated ha-tred" at Janet when he sees the clothes on the floor and his ringing for the servant to remove them without "looking at her again" frighten her. Janet's conflict during the dinner party—attending to her role as hostess while watching Dempster, who is steadily becoming more drunk, and feeling "as if she had defied a wild beast within the four walls of his den" (273)—illustrates the psychological complexity reviewers praised in com-paring the story to a biography. The complex interaction between hus-band and wife in this central installment is the story's finest example of the psychological realism that announced to reviewers the appearance of a new and unusual author.

Eliot did not show Janet "staggering in the streets," as Robertson claimed, because to have done so would have turned the focus to external events rather than her inward struggle.[38] The many weeks in which both Janet and Dempster have been drinking are summarized rather than dramatized. Dempster's drunkenness is depicted to show its effect on Janet, who struggles toward the self-esteem that will help her overcome her dependency. In the final scene of installment 3, Dempster is drunk, but the climactic stress is on Janet's suffering rather than on her, or his, addiction. Readers see her initial relief that Dempster has not killed her and then her consciousness of her predicament—her inability to awaken the servants without her husband's knowledge, the absence of a friend to whom she might turn. In the final paragraph, physical details image the loneliness and negation of the battered, alcoholic woman's life: the "dead silence" but for the wind; the closed doors and dark windows; "no ray of light" to fall on her, "no eye" to see her. The "cold stone" and "dismal night" are symbols of her own "blank future" (275). This dramatic ending in which Dempster pushes her out the door at midnight, clad only in her nightdress, is the nadir toward which the story has been moving. Like Janet herself, readers experience both shock and relief.[39]

Blackwood's enthusiasm for "Janet's Repentance" begins with this conclusion. Sending proofs, he pronounces the installment "first rate." The "religious feeling" of the beginning is just right, and the dramatic ending redeems the problems in the first two installments. "In spite of the objections I mentioned I had a conviction from the first that Janet would turn out something very wonderful and I could not have anticipated anything more powerfully interesting and exciting than the close of this part. I look with great impatience for the rest of the M.S." (*Letters* 2: 373). Blackwood's taste, like that of many readers, ran toward the dramatic, emotional close; the ending in "Gilfil" that gained his approbation was the finding of Anthony's body in part 3. With Wybrow's heart condition outside the psychology of the character, this denouement is almost gratuitous. His heart palpitations prepare readers for his death, but they affect his life only slightly, increasing his pampered self-centeredness; their principal role seems to be to resolve the plot.[40]

In "Janet," however, the outcome stems not from happenstance, incidental medical history, but directly from her characterization as an alcoholic woman married to an alcoholic and abusive man. Dempster's violence, aggravated by his "drinking more than ever" (266), makes the ending of part 3 both inevitable and effective. It realizes what readers have foreseen and dreaded, and yet relieves their fear of a worse outcome. Janet imagines this alternative as her husband threatens, "If you don't come, I'll kill you." Then "fierce with drunken rage," he approaches. "What was he going to do to her? She thought every moment he was going to dash her before him on the ground." When instead he pushes her out and slams the door, she feels a "sense of release from an overpowering terror" (274). This release also comes to readers, who undoubtedly shared Blackwood's feeling of being "in a horrid funk for poor Janet [but] like her self . . . rather relieved when the door was closed upon her" (*Letters* 2: 371). Dempster's slamming of the door reverberates beyond the closure of the installment, as relief gives way to speculation on the next threat to Janet's new resolve and, perhaps, to her life.

Readers contemplating Janet's fictional situation in September 1857 could recall factual narratives of wives reclaimed by brutal husbands, forced by law to return home where they were beaten, sometimes to death. Thus, the narrative's careful handling of Janet's alcoholism to retain readers' sympathy is important. Victorian reticence did not prevent newspapers from publicizing murders of all kinds, including those by alcoholic, abusive husbands. Indeed, as Richard Altick points out in *Victorian Studies in Scarlet*, the public's fascination with murder had begun even before Victoria's accession, as the growing popular press stood ready to exploit reader interest in the crime: "A series of murders [between 1823 and 1837], and a nascent popular press: it was . . . a fated combination" (17).[41] The increase in newspapers and newspaper readers during Victoria's reign, and especially during the 1850s, meant that Eliot's readers had examples of murder and other domestic violence constantly before them.[42] Parliamentary deliberations in the 1850s also focused on wife abuse. Until the middle of "the nineteenth century the husband was entitled to use violence and physical restraint to secure the person and services of his wife (her *consortium*)" (Thomas 202–03).[43] In 1853 Parliament passed "the first law against wife-beating . . . but since the penalties provided by the bill—whipping and short-term imprisonment—did nothing to ameliorate the drunkenness, poverty, and misogyny that were the causes of abuse, and made no provision to prevent repeated attacks, little changed in consequence. Women continued to be mistreated at home and found the law virtually powerless to help them" (Morris 38).

The Caroline Norton case brought public attention to the powerlessness of abused women at the higher levels of society. Many other, ordinary women who suffered the same abuse were only noted briefly in the press, usually after having been seriously injured, and sometimes even to the point of being battered to death. A year and a half before "Janet's Repentance," Eliot's awareness of the issue is apparent in a letter to Sara Hennell mentioning the "Petition to be presented to Parliament praying that married women may have a legal right to their own earnings, as a counteractive to wife-beating and other evils" (*Letters* 2: 225). Other legislative proposals of 1856 addressed the problem of abuse more directly and occasioned much discussion in the national press. In an essay called "Outrages on Women," the *North British Review* debated the merits of a bill to substitute flogging for a six-month prison term for men who battered their wives (Kaye).

The problem did not disappear. A powerful spokesperson on the subject was Frances Power Cobbe. Her comments in the *Contemporary Review* more than twenty years later on "Wife-Torture in England" are as applicable to the period of "Janet's Repentance" as to 1878.

Sometimes, it is true, there are men of comparatively mild dispositions who are content to go on beating their wives year after year, giving them occasional black-eyes and bruises, or tearing out a few locks of their hair and spitting in their faces, or bestowing an ugly print of their iron fingers on the woman's soft arm. . . . But the unendurable mischief, the discovery of which has driven me to try to call public attention to the whole matter, is this—Wife-*beating* in process of time, and in numberless cases, advances to Wife-*torture*, and the Wife-torture usually ends in Wife-maiming, Wife-blinding, or Wife-murder. (72)

While her essay overstates the difference between classes, her appeal for legislation to protect battered wives is cogently argued. Cobbe points to the ineffectiveness of the 1853 statute prescribing a prison sentence of less than six months and "a fine not exceeding £20" (77) and the equally inefficacious proposal revived by Colonel Egerton Leigh in 1874 to add flogging to the penalties. Such solutions are even counterproductive. The husband, angry from his imprisonment, is more likely to endanger the wife's health and existence. Wives are reluctant to testify when "the husband will return to them full of fresh and more vindictive cruelty" (80). (The *North British Review* had also argued in 1856 that "no tender-hearted woman" would testify to abuse if this punishment were the result, and "public opinion . . . will be against the woman who swears her husband's back into a jelly" [242]).

Cobbe condemns society for making the battered wife a subject for joking and for blaming the victim instead of the perpetrator. Wife beating is given "a particular kind of indulgence . . . by public opinion. The proceeding seems to be surrounded by a certain halo of jocosity which inclines people to smile whenever they hear of a case of it (terminating anywhere short of actual murder), and causes the mention of the subject to conduce rather than otherwise to the hilarity of a dinner party." This is not a new situation. "Certainly in view of the state of things revealed by our criminal statistics there is something ominous in the circumstance that 'Punch' should have been our national English street-drama for more than two centuries." As part of this tradition of "jocosity," she adds, "The 'Taming of the Shrew' still holds its place as one of the most popular of Shakespeare's comedies" (56–57).

Almost as if she were thinking of "Janet's Repentance," Cobbe condemns Victorian society for blaming the abused wife, as if nagging, ill-temper, or other faults (even when they exist) justify her abuser.[44] In fact, an abused woman is usually a "depressed, broken-spirited creature whose mute, reproachful looks act as a goad . . . to the passions of her oppressor" (68). Cobbe blames alcohol, especially adulterated alcohol, "poisoned drink" (65), as the first cause of brutality in men. When a woman joins him in drink, society is quick to feel that she "deserved the blows she receives" (58).

This is the essence of the debate between Mrs. Pettifer and Miss Pratt in installment 1. Mrs. Pettifer excuses Janet: "When a woman can't think of her husband coming home without trembling, it's enough to make her drink something to blunt her feelings." Miss Pratt, however, retorts, "Speak for yourself. . . . Under no circumstances can I imagine myself resorting to a practice so degrading. A woman should find support in her own strength of mind" (216). Cobbe, like Mrs. Pettifer, calls for sympathy and understanding.

> One word . . . even for that universally condemned creature, the drunken wife. Does any save one, the Great Judge above, ever count how many of such doubly-degraded beings have been *driven* to intemperance by sheer misery? How many have been lured to drink by companionship with their drunken husbands? How many have sunk into the habit because, worn out in body by toil and child-bearing, degraded in soul by contempt and abuse, they have not left in them one spark of that self-respect which enables a human being to resist the temptation to drown care and remembrance in the dread forgetfulness of strong drink? (69)

Janet is not worn out in body like the poor, working-class women whom Cobbe considers to be victims of the most violent abusers. However, Dempster's contempt and abuse have worn his wife out in spirit, as the narrator's lengthy analysis of Janet's feelings at the beginning of installment 4, chapter 15, shows. In his delineation throughout "Janet's Repentance," Eliot's narrator repudiates the position of Victorians who, as Virginia Morris points out, were sympathetic to abused women but still "expressed the traditional view that most women who were abused 'asked for it' by not being good wives" (Morris 37–38). Morris's brief chapter on Eliot does not speak of this feature of "Janet's Repentance," but the story supports her premise. Milby can ignore the Dempsters' domestic situation because Janet is an alcoholic, and therefore a "bad" wife.

Abuse was even justified in pseudoscientific terms by Herbert Spencer in *The Study of Sociology.* Applying Darwinian concepts to the power relationship in marriage, he argues that women's admiration of strong men has resulted in the production of children more likely to survive than children of weaker men. Apparently wife abuse is an unavoidable by-product of this happy evolutionary circumstance. "To this admiration for power, caused thus inevitably, is ascribable the fact sometimes commented upon as strange, that women will cling to men who use them ill, but whose brutality goes along with strength of body or mind, more than they will cling to feebler men who use them well" (373). Eliot gives a different picture of the consequences of women's admiration of the "strong" man in *Daniel Deronda*, published a few years after Spencer wrote.[45]

When gossips like Miss Pratt blame Janet, they reinforce her own sense of guilt and her readiness to be victimized. Eliot is aware of readers' prejudices. Her narrator poses several "popular" answers to the question, "Do you wonder . . . what offense Janet had committed in the early years of marriage to arouse the brutal hatred of this man?" Janet's mother-in-law "thought she saw the beginning of it all in Janet's want of house-keeping skill and exactness" (267). Other women recall the "dreadful stories about the way Dempster used his wife; but in Mrs Phipps's opinion, it was six of one and half-a-dozen of the other" (269). The narrator regulates readers' responses to popular opinion by describing the abusive personality:

> do not believe that it was anything either present or wanting in poor Janet that formed the motive of her husband's cruelty. Cruelty, like every other vice, requires no motive outside itself—it only requires opportunity. You do not suppose Dempster had any motive for drinking beyond the craving for drink; the presence of brandy was the only necessary condition. And an unloving, tyrannous, brutal man needs no motive to prompt his cruelty; he needs only the perpetual presence of a woman he can call his own. A whole park full of tame or timid-eyed animals to torment at his will would not serve him so well to glut his lust of torture; they could not feel as one woman does; they could not throw out the keen retort which whets the edge of hatred. (268)

Eliot develops this type more fully in *Daniel Deronda*, where Grandcourt needs no alcohol to stimulate him to more subtly abuse his wife. His abuse has been perfected through practice on his dogs, his lackey Lush, and his former mistress, Mrs. Glasher.

In part 5, Eliot continues to juxtapose the narrator's sympathy with

Milby's conventional reactions. Mrs. Lowme, for example, objects to "'Tryanite cant . . . in a woman of her habits; she should cure herself of *them* before she pretends to be over-religious.'" Even her "repentance" does not alter her detractors' views. Mrs. Phipps undercuts her claim to be pleased at the "likelihood of improvement in Mrs Dempster" by ascribing it to Janet's guilt: "'I think the way things have turned out seems to show that she was more to blame than people thought she was; else, why should she feel so much about her husband?'" (315). One might here extend Altick's point about the public interest in murder being conditioned by class bias, "the assumption being that respectability or its converse somehow qualifies the abstract consideration of guilt or innocence, a crime being more heinous and punishment more urgent if the victim was 'respectable' and therefore less deserving of being murdered" (*Studies in Scarlet* 12). And Dempster, despite his alcoholism—or sometimes because he can carry his liquor as a man should—is a respected figure in Milby. As Tomlinson, "the rich miller," says "admiringly" of him: "I never see Dempster's equal; if I did I'll be shot. . . . Why, he's drunk the best part of a bottle o' brandy since here we've been sitting, and I'll bet a guinea, when he's got to Trower's his head'll be as clear as mine. He knows more about law when he's drunk than all the rest on 'em when they're sober" (195). But in keeping with the gender double standard, Janet's alcoholism degrades her. Even after she is recovering, Milby gossip shows that her alcoholism, which, especially in women, is more readily associated with the lower classes, threatens her "respectability" and hence public sympathy. From the serial standpoint, this danger is as much a threat to Janet at the end of part 3 as the potential for her death from cold or from later brutality. Lest readers adopt the judgmental stance of her mother-in-law and other Milby women in part 3, its last chapter has been carefully crafted to stress her attempt to stop drinking and reform her life, and the ending shows the futility of her attempt. Dempster becomes more brutal as she attempts to placate him.

Part 2's conclusion describing Janet as a mourner at Tryan's funeral makes it unlikely that her repentance was to be a deathbed one, but newspaper narratives also offered outcomes just short of death. Like Janet herself, readers had reason to fear for her, should Dempster reclaim her as the law allowed. The unequal number of parts in the first two stories, two installments for "Amos" and four for "Gilfil," meant that serial readers could make no predictions about the course of Janet's eventual repentance based on the assumed length of the work.[46] The openness of possibilities to be speculated on during the intervening month adds to the interest and excitement of the dramatic closure.

In a pattern unusual in *Scenes of Clerical Life*, though common enough in other serial stories, the first paragraph in the next installment returns precisely to the place at which the story had broken off the month before. It also repeats the words of the conclusion: "cold stone" becomes "stony street"; the "harsh north-east wind, that blew through her thin night-dress, and sent her long heavy black hair streaming" becomes "the bitter north-east wind and darkness—and in the midst of them a tender woman thrust out . . . in her thin night-dress, the harsh wind . . . driving her long hair away from her half-clad bosom" (274–75). This opening stresses the pathos that was subsumed by dramatic excitement at the close of part 3. Then Eliot reverts to a structure frequent in the installment openings of *Scenes of Clerical Life*: the narrator generalizes on the conclusions to be drawn from the story. This pause fills the blank before the stunned Janet becomes conscious of "being seated on the cold stone under the shock of a new misery" (276). Part 4 focuses on Janet—her shelter with Mrs. Pettifer, her confession to Tryan, and her reconciliation with her mother. Only briefly does the narrative depict Dempster's waking expectation that "She'll be back again before night," his driving out, and, in a dramatic conclusion, his body being carried home.

This final scene in part 4 resembles the most dramatic serial break in "Gilfil," Caterina finding Anthony's body. One might have expected an enthusiastic comment from Blackwood on this ending as well, but no letter is extant on the matter.[47] As Blackwood had wondered if Anthony really were dead, a similar ambiguity is introduced in the final paragraph here: "It is Dempster's body. No one knows whether he is alive or dead" (300). Readers were likely to care even less for Dempster than they had for Anthony Wybrow. The effect of the event on others, especially Janet, would have formed the principal ground for speculation about the outcome before the November *Blackwood's* appeared. Neither reticence nor a sense of propriety prevented Victorian readers from hoping for the death of inconvenient fictional characters; the extensive serial reviews occasioned by *Middlemarch* and *Daniel Deronda* expressed hopes for the "demise" (to use Mr. Vincy's neutralizing term for the death of Featherstone) of Casaubon and Grandcourt. No doubt early readers of George Eliot felt the same about Dempster and hoped for his death, as both his "just deserts" and a release for his wife.

The ending supplies drama and satisfies probability. In part 3, townspeople predict, now that he has stopped driving himself, that he will end in "meningitis and delirium tremens" (270). In part 4, the narrator links Dempster's accident with his treatment of Janet the previous night. The remembrance of "what Janet had done to offend him the evening before . . . gave him a definite ground for the extra ill-humour which had attended his waking every morning this week, but he would not admit to himself that [her absence] cost him any anxiety" (283). In this ill humor, he berates his driver and winds up driving himself. Despite foreshadowing, the accident is almost too fortuitous—a Providential intervention. To abstain from alcohol, Janet must prevent Dempster from forcing her to return home, where she fears both alcoholism and abuse will resume. His accident offers Janet—and speculating readers—new possibilities: Dempster's remorse and recovery or his death, the only "divorce" available to most abused women.

Neither of these possibilities is precluded by the narrator's early hints about Janet at Mr. Tryan's funeral. Romantic readers might hope for Dempster's death and Janet's union with Mr. Tryan, even if that union were only a short one, as Gilfil and Caterina's was. Or they might hope for Dempster's "repentance" as well as Janet's, with the happy reconciliation of the couple who had married with high expectations and love. More realistic readers would have noted in the other two stories Eliot's refusal to compromise the realism with a conventional happy ending. Obviously, Janet's alcoholism complicates the potential outcomes. How will Dempster's recovery or death affect this part of her life? Will she, in a rush of sympathy, return home to encounter her temptation without the protection of Mrs. Pettifer or her mother, to whom she says, "'don't let me have anything if I ask for it'" (300)? Will Dempster recover, unreformed, and renew his violence and alcoholism? Will she follow the pattern of many abused women and return to accept the abuse as something she deserves?

The resumption of the story in part 5 appeals to readers' primary interest by returning to Janet in three long narrative paragraphs. Dempster's accident is described through a conversation between Mr. Tryan and Mr. Landor, whose first concern is Janet. Their discussion of her options forestalls any too simplistic equation between the accident and Janet's possible release from her husband. The complications of ordinary human life replace the dramatic excitement of the serial ending. Janet's dilemma is first articulated in chapter 22, before she knows of his accident. She weighs her options in the paragraph beginning "'I feel so uncertain what to do about my husband.'" Society can enforce her return to her husband; her own mingled sense of guilt and duty bids her to return on her own initiative. But society also condemns her "unwomanly" dependence on alcohol, and she too fears that dependence, as Mrs. Pettifer points out in recommending that Tryan not inform her immediately of the accident (304). Part 5 offers no easy resolution of Janet's struggle with alcohol, gossip, and guilt. Her husband dies a terrible death with no sign of reconciliation to her. Mr. Tryan's death, though delayed enough to give her time to shape her new life, leaves her fearful and alone. Like Gwendolen Harleth, she must depend upon herself.[48]

That the installment endings focus on the suffering Janet, rather than depicting her alcoholism graphically, does not mean that her alcohol dependency is not presented as a serious matter. The power of part 5 stems from the vividness of her temptation as well as from the pathos of Tryan's death. In the first chapter, she describes her dread of abuse and her temptation to drink:

> "This morning, when I felt so hopeful and happy, I thought I should like to go back to him, and try to make up for what has been wrong in me. . . . But since then . . . I have had the same feelings I used to have, the same dread of his anger and cruelty, and it seems to me as if I should never be able to bear it without falling into the same sins, and doing just what I did before."
> (305)

Her dilemma is one Eliot had articulated a year and a half earlier in "The Antigone and Its Moral": "two principles, both having their validity, are at war with each" (*Essays* 263). When Dempster is injured, the conflict between Janet's two valid duties, to herself and to her marital vows, appears to be removed. Janet can now return home safely. And yet her "repentance" is not a simple, or moot, matter. Janet's only depicted confrontation with alcohol occurs a month *after* Dempster has died, when her desire for drink can no longer be linked directly to Dempster's abuse. What twentieth-century readers would call her support system has momentarily deserted her,[49] and in one of those "vague undefinable states of susceptibility . . . that determine many a tragedy in women's lives" (318–19), Janet finds a decanter of brandy while searching Dempster's desk for some papers. She "dashe[s] it to the ground" (319), but the narrator notes that the "temptation would come again" (320). Readers like the *Quarterly Review*'s Robertson, who takes a sentimental view of women and disdainfully quotes this incident as an example of the coarse and repulsive in Eliot, find the scene distasteful. But Eliot the realist refuses to compromise the truth with a sentimental or simplistic view of Janet's alcohol addiction. Janet's struggle continues even without Dempster's abuse and provocation.

Alcohol and abuse figure largely in the serial structure, but the dramatic endings depict Janet as a suffering or sorrowing individual; she is a victim whose struggle merits readers' sympathy. By this careful handling of the serial structure, Eliot regulates readers' responses and nullifies Blackwood's objections. At the same time, chapters within the installment establish Janet's alcoholism and her need to take responsibility for her recovery. This skillful balancing of the complex issues within the demands of the serial form helped make "Janet" the most psychologically interesting of the three stories and a favorite of many reviewers and discerning friends and acquaintances.

Eliot's experiments with the techniques of serial fiction writing in *Scenes of Clerical Life* are part of her apprenticeship in her new craft. "Amos Barton" demonstrates her ability, as Lewes said, to do comedy and pathos, and establishes the new realism that reviewers heralded from the first installment. But the drama is slight, and her serial break makes little attempt to exploit the dramatic potential of the story. In "Mr Gilfil's Love-Story," she is more skillful in using the serial structure to enhance the dramatic action. The virtues that reviewers noted—her "exquisite" pathos, her "delicacy and depth of moral insight" (*Leader*, Nov. 7, 1857; 1072), her "conscientious truth to real life" (*Nonconformist*, Feb. 10, 1858; 115)— are accompanied by "striking situations" and "thrilling incidents" missing in "Amos Barton." Finally, in "Janet's Repentance," she makes the drama more integral to the whole by focusing the serial endings on her principal character and using them to regulate readers' sympathy. At the same time, she presents complex psychological characterizations and delineates a critical social issue concerning women's lives. The latter two stories also show Eliot's careful balancing of audience expectations with a determination not to alter what she considers essential. Paradoxically, she risks the suspense by the early revelation of Caterina's and Tryan's deaths, while employing suspenseful, even melodramatic serial closures.

By the time she was ready to write *Adam Bede*, she knew what the serial form required and what to avoid. This awareness enabled her to resist Blackwood's pressure to begin early publication of her story in

Maga and to understand his viewpoint when finally, by mutual agreement though for different reasons, they realized that it would be unsuitable in that format. Though she and Lewes flirted with prospects for serializing *Adam Bede* and *The Mill on the Floss*, not until five years later with *Romola*, in George Smith's new *Cornhill Magazine*, would Eliot again try her fortunes with this difficult and challenging mode of publication.

3

"An Unfortunate Duck Can Only Lay Blue Eggs": Negotiations to Serialize *Adam Bede* and *The Mill on the Floss*

AFTER READING volume 2 of *The Mill on the Floss*, John Blackwood expressed his delight in the continued humor and actuality of the work: the vividness of Tom's life at Mr. Stelling's school and the "darkening of old Tulliver's days and the whole scene drearily settling over the Mill form[ed] a very pathetic picture." Blackwood here again shows his Victorian appreciation for pathos. But he particularly liked happy endings and added, "I shall be glad when sunshine brings Tom more back to young life. I wish noble Maggie had a more goodly lover." Anyway, "she does not seem really in love," he consoled himself, and he awaited volume 3 eagerly: "The ground is beautifully laid for the third volume and my expectations are great" (*Letters* 3: 263–64). Although it was not yet written, Eliot knew that volume 3 would produce quite a different kind of lover, not the goodly one Blackwood hoped for; rain, not sunshine; and death, not a return to young life for Maggie and Tom. Eliot gave Blackwood playful warning in her next letter: "I am preparing myself for your lasting enmity on the ground of the tragedy in my third volume. But an unfortunate duck can only lay blue eggs, however much white ones may be in demand" (*Letters* 3: 265).

Throughout her career, Eliot was to be such an unfortunate duck. While she was attentive to the narrative structures necessary in a successful serial, she refused to compromise on matters she thought were essential to her artistic vision. Serialization, despite its potential for great monetary rewards, at times threatened her power to present her "own conception of life and character," as she had told Blackwood in suggesting that "Janet's Repentance" be published as a volume rather than in *Blackwood's*; she preferred to lose the money rather than alter her artistic vision. As a result, her next two works, *Adam Bede* and *The Mill on the Floss*, were published first in the standard Victorian three-volume format, even though they were originally planned for serialization. For *Silas Marner*, serialization does not seem to have been considered, even though, of the three, it lends itself most readily to the serial format. It could have been, in Maga, almost a fourth scene from clerical life, such as Blackwood had hoped for in 1857.

After Eliot told Blackwood she would end the clerical series with "Janet's Repentance," her memories of his lukewarm reaction to parts of the story determined her to avoid premature judgments in the future. "In the case of my writing fiction for Maga again," she wrote him on September 5, two months before its final installment, "I should like to be considerably beforehand with my work, so that you can read a thoroughly decisive portion before beginning to print" (*Letters* 2: 381). Believing Blackwood would have understood her intentions better could he have read more, she explains on October 17 that the possibility of publishing her next work in installments can be decided later. She will not "ask you to look at [the new story] till I have written a volume or more, and then you will be able to judge whether you will prefer printing it in the Magazine, or publishing it as a separate novel when it is completed" (*Letters* 2: 387–88).

Blackwood's response to "Janet" continued to distress her. Her journal entry, "How I Came to Write Fiction," on December 6, 1857, reiterates her "annoyance at Blackwood's want of sympathy [which] determined me to close the series and republish them in two volumes" (*Letters* 2: 409–10). Given that *Adam Bede* was her next fiction, one can hardly regret that she did not try to confine this story to the relative brevity of the novellas in *Scenes of Clerical Life*. At the same time, though, one would like to have seen the further development of her serial technique at this early stage in her fiction-writing career, especially for relatively short installments—a type of serial writing she never resumed despite offers from Blackwood and others.

As *Adam Bede* took shape during the fall and winter of 1857–58, Eliot wrote with serial publication in mind. Work on the novel progressed well. She began writing on October 22, and by December 17, she had completed the first installment (GE Journal). By early March, she had written three serial parts, and although she had said she would not give Blackwood less than a volume, she allowed him to carry these three parts, chapters 1 to 13, away with him on March 4, 1858. By March 27, confidence with her progress led her to suggest beginning the novel in Maga whenever Blackwood wanted: "before I go [to Munich] I shall send you a small packet of M.S. forming the fourth part of 'Adam Bede,' if he is destined to appear in parts, which your last pleasant letter has made me regard as probable. In that case, I leave entirely to you the decision when he shall make his debut. I feel ready to begin now at any time" (*Letters* 2: 442).

Blackwood's reaction was disappointing. He wrote to Lewes on March 11 that he found "Adam Bede all right, most lifelike and real" but that he "wish[ed] to read the MS quietly over again before writing in detail about it. . . . Is there much more written or is it merely blocked out?" (*Letters* 2: 439n4). His next letter on the subject was not until March 31. This unusually long delay in responding to her work in itself indicates Blackwood's hesitation. Just as he had feared that readers would find alcoholism and wife abuse offensive in "Janet's Repentance," he responded with apprehension to the sexual implications of *Adam Bede*. Noting cautiously that the story would be "far different from anything that has ever appeared in the Magazine and as far as I can at present judge will do well there," he preferred to wait to "decide on the form of publication until I have seen more." Despite positive remarks in this and his initial letter, Blackwood expresses unease about the scenes between Hetty and Arthur: "The Captain's unfortunate attachment to Hetty will I suppose form a main element in the Tragic part of the story. I am not quite sure how far I like the scenes in the wood and I hope things will not come to the usual sad catastrophe!" He concludes by asking Eliot to give him a sketch of the story when she sends the next part (*Letters* 2: 446).

She refused this request, which she apparently interpreted as an objection to a seduction and illegitimate child ("the usual sad catastrophe") as unsuitable for Maga's readers, especially young girls. Explaining that the treatment of the story makes all the difference, she hypothesizes a contrast between Sir Walter Scott's *The Heart of Mid-Lothian* and a similar story "told by a Balzacian French writer." The latter "would probably have made a book that no young person could read without injury. Yet what girl of twelve was ever injured by the Heart of Midlothian? Of artistic writing it may be said pre-eminently—'to the pure writer all things are pure.'" However, she is not "arguing against your hesitation to publish 'Adam Bede' in Maga," but simply explaining why an outline of the story would be of no use, and reminding Blackwood that he "can certainly not be more solicitous about the moral spirit of what you publish in the Magazine, than I am about the moral spirit of what I write" (*Letters* 8: 201–02). In this letter, she begins to be tentative about serialization: she is not forwarding a part, but the *amount* of a part. Perhaps at this point, she began to dread a recurrence of the problems she had encountered with Blackwood over "Janet's Repentance."

Eliot's reference to *The Heart of Mid-Lothian* must have made it clear to a Scotsman like Blackwood that the story *was* leading to "the usual sad catastrophe." Perhaps this led to his eager acceptance of her suggestion "definitively to give up the idea of monthly publication, and await the printing of the book in three volumes" (*Letters* 8: 202). If he remembered this allusion, he does not mention it almost a year later in sending her a portfolio of reviews, of which "The best I have seen is that in the Edinburgh Courant" (*Letters* 3: 20). Eliot's response mentions the "ring of sincere enjoyment in [the review's] tone" (3: 25), but nothing about the Edinburgh *Evening Courant*'s comparison of the new novel with Scott. The review points to the novel's "singular *reality*" and "the author's power of unravelling the tangled web of motives which determine human action, and tracing every turn of the conflict between good and evil, between passion and duty. . . . [S]ince the *Heart of Mid-Lothian* we doubt if there has been a tale where the pathetic emotions are touched with deeper effect or to truer and higher purpose, than in this of *Adam Bede*" (Feb. 15, 1859; 3). In retrospect, Blackwood could see in this and other reviews no misapprehension of the moral tone; but with most of the book unwritten, his anxiety led him to resist serialization in Maga.

In her recollection, Eliot identifies this moral issue as the critical one, though other factors were also involved. Her journal registers the reluctance behind Blackwood's carefully chosen words; after he received the first volume he

> seemed to hesitate about putting it in the Magazine, which was the form of publication, he, as well as myself, had previously contemplated. He still *wished* to have it for the Mag., but desired to know the course of the story; at *present*, he saw nothing to prevent its reception in Maga, but he would like to see more. I am uncertain whether his doubts rested solely on Hetty's relation to Arthur, or whether they were also directed towards the treatment of Methodism by the Church.

She refused to have the story "judged apart from my *treatment*" and "ultimately I proposed that the notion of publication in Maga should be given up" (*Letters* 2: 503–4).[1] Months after the event, Blackwood's lack of confidence still rankled.

On April 2, Blackwood wrote Lewes that he knew she would not wish to give such a summary and had "very nearly said so when I made the request. On the whole I think he [Eliot] is right. What he says of the treatment of a subject being the essence of art is very true" (*Letters* 2: 447).[2] After this letter, Blackwood's published letters to Lewes cease until April 30,[3] but two letters from Lewes to Blackwood, April 3 and 14, have been published. The first treats Lewes's own business and then discusses Eliot: "You are the right sort of person to deal with him, for you perceive his Pegasus is tender in the mouth, and apt to lay back his ears in a restive ominous style if even the reins be shaken when he is at work."[4] On April 14, Lewes merely announces their arrival in Munich and sends Eliot's "kind regards."[5] One could conclude from these published letters that Blackwood's hesitation caused Eliot to suggest volume publication, and that Blackwood was happy to acquiesce.

Another letter, however, gives a different picture. On April 3, Blackwood wrote Eliot an encouraging letter the original of which is no longer extant. But a copy is recorded in the firm's letter book for 1857 and 1858 (NLS MS. 30,358).[6] This letter shows that Eliot, rather than Blackwood, made and held firm to the final decision not to publish *Adam* in Maga, but it does not explain just why or how that decision occurred. Blackwood has "just finished the perusal of the 4th part of Adam Bede which arrived a few hours ago," and he comments at length on characters and plot, concluding that "There is an atmosphere of genuine religion and purity that fears no evil about the whole opening of the Story," a comment that obviously attempts to reassure her on the point she had raised in her "Heart of Mid-Lothian" rejoinder. And, he assures her, "I think It [*sic*] must go into the Magazine. It will be the best thing for both parties. I would not wish to commence for some months so I was glad to hear that you were not anxious for early publication. Send me more M.S. when you can." His assurance that it "must" go into Maga is somewhat undercut by his wish not to begin too soon—or did he simply not want her to feel pressured as she had with *Scenes*? In either case, this letter shows that Blackwood remained interested in serialization.

Probably Blackwood was concerned about her response on April 1 and wrote as soon as he could to allay any fears arising from his negative comments and his request for a plot summary. And yet, despite this encouragement to the diffident "Pegasus," Blackwood's next published letter, dated April 30, asks Lewes to tell George Eliot "that he will find me quite ready to meet his wishes by the publication of Adam Bede as a separate work at once" (*Letters* 8: 203). In addition to the unpublished April 3 letter, at least one more letter appears to be missing from the record: a letter from Eliot between April 3 and April 30 that would show how the decision against serialization was reached and what led to Blackwood's April 30 response. Without the April 3 letter, the published record suggests that Blackwood's unwillingness to risk a controversial subject led to the decision.[7]

Nonetheless, Blackwood's fear that the story would be unsuitable for family reading initiated the questions about serializing; even though some reviewers repeated views that Eliot had espoused months before publication, others validated Blackwood's hesitation.[8] But here as elsewhere, Eliot held fast to the doctrine of realism as allowing, even demanding, a more explicit presentation of human weaknesses than some readers and publishers found acceptable.

Apart from these commercial issues, it is uncertain how *Adam Bede* would, from an artistic standpoint, have borne serialization. The plot seems to develop slowly, and slow development is inimical to serial fiction's requirement for frequent climactic endings, especially in a magazine like *Blackwood's* that featured relatively short installments. At the beginning, *Adam Bede* shares the placid country setting of "Amos Barton," though the latter's brevity and the charm and novelty of Eliot's style brought it a positive reception as a two-installment sketch despite the absence of striking incidents or strong plot development. Nonetheless, the structure of the early parts of *Adam Bede* suggests that Eliot not only attended to the larger canvas of three-volume publication but planned her installment breaks to include the drama requisite in a serial's smaller units. Her journal, her correspondence with Blackwood, and the manuscript of *Adam Bede* provide information about her plan for ending the first, third, and fourth installments, and, with less certainty, the second. These breaks show that despite the cumulative impression of a slowly unfolding plot, the individual parts would have evoked suspense effectively and drawn readers back for future installments. The excitement of the love affair would have sustained interest through book 2, and book 3 would have had the sensation of Hetty's pregnancy and the child murder to keep readers returning.[9]

The manuscript for *Adam Bede* is explicit about only one serial break; the notation "End of part I" appears at the end of chapter 4, which concludes with the finding of Thias Bede's body. Besides definitively marking the conclusion of her first installment, this notation indicates the approximate length of the installments as Eliot projected them. "End of Part I" occurs at the bottom of the page marked as 86 in the British Library numbering, but the actual text pages in this first part number 82,[10] the first four pages being Eliot's dedication and a three-page listing of book and chapter titles written after the manuscript was completed. The eighty-two pages comprise chapters 1 through 4, which introduce the Bede family and Dinah Morris.

A woman preacher is a novelty that would have caught serial readers' attention, and the part contains both a love interest and pathos, staples of the attractive serial of the late 1850s. Pathos would have dominated readers' impressions because of the final event of chapter 4—Adam and Seth's discovery of their father's body in the overflowing creek. The tapping of the willow wand adds a touch of mystery never amiss in a serial. Blackwood was enthusiastic: "Adam's dreary night work, the rap of the willow wand, and the brothers carrying the coffin in the lovely morning most skilfully throw in the shadows, preparing one for the coming catastrophe. The wind up of the first part and Adam's reflections are admirable" (*Letters* 2: 4).

Instead of beginning again where she left off, Eliot employs a device familiar in other serial writers, opening the new part with new characters and setting. Linking the parts are references to unusually wet weather. Chapter 5 opens by noting the heavy rainfall, which helped to swell the creek and drown the inebriated Thias Bede in chapter 4. Where this installment was to begin is certain. Its ending is less so, but several kinds of evidence—the manuscript, Eliot's journal and letters, and traditional serial practices—suggest that the second planned installment ended after chapter 9, "Hetty's World."

The length of the planned part 1, as well as the total number of pages in the first three parts, limits the possible points of closure for installment 2. If Eliot aimed for installments of approximately equal length, 82 pages per part would put the second break at or near page 168, where chapter 10 begins (4 introductory pages plus 82 pages each in parts 1 and 2). Dramatically, this is an excellent breaking point, and Eliot paid special attention to the close of this chapter, where three lines of Arthur's conversation are blacked out and overwritten.[11] What is underneath the blottings is impossible to decipher. The new text contains Arthur's speech in the chapter's penultimate paragraph, where he abruptly changes the conversation to avoid discussing with the Rector his intentions toward Hetty. Coming at the end of an installment, Arthur's reluctance to strengthen his willpower by the aid of a second "conscience" emphasizes the possible seduction that Blackwood feared—but it provides excellent suspense.

More conclusive evidence comes from Eliot's correspondence and her journal, which also establish that part 3 ended with chapter 13. When Blackwood called on March 4, 1858, she gave him the manuscript of *Adam Bede* "to the end of the second scene in the wood" (*Letters* 2: 436), that is, through chapter 13. Writing about it March 31, Blackwood refers to 219 manuscript pages; Eliot's first 13 chapters end on 219 in her pagination (the only pagination, of course, available to Blackwood). These appear to be all she had completed; on March 13, Lewes had written in response to Blackwood's question about whether there was more: "no more is yet *written*; although all is laid out; but before he [Eliot] goes away he will send m.s.s. for another *part*" (2: 440). Lewes is not quite accurate; Eliot's journal for March 8 notes, "Wrote Chap. 14 up to the going to bed."[12] Nonetheless, corroborating that she had given Blackwood all the manuscript she had, whenever Eliot returned to writing— March 8 or later—she misremembers her pagination and misnumbers the first page of chapter 14 as 120 instead of 220. On March 27 she will send Blackwood "a small packet of M.S. forming the fourth part of 'Adam Bede'" (2: 442).[13]

Eliot's journal also supports the idea that part 2 concluded with the end of chapter 9. On December 17, she read *Adam Bede* to Lewes "to the end of the third chapter." Her next entries on the subject are January 6, "Finished chapter 4 of my novel"; January 17, "Cold and sore throat, but enjoying the writing of my 5th chapter"; and January 20, "Read aloud the additional dialogue in the chapter of 'The Hall Farm.' G. admired it very much." "The Hall Farm" is chapter 6 in the published novel, but it is probably the chapter she refers to as 5 in her entry on January 17. It is unlikely that she was in the midst of chapter 5 then and reading chapter 6 to Lewes just three days later. The manuscript pagination shows that chapter 3 was not divided into a separate chapter until after the first three parts were written; hence, the chapter 4 referred to on January 6 was published as chapter 5.

On January 31, 1858, she records, "Finished Chapters 7 and 8—the dialogue between Dinah and Mr. Irwine, and the rest up to the arrival of the Rector and Captain at Adam's Cottage." What she describes are the events from chapters 8 and 9 as published, not 7 and 8. This journal entry treats these two chapters as a unit; in fact, they were for a short time a single chapter in the manuscript. This unity outweighs the one possible argument—balancing the length of parts—against division of part 2 after chapter 9. Since part 3 ends at page 219 in the manuscript, having the second break at the end of chapter 9 makes part 3 considerably shorter than parts 1 and 2, at 59 manuscript pages instead of 82. However, one or both of the second and third parts had to be shorter than part 1, since that part is unquestionably 82 pages long, leaving only 140 pages to be divided among parts 2 and 3.

The possibility outlined above, that part 2 was to end with chapter 9, is stronger than the likelihood of a more equal division. Dividing the 140 pages exactly in half would bring part 2 up to BL page 156, on which chapter 8 ends. In this case, the break would fall with Hetty's indifferent response to the sudden news of Thias Bede's death. This chapter break is, however, an insertion in the middle of a paragraph. The first word on the line closes the preceding sentence; then, above the phrase "While she adjusted the broad green leaves" is the notation "Chapter 9. Hetty's World." Although chapter 9's repetition of the closing words of chapter 8 is a typical serial device, the chapter designation was made after Eliot wrote the verbal echo, which is unaltered in the manuscript. Furthermore, her journal suggests that she thought of the story line in a smooth flow from Dinah and Irwine's conversation to the departure for "Adam's cottage"—a phrase that constitutes the final two words of both her journal entry on this topic and chapter 9 (as published).

Neither does chapter 8 have the drama of a good serial break. Hetty's repetition of the old news of Thias Bede's death is pallid compared to Irwine's warning to Arthur about the dangers of turning her head by his attentions and "spoil[ing] her for a poor man's wife." Hetty's "pleasant delirium" and Arthur's consciousness of flaws in his behavior provide promising directions for a serial story, and chapter 9 ends on an ominous note. Irwine sagely advises Arthur to notice who Mary Burge is, in which case "'You needn't look quite so much at Hetty Sorrel then. When I've made up my mind that I can't afford to buy a tempting dog, I take no notice of him, because if he took a strong fancy to me, and looked lovingly at me, the struggle between arithmetic and inclination might become unpleasantly severe.'" Unwilling to face this "unpleasantly severe" battle of conscience, Arthur changes the topic: "'Thank you. It may stand me in good stead some day, though I don't know that I have any present use for it. Bless me! how the brook has overflowed. Suppose we have a canter, now we're at the bottom of the hill.'" This is the paragraph that Eliot revised in manuscript—and the narrator's final comment stresses the point: "one might even have *escaped* from Socrates himself in the saddle" (147; emphasis added).

If installment 2 closed with chapter 9, then part 3 would have been much shorter than the first two parts.[14] However, once readers had been drawn into a story, equivalent length in installments seems to have been less important than at the outset. Blackwood's views on longer early installments appear in a letter to Lewes on December 31, 1858, regarding the latter's *Physiology of Common Life*. Sending proofs of parts 2 and 3, Blackwood writes, "You will see that they rather exceed the quantity we fixed upon for each number, but it is no disadvantage to have the early parts portly" (*Letters* 2: 513). A part 3 consisting of chapters 10 through 13 in a serialized *Adam Bede* would have been only three pages shorter than part 4, as described below, and would have met several requirements of a good serial. It reintroduces the main figures and plot lines, and it ends (like part 2), with hints calculated to increase reader anxiety and suspense, as Arthur reflects on his dilemma: Hetty's reputation will be irrecoverably damaged if their meetings become known, but "No gentleman, out of a ballad, could marry a farmer's niece." He determines to tell Irwine on the morrow, and therefore, chapter 13 concludes, "there was no more need for him to think" (184). This chapter repeats the focus on Arthur and Hetty's infatuation with which chapter 9 ended.

If the seduction potential of these three parts worried Blackwood, his views were going to be reinforced, and not "modified" as Eliot hoped, when he received part 4 (*Letters* 8: 202). There is no manuscript notation stating, "End of part 4," but Blackwood's April 3 letter describes the installment content thoroughly.

Installment 4 opens by reminding readers where the preceding installment closed. The final two chapters of part 3 were titled "In the Wood" and "Evening in the Wood." The first sentence of part 4, chapter 14, "While that parting in the wood was happening, there was a parting in the cottage too," recalls these chapter titles and the Hetty-Arthur meetings, while returning readers to the Bede household. The story then mingles the two narrative threads as Dinah and Hetty meet on their way to the Hall Farm in the late evening.

Linking devices with the preceding installment also recur later in part 4, when, after two chapters at Hall Farm, Eliot shifts to Arthur Donnithorne in chapter 16. "Arthur Donnithorne, you remember, is under an

engagement with himself to go and see Mr Irwine this Friday morning."
This narrative reminds readers of part 3's closure, where he had resolved
to "go and tell Irwine." Although the "you remember" locution is sometimes used by serial writers to restart their story at the beginning of an
installment, here it simply reminds readers where *Arthur's* story left off.
Chapters 14 and 15 of part 4 have only the slightest opening reference,
described above, to the scene in the wood, and none to Arthur's determination to arm himself against temptation by confessing to Irwine. For
a non-serial audience who had read of Arthur's resolution only three
chapters earlier, this reminder would be unnecessary. For serial readers,
however, the direct address in chapter 16—"you remember"—creates a
comfortable sense of shared knowledge between narrator and readers—
who may, in fact, not have remembered. Like the teacher using the phrase
"as you know" to introduce something that should be known but probably isn't, the narrator deftly recalls a detail from the preceding installment, while seeming to assume that, of course, readers hardly need this
reminder. It is a bridge not from the end of one part to the start of a new
one, but from the end of the earlier part to the middle of the new one,
when the narrative shifts its focus.

The close of part 4 once again focuses on Arthur's attempt at self-
discipline, and on his failure, echoing what readers have seen at the end
of parts 2 and 3.[15] The cumulative effect is to heighten readers' apprehension of danger to Hetty, whose illusions are so obviously foolish. The
close continues the ominous tone of the chapter's opening, in which
Adam confidently expects the best from the young squire even as Arthur
toys with the woman Adam loves. Chapter 17, with its pause in the story,
would have been appropriate to resume an installment, but it was never
called upon to take this role.

Contemporary reviewers, who read *Adam Bede* in the context of the
author's serialized first work, had no way of knowing that Eliot ever
considered serializing this second work. However, they sometimes commented on its unsuitability for part publication. The *Critic* makes a direct
statement: this "author has no startling effects, no spasmodic ebullitions
of passion, no ecstatic descriptions, no odd, eccentric, angular characters, no villains that are too villanous [*sic*], no village maidens artistically
perfect," such as a serial requires. "His story would hardly cut up into
twenty portions for the benefit of weekly or monthly serial readers. It
would puzzle too much the dissector to find the points of the narrative at
which the incidents were so exceptionally striking as particularly to jus-

tify a pause" (Apr. 9, 1859; 18:347). Other notices, without the direct reference to serialization, observe the subdued nature of the narrative. The *Morning Chronicle* says that the author "Hitherto . . . has shown a great—we might say an utter—want of invention. Nothing could be more meagre than the plots of his former work. The plot of the present is as common-place as possible" (Feb. 28, 1859; 6). The *Daily News* enjoys the serene, commonplace depiction of the past: the novel "take[s] us away from the conflict and excitement of our own 'high-pressure' age, with its extreme theories and extreme reactions" and "into a society which, if no less earnest and trying to those who composed it, has been rounded by time into an aspect of comparative simplicity and peace" (2).

But conflict and excitement, not simplicity and peace, are the center of a good work, serial or not, as the press noted. The *Illustrated Times* observes that "Circulating-library readers will be staggered when we tell them the story out of which these three volumes are made" and summarizes the plot, upon which "very slight basis is constructed a three-volume story of almost always strong, and sometimes very painful interest" (Feb. 19, 1859; 123). The *Leader* also places *Adam Bede* in the context of current reading, arguing that the "mere reader of fashionable novels will not very much like this work; and the admirer of the 'fast' school of literature will think it 'slow,'" but readers who appreciate quieter effects will read and reread this work (Feb. 26, 1859; 270). The *Guardian* disapproves of Arthur's last-minute reprieve, but otherwise, "This book is sterling stuff, and we think will live. It deals with gentle and simple, and speaks to the general heart of humanity. We should advise Mr. Eliot to beware of startling situations, and to cultivate the admirable style of which he is master, and he may become a classic" (Mar. 2, 1859; 207). Although there is no mention of *Scenes of Clerical Life*, several reviews recall Eliot's own "striking situations," which she knew were the ordinary stuff of which serial novels are made.

Eliot did not begin volume 2 until she was in Munich in April. Her journal for that month says nothing of *Adam Bede*, but describes at length the scenery, art, music, and people she encountered. On May 4, she mentions *Adam* in connection with Blackwood's noncommittal April 30 letter; even though Eliot apparently made the final decision not to serialize, she was disappointed that he failed to see her purpose. It is tempting to hypothesize that she made her decision to write chapter 17 at this point. (See Anderson, "George Eliot Provoked" for fuller development of the idea that Chapter 17 was written as a response to Blackwood.) Time would have allowed her to write chapters 17 and 18 between May 4 and 18, since she wrote two more, 19 and 20, in eight days: "Read the 18th chapter of Adam Bede to G. He was much pleased with it" (May 18); "This evening I have read aloud 'Adam Bede' Chap. 20" (May 26). And chapter 17's allusions to painting would have been especially likely to come to mind as she and Lewes visited the art galleries of Germany, to which—along with the people, scenery, and music—she devoted thirty pages of her journal before her May 4 entry.

Overall, given the novel's stunning reception after the public's positive but mild response to *Scenes of Clerical Life*, one cannot resist thinking that it was fortunate *Adam Bede* did not appear first in Maga. The effect of the story might have been diminished by its publication in small bits. Perhaps George Eliot realized this, for she is firmer in her own opinion in dealing with Blackwood a year later regarding *The Mill on the Floss*.

With *The Mill on the Floss*, the publishing decisions were more complicated. The monetary benefits of publishing in parts as well as in volumes were attractive to George Eliot, and Blackwood was not the only publisher interested in the now-famous author of *Adam Bede*. Other editors and publishers began to court her, often through Lewes. Dickens hoped she would provide a serial to follow Collins's *The Woman in White* in *All the Year Round*. Competitor Samuel Lucas wrote Eliot for a contribution to *Once a Week*, which Bradbury and Evans established after Dickens bought their share of *Household Words* and incorporated it in *All the Year Round* (*Letters* 3: 43). Eliot declined both offers, though Dickens was importunate, and she valued his praise for her work. Her first expectation had been to remain with Blackwood and Sons. However, her relationship with the sons was changed not only by her increased assertiveness, but by the revelation of her identity forced upon her (she felt) by the Liggins controversy. William and John Blackwood opposed this revelation, and misunderstandings developed between them and Eliot as a result. After a period of strained relations, months of negotiations, and a growing disinclination to break her novel into small parts, Eliot determined once again to avoid this fragmentary method of publication; and they mutually agreed to publish *The Mill on the Floss* only in volume format.

At first John Blackwood assumed that she would publish the new novel in Maga, which in late 1859 and early 1860 faced competition from two new monthlies, *Macmillan's Magazine* and the *Cornhill*. He broached the topic of serialization soon after *Adam Bede* appeared. Reporting on the sales of *Scenes* and *Adam* on March 30, 1859, Blackwood concluded, "I put a query as to what you were doing with the new Tale. I am very anxious to hear about it. I want a Tale for the Magazine and I know I can trust to George Eliot" (*Letters* 3: 40). Eliot responded cautiously the next day, "About my new story, which will be a novel as long as Adam Bede, and a sort of companion picture of provincial life, we must talk when I have the pleasure of seeing you. . . . It will be a work which will require time and labour" (3: 41). To fill just one number, she promises him a "slight story," which he published as "The Lifted Veil" in July 1859. This story (which he did not like) did not deter Blackwood from hoping for her next full-length work. Her description of this future work as a "companion picture" to *Adam Bede* would only have increased its desirability. On June 24, John Blackwood wrote to William that he would see Eliot the next day: "I half venture to think that before I leave London I should do something decisive about the new Novel. I have very little doubt that at present a new work by George Eliot might affect the sale of the Mag. most materially especially when there is an upward tendency already" (*Letters* 3: 92). On August 15, John Blackwood asked, "How is the new Tale? I long to see more of it. Every bit of what I read is distinctly before me now" (3: 131). Eliot's reply shows she had serialization in mind: the new story "is only in the leaf-bud. I have faith that the flower will come. Not enough faith, though, to make me like the idea of *beginning to print* till the flower is fairly out—till I know the end as well as the beginning" (*Letters* 3: 133; emphasis added). With her new story having such personal resonance, she would have been especially fearful that her experience with *Scenes of Clerical Life* might be repeated—that Blackwood would misjudge the work based on partial knowledge. Blackwood's next business letter to Lewes, on September 2, asks: "How does the new Novel get on? Do you think we can start before the end of the year?" (3: 143).

Her reply on September 13 shows that she was not as sanguine as Blackwood that she *would* serialize the new novel. Describing at length the difference between the desirability of serialization for an unknown author and its potentially negative effect on sales following a well-known book like *Adam Bede*, she gives both commercial and artistic reasons for her reservations about serializing "Maggie" in *Blackwood's*. "The very large sale of 'Adam Bede' has necessarily modified my prospects as to the publication of my next book." Now that she has "so large and eager a public," she argues, "if we were to publish the work without a preliminary appearance in the Magazine, the first sale would infallibly be large, and a considerable profit would be gained." Recognizing the vagaries of public favor, the still diffident author is compelled to add a qualifier: "even though the work might not ultimately impress the public so strongly as 'Adam' has done." Publication in Maga, on the other hand, by a "new writer concerning whose works there is some expectation and curiosity, would inevitably reduce what would otherwise be the certain demand for three-volumed copies. The Magazine edition would be devoured, and would sweep away perhaps 20,000—nay 40,000—readers who would otherwise demand copies of the complete work from the libraries" (*Letters* 3: 151).

She also anticipates Anthony Trollope's later concern regarding *Romola*, discussed in chapter 4, whether the general public will perceive the book's artistic merits if it is published as a serial: "Again, the book might be in some respects superior to Adam, and yet not continue in the course of periodical reading to excite the same interest in the mass of readers." As a result, "an impression of its inferiority might be spread before republication:—another source of risk." Finally, she notes the irrelevance of the advertising value that usually accompanies magazine serialization: "The large circulation of 'Adam' renders the continual advertisement afforded by publication in a first-rate periodical—an advertisement otherwise so valuable—comparatively unimportant." Her failure to allow Lewes to undertake this business (as he usually did), her stress on artistic questions, and her unwillingness to be driven to write for the sake of money[16] demonstrate Eliot's sensitivity and serious consideration of the business of serialization.

Blackwood's reply on September 21 addressed only the monetary issues and not the artistic matters that were important to Eliot. He blundered in his treatment of the anonymity, either through not having read carefully her comments about the value *Adam Bede* had given her name, or through a blind fear that the revelation of her authorship would damage sales. Just then she felt particularly vulnerable. Six letters[17] passed between Eliot/Lewes and Charles Bray/Charles Bracebridge from September 26 to the end of the month, regarding Bracebridge's adherence to the Liggins imposture. In her journal, she refers to "a *crétin* named Bracebridge . . . who undertakes to declare the process by which I wrote my books," and "It is poor George who has had to conduct the correspondence, making his head hot by it, to the exclusion of more fructifying work" (Oct. 7, 1859). This unpleasantness made Eliot especially sensitive to Blackwood's suggestion that he would publish the new tale anonymously and that "it would be great fun to watch the speculations as to the author's life." As Haight observes, it would be "No fun for GE. This is an unusual lapse of tact in Blackwood" (*Letters* 3: 161 and n3).[18]

This lapse may have settled the fate of "Maggie" as a serial novel. Eliot's response the next day is sharper and colder than her usual tone to her publisher. Beginning with the statement that she "felt no disposition to publish in the Magazine beyond the inclination to meet your wishes— if they still pointed in that direction, and if I could do so without sacrifice," she repeats her opinion that serialization will damage the reception of the three-volume edition: "Your letter confirms my presupposition that you would not find it worth your while to compensate me for the renunciation of the unquestionable advantages my book would derive from being presented to the public in three volumes with all its freshness upon it." Her sensitivity is clear in the stiff formality of her charge against him: "I infer that you think my next book will be a speculation attended with risk [and] I prefer incurring that risk myself." The letter's long final paragraph details the troubles she is still having over the Liggins business (*Letters* 3: 161–62).[19]

More than three weeks elapsed before Eliot and the Blackwoods exchanged any further correspondence, but letters to others reveal mutual irritation. William Blackwood on October 5 expressed to John his displeasure with her response. Eliot's vulnerability is apparent in her letter of October 6 to Blackwood's London manager, Joseph Munt Langford, requesting the name of a lawyer to give an opinion on a detail in her new work: "Is it quite an irrational supposition, that among the hard-headed admirers you alluded to, there may be one to whom you could mention my want, and who would not be *too much disgusted* by the *painful certainty* that *the author of 'Adam Bede' is a woman*, to be willing to be consulted by her?" (*Letters* 3: 173; emphasis added). Her uncharacteristically bitter tone reveals her frustration not only because of the Liggins imposture, but because her relationship with Lewes made her susceptible to special criticism beyond even the extraliterary standards that generally plagued women writers. John Blackwood recognized only part of the cause for her mental perturbation. Sending news that 2,000 additional copies of *Adam Bede* were being printed, he regrets "that you should allow yourself to be so disturbed by an old fool like Bracebridge" and alludes to the new novel, but with a distant grace: "The Major and I are very sorry indeed that you cannot entertain our proposal for the new

Tale. I hope Maggie gets on as gloriously as she promised" (*Letters* 3: 182–83). A cordial letter to Lewes the same day does not mention Eliot or the novel (*Letters* 8: 249).

Two days later, Eliot tried to be equally cordial. Admitting her sensitivity and wishing he could share in her progress on the new book, she assumes that Blackwood will remain her publisher, even if they have not yet come to an agreement.[20] However, she reiterates her fear of beginning prematurely: "And I think I should worry myself still more if I began to print before the thing is essentially complete. So on all grounds it is better to wait" (3: 184–85). The novel had, in fact, progressed to the point at which she had been willing to start the serialization of *Adam Bede*, the end of volume 1. Her journal for October 16, the same day as this letter, records confidently, "I have finished the first volume of my new Novel, 'Sister Maggie,' have got my legal questions answered satisfactorily, and when my headache has cleared off must go at it full speed." Her increasing reluctance to break the novel into parts was undoubtedly as significant to her hesitation as its unfinished state. This abhorrence of small parts may be inferred from Lewes's letter one day earlier telling Blackwood, "Maggie grows slowly into womanhood—and since she is to rival Adam—she had better take her time, and not be outgrowing her strength. I have just heard the first volume over again, not bit by bit as heretofore, but en masse; and my admiration increases with familiarity" (3: 183). Lewes attributes his increased admiration to "familiarity" but if Eliot, in one of their frequent discussions of her work, compared his initial reaction to "bit by bit" reading with his great enthusiasm after hearing her read a whole volume, her fears about breaking the novel into parts could only have been reinforced. Nevertheless, the shrewd businessman Lewes was not to give up so easily the possibility that Maggie's readers might first encounter the tale themselves "bit by bit."

George Eliot's sensitivity about *Adam Bede*'s being revealed as a woman's book was outweighed by her annoyance with the Liggins imposture and then by the appearance of a "sequel," *Adam Bede, Junior*, advertised by Newby. She and Lewes determined to reveal her identity: for the first time in a letter to her publishers, dated October 16, 1858, she signed her name "Marian Evans Lewes" rather than "George Eliot." William Blackwood opened this letter first, sending it on to his brother with a note that began, "I send you a letter from G.E. I am rather sorry to see the change of signature," which signaled Eliot's determination to end the incognito. This, William Blackwood added, "is one reason for [the new book's] not appearing [in Maga] to which considerable weight may be due: and another is the author's strong feeling about the advantage" that it should be publicized as by the author of *Adam Bede*. William Blackwood still thought "we are right as to the mode of publication we recommended" and he "would not, were the author's position different, mind about pressing our ideas on him. But considering how that position may possibly affect the new book I think we might be placed in disagreeable circumstances by doing so" (3: 188). William's discreet reference to "that position" and its effect would not have been lost on John Blackwood, who understood the need to placate the prejudices of a family audience, prejudices that he sometimes shared, as his response to "Janet's Repentance" shows.[21]

Both sides were now reluctant to serialize, though for quite different reasons. Both felt misunderstood and mistreated, and *Blackwood's Magazine* lost the novel just as it faced formidable new rivals. While Eliot was made anxious by the Liggins and Newby frauds and her vulnerable position as a woman author, members of Blackwood's firm were anxious because of two new periodicals, *Macmillan's* and the *Cornhill*. George Simpson wrote to Langford on November 3 that "Mr. John said he was determined to have it [Eliot's new novel], *so much would it help Maga to have it in her pages*" (3: 193; emphasis added). John Blackwood was both disappointed not to acquire it and "disgusted" (Simpson's word for the reaction of both John and William Blackwood) at the coolness with which Eliot seemed to receive their voluntary payment—£800 more than agreed upon for *Adam Bede*. His dismay and sense of betrayal are recorded in George Simpson's correspondence with Langford as well as in his own letters.

John Blackwood, aware that his remarks about the anonymity might have offended Eliot (3: 206), tried with Langford to puzzle out what had gone wrong. On November 18, Langford wrote encouragingly:

> if you still wish to have the book a little judicious reticence may bring back the author to you. The idea of putting it into Maga seems not to be liked. I told Lewes that I could understand an insuperable objection to that upon artistic grounds but that I could not understand such an objection of that sort as could be overcome by money. He seemed to have some crotchet about your having said that you would give *as much* for the tale for Maga as for original separate publication and that you ought to give more for so making use of it to suit your own purpose. (3: 207)

Other comments respond to Blackwood's expressed curiosity about the new periodicals. Simpson is reassuring: "I am pleased to hear that you have good things in prospect for Maga—the opposition is strong just now but there is no fear that she will be shaken from her pre-eminence." But the new competition, monthly magazines aiming at a well-informed audience like that of *Blackwood's*, continued to cause anxiety. Further in his letter, Simpson appears to protest too much: "Macmillans have sold 10,000 and are reprinting—still the thing is a failure and has made no impression. Thackeray's name [as *Cornhill* editor] has not met a single approval in my hearing" (3: 207). The level of the firm's anxiety is also evident in Simpson's November 19 letter to Langford, where he juxtaposes discussion of their disagreements with Lewes and Eliot and the subject of the two magazines. He leaps from the revelation of Eliot's identity and Blackwood's response to, suddenly, the *Cornhill*: "The title of Thackeray's Magazine conveys to me the idea of Banks Stockbrokers, and Assurance Companies not of Literature. How lucky for Macmillan that this has at once realised a perfect failure. Had it gone on dubiously they might have been led into a heavy loss. Of course they will stop in time.?" (*Letters* 3: 210).

As the *Cornhill's* January first number approached, the firm's anxiety increased. John Blackwood wrote to his brother from London on December 20, "The Cornhill Mag. contents do not look very alarming on the contrary there is a sort of trifling look about the whole concern," to which William replied that "It's a beastly vulgar looking thing whatever it's [*sic*] contents may be" (Dec. 24; Letters in the National Library of Scotland). On December 21, Simpson sent John Blackwood a self-congratulatory letter that reveals their awareness that the press would make comparisons: "I am indeed elated at the prospects before us. What will the public say to the January No of Maga! The extent of his resources and great superiority to all his rivals surely ought to be the subject of universal acclaim." Simpson apparently wanted to enlist some help in producing that acclaim, for William wrote again on December 28, "Simpson has been anxious for me to send our paper of extracts to the press generally rgding this N°. I have taken such a disgust however at the way the newspapers speak of the Cornhill Macmillan and other rubbish that I think in the case of such a good N°. as this it's better policy to let the public alone to see what good stuff there is in Maga that is not puffed if the papers cant of themselves point it out" (NLS).

Reviews of the new periodicals were mixed. The *Illustrated Times* begins its January 1860 "Magazines" column by marveling at the large number of notable new magazines, naming the *Cornhill* and *Macmillan's*, but it also offers the consolation that "With all the rush of novelty there seems no likelihood of stern, tough old *Blackwood* giving ground. His number for the New Year is replete with good things" (Jan. 7; 11). The March notice predicts "wide popularity" for the *Cornhill*, which "bids fair to achieve a very extended permanent circulation." However, it is unlikely that "either of the newcomers [will] allure one subscriber from his monthly payment to *Blackwood* or *Fraser*."[22] *Blackwood's* has "an honest, hearty, bluff outspokenness, an unswerving, uncompromising belief in the impossibility of error in its political creed, a fierceness and a thoroughness in its criticisms on art, literature, and passing events which you would seek for in vain in the temporising politeness of the *Cornhill* or the would-be earnest, but often dreamy, principles of *Macmillan*" (Mar. 10, 1860; 153).

By May, however, the column is less reassuring. This time it begins, "The current number of *Blackwood* will fail to create an impression that the old-established magazines are endeavouring successfully to contend with their younger brethren. Its contents are unusually heavy, and what light matter there is lacks point and spirit" (May 5; 281). June's verdict is similar: "Is it by comparison with its younger brethren that *Blackwood* begins to read heavily, or does it really require not merely a little fresh blood but a new arrangement—a different supervision? Certainly the past few numbers have been dull enough, and the present shows but little improvement" (June 9; 361). July's column is more positive, "Still let us give the post of honour to *Maga*—still let the pictured presence of stern old Buchanan walk in the van of our notices, 'though younger competitors are now striving hard to 'push him from his stool'" (July 7; 10). The timeliness of the contrast seems to have ceased after this month, and the competition drops from the column, but these comparisons during the first half of the year indicate that the Blackwood firm's fears had foundation. If *Blackwood's* was the royal father of the magazines, there were several Prince Hals trying on the crown.

A comment in Simpson's November 19 letter validates Eliot's fears about the way her authorship would be treated when her liaison with Lewes became known. On November 18, Lewes had sent Blackwood a letter that must have added to the latter's annoyance: "What days these are for furious speculation in the periodical world! My precious time is occupied with declining offers on all sides—every one imagining that he can seduce George Eliot, simply because he (the everyone, not G.E.) *wants* that result!" (3: 208). The bitterness of the members of Blackwood's firm shows forth in Simpson's crude response to Langford the next day: "I say no wonder when Mr. Lewes has shown them the way" (3: 209).[23] At this time, speculation about the authorship had begun to connect the "morals" (or lack of) in the author with the effect of her book. If her publishers—albeit during a difficult period in their relationship—express such blatant sexism, what could Eliot expect from critics and the reading public?

In a November 18 letter, Langford alludes to not telling Lewes something Mudie had said, to which Simpson responds that he wishes Langford had done so, adding, "I am sure you are right that the secret was published by him [Eliot] to gratify his vanity, but I think the penalty will be enormous" (3: 309–10). Haight clarifies: "Mudie, who was notoriously prudish, may well have felt that the irregularity of GE's relations with GHL would compel him to boycott her next novel. Langford wrote John Blackwood 23 August 1859: 'Williams has read Adam and is delighted, but will not believe the story [of its authorship], not thinking it possible that such a book can come from a polluted source'" (3: 209n2). Langford wrote again on November 23, describing a talk with Mr. Watson of Nisbet & Co., who "says that the story of the authorship has most certainly affected [sales of *Adam Bede*] with their customers—that it was taken up remarkably by the religious world and that people who were not in the habit of reading works of fiction at all were delighted with it— but that all that had ceased" (NLS). Watson also described a manuscript proposed to him—"an elaborate critique written by a lady addressed to the women of England on the grounds of the reputed authorship and aiming to show from internal evidence that the work was written by a woman of loose morals!" (NLS; Haight quotes part of this letter in 3: 221n6).

Despite such rumors, the Blackwood's firm remained interested in the new novel. Letters between John Blackwood and Eliot in late November and early December cleared up the misunderstanding,[24] though these letters, especially in conjunction with a letter from William to John Blackwood, show that the removal of the incognito continued to make the brothers uneasy. They determined not to renew their offer to include the story in Maga, but to publish it in volumes only, though Mudie's threat would have been disastrous if carried out.[25]

Although John Blackwood reassured Eliot that any disadvantage resulting from the end of the incognito would be overcome,[26] its removal decided the brothers against including *The Mill on the Floss* in Maga. "I would not have it now for Maga. Any failure or fancied failure of it in that case would be most disagreeable. Our practice of never giving an author's name in Maga should be strongly dwelt on [in John's letter to Eliot] and our reason for it. It will soothe his feelings," William Blackwood wrote to John on December 1, adding, "The dropping of the incognito is the most serious part of the business and will, I feel satisfied, *affect the circulation in families of any future work*" (3: 221; emphasis added). Though John Blackwood had early demonstrated his respect for Eliot by taking his wife to call upon her, the brothers understood the realities of Victorian prudery and feared the effects on readers who might regard the author as "polluted."[27]

Following William's advice, John Blackwood explained to Eliot why he had proposed anonymous publication in Maga. It was the practice Maga had always followed, although he had to admit two exceptions were made for Bulwer Lytton. Eliot would have been especially aware of the exception for *What Will He Do With It?*, since this novel ran in *Blackwood's* concurrently with the final installment of "Gilfil" and all of "Janet's Repentance."[28] In her brief, cordial note of December 5, inviting Blackwood to lunch, Eliot, perhaps in a spirit of reconciliation, made no comment on this inconsistency in their treatment of herself and her more famous (or less infamous) contemporary. This lunch was evidently a success, for it led to Blackwood's being entrusted with a volume and a half of *Mill* to read prior to making an offer. John's letter to William, written immediately afterward, shows Lewes's and Eliot's different views on serialization. Lewes still hoped to serialize, if not in Maga, then in one-shilling numbers; and he had explained to Blackwood the costs and profits as calculated by Bradbury and Evans. Eliot opposed the one-shilling plan and serialization in a periodical; she had already refused an offer of £4,500 for serialization in a magazine and "two editions afterwards," Blackwood reported. When he told her that he "would not offer any wild sum such as I was sure people trying to start a periodical and help off other things would give," Eliot responded that she wanted only "a fair profit to myself [Blackwood] with a good sum to her" (3: 232–33). What Blackwood found in the first volume and a half reassured him about the wisdom of the firm's plans. The book was "wonderfully clever" but wanting in "the hurrying on interest of a taking narrative." After summarizing the plot, John Blackwood adds, "I would not advise serial publication unsupported by the prestige of the Magazine and [given that the brothers were reluctant to have the story in Maga] shall make such an offer as you propose"—that is, for volume publication only (3: 233–34).

A letter on December 14 made this offer (3: 235), but Eliot did not immediately accept. Lewes still held to the one-shilling scheme: "Lewes has a notion that from 5 to 10 thousand may be made by publishing in the shilling numbers, and it is quite possible," John Blackwood wrote William on December 15. However, Eliot "is dead against it and I think will have her way. She fears the nervous excitement of the trial and thinks her story will tell better in a mass" (3: 235–36). Blackwood was right. Eliot prevailed against what she termed "the Nightmare of the Serial" and wrote on December 20 to accept the offer (3: 236). But she continued to fear the negative effect of the novel's being read in small parts, even in manuscript. As late as March 15, when *Mill* was nearly completed, Lewes sent Blackwood "more m.s.," with the warning that "Mrs. Lewes . . . makes a point of none of you reading any more of the book until you can go to the end, as this fragmentary mode of sipping the champagne allows the effervescence of interest to go off" (3: 273).[29]

The offers that Blackwood had heard about for serializing *The Mill on the Floss* in separate parts or in a periodical had come from two sources. In mid-November, Dickens solicited Lewes for a story from Mrs. Lewes to follow *The Woman in White* in *All the Year Round*. She is to name her monetary terms; she will retain the copyright; and she has "perfect liberty to select her own publisher for the completed story." And Dickens added the inducement that "An immense new public would probably be opened to her" (*GE Letters* 3: 203). Lewes recorded in his journal the next day, November 15, "we have turned the matter over and almost think it feasible." Three days later, however, Eliot's journal notes: "We have written to Dickens saying that Time is an insurmountable obstacle to his proposition as he puts it" (3: 205). Nonetheless, Lewes just a few days afterward "Called on Dickens to arrange about Polly's story which he wishes her to write for him" (GHL Journal, Nov. 22, 1859).[30] Their attempt to decline Dickens's offer must have been somewhat ambiguous, because as late as February 13, 1860, he still hoped for a story from her, writing to Lewes that his "letter has perfectly amazed me. I had not the least idea and I assure you—not the faintest notion—that there was any postponement, far less a postponement sine die."[31]

At the same time, autumn 1859, Lucas and Evans of Bradbury and Evans also asked Lewes for a novel "on my own terms" for *Once a Week*, perhaps as a pretext for inquiring about Eliot's work.[32] They also "wanted to know whether [Eliot's] new novel was in the market"; Lewes told them "that she felt bound to give Blackwood the refusal," but they promised to give more than whatever Blackwood offered. "We parted," Lewes concludes, "on the understanding that they were to make an offer" (*Letters* 3: 204). Magazine serialization had apparently not been ruled out. Eliot's journal for November 18 records that she and Lewes are still considering *Once a Week*: Evans and Lucas "were to write and make an offer, but have not yet done so" (*Letters* 3: 205). By December 1, the offer was made: "Bradbury and Evans have offered me £4500 for my new novel. i.e. for publication in 'Once a Week' and for two subsequent editions" (GE Journal, Dec. 1, 1859). Even though they did not accept this offer, Lewes's proposal to Blackwood for one-shilling numbers of *The Mill on the Floss* was a result of these negotiations.

Blackwood was right in seeing that the action of this novel would not have suited serial publication in Maga or in one-shilling monthly parts, which typically were thirty-two pages long. It would have been even less appropriate for briefer weekly installments. If one looks at the climactic incidents of the first part, they have little cliff-hanger excitement or even the milder enticement of some endings in *Scenes of Clerical Life*. Approximating the length of the *Scenes*' installments in *Blackwood's*, the first break in *Mill* would have had to occur after chapter 4 or chapter 5. Chapter 4 ends with a major drama in Maggie's young life: her discovery that she has forgotten to feed Tom's rabbits and they have all died. His homecoming will be spoiled, and it is all her fault. The incident, however important for characterization and theme, is not the cliff-hanger ending that readers expected. If an installment had stopped after chapter 5, it would have been as long as one of the longer parts of *Scenes*, with an ending even less dramatic than the death of the rabbits. This chapter's closing section intimates that things will change in ways that the parties themselves don't see, rather like the prediction about Countess Czerlaski at the end of installment 1 in "Amos Barton." But in the latter, the comment is brief and pointed and creates mild suspense, whereas in chapter 5 of *The Mill on the Floss*, the theme is so generalized that readers' attention is directed away from Maggie and Tom altogether.

The early parts of the novel include other little incidents that help form Maggie's consciousness, but none of a kind to attract interest in isolation or carry much dramatic weight. One need only compare the way in which Oliphant handles suspense and interest in *The Athelings* by avoiding any focus on the young twins, however useful they were for intermittent pathos. Instead, she moves the marriageable sisters into high society early in her installments. A child's ordinary family life was not likely to contain the stuff of which good serials were made. David Copperfield, Oliver Twist, and Pip only prove the rule by being children with rather un-ordinary childhood experiences—excellent material for installment fiction.

To see how this argument is not negated but rather reinforced, one might consider Pip, a child also growing up in the country in *Great Expectations*, which began serially in *All the Year Round* on December 1, 1860, a few months after *The Mill on the Floss* appeared in three volumes. Contrasting the incidents of the first third of Eliot's novel with those of Dickens's, one can see how much more likely readers would have been to return to Pip than to Maggie had she also been presented in parts. In Dickens, "striking incidents" begin immediately as Pip encounters the convict in the graveyard. On the other hand, when the reader first meets Maggie, she is sitting in a corner of her drawing room listening to a conversation about her brother's schooling and her being too "'cute for a wench." Pip and Maggie alike soon feel guilty for acts that they could hardly have avoided; Pip steals food and drink for Magwitch, and the dreamy Maggie forgets the rabbits. What follows each "offence" points to the difference between their stories' suitability for serialization. In *Great Expectations*, just when he thinks he has been found out by his sister and expects to be arrested by the soldiers, Pip is taken on an exciting chase through the marshes. In *Mill*, Tom simply refuses to take Maggie fishing—and eventually relents about that. Most of the exciting moments early in Eliot's novel come from Maggie's disobedience to small behests—she cuts her hair, she is driven by jealousy to push Lucy into the mud, she runs away to the gypsies. Where Pip's childhood record focuses on the extraordinary—encountering a convict and later the secretive man with the file, visits to Miss Havisham, a mysterious benefactor, even an early promise of a love interest—Maggie's contains more ordinary incidents. Eliot was undoubtedly right in seeing that, as a serial, the novel would have had even less appeal than early parts of *Adam Bede*—which at least featured the novelty of a woman preacher, a sudden death by drowning, the supernatural rapping of the willow wand, disappointed love, and a possible seduction, along with a modicum of silver-fork appeal in the Irwines and Donnithornes. John Blackwood correctly identified the problem as a lack of "hurrying on" of the interest, an essential ingredient of a strong serial.

Reviewers generally agreed. Several notices in the popular daily and weekly press provided reassurance that Eliot had lived up to her "responsibility" as the author of *Adam Bede*. *The Mill on the Floss* was a worthy successor, and, some felt, even superior. The London *Sun* was especially fulsome, but otherwise typical: "The author of 'Adam Bede' may well be congratulated on having so triumphantly passed the ordeal of a second [*sic*] publication after a first of such marvellous renown as that which was sounded through the length and breadth of the land by the voice of fame" (2). Some, however, thought the plot was slow, and the incident negligible. The *Morning Chronicle* puts it bluntly, "The interest of the new tale is far less absorbing" and the "pathos less subduing" than in *Adam Bede* (6). The *Illustrated Times* notes that the "minute character-sketching" of volume 1 has little connection with volumes 2 and 3. "Any one who pleases may begin the reading literally with the third volume, and feel little sense of incompleteness" (345). According to the *Press*, the novel has "no plot in the common acceptation of the word" (335); the *Daily News* explains that Eliot does not work "from the theatrical point of view" (5), and *John Bull* finds this a better novel, even though "the mere narrative part of the story is but a subordinate feature in the composition." Rather, it "is more as a piece of artistic biography than as a story that the history of Maggie absorbs our interest" (235). The presence of "mere narrative" is, of course, a key item in a serial novel. *Adam Bede* is "more interesting," but *The Mill on the Floss* is "better constructed," agrees the *Morning Post*. We never "love any of the characters portrayed but we know them all. . . . The writer even does not love any of the people—that is quite clear and the story derives a loss of interest and an increase of value from that circumstance" (6). This assessment of the subordinate characters appeared April 19, 1860, exactly a month before a similar one in the *Times*, in which E. S. Dallas asks why a "brilliant novelist" gave her readers "these mean, prosaic people, the Dodsons" (*Critical Heritage* 136). Eliot appreciated the "generous spirit" and "intelligence" of this review, but regretted that her own good opinion of the virtues of the Dodsons has been missed (*Letters* 3: 299).

The *Weekly Scotsman* also regards *Mill* as superior to *Adam Bede* "though some will say otherwise," and has a simple, but insightful, explanation for the lack of exciting incidents: "Maggie's life was deadening, her youth was passing in this dreary circle." But this reviewer, defining the word "passion" narrowly, ignores the lifelong passionateness of Maggie manifested in her earliest conflicts: "The passion of the story is concentrated toward its close" (6). This analysis—of greater excitement and passion near the end—was frequent. Other reviewers found that the story's interest increased as it progressed, though the precise point where it picked up is disputed. The Edinburgh *Evening Courant* says that the story moves "along somewhat sluggishly at first," but then "deepens in interest." The final book's focus, the "love affair" between Maggie and Stephen, "is not a pleasant one to contemplate. We are bound to admit, however, that this episode has been treated with wonderful dramatic force." Overall, the novel is "superior to 'Adam Bede' as a continuous narrative." This phrase is not explained, but perhaps refers to the almost constant focus on Maggie. This narrative changes "its character" in the second part; "losing the subtle humour which pervaded the earlier part, [it] becomes grander and more rapid. . . . The sad era of Maggie's life occupies the second volume. With the third the stormy season begins." One of the few negative reviews agrees that there is "no interesting story" until volume 3, "when the narrative really commences, and the incidents are hurried on with perhaps too much rapidity. There is no incident of any kind whatever for the first two hundred pages" until Maggie runs away to the gypsies (*Atlas* 291). The *Press* pointed out that "the third volume has plot of its own sufficient in itself for an ordinary novel" (336). These remarks indicate that George Eliot was right in her initial assessment that the book might be stronger than *Adam Bede* and yet not be perceived so in part publication.

Eliot's next two novels overlapped each other in composition. The idea for *Romola* began on the trip Lewes and Eliot made to Florence as soon as *Mill* was finished. She interrupted this work, however, to write *Silas Marner*, the one novel between *Scenes* and *Romola* that she seems never to have thought of serializing, despite the fact that it would have been better suited to this format than either *Adam Bede* or *Mill.* In terms of incident, *Silas Marner* contains several fine potential serial endings. Chapter 4, for instance, closes with Dunstan Cass robbing Silas's cottage; the final line is equal in vividness and dramatic force to anything by Wilkie Collins. Clutching his riding whip and the money bags, Dunstan "stepped forward into the darkness." These first four chapters are almost the same length as one installment of *Scenes of Clerical Life.* A second installment of similar length would have brought readers to the end of chapter 9, with its impending crisis in which Mr. Cass urges Godfrey to marry, not knowing that he already has an alcoholic, lower-class wife. Chapters 10 to 12 would have formed a slightly longer installment, with a conclusion combining drama and pathos, as the toddler Eppie leads Silas to her mother, dead in the snow. Chapters 13 to 18, another potential installment, close with the discovery of Dunstan's skeleton and Godfrey and Nancy's decision to adopt Eppie. In a highly laudatory review, the *Morning Post* observed the story's "faultless" construction:

> it is as devoid of trick in contrivance as of tameness in conception; it is neither far-fetched nor incongruous. It is admirably proportioned; and for harmony and symmetry of parts, might please the fastidious Mr. Curdle, who described the dramatic unities to Nicholas Nickleby as a 'sort of universal dove-tailedness.' It impresses the reader with its having been carefully studied, almost as a piece of patchwork, or a puzzle might be, and each individual and event critically sorted into their right places.

While "the story, gathering persons and events in its rapid, steady roll, has to do with many others, still Silas is always the centre of attraction." This is practically a description of the formula for a good single-plot serial story: proportion, steady movement, main character(s) as the central focus even when others are being portrayed—all the pieces of the puzzle, which are the individual serial parts, fitting together. The exciting, pathetic, and yet natural events and the direct line of the plot of *Silas Marner* would have made it an excellent companion piece to the stories in *Scenes of Clerical Life* and a fine contribution to *Blackwood's*.

Yet the possibility apparently never presented itself either to Eliot or to her publisher. As far as the letters and journals show, she seems to have determined the format without Blackwood's advice, "I have reached p. 209 of my story, which is to be in one volume," she wrote in her journal on February 1, 1861. Lewes wrote the day before: "she thinks it will not be more than one volume" (*Letters* 3: 375). By February 15, she has sent Blackwood 230 pages; in another 100 pages, she expects to complete the work. Perhaps a factor was her opinion that "nobody will take any interest in it but myself, for it is extremely unlike the popular stories going" (*Letters* 3: 371). The sensational nature of "popular stories" such as *The Woman in White*, which had concluded half a year earlier, and *Great Expectations*, then running in *All the Year Round*, might have made Eliot feel that her story as a serial would have had nothing comparable to offer. However, the incidents of *Silas Marner*— clandestine marriage, alcoholism, robbery, violent death—were the popular ingredients of sensation fiction. In anticipation of Blackwood's doubts about the suitability of these details in his family magazine, she may have decided not to raise the issue of serialization. Though Blackwood's response makes no direct mention of earlier problems, it does reiterate complaints he had had about the stories in *Scenes*, especially "Janet's Repentance": he laments Silas's "want of brighter lights and some characters of whom one can think with pleasure as fellow creatures" (*Letters* 3: 380). However, when Eliot writes that "the Nemesis is a very mild one," he looks forward to the conclusion "of the character of which I am delighted to hear" (*Letters* 3: 382, 383). "Relieved" would probably have been as good a word, for *Silas Marner* has a conclusion to please those who like white eggs.

After receiving the first 230 pages, Blackwood proposed a single post octavo volume, or two smaller volumes should the story prove to be longer than Eliot expected. He then waited for Eliot to state her preferred mode of publishing. Perhaps still wary from the bad feelings that had developed in the negotiations over *The Mill on the Floss*, he was certainly distracted by the final illness of his brother, who died April 8, 1861, six days after *Silas Marner* appeared. Even if the story had presented itself as a good one for serial structure, Eliot's nervousness about watching the reception of the parts, her fear of parts not living up to the promise of the whole, and the economic arguments would have remained. For her next novel, *Romola*, already under way, special reasons overrode these considerations, and Eliot herself first proposed that it be serialized. The Blackwood brothers greeted this suggestion enthusiastically, as will be discussed in the next chapter.

4

The Serialization of *Romola*:
"A More Surprising Thing than
Pine-apple for the Million"

W̶HEN GEORGE ELIOT decided not to publish *The Mill on the Floss* as
a serial novel, she breathed a sigh of relief that the prospect of the
"Nightmare of the Serial" had vanished. With *Romola*, the nightmare
reappeared. This novel, her second serial work, was issued under circumstances very different from the quiet and anonymous publication of her
three novellas in *Scenes of Clerical Life* in *Blackwood's* in 1857. These
first stories were written by a diffident author who needed anonymity
even more than most Victorian women writers who wished to be judged
for their work and not for their gender. But by July 1862, when *Romola's*
first installment appeared in the *Cornhill Magazine*, Eliot was famous for
three enormously popular successes: *Adam Bede*, *The Mill on the Floss*,
and *Silas Marner*, all of which were published initially in volume form.
Instead of offering quiet anonymity, *Cornhill's* editor, George Smith,
advertised widely a "new work" by "the author of Adam Bede."

The lure of the new magazines—what Lewes and Eliot had been
tempted by, and Blackwood had feared for *The Mill on the Floss*—came
true with *Romola*. Two years before, Lewes had described *Blackwood's
Magazine* to his son Charles as "the first and best magazine [though it]
only sells 8,000" copies (*Letters* 3: 275). Eliot praised Blackwood as a
man of "such high character that few authors can get their business
transacted more simply than I do" (*Letters* 3: 426). But with *Romola*,
Eliot and Lewes accepted a proposal from a relative newcomer to the
field, the *Cornhill*, which Lewes had called, in the same letter to his son,

"the greatest success of any magazine ever published in this country. It sells 100,000 copies" (*Letters* 3: 275).

In spring 1862, when he made the irresistible offer that caused George Eliot to desert Blackwood, Smith needed to shore up those spectacular sales—which had slipped to 70,000 by January 1862 and 60,000 by July, when *Romola* began (Sutherland, "*Cornhill's* Sales" 106). Trollope's *Framley Parsonage* had concluded its popular run a year before, and nothing else had had quite the same effect.[1] Thackeray's *The Adventures of Philip* was episodic and slow. Harriet Beecher Stowe's flowery romance, *Agnes of Sorrento*, contained "proper" religious sentiments and fine descriptive touches but lacked the dramatic excitement that a serial needed. Eliot might have seemed an odd choice of author to redeem the situation, her fame not having derived from her one prior serial work but from *Adam Bede* and *The Mill on the Floss*. But Eliot's name was the critical factor. Her work was so highly regarded—the Queen "commanded two pictures to be painted from Adam Bede" and spoke "in great admiration" of *The Mill on the Floss* (*Letters* 3: 249, 360)—that even concerns about her liaison with Lewes were diminishing. As evidence of the fact, Mudie "intended to send a card to Mr. and Mrs. Lewes for the opening of his new rooms on December 17th, when he gives a soiree there" (*Letters* 3: 360n6a, from a letter from Langford to John Blackwood). Just as Dickens solicited her work to boost sales of *All the Year Round*, so Smith hoped her novel might reverse his declining sales figures.[2]

Eliot's letters demonstrate once again her distress in confronting publication decisions, and the constant tension produced by serial deadlines. Especially when writing was not proceeding rapidly enough, serialization was a nightmare. Although she never came as close to missing a deadline as she had when Blackwood received installment 3 of *Scenes* only eighteen days before it was to appear, her letters and journal express frequent concerns about *Romola*'s deadlines. The challenge was actually greater. While the interval between parts was the same—one month—*Romola*'s installments were generally longer,[3] and Eliot also had to allow Frederic Leighton time to read the part and prepare the two illustrations that accompanied each number.

Her defection from Blackwood was not her original plan. Initially she and Lewes assumed the story would appear in installments in *Blackwood's Magazine*. On June 23, 1860, almost two years before she concluded her negotiations with George Smith, Eliot had hinted to Blackwood her idea for a new book. She could not "venture to tell you what my great project is by letter, for I am anxious to keep it a secret. It will require a great deal of study and labour, and I am athirst to begin" (3: 307). Eliot and Lewes's anticipated pleasure in sharing the secret with Blackwood is evident in several letters. On August 6, Lewes wrote that he hoped to see Blackwood in Edinburgh and tell him "'the secret'—among other things" (3: 327). Four days later, he expects a visit from William Blackwood that would enable him to reveal it (3: 330). When neither of these meetings materialized, Eliot described her plan to publish her "next English novel [*Silas Marner*] when my Italian one is advanced enough for us to begin its publication a few months afterwards in Maga. It would appear without a name in the Magazine, and be subsequently reprinted with the name of George Eliot." She justifies this renewed anonymity with an argument that Blackwood also made when authors ventured into new territory. "I need not tell you the wherefore of this plan—you know well enough the received phrases with which a writer is greeted when he does something else than what was expected of him" (3: 339). John Blackwood also viewed anonymity as useful when an author changed course. Trollope's first novel in Maga, *Nina Balatka*, appeared under similar circumstances:

> The introduction of Anthony Trollope to the readers of the Magazine was through one of those mysterious literary surprises to which 'Maga' has often been addicted. Anonymous writing lends itself readily to an author wishing to try a new venture; and when the popular chronicler of the Cathedral Close forsook it for a change, he turned to 'Maga' as the open door by which to escape the reproaches of those who might have resented his departure from that pleasant neighbourhood. (Porter 361)

Eliot, too, had become identified by readers as the chronicler of English life in the Midlands, and she and Blackwood recognized the difficulties *Romola* faced in departing from that well-loved terrain. Anonymity made sense, and she was initially content to let *Romola* appear "without a name," as was customary in *Blackwood's*. Smith, however, sought her precisely for her name. Even though *Cornhill's* pages listed no author's name, Smith advertised its authorship widely, and most reviewers discussed it in the context of her previous work—especially *Adam Bede*. In retrospect, this association was a drawback, since *Romola* was so different from its predecessors.[4]

Eliot's enthusiasm for and expectation of working with Blackwood continued. In her New Year's Day letter, 1862, she wished him "All happiness . . . in this coming year. I wish I could believe that I shall contribute to it by writing a book you will like to read" (*Letters* 4: 3). The second sentence reveals her characteristic lack of confidence, which was intensified by the period and setting, fifteenth-century Italy. Long before any publication deadlines were set, writing *Romola* was a struggle. Her journal during the second half of 1861 tells of frequent depression and despair. In July, she read Florentine history or fiction, such as T. A. Trollope's *La Beata*; some days, she was too depressed to work. On July 30, she records: "Read little this morning—my mind dwelling with much depression on the probability or improbability of my achieving the work I wish to do. I struck out two or three thoughts towards an English novel. . . . I am much afflicted with hopelessness and melancholy just now: and yet I feel the value of my blessings" (GE Journal). Two days later, she was "struggling constantly with depression" (Aug. 1, 1861). She continued to read—now Bulwer Lytton's *Rienzi*, "wishing to examine his treatment of an historical subject"—and she talked with Lewes of her "Italian novel" (GE Journal; Aug. 4, 10). Despair and discipline are juxtaposed almost humorously in another entry: "Got into a state of so much wretchness in attempting to concentrate my thoughts on the construction of my story, that I became desperate, and suddenly burst my bonds, saying, I will not think of writing! Read Sacchetti and began Pulci" (GE Journal, Aug. 12). But three days later, after discussing her plot with Lewes, she "struck out an idea with which he was thoroughly satisfied as a 'backbone' for the work" (GE Journal, Aug. 15), and "conceived the plot of my novel with new distinctness" (Aug. 20). During much of September, she was correcting her earlier books for a new edition; but finally she "Took up again the MSS. connected with my Italian novel, and made various arrangements towards work" (Sept. 30). By October 7, her journal records, "Began the first chapter of my novel," but renewed doubt and despondency follow:

> [Oct.] 28–30. . . . Utterly desponding about my book.
> [Nov.] 2. Spent my morning in brooding—producing little.
> [Nov.] 5. . . . *Dreadfully depressed about myself and my work.*
> [Nov.] 6. . . . So utterly dejected that in walking with G. in the Park, almost resolved to give up my Italian novel.

The English novel looms as a refuge: "Yesterday, I was occupied with ideas about my next English novel; but this morning the Italian scenes returned upon me with fresh attraction" (Nov. 10). She persevered and records a second beginning on New Year's Day, "*I began my Novel of Romola.*"

Ill health slows her progress in January 1862. She is still writing the "introductory chapter" on January 14, and on January 31, she "read to G. the Proem and opening scene." By February 17, she had completed only the proem and two chapters, that is, forty-seven manuscript pages; she records "an oppressive sense of the far-stretching task before me, health being feeble just now" (GE Journal). Again on February 26, she mentions illness and discouragement: "I have a distrust in myself, in my work, in others' loving acceptance of it which robs my otherwise happy life of all joy. I ask myself, without being able to answer, whether I have ever before felt so chilled and oppressed. . . . I have written now about 60 pages of my romance. Will it ever be finished?—ever be worth anything? (qtd. in *Letters* 4: 17). She uses the word "about" because she began numbering the pages of her proem with Roman numerals, pages [I]-XIV, and only used Arabic numerals in beginning chapter 1. Hence, in calculating pages, Eliot could not simply look at her page numbers, but had to add to her own Arabic numbers the fourteen pages of proem. The numbering was further complicated when Eliot made major additions or rearrangements, in which case she would sometimes duplicate page numbers and affix an "a" (and even a "b" or "c") to them to keep the order clear.[5] Sixty actual pages would at this point have put Eliot at 46/61, that is, twelve pages into chapter 3.[6] The first installment ends on 82/99,[7] so Eliot had still to complete more than a third of this part when George Smith appeared February 27 with his "most magnificent offer" for a story to begin in April or May (recorded in Lewes's journal; see *Letters* 4: 17–18). Eliot does not mention timelines, but merely Smith's "proposition to give me £10,000 for my new novel—i.e. for its appearance in the Cornhill and the entire copyright at home and abroad" (GE Journal, Feb. 27, 1862). The prospect of early serialization was daunting, given the retardation of her writing that resulted from her greater-than-usual diffidence and her ill health. Lewes's journal records: "she felt it impossible to begin publication in April or May. . . . Unless she sees her book nearly completed and such as she considers worthy of publication she objects to begin printing it." Smith, however, needed the story soon, "April or May being the months when the Magazine will stand in need of some reinforcement as Thackeray's story is quite insufficient to keep up the sale."[8] Consequently, he proposed to consider whether "Brother Jacob," a story

Eliot had completed two years earlier, could be divided into three parts and carry *Cornhill* over to a time when she would feel comfortable starting her new work. "If not," Lewes concludes, "some other proposal will be made by him" (GHL Journal, qtd. in *Letters* 4: 18). The expectation of either acceptance of this plan or a new proposal may have led Eliot to avoid any mention of the new work in a letter to Blackwood the next day, February 28.

Smith wasted no time, for he reappeared on March 1. "On examining his engagements he finds it impracticable to delay the publication of Polly's new work in the Magazine till August or September," Lewes records (qtd. in *Letters* 4: 19). His examination must have reminded Smith that, by June, the only novel would be the lackluster *Adventures of Philip*; and he knew that a periodical needed a continuing serial novel, not just a short story or two (with which he was already supplied). However, Smith still wanted to publish George Eliot's next work, and he and Lewes contemplated other options:

> the plan of a sixpenny serial,[9] also of publishing the book at once at 6/.[10] On these points he is to make calculations and then make a new proposal. Although I regret the loss of such an opportunity of £10,000, I am just as well pleased that Polly should not be hurried and flurried by being bound to appear at an earlier date than she would like. (GHL Journal, qtd. in *Letters* 4: 19–20)

Eliot's journal reveals her reluctance to serialize and almost a sense of relief that "The idea of my novel appearing in the Cornhill is given up, as G. Smith wishes to have it commenced in May, and I cannot consent to begin publication until I have seen nearly to the end of the work" (GE Journal, Mar. 1, 1862). Smith returned on April 8 to propose "weekly numbers at 6d with one plate" (4: 24), and then the journals and letters are silent on the subject for more than a month.

Eliot's journal during this period is full of references to ill health and her consequent inability to write. On March 24, she began "the Fourth chapter of my novel, but have been working under a weight."[11] On March 24, 27, 30, and 31, she refers to writing little because of ill health. By April 2 ("Better this morning"), she had reached the seventy-seventh page (63/78), only five pages into chapter 5 (as published), and only seventeen pages more than she had completed at the end of February. By this time, her views on anonymous publication of *Romola* have changed.

Denying that she is "the author of the Chronicles of Carlingford" running in *Blackwood's*, she chides Sara Hennell: "A little reflection might,
one would think, suggest that when a *name* is precisely the highest-priced
thing in literature, any one who has a name will not, except when there is
some strong motive for mystification, throw away the advantages of that
name. I wrote anonymously while I was an unknown author, but I shall
never, I believe, write anonymously again."

In addition to the "monetary question," she articulates the importance
of being responsible for her views, and therefore announces that "I
should not, without important reasons, put forth anything that was not
virtually declared to be mine" (*Letters* 4: 25). She probably had in mind
George Smith's generous monetary offer, which required that the new
story be "virtually declared" as hers. Her annoyance that Oliphant's
picture of Dissenters has been attributed to her may account for her
severe tone,[12] although a week later, she apologizes for writing "pee-
vishly and irrelevantly," blaming her poor health and her special sensitivity following the *Adam Bede* authorship controversy. Nonetheless, in
more measured words, she reaffirms her decision not to publish anonymously: "in general, you may be sure that whenever a fiction is mine it
will bear the name of George Eliot, or at least be formally and officially
announced as written by George Eliot." Her next sentence alludes to
Smith's offer: "I have refused the highest price ever offered for fiction"
(*Letters* 4: 28). Though she had declined it, Eliot knew from Smith's
persistence that he would probably be back—as indeed he was.

On May 17, Lewes records Smith's final offer. Eliot had "one evening
read several chapters" to Smith to enable him to get a sense of the work
and thus decide on the best publication method. "He dissuaded us from
the notion of a serial, believing that it would not *tell* in small portions. He
wishes to publish it in the 'Cornhill Magazine,' but in considerable instalments—of 45 or 40 pages each number, with two illustrations" (qtd.
in *Letters* 4: 33–34). Eliot wrote to Blackwood on May 19 to tell him the
"abrupt" news that the novel that had been so long a treasured "secret"
would not in fact be his (*Letters* 4: 34–35). On May 21, she and Lewes
signed the agreement stipulating "a novel of sufficient length to fill 384
pages of 'the Cornhill Magazine' . . . in twelve monthly portions." Eliot
would receive £583.6.8 for "each portion of the Manuscript" (*Letters* 8:
301). The total, £7,000, was £3,000 less than Smith's offer in February,
but Eliot preferred to lose the extra money rather than write the sixteen
shorter installments originally proposed. Twelve parts totalling 384 pages

meant an average of 32 pages each. Where Lewes got the "45 or 40 pages" that his journal records as the length of each installment is unclear. Perhaps he was thinking of the fact that *Romola*'s one completed installment filled 98 manuscript pages and, with characteristic shrewdness, had calculated that it would make up 40 to 45 magazine pages. If so, he was an uncannily accurate estimator; it filled 44 *Cornhill* pages. This first was, however, the longest installment; and number 2, much of which was written by late May, is next at 42 *Cornhill* pages.

Attractive as this arrangement was, it meant that not only did Eliot have to write installments longer than those of *Scenes of Clerical Life*, but she had also to have her copy ready early so that Frederic Leighton could prepare his illustrations. These considerations and the imminent deadlines notwithstanding, Lewes wrote optimistically to Charles Lewes the day they signed the agreement that "Smith is in high glee at such an attraction for the Magazine, and mutter is less desponding than usual." Lewes adds that since Eliot was "only three numbers, or less, in advance she will have to work steadily now to keep well ahead in case of illness, or other contretemps" (*Letters* 4: 37). She was very considerably less than three numbers ahead; on May 21 she was ten days away from completing installment 2. Her April-May pace was slightly more rapid than that of the first three months of 1862, but not rapid enough. Three-quarters of part 1 had taken three months, and its last quarter and all of part 2, two months—i.e., she wrote only two installments in exactly five months, from New Year's Day to May 31. Even at a writing rate of one installment every two months, and with two completed, she would have run out of copy by the November 1 issue of the *Cornhill*.

Despite this fact, Eliot's four letters to Leighton in late May and early June justify Lewes's optimism by being surprisingly cheerful, though she does say she is "more gratified . . . by your liking these opening chapters than I have yet been by anything in these *nervous anxious weeks of decision* about publication" (*Letters* 4: 40; emphasis added). By June 10, perhaps as a consequence of the distraction and time that the illustrations entailed, her journal records, "I have not made quite so much way in my new part as I had hoped to do in these first 10 days" (*Letters* 4: 42). By June 22, part 3 was substantially completed: "Read the third part to G. ending with Tessa's marriage [chapter 14, the last one in part 3]." During the next two days, she made "a few additions to the part, having a headache which prevented me from working vigorously," and Lewes took it to the printer on June 24. The next day, she began part 4 (*Letters* 4: 45).

Completion of an installment in only twenty-four days seems to indicate an amended pace that would enable her to meet the monthly deadlines, but the actual number of manuscript and published pages in installment 3 tells another story. The installment begins on 183/201 and ends at 254/274, and hence fills only 74 manuscript pages in contrast to approximately 100 in each of the first two installments—or 44 and 42 published pages (exclusive of illustrations). Installment 3 was only 30 published pages. As Appendix 2 shows, after installments 1 and 2, the number of published pages ranges from a low of 24 in April and May 1863 (56 and 57 manuscript pages respectively) to a high of 38 in October 1862 (97 manuscript pages). Following the first two parts, Eliot never again produced the "45 or 40" pages that Lewes had recorded as the expected length. Five installments run from 30 to 38 *Cornhill* pages, and the other seven from 24 to 29 pages. The original agreement with Smith was for twelve numbers totaling 384 pages, or an average of 32 pages per part. But after part 6, she only once wrote as many as 32 pages per part (35 in installment 13). At the end of twelve installments she had 379 pages, 5 short of her goal. Since *Romola* actually appeared in fourteen installments, Eliot exceeded the contracted length, but only because of the longer early parts and the extra two installments. With fourteen installments, the *average* is just over 31 pages per part. If she had divided her text into twelve parts, she would have averaged 36½ pages per part.

These totals are significant in retrospect, but in summer 1862 she could not divide a text that was not yet written. With her customary care for the artistry of her work, she was more interested in coherent installments than in achieving a particular average number of pages according to a contract.[13] The length of individual installments was to be determined by aesthetic considerations, with an important secondary factor being the state of Eliot's health in the winter and early spring of 1863. The frequent references to illness at that time indicate that her curtailed ability to work resulted in briefer installments.

In the summer of 1862, however, work generally proceeded well. It is true that in late June she worried that her writing was not going as rapidly as she wished: "June 30. I have at present written only the scene between Romola and her brother in San Marco towards Part IV" (*Letters* 4: 45). This scene occupies most of chapter 15, which runs to 17 manuscript pages. With the third installment's 74 pages, Eliot completed a total of 91 pages that month. Thus, her June pace is better than the rate of 77 pages in three months, or even than 199 pages in a total of five months

(98 pages of installment 1 plus 101 pages of installment 2). When the first installment appeared on July 1, she had the comfort of knowing that she was prepared for the two months ahead. With her initial installments so much longer than the average length contracted for, Eliot could feel she was meeting her agreement even if one or two later installments fell short.

Completion of an installment in only three weeks in June 1862 gave her but momentary relief. Her journal entries in July reveal constant awareness of writing to a deadline:

> July 6.* The past week has been unfruitful from various causes. I have not been sufficiently determined in my resistance to sensational and external hindrances. The consequence is, that I am no farther on in my MSS. and have lost the excellent start my early completion of the 3rd part had given me.
>
> 10. A dreadful palsy has beset me for the last few days—I have scarcely made any progress. Yet I have been very well in body. . . .
>
> 11. At p. 30 of Part IV. . . .
>
> 21. At p. 59 of P. IV.
>
> 31. Finished P. IV pp. 94. . . .[14]
>
> [August] 6. Having had a new scene to insert in Part IV, and not having been well, I have not yet begun Part V.

Part 4, totalling ninety-seven manuscript pages (thirty-eight in *Cornhill*), took six weeks to complete. Although Eliot's mention of the ninety-four pages on July 31 shows that she knew it to be longer than part 3, her principal concern was the installment's completion, not its length.

In early July, a letter from Lewes to Mr. and Mrs. W. M. W. Call reiterates the reason behind Eliot's early plan for anonymous publication (her change of subject and period), discounts money as the only reason for serialization, and, incidentally, shows Lewes as the guiding hand behind the decision:

> My main object in persuading her to consent to serial publication, was not the unheard-of magnificence of the offer, but the advantage to such a work of being read slowly and deliberately, instead of being galloped through in three volumes. I think it quite unique, and so will the public when it gets over the first feeling of surprise and disappointment at the book not being English, and like its predecessor. (*Letters* 8: 304)

Evidently regarding this viewpoint as specious, R. F. Anderson argues that "a serial reader might be just as much a 'galloper' as a three-volume reader who was a borrower from Mudie's Select Library or the like; the former in order to get on to the rest of the periodical, and the latter to other borrowed novels" ("Things Wisely Ordered" 24).

Readers' responses to the change in subject matter were probably part of the "sensational and external hindrances" that affected Eliot's concentration in early July. The weather was also "most oppressive—rainy and heavy," Lewes's health was poor, and a visit from Thornton Lewes, though welcome, brought "a general impression that life is made up of large boys with robust voices and bright spirits" (*Letters* 4: 46). Reviewers' doubts about the new setting and time period were offset a little by encouraging comments from friends like Anthony Trollope (*Letters* 8: 303) and Sara Hennell. But despite Sara's favorable response to part 1, Eliot fears that later parts will "disappoint" her. She is both apologetic and defensive: "If one is to have freedom to write out one's own varying unfolding self, and not be a machine always grinding out the same material or spinning the same sort of web, one cannot always write for the same public." She had "forewarned the proprietor of the Cornhill on that point, read a large portion to him, and made him fully aware what the book was to be," and so, she concludes, her anxiety about the new subject and her responsibility to Smith is relieved (*Letters* 4: 49).

A letter on July 17 reveals the extra attention needed to coordinate the illustrations. Leighton wanted to plan his summer holiday, and Eliot suggested to Smith that "The two chapters [15 and 16] from which I wish the illustrations for Part IV to be taken might now be put in type for Mr. Leighton, if you would be kind enough to send for the M.S." (*Letters* 4: 50). A letter on July 25 asks for additional proofs of these chapters because she has had to pass her proofs on to Leighton (4: 51). This early typesetting of chapters 15 and 16 explains a notation on manuscript page 44/318. The words "Part IV" appear in the upper left, after an ink blot under which is just decipherable the phrase "Continuation of." This notation complements the letters' evidence that Eliot gave Smith chapters 15 and 16 early. She probably needed the proofs to refer to these early chapters, and when she completed the part, she marked its continuation for the typesetter. Leighton's two illustrations come, one each, from chapters 15 and 16; they even bear the chapters' titles.

On the surface, Eliot still had plenty of time, since part 4 would not appear until October. If by July 17 she had completed only the forty-three manuscript pages in chapters 15 and 16 (seventeen of which were written in the last six days of June), her pace in July had slowed again, to less than a page and a half per day. Pressed by deadlines, she declined to accompany Lewes to Spa. As he wrote to Blackwood, she "can't be seduced to leave her work. . . . She continues pretty well, but anxious as ever, and till her book is finished will know no peace." His next remark is ironic, considering how much she still had to write: "May it be soon!" (*Letters* 4: 50). However, after Lewes set off on the 17th, she worked quickly, being at page 59 by July 21 and completing page 94 by July 31. She greeted his return August 2 with elation, evident in the underlining in her journal: "*This evening G. Returned bright and well from Spa.*" However, her writing slowed again as she revised part 4: "Having had a new scene to insert in Part IV. and not having been well, I have not yet begun Part V" (GE Journal, Aug. 6, 1862). On August 24, she "Read aloud part V. to G. up to p. 45"; revised its first chapter on August 26;[15] and on September 3, sent "Part V. to press" (GE Journal). It was her shortest installment to date, at sixty-eight manuscript and twenty-eight published pages. She remained slightly less than two months ahead of her deadlines.

By September 10, she had begun part 6, telling Leighton that "The initial letter of the December part [installment 6] will be W" (*Letters* 4: 56). On September 23, she was only "At p. 54"; and on the 26th, "At P. 62." Her journal on September 30 again shows her conscious of needing to remain two months ahead: "The last day of the month. At p. 72—not yet at the end of my December part." The weather cleared—October 1 was a "delicious, clear day," and the next day she was "At p. 85. Scene between Tito and Romola." On October 3, she completed the part, which totaled ninety-four pages; and on October 6 "Began part VII. having occupied the intermediate days in planning." For the next two months, she stayed precisely on schedule, completing a part on the final day of each month, despite occasional illness:

> [October 13] Read aloud to G. up to p. 37 of Part VII. . . . [Page 37 is the last manuscript page in chapter 34.]
> 18. An unfruitful week. Only at p. 45 of P. VII. [MS. page 45 begins chapter 36.]
> 20. Wrote nothing because of indisposition. . . .
> 24. Only at p. 51, having rejected a chapter wh. I had begun, and determined to defer it to the next Part.
> Oct 31. Finished Part VII, having determined to end at the point where Romola has left Florence. (GE Journal)

Her next entry is November 10, when she is "Only at p. 18, not being in working order." By November 18, she is on page 42; and by the 25th, page 59. Despite a "Wretched headache" on November 28, two days later she completed part 8, the shortest thus far at sixty-seven manuscript pages (GE Journal). While she was keeping steadily to an average of a part a month, writing six parts (numbers 3 to 8) in six months (June to November), the parts themselves generally continued to get smaller, as Appendix 2 shows. Of these six parts, only two were over ninety manuscript pages (4 and 6), two just over seventy pages (3 and 7), and two under seventy (parts 5 and 8). With the exception of part 13, at eighty-three manuscript pages, subsequent parts were to be even smaller.

Despite this adherence to her monthly deadlines, Eliot still felt burdened by her task. Four days before completing part 8, she tells Barbara Bodichon that she looks "forward with some longing to that time when I shall have lightened my soul of one chief thing I wanted to do, and be freer to think and feel about other people's work" (*Letters* 4: 65).[16] But the most difficult period since the winter and spring of 1862 was still to come. From December until *Romola*'s completion in June 1863, ill health meant a constant struggle to stay on schedule. She managed to complete most installments just a few days beyond the end of the month, but only because they were shorter than earlier parts. The one exception is the eighty-three manuscript pages of part 13, which she did not complete until May 16.

In early December she was headachy and ill. By December 17, she was "At p. 22 only" and very discouraged:

> I am extremely spiritless—dead, and hopeless about my writing. The long state of headache and disordered liver has left me in depression and incapacity. The constantly heavy, clouded and often wet weather, tends to increase the depression. I am inwardly irritable and unvisited by good thoughts. . . . I read aloud what I had written of Part IX to George, and he to my surprise entirely approved it. (GE Journal)

Illness continued, and her writing pace is slow:

> [December] 22. At p. 33. . . .
> 27. Making little way. Only at p. 44!
> 31. . . . At p. 58 of my 9th Part which I think will be the darkest that has yet come. . . .

She concludes her year-end reflection by noting that "I have had more than my average amount of comfortable health until this last month in which I have been constantly ailing and my work has suffered proportionately" (GE Journal, Dec. 31, 1862).

She did not complete the seventy (or seventy-six)[17] manuscript pages of part 9 until January 4, when she "Read it aloud in the evening, and brought on a dreadful headache, which lasted nearly all the next day." This was also a low point in the serial notices. Lewes kept a close watch on reviews; therefore the encouragement of friends, given its absence in the press, was especially welcome: "Pleasant words from Anthony Trollope"; Arthur Helps regards *Romola* as "the finest thing I have done" (GE Journal, Jan. 4, 8).

Planning part 10 delayed the start of its composition until January 10. On January 26, she had "still about 25 pages of my Xth part to write." Although she postponed some of her material until the next installment (GE Journal, Jan. 30), she completed part 10 on February 4. Two days earlier, George Smith had passed along the heartening news that a party at Lady de Grey's felt it was the "finest book [they] had ever read," to which she adds a triumphant "Ebenezer!" (GE Journal, Feb. 2, 1863). This news and increasingly positive reviews helped offset her discouragement at being only at page 22 of part 11 almost halfway into the month: "Mr. Smith brought pleasant news about Romola, saying that the opinion of it in high quarters was getting past [*sic*] downwards, two of the papers this week having called it a 'masterpiece'" (GE Journal, Feb. 11, 1863). To relieve her health, she and Lewes went again to Dorking on February 24, where they had also been from January 23 to 26. On their return, "I had headache as usual, as my introduction to town life,"[18] but she had completed part 11, which was the second shortest at fifty-seven manuscript pages (GE Journal, Mar. 3). Two of these pages contain so little writing that the number of *Cornhill* pages, twenty-four, is the same as in part 10.

She did not reach page 22 in the next part until March 16, when she was "Wretchedly oppressed and ailing—feeling as if I should never get my work done so as to satisfy me." By March 22 she was "Better: wrote up to p. 32." But she continued to be unwell throughout the month, and did not complete part 12 until April 5.[19] Despite her pleasure at Lewes's being "highly contented" with the part, deadline anxiety continued, as indicated by her page counting: "[Apr.] 13. Only at p. 13! [Apr.] 16. At p. 20" (GE Journal).

Throughout the winter and spring of 1863, she remained almost two months ahead of publication only by writing less. The parts she wrote from January into early April, numbers 10, 11, and 12, are the shortest in the novel—with fifty-six, fifty-seven, and sixty-one manuscript pages respectively. Number 13, at eighty-three pages, closer to the length of the early numbers, took nearly a month and a half to write, from April 6 to May 16. On May 18, she "Began Part XIV—the last!" (GE Journal). The exclamation point shows her elation that *Romola* is almost finished, but even this last part is written amid discouragement and illness:

> [May] 25. Heavy and good for nothing. Only at p. 18.
> June 1. I have not yet finished Romola, and am made stupid and depressed by a slight cough. I have written up to the moment when Tessa and the children are taken home by Romola.
> June 6. We had a little evening party . . . to celebrate the completion of Romola, which however is not absolutely completed, for I have still to alter the Epilogue. (GE Journal)

On June 7, she was "Ill with hemicrania, unable to do anything all day"; and on the 8th, "Still suffering from my cough and headache." Finally on June 9, she wrote "*Ebenezer!*" in delight that she had "Put the last stroke to Romola." This installment, including the epilogue, is only 65 manuscript and 25 printed pages, one printed page longer than either installment 10 or 11.

While Eliot was struggling with the composition of *Romola*, readers had to make two adjustments to their expectations from a work by "the author of *Adam Bede.*" Despite *Scenes of Clerical Life*, they did not expect a serial novel from George Eliot, and they did expect homely English settings. The London *Globe and Traveller* illustrates the first point amusingly in the lead sentence of its *Romola* review: "A more surprising thing than pine-apple for the million was the publication of 'Romola' in a shilling magazine. We read it there with mingled admiration and doubt of its being the right thing in the right place." By the date of this notice, September 21, 1863, the reviewer has read it again in volume form and judges that "no work of prose-fiction in English is better." The outcries against *Romola*, according to the review, came from its being presented initially to the wrong audience, who were readers with other expectations and who were naturally disappointed:

Its first appearance in a cheap and popular miscellany was a disadvantage, undoubtedly—so refined and highly-finished a masterpiece did not find its proper public immediately, and the wrong sort of readers cried out, "This is *hard* reading, dull reading." "It is not a bit like 'Adam Bede.'" "What do we care about mediaeval Florentine history? Is it not all written in the books of Sismondi, &c. Historical novels are a nuisance. Nobody but Walter Scott can make them endurable."

This was true of "the majority of the readers of the *Cornhill*." A minority read it "there, with more or less of discriminating appreciation, [and] have now the pleasure of hearing their opinion echoed" by those who refuse to read "a work of art in monthly sections. [These] protest against it; they will have the whole book, and nothing but the book" (1). This *Globe and Traveller* account accurately reflects the opening response of those newspapers and journals that gave brief notices to the early numbers. The *Spectator* initially disapproved but was converted midway. The *Guardian* and the *Illustrated Times* disliked it as a serial, but changed their views after the three volumes appeared. *John Bull* began more neutrally, but soon wished for another "English" novel from the author of *Adam Bede*, and finally declined to join the appreciative minority cited by the *Globe*. Other serial notices were mixed.

Behind the *Spectator*'s July 1862 notice of *Romola* looms reviewer R. H. Hutton's admiration for *Adam Bede*:

> The *Cornhill* begins with "Romola," advertised as George Eliot's, on which we are unable even to form an opinion; the writing is admirable, but we fear that the author in laying her scene in mediaeval Italy quits the soil on which she is strong, and will write too much as a painter might, wasting power on the effort to *drape* characters into whom on English ground she would have infused the breath of life.

Hutton's attention has been caught by Romola and her father, but thus far they are "lay figures, marvellously attired," and Leighton's drawings fail to realize them fully. The book recalls *Agnes of Sorrento*, "one of the most decided failures in literature" (July 5, 1862; 752).[20] In August, the *Spectator* is even more decided: "George Eliot has made a mistake," and the work is "a failure." While two installments are not enough to give a clear idea of either plot or characters, they are "sufficient to prove how completely the authoress has fettered herself." She has spent too much effort on historical context; as a result, the book "is dull, almost unreadable, and though there are touches here and there which make the reader savage at such waste of power, there are also descriptions and dialogues tedious to admiration." Hutton quotes Bardo's dialogue at length to demonstrate its unreality and notes that Thackeray's *Philip* "ends with this number somewhat hurriedly" (864). Next month a work by Trollope would replace *Philip*; for which George Smith, as well as this reviewer, must have been grateful.

The September *Spectator* did not discuss that month's installment. By October, Hutton is discovering *Romola*'s merits, though he repeats the words of his first two notices, especially about "wasting power," in wishing that the book were other than it is. It "decidedly improves. The characters are becoming human" as one gets beyond the historical "drapery." But Eliot's "great power is sadly wasted" (Oct. 4, 1862; 1117). Reviewing the December magazines, Hutton alludes to the waste of power in different words: "The *Cornhill* for this month has only three papers besides 'Romola,' which becomes more powerful with each number, and more annoying to those who detest *wanton throwing away of material*" (Nov. 29; emphasis added). In February, the month that George Smith noted the change in critical reception, Hutton begins to concede that the novel may have its own special qualities even though it fails to fulfill his expectations: "'Romola' improves as it advances; and we may end, in spite of feeling and judgment, in becoming interested in the wonderful portrait of Tito, the goodnatured, sweet-tempered, intellectual Greek, whose love of things pleasant makes him traitor to father, wife, and friends, and whose crave [*sic*] to be cushioned round with goodwill is based on cowardice and not love." This perceptive summary of Tito's character is elaborated in the next month's notice, in which Hutton acknowledges the error of his views. Other magazines for the month contain nothing so "pleasant" as the *Cornhill*'s serialization of *The Small House at Allington*, "and nothing which displays such intellectual power as 'Romola.' We shall be forced, after all, to retract our criticisms upon that extraordinary performance." In the next sentence, he refuses to relinquish his favorite phrase, but grudgingly admires: "It *is* a waste of power, but then the wealth is wasted by one the residue of whose abundance is greater than other novelists' riches." Tito is the cause for this reversal: "Such an intellectual study, to use an artists' [*sic*] phrase, as 'Tito Melema,' has not been placed before the world in this generation, and we know not which to wonder at most, the accuracy of the anatomical knowledge displayed, or the art with which that knowledge is infused—

there is no other fitting word—into the readers' [*sic*] mind." Even though the story is still as "unreal as ever," and too much occupied with historical matter, "the marvellous figure in the centre, the gentle, intellectual, soft-hearted villain, is redeeming all." The reviewer wonders, "where can George Eliot have seen the working of a mind exquisitely refined, and even broad, yet so rotten with cowardly selfishness, that even in hatred, 'that cold dislike, which is the anger of unimpassioned beings, does but harden within him?'" (Mar. 7; 1729).[21] After this change of heart, Hutton waits until *Romola*'s completion to publish a notice so closely touching Eliot's intention that she wrote to thank him for it.

The *Reader* was probably one of the papers Smith had in mind; it is the only one I have discovered that uses the word "masterpiece" by early February. A month before Hutton, it perceives the centrality of Tito's character and the overall excellence of the work: "The critics of 'Romola' must by this time have discovered that they have been cavilling at a masterpiece. Not only is the character of Tito Melema an entirely new one in the realm of fiction, but it is one wrought out—considering its difficulty—with a firm and subtle truth never yet equalled." The review acknowledges the initial strangeness of the setting, but argues that Eliot "has now thoroughly realized to herself her own picture." Tito is the center of a work beside which "Every other paper in the *Cornhill* must appear tame" (Feb. 7; 152). In March—when Hutton acknowledged his altered view—the *Reader* simply noted that "'Romola' continues to spin its subtle thread, bringing out this time with marvellous skill the widening of the breach between Tito and his once fond wife" (Mar. 7; 245).

The *Reader*'s final notice continues to place Tito in this central position and devotes two columns to defending the historical setting. It reiterates that "Tito is the most elaborately and subtly wrought-out character in the book." Regarding the objections many have made to the setting, "On the whole, we partly sympathize with the feeling that, in ordinary, British novelists should keep to British scenes and subjects." But there are two areas of exception: first, when a writer attempts a historical novel, and second, when the novel "is one of that higher order of ideal phantasy in which the author, having already some notion in his mind of a story of what may be called 'elemental' or 'universal' as distinct from 'circumstantial' life," chooses, like Shakespeare, to change the setting to a remote place, "or else . . . finds some actual moment in the past in which nature and history have anticipated him by furnishing a real combination of scenery, incident, and character, in the imaginary representation of which his end will be most emphatically served." Eliot's novel fits both categories. The proem establishes a setting both "natural and valid." And as a historical novel, it is rich and learned, comparable to Scott's achievements (July 11, 1863; 28).

The *Examiner* published just two notices of the novel. On December 6, 1862, a single sentence refers to the "undiminished vigour and truth of local colour [in] the Florentine romance of 'Romola.'" On December 26, 1863, it enthusiastically recommends the book as "the best novel and the Christmas novel of the year," calling it a "genuine prose epic." It will excite neither laughter nor tears, but then neither do Dante's or Milton's depictions of "a true spiritual life" (820). Despite the historical setting, the novel has "not a trace of antiquarianism." Rather, it shows "a fine mind grappling worthily with a great living thought, and in a form that restores to the prose fiction of our day some of the dignity it has of late been losing" (821). The Edinburgh *Evening Courant*'s one serial notice called it a "singularly powerful story" (July 7, 1863; 6), and its final review was brief and positive.

Several papers that were disappointed with the novel during its serialization found rereading it in volumes a different experience. The *Guardian* contained ambivalent serial notices but ended with an enthusiastic review of *Romola* in volumes. Two weeks before the first installment, the *Guardian*'s "Table-Talk" column anticipated its publication: "It is said . . . that [Eliot] will leave the pleasant English villages, and cosy parsonages, and quaint farm-houses and sluggish rivers which she has hitherto delighted to depict, and try her hand on an Italian scene" (June 18, 1862; 595). The descriptive details suggest that the reviewer also delights in these English scenes. The *Guardian*'s earliest serial notice is uncertain about the Italian setting "when the 'revival of learning,' as it was called, was rooting up all the old traditions in literature, art, and religion." *Romola* has "a strange, unreal, and somewhat tame effect, coming after a tale conversant entirely with the every-day realities of the nineteenth century" (Aug. 6; 763).[22] The next notice repeats the idea that *Romola* is "a tale of times far removed from modern comprehension or interest" (Dec. 31; 1247). As late as April, with four installments remaining, the reviewer is negative: "'Romola' still continues to present a somewhat faded picture (whether a true one or not who can tell?) of Florentine society in the days of the Medici and Savonarola" (Apr. 1; 315). It is surprising, then, that the *Guardian*'s final, lengthy review (nearly two columns long), published on September 16, 1863, is enthusiastic about everything except (predictably) Romola's lack of true religious feeling and trust in a higher being.

The *Illustrated Times* also withheld approval until volume publication. Despite—or perhaps because of—pride in having been among the first to recognize Eliot's superiority, starting with installment 1 of *Scenes of Clerical Life*, this reviewer anticipates that the setting "will be a disappointment to many who have followed this lady through her most marvellous descriptions of English scenery and English home life—pictures recognisable by most of us." This is not what readers expect of serial fiction: "To modern novels, and specially to modern novels published in the serial form, the description of existing life and character, of the railway-using, mammon-worshipping, nineteenth-century world has become almost an absolute necessity, and therefore the experiment to interest us in bygone days, made though it is by a masterhand, is not unfraught with danger." Having "hailed the new author as a bright, particular star" since the appearance of *Scenes*, this critic may "be saved from the accusation of warped judgment" in believing that the new story "will not achieve popularity." Despite "wonderful" writing, "the story is dull and flat; it takes no grip of the mind, it arouses no special interest, and . . . it is extremely difficult reading" (July 5, 1862; 159). The second installment is so disappointing that the reviewer resolves to say no more until it "is concluded, save in reiteration of my previously expressed opinion—that the period of action, the location, and style of the story have been unfortunately chosen" (Aug. 9; 239). By December, however, the reviewer is tempted into an echo of the *Spectator*: *Romola* "is generally allowed to be a striking example of extraordinary power applied to an utterly ungenial subject" (Dec. 13; 535). He is silent on the subject until June, when he praises *The Small House at Allington*, but calls the rest of the *Cornhill* "simple twaddle." But "Of course, one excepts 'Romola,' of which everyone says, 'What a pity it's so uninteresting, when it's *such* a picture of Italian life,' which, being interpreted, means that no one reads it" (398). With volume publication, the reviewer's change of heart suggests that the fault lies with both the initial publication format and the readers. The review begins by noting the surprise that greeted its appearance:

> One of the strangest things that ever startled magazine-readers was, surely, the appearance of a second Italian story of the times of Savonarola, directly after Mrs. Stowe had finished "Agnes of Sorrento," in the *Cornhill*. During its progress nearly everybody has found "Romola" dull—*dull* is the word

which has invariably been used about it; and it now remains to be seen what will be said by the large numbers of people who will sit down to read it through connectedly.

When they do so, they will "come to the conclusion that, if they have before found 'Romola' dull, it is because they have not done their own part in reading with an earnest imagination what has been written with such intensity and skill." It is a "solemnly magnificent book," and one that has affinities with present-day life, including "the records of Sir Cresswell Cresswell's court" (July 25, 1863; 58).[23] This is one of several instances in which readers found the novel a different book in volume format than in installments.

Some serial notices decrease rather than increase in enthusiasm, and present no final review reversing their negative opinion. *John Bull*, the *Critic*, and the *Nonconformist* each published at least one comment before the book appeared in volume form, and all expressed disappointment. *John Bull* had the most frequent notices, attempting at first to be open-minded even while expecting the usual setting in the English Midlands. The reviewer's expectations are evident from the outset: *Cornhill* readers "will naturally be attracted . . . by the new story which *the author of 'Adam Bede'* has commenced in this number" (emphasis added). In it are "scenes very different from that homely life in the midland counties, in which the writer obtained her earlier renown" (428). In part 2, the story "fascinates the reader more completely, and those who have commenced it will be looking forward diligently for the next number, which is, we suppose, the proper state of mind for the reader of serial tales to be in" (Aug. 5; 492). By September, opposition to the new terrain is less tentative: "we still think that she draws a better inspiration among the farmsteads of the Midland counties than amid all the pageantry and picturesqueness of old Italy in the days of the Borgias" (571). October's single sentence makes the point: "We . . . cannot help wishing that the writer was *at home*" (635).

For several months thereafter, *John Bull's* notice of the monthly magazines includes at most a brief mention of *Romola*. On July 4, 1863, a review of the penultimate installment still reflects disappointed expectations: "In the *Cornhill* the story of 'Romola' assumes a more tragic and 'sensation' [sic] aspect, but still fails to attract us with the spell of George Eliot's other works" (427). *John Bull's* final review believes that only the author's skill has kept *Romola* from being "ponderous" and still desires

to "welcome 'George Eliot' back to her own people and her own country." The xenophobia that underlies some of the response in this conservative paper (which Charlotte Brontë had thirty-four years earlier called
"high Tory, very violent" [Brown 27]) is particularly evident in the final
line, which follows a direct quotation from Romola's advice to Lillo in
the epilogue, that the "highest happiness" can only come with pain: "A
lesson which the fair South is not apt to teach" (Aug. 1, 1863; 491).

The *Critic* greeted the first installment of *Romola* with "regret" at the
setting, since *Cornhill* readers "have already had quite a sufficient dose of
quasi-Italian habits and customs from the prolific pen of Mrs. Beecher
Stowe, in her tedious 'Agnes of Sorrento.' Authors in general when they
get on the subject of Italy, seem to think they must indulge in highflown
prose; and even Miss Evans seems to think that the land of poetry must
be described in 'poeticals.'" Thus far, the reviewer prefers "the authoress's
pictures of home life to anything we have as yet in the *Cornhill*" (July 15,
1862; 20). In the penultimate review, "*The Cornhill Magazine* still makes
us regret in 'Romola' that the author has wandered out of the tracks in
which she shines so brightly" (July 1, 1863; 399).[24]

The *Nonconformist*, having "necessarily omitted" reviews for several
preceding months, first notices *Romola* on March 4, 1863. It has "but
little true vitality, and by very few, we fancy, can it be enjoyable in the
highest degree" (177). The April number "is full of truth and human
feeling" (259), but by July the novel is compared unfavorably with *The
Small House at Allington*: "We continue to enjoy greatly the truthful real-
life story of Mr. Trollope: but 'Romola' chiefly impresses us with the
value of that recent life of Savonarola from which it transplants so much"
(554).

This early negative response had a discouraging effect on the author,
especially during her struggle with illness and despair in the early months
of 1863. Even though Eliot and Lewes promoted the idea that she did not
hear what was said about her work, and though he at times did protect
her from unfavorable comments, her supposed unawareness of reviews is
a myth. In fact, she took a lively interest in readers' responses throughout
her career, as her letters and journals attest. Her letter to R. H. Hutton on
his intelligent review in the *Spectator* is unusual only in that she took the
trouble to respond. Both Eliot's and Lewes's journals show them assid-
uous in looking for notices of her latest work, despite the latter's disclaimer that he alone seeks out reviews of her work and shields her from
them (Letter to Sara Hennell, Sept. 12, 1862; 4: 58–59).

A few reviews of the volume publication reflect the ethnocentric view that the historical Italian setting is too distant to interest English women and men. The *Weekly Dispatch*'s theory of art holds that "A novel, like other forms of art, must appeal to the knowledge and the sympathies of those to whom it is addressed; otherwise executive skill is used in vain, and effort results, so far as popularity is concerned, but in failure." This reviewer's theory seems to be founded on commercial success and the idea that fiction should reproduce the safe, comfortable, and familiar rather than challenge readers' expectations. The reviewer elaborates the second point: *Romola* "fall[s] flat upon the ear of the English public"; "to the general reader the tangled web of Italian fifteenth century policy is utter weariness and vexation of spirit"; "we hope that in future the author will illustrate the life around her, and leave foreign themes to those whom they more immediately concern." Foreigners, presumably. Just before the last quotation, the reviewer acknowledges that "Regarded as a work of art the tale has rare merit" (July 26, 1863; 6). He never relates this remark to his opening statement on fiction's role.

On August 3, 1863, the *Daily News* argues that in setting her novel in fifteenth-century Florence, Eliot "has placed her genius at some disadvantage with an English public." Despite the conscientiously drawn historical background, she fails to revive a dead era, "separated in its interests, its hopes, and fears by the whole distance of a different country, a different language, a different religion, and a new epoch in the history of our race." An analogy with the visual arts emphasizes that the duty of art is not to encompass the strange and unfamiliar: "It is as if Sir Edwin Landseer should employ his wonderful talent not upon the horses and dogs, and deer with which we are familiar, which blend themselves with the memories of our life and are objects of our fondness and admiration, but upon the denizens of a preadamite world" (2). Such matters interest historians and had better be left to them, the writer concludes.

These were minority views regarding the volume edition, which received a better critical reception than one is sometimes led to believe. Readers could now contemplate Eliot's purpose in its entirety. David Carroll, in his introduction to *George Eliot, The Critical Heritage*, recalls Lewes's later comment that *Romola* was received with "'a universal howl of discontent.'" *Romola* was, Carroll adds, her first novel to divide "her reading-public into those who welcomed the latest unfolding of her genius and those who persisted until the very end in their nostalgia for the world of the early novels." The critical confusion occurred because "critics were caught awkwardly between" these two publics. "They belonged for the most part to the first audience, but they were writing for the second, and this is reflected in their reviews" (19). Carroll's comments are based on reviews from the more prestigious literary journals and not the more ordinary daily or specialized newspapers included here. What role the historical setting played in the reception of the serial installments, however, is less clear than Carroll's remarks indicate. Despite expectations of another English book and readers' natural disappointment when *Romola* proved to be otherwise, there are indications that the historical setting was only an initial obstacle and that more serious problems were posed by plot, character development, and mode of publication—the fact that serialization was simply wrong for *Romola*.

Even among the favorable notices, reviewers of *Romola*—much more than for either *Middlemarch* or *Daniel Deronda*—agreed that the work did not bear the serial format well. One of the most positive reviews, in the *Morning Post* on August 25, begins with a discussion of *Romola*'s publication circumstances (including the erroneous assumption that this was Eliot's first attempt at serialization):

> The number of those books which, having been published in a serial form, come before the public on their completion as a whole, and are admirable in both shapes, is very small. The ordeal is a trying one for any author; and when one has enumerated "The Newcomes" and "Vanity Fair," by Mr. Thackeray; and "Barnaby Rudge," and "A Tale of Two Cities," by Mr. Dickens, the catalogue of works successful under both conditions is well-nigh exhausted. The author of "Adam Bede" has now for the first time made this perilous experiment, and with success as marked as that of her above-named predecessors, and distinguished from theirs by one great difference. "Romola" is far more delightful when read in its complete form.

The historical setting is managed "with the same ease and dignity which marked her treatment of her former themes," and in the story's "completed form . . . the reader recognises [its] full beauty" (3).

Among the reviewers who found the format problematic, several others shared the *Post*'s enthusiasm. The *Globe*'s comment on the surprise of serialization being greater than "pine-apple for the million" has been quoted above. Its long and favorable review acknowledges that the reader may at first be overwhelmed by the setting, but George Eliot makes "her reader, if not *at home* in mediaeval Florence, yet able to understand and to take a deep interest in all that she shows him there" (Sept. 21, 1863; 1). The *Englishman* mentions *Romola*'s early negative reception and predicts its more successful future.

> The general impression at one period was against the book, but this has gradually been changing, and we should not be surprised to see Romola take its place side by side with the first successful works of George Elliot [*sic*]. The book must be read as a whole before a fair estimate of its merits can be formed, and we have no doubt it will receive every justice at the hands of the press and the public. (Aug. 15, 1863; 1)

The *Nonconformist*, too, found that reading it as a whole gave "new impressions of its power, and beauty, and truth," and the historical background is well studied, even though the reviewer "Still . . . could almost wish she had remained on the special English ground and amidst the peculiar classes which she so livingly [*sic*] pictured in 'Adam Bede,' and 'Silas Marner'" (Aug. 12, 1863; 654). The tentatively proferred "Still . . . could almost wish" indicates the reviewer's doubts about his initial judgments; he is still evaluating his position. The *Observer* argued that "it is not a novel suited by any means to a monthly periodical," but it expected that "From the publicity which *Romola* has already acquired it is probable that many will . . . read it now for the first time, and those who have perused it in parts will be glad to have the book for study in a complete form" (July 19, 1863; 7). One thing is certain: *Romola* in volumes created a different impression from *Romola* serialized.

R. H. Hutton did not regard the historical background as the major feature inhibiting successful serialization. Rather, Eliot's work generally is of a sort to defy success in this format. Denying that he wishes to "vindicate" his mistaken initial judgment, Hutton nonetheless suggests that the fragmentary nature of the publication is "perhaps . . . one reason for the inadequacy of the first impression. George Eliot's drawings all require a certain space, like Raffael's Cartoons, and are not of that kind which produce their effect by the reiteration of scenes each complete in itself. You have to unroll a large surface of the picture before even the smallest *unit* of its effect is attained." Though this is true of her "English tales," it is even "more true of this, probably the author's greatest work." Although it takes some time to get to know the characters in *Adam Bede*, "in the meantime, the vivid detail, the dry humour, the English pictures with which we are all so familiar, fascinate and satisfy us." In "the light

Florentine buzz" of *Romola*, Eliot has not this advantage; unlike Walter Scott, whose "art for revivifying the past" she shares, she does not create a momentum that entangles and involves her readers. Here Hutton pinpoints the essence of the good serial story and the unsuitability of Eliot's novels for short installments. "She does not carry her readers *away*, as it is called; it is generally easy to stop reading her; she satisfies you for the moment, and does not make you look forward to the end" (July 18, 1863; 2265).

Hutton's charge is more complex than Blackwood's complaint that Eliot reveals the outcome in the early installments of *Scenes*. In *Romola*, Eliot does not state explicitly the fate of her characters, as she does in "Mr Gilfil's Love-Story" and "Janet's Repentance," thereby narrowing the field for readers' speculation about possible outcomes. True, readers know Savonarola's history from other sources, but that knowledge pertains only to *his* fate; it gives no indication of the outcome for Romola or Tito. Hardly knowing where to begin imagining their futures, readers are, as Hutton says, content with the richness of what is immediately before them. Except when the overzealous Piagnone boys try to extort her necklace, we anticipate and fear little for the simple Tessa. For Romola, there are no titillating expectations about "another man" once the unhappiness of her marriage is apparent, such as were conventional in the sensation fiction of the 1860s (and such as readers in 1876 anticipated regarding *Daniel Deronda*'s Gwendolen). Rather, there is only the slow unfolding of Romola's disillusionment. As they encounter each new instance of Tito's treachery, readers may wonder, "What will she, what can she do?" Romola herself hardly knows, and it is easier to await events patiently with her, than to define expectations.

The historical setting plays a part in this indefiniteness. When Romola sets forth "to go to the most learned woman in the world, Cassandra Fedele, at Venice, and ask her how an instructed woman could support herself in a lonely life there" (327), most Victorian readers would not have known what Eliot (in 1854) had called those "awful women of Italy, who held professional chairs, and were great in civil and canon law" (*Essays* 54). Eliot admits to not knowing much of them herself. As Deirdre David points out, Fedele was one of a significant minority of women humanists, who "came from prominent families located in court cities and, of course, were educated by men (often their fathers) in the languages, literature, history, poetry, and moral philosophy of Greece and Rome" (190). Not only would readers have had difficulty envisioning

Romola in a scholarly, independent life as a Florentine woman, but to place her in such a role would have removed her from Florence and distracted attention from Tito at a time of increasing enthusiasm for his characterization.

Victorian readers' models were more likely to be devout peasant girls like Agnes of Sorrento than Renaissance women humanists.[25] Stowe's *Agnes of Sorrento*, which the *Cornhill's* readers would recently have read, includes no learned pagans or churchwomen. Its women are pious, unlettered nuns and peasants, and one noblewoman; its heroine, Agnes, resembles Tessa, not Romola. The novel sprang from Stowe's happy sojourn in Italy in 1859–60 rather than from the intimate knowledge of social conditions that informed her powerful statements on nineteenth-century American life. It is neither realistic in the traditions of Eliot or Dickens nor historical in the tradition of Scott, to whose work reviewers compared *Romola*. Stowe describes her story as "a child of love in its infancy, and its flowery Italian cradle rocked it with an indulgent welcome." It is "a mere dreamland . . . [and] merely reproduces to the reader the visionary region that appeared to the writer. . . . All dates shall give way to the fortunes of our story, and our lovers shall have the benefit of fairyland; and whoso wants history will not find it here, except to our making, and as it suits our purpose" (viii-ix). Inanimate characters and imprecise historical setting notwithstanding, *Agnes of Sorrento* has the strong love interest important to a Victorian serial audience. Agnes falls in love with a mysterious stranger of noble lineage, who leads a band of outlaws because he has been dispossessed by corrupt and powerful Church rulers who linger in the background like villains in a melodrama. During a pilgrimage to Rome to save her lover's soul, Agnes attracts the attention of the papal retinue and is only saved from infamy by her lover's vigilance and his band of soldiers. *Agnes of Sorrento* is indeed a "dreamland."

Romola, too, has its love affairs. Tito, after all, courts two women, Romola and Tessa. But neither these affairs nor the possibility that Romola will discover his left-handed marriage dominates reader interest, which focuses instead on Tito's developing personality.[26] The love passages between Romola and Tito are incidental to the larger moral and psychological scheme. For a love story, as the *Morning Post* asserts, there is "a singular absence of passion" (Aug. 25, 1863; 3). Tito's "passion" is his constant fear of Baldassarre's return and vengeance, while Romola's self-control is stronger than any passion. Eliot never portrays her with the passionate vulnerability of Lydgate, for example, although at several points *Romola* anticipates the Lydgate-Rosamond relationship. Like Lydgate, Romola blinds herself rather than face a marriage without love; she blames herself for demanding monetary self-sacrifice. Romola "strangle[s] . . . every rising impulse of suspicion, pride, and resentment; she felt equal to any self-infliction that would save her from ceasing to love" (251).[27]

But Romola has none of the "spots of commonness" that humanize and particularize Lydgate. She is too ethereal, too dignified, too self-controlled for passionate love.[28] Even her love for her father and mixed emotions about her brother are kept in check. It is ironically appropriate that Tito and Romola acknowledge their love as they search out a book for Bardo. No strong passion bursts forth in this recognition scene. Instead, the narrator says, their "first blissful experience of mutual consciousness [is] all the more exquisite for being unperturbed by immediate sensation" (123). Romola idealizes Tito as a new brother to her and a new son to her blind father. In their first meeting after Dino's death, Romola tells him that she had read about love in "the poets" but never expected it for herself. But "'then *you* came, Tito, and *were so much to my father*, and I began to believe that life could be happy for me too'" (183; second emphasis added). Tito's attention to her father is the seed of Romola's affection for him. Its destruction begins when she must find excuses for Tito's neglect of Bardo several months after their marriage and is complete when he sells Bardo's library to the French.

Tito's ruling passion is not sensual love. His relationship with Tessa results not from the lusts of a seducer but from inadvertence and his inability to face the disappointment even of a contadina. R. H. Hutton suggests that the scene in which Tito locks the crucifix in the Bacchus and Ariadne triptych "fondly calling her 'Regina mia,' . . . somehow conveys that he less *loves* the woman than passionately admires her" (*Spectator*, July 18, 1863; 2266). As early as installment 2, the narrator describes him as "in his fresh youth—not passionate, but impressible: it was as inevitable that he should feel lovingly towards Romola as that the white irises should be reflected in the clear sun-lit stream." These images—white irises, clear sunlit stream—prepare for the idealization of the next line: Tito "had an intimate sense that Romola was something very much above him" (95). Romola is the white iris, also called the Florentine iris, an appropriate flower here. The clear, reflective stream images both Romola and her love for Tito, which mirrors her own ideal, aspiring nature rather than his innate qualities. Ominously, the white flowers and the clear, reflective stream also recall the mythic Narcissus, an appropriate image for Tito—whose first love is for himself. In installment 4, as Tito, fearing that Dino's deathbed message has estranged them forever, waits for Romola under the loggia, the sunlight image recurs: he "awaited her, with a sickening sense of the sunlight that slanted before him and mingled itself with the ruin of his hopes. He had never for a moment relied on Romola's passion for him as likely to be too strong for the repulsion created by the discovery of his secret" (179). His death, alongside the fast-flowing river, ironically completes the images of sun and water surrounding this new Narcissus.

Despite his frequent association with Dionysus, Tito's ruling passion is not Bacchic joy but Pentheus-like fear. He at first experiences this fear intermittently and mildly, but it becomes a "passionate fear that possesse[s] him" after he finds himself in the clutch of Baldassarre on the steps of the Duomo (225). Fear, rather than love, provides the suspense; when Baldassarre appears, his fear loses its intermittent quality and becomes a consuming dread. The subtle, gradual building of suspense around the hero's equivocations with his duty and his conscience went beyond the expectations of Victorian readers, who looked for a more traditional story of love thwarted, woman deceived. It is not merely the external setting that is strange, but the landscape of the conscience, a landscape with which installment presentation is especially incompatible.

The novelistic tradition, especially the serial sensation novel of the sixties, might have provided a love triangle in which a jealous Romola discovers Tito's bigamy and flees from him. For Eliot, however, his infidelity is only another facet of his treachery. It has little connection with sexual jealousy. The *Morning Post* described Romola as "goddess-like," a "majestic ideal of womanhood." When her trust vanishes, her love vanishes, "and in her sublime scheme of duty and resignation pique and jealousy can find no place." Romola is a rare character in literature; her "tranquil acceptation of the fact of her husband's infidelity, and her instant decision to shield the girl whom he has deceived, and the children whom he may any day forsake . . . are sketches which no other hand could have so perfected" (Aug. 25, 1863; 3). This "tranquil" response stems from the absence of passion noted by the *Post* reviewer.

The situation is obviously more complex than the *Morning Post* review suggests, but the *Post*'s assessment indicates a likely response from Victorian readers: surprise at Romola's reaction and a sense that it marks her as an unusual woman. Baldassarre himself reads the situation like a Victorian audience. He hopes that his news of Tito's infidelity will cause Romola to believe his own story of Tito's treachery. "The tall wife was the noble and rightful wife; she had the blood in her that would be readily kindled to resentment. . . . She could believe him: she would be *inclined* to believe him, if he proved to her that her husband was unfaithful. Women cared about that: they would take Vengeance for that" (437). But, after the "first shock . . . of anger" in which "The woman's sense of indignity was inevitably foremost" (455), Romola's response is not jealousy but wonderment whether "that other wife" may be Tito's legal wife (456). By the time she meets her, Romola hopes Tessa will prove to have been legally married to Tito before her own nuptials: "A strange exultation for a proud and high-born woman to have been brought to! But it seemed to Romola as if that were the only issue that would make duty anything else for her than an unsolvable problem" (471). After Tessa describes her "marriage," Romola feels "the chill of disappointment that her difficulties were not to be solved by external law" (472)—a reaction that reinforced readers' awareness that this was no ordinary novel about an ordinary woman.

The *Globe and Traveller*'s description of Romola's love for Tito as "trusting, unselfish, and thorough—no love was ever told so well in so few words" uses adjectives that apply as well to her father, godfather, and brother as to her lover. When she is betrayed by the men she trusted, Tito and Savonarola, "She is compelled to hate evil men more strongly than she can love good ones" (Sept. 21, 1863; 1). When treachery or death removes those she loved and trusted, Romola accepts that she must trust in herself. R. H. Hutton argues that within her character there is a "*soupçon* of hardness" (July 18, 1863; 2266).

In the absence of passion, jealousy, and other perils and rewards of love that delighted Victorian readers in sensation fiction, the novel focuses on Tito's moral decline. Even Romola, despite her titular primacy, becomes secondary. More subtly and extensively than Eliot's other works, *Romola* delineates a character who begins in moral neutrality and gradually becomes a moral pariah. Tito is *the* fascinating study in the novel. Until he began to perceive Tito's development, R. H. Hutton could see little merit in the work, and other reviewers were of a similar mind. As a Victorian villain, Tito is unusual. He commits no overtly violent deeds; he is gentle and sweet-tempered. He is not a dissolute seeker of gross pleasures. He wishes no ill luck to others—except when his own comfort is at stake, and then he can wish death on Fra Luca or Baldassarre with nonchalance. Like other Eliot villains, he is no moustache-twirling stereotype. But he has the essence of villainy as Eliot delineates it throughout her fiction. He cares only about himself and rejects that wide fellowship with other human beings that her best characters achieve through suffering. The *Morning Post*'s analysis of Tito calls attention to this difference between Eliot's work and other current fiction. Eliot "has never set forth the ordinary villain of the modern novel; in her delineations of life, men are rather selfish and weak than deliberately and heroically wicked. She carefully eschews the Rochester type, though her heroes are as bad men as Miss Brontë's." Their villainy comes from another source. "They are easygoing sinners, whose moral sight is hopelessly oblique, and whose systematic pursuit of ease and pleasure is attended with consequences as fatal as though they were produced by the darkest and most guilty motives."

The *Post* sees Eliot's presentations of evil as gender-specific. Eliot "has a profound appreciation of the moral weakness of men, and their normal deficiency in the power of self-sacrifice. This reading of the proclivities of male human nature lends to all her sketches of character a keen analytic power, and separates them utterly from the productions of the sensation writers." Despite being from the start "in the author's confidence about the real nature of the man," the reader "has much ado to keep from liking him very much indeed." While fully cognizant of the man's true nature, readers understand his attraction: "In every relation of life Tito is worse than worthless, but in all, his sweet temper, which is unwillingness to incur a disagreeable sensation by being angry, and his gentleness, which is a mere accident of temperament, make him irresistible, when taken into consideration with his beauty, his grace, his popular manners, and his easy-going ways" (Aug. 25, 1863; 3).

Tito fascinates the reader as he fascinates his Florentine companions. His lack of opinion and allegiance, which guarantees his constant good nature even in the face of opposition, is a virtue his companions appreciate. As Giannozzo Pucci tells him, "Niccolò Macchiavelli might have done for us if he had been on our side, but hardly so well. He is too much bitten with notions, and has not your powers of fascination" (351). Tito has no notions to interfere with his plans for *self*-betterment. His companions know his game, and so do readers, who nonetheless continue to hope that he will change, despite the narrator's warning that "Our lives make a moral tradition for our individual selves" (353). But Eliot knows the nature of moral decisions too well to contrive a happy solution such as Stowe does in her Italian novel.

Tito's attraction comes despite his secretiveness. Sometimes he seems unaware of his own moral maneuvering: "Tito had an innate love of reticence . . . [and] would now and then conceal something which had as little the nature of a secret as the fact that he had seen a flight of crows" (94). At times his secrecy is strategic. He can try to conciliate his father in the hut behind Tessa's house because "there would be *no witness by*" should he fail. He repents in order to "make all things pleasant again, and keep all past unpleasant things secret" (310). Tito's charm is such that, even at this point, readers hope Baldassarre will relent and Tito be unscathed by any public scandal; he almost convinces us, as he convinces himself, that he deserves little blame. The *Morning Post* was one of the first to observe his complex rationalizing: "His dilemmas of feeling are charming, and his soothing of his own intrusive scruples and attempts to mitigate results where he has actively produced causes, are triumphs of inverted reasoning" (3). His secretiveness permits this inverted reasoning. If his actions were public, he could not reason away his culpability. Consequently, whenever discovery seems imminent, he contemplates flight. Hutton's *Spectator* review distinguishes Tito as the most successful character in the romance novel tradition: "There is not a more wonderful piece of painting in English romance than this figure of Tito" (2266). Such a "character essentially treacherous only because he is full of soft *fluid* selfishness is one of the most difficult to paint" (2266).

The fact that Tito is *not* a stereotypical melodramatic character is partly what made *Romola*'s serial reception problematic. For the serial reader in the era of sensation novels, it lacks the spectacular outward incident that ought to accompany and manifest the villainy of the malefactor. Tito Melema is not an open villain like Count Fosco in *The Woman in White*, whose machinations threaten the life and liberty of Laura and Marian and who ends as a huge corpse in the Paris Morgue, drawing queues of curious spectators. Nor is he a simple hypocrite like Godfrey Ablewhite, whose unmasking is played not only to an audience of appreciative readers but, with great dramatic effect, to the audience gathered around the bed at the "Wheel of Fortune" (*Moonstone*, Fifth Narrative). Tito's unmasking comes when "Florence was busy with greater affairs," and the public display of the bodies is accompanied by no public disclosure such as that in Collins's sensational close. As Bernardo Rucellai says, "there is no knowing the truth now" (555–56).

The evil that Tito causes is subtle and hardly appears wrong, as his elaborate rationalizations prove to his own satisfaction. What does Tito do after all? He refuses to search for a foster father who gave him everything. But then how, at first, could he know that that foster father, elderly and suffering privations, remained alive? He "marries" an innocent peasant girl in a specious ceremony and eventually fathers two children by her. But he does it on impulse with no original intention to seduce or deceive. He wants to keep Tessa's goodwill should he lose all others'. Anyway, she should have known it was a sham. And he cares well for her afterward, so that she is perfectly contented and much happier than she had been with her abusive stepfather. He sells the precious library that his late father-in-law had wanted to be kept intact. But Bardo is a rather selfish old man whose own peers found him "tiresome" (193). Even Bernardo del Nero doesn't see the necessity of keeping the library intact although he sympathizes and supports his old friend's wish. After Bardo's death the library is, Romola knows, Tito's property because of his rights as her husband. By such reasoning, Tito convinces himself— and appealed to his Victorian readers to believe—that all his actions were perfectly reasonable.

The study of the human conscience reasoning its way to evil is not the stuff of which good serials are made. Tito slowly "experienc[es] that inexorable law of human souls, that we prepare ourselves for sudden deeds by the reiterated choice of good or evil" (224), but serial readers look for the "sudden deeds," not the process leading to them. The situation from which this narrative comment arises is a good example of the novel's subordination of outward event to interior effect. On the surface, the escape of prisoners and the sudden seizing of Tito by the man he most fears to meet are materials that a sensation novelist might have presented with great dramatic force. Eliot declines. Instead, the prisoners' escape is briefly recounted; it has no notable consequences for the soldiers or the public. Even the encounter is outwardly calm. Baldassarre clutches Tito's arm to avert a fall, but backs off at Tito's impetuous words and retreats quietly into the church. Among the crowd on the steps, Tito alone sees and comprehends the "magical poison [that] darted from Baldassarre's eyes" (222). Then Eliot's narrator, briefly disposing of the characters—Piero goes into the church, and Tito to the Segretario's—turns to Tito's thoughts: his half-wish that he had been ready with "a timely, well-devised falsehood [that] might have saved him from any fatal consequences," his chagrin at the momentary loss of self-command (224). The incident itself is secondary to the contortions of Tito's moral reasoning.

Internal psychological development could not, however, dominate to the exclusion of external events, which were usually what brought serial novel readers back to future parts. Ideally, each installment contains at least one new event that engenders danger, excitement, or uncertainty on which readers can build expectations for the parts to come. Each new part needs a bridge to connect readers to the previous month's conclusion, but the bridge cannot be obtrusive when reproduced in the volume publication, where readers are not likely to make the same pauses as the installment publication initiated.[29] And if there are multiple plot lines, or at least important characters moving in different directions, each plot line should be given some attention during the part. If multiple plot lines are introduced early, when one plot flags momentarily, interest remains strong in another. Gradually readers see the parts coming together.

Writing just two installments ahead of publication, Eliot managed to attend to the structure of both part and whole remarkably well. In installment 1, she weaves several narrative threads together so that all the main characters except Savonarola are introduced, and the story is well under way. Suspense builds on four points: the mystery of Tito's background, the exact nature of Bardo's son's treachery, the fate of Bardo's library, and the dowerless Romola's marriageability. Beginning with Tito, the installment highlights the mystery of his appearance; Bratti and then Nello inquisitively probe the shipwrecked stranger to determine how, with his jewels and princely airs, he came to sleep on the pavement in travel-stained clothes. Readers glimpse something amiss when Bratti chances to remark that "Anybody might say the saints had sent *you* a dead body; but if you took the jewels, I hope you buried him" (11). The narrator remarks a "painful thrill . . . dart[ing] through [Tito's] frame" (11), to which Bratti is oblivious. In chapter 3, this touch of mystery recurs when Nello alludes to the Christian Greek who "is of so easy a conscience that he would make a stepping-stone of his father's corpse." The narrator adds, "The flush on the stranger's face indicated what *seemed* so natural a movement of resentment, that the good-natured Nello hastened to atone for his want of reticence" (37; emphasis added). In both instances, as noted by the *Morning Post*, readers share with the narrator a secret the Florentines miss.

Likewise, Dino's desertion is discussed elliptically, as befits a subject that Romola and her father know well. Readers would have responded variously, depending on their religious affiliations, to Bardo's strictures on the Church that deprived him of his son; but many no doubt shared his indignation, endorsing Carlyle's and the novel's viewpoint on doing the duty nearest them.[30] And, just a few years after the Oxford movement, partisan sentiment regarding religion would have led some Victorian readers to a nodding agreement with Bardo's objections to the Roman Catholic church's "fanatical dreams."[31] Similarly, Anthony Trollope could refer without irony to Arabin as "a High Churchman at all points— so high, indeed, that at one period of his career he had all but toppled over into the cesspool of Rome" (*Barchester Towers*, Chapter 14; 126– 27).

Two other threads are closely intertwined. The preservation of Bardo's library is not a burning issue for readers until it assumes importance later in Romola and Tito's disintegrating relationship. The question of Romola's fate is of more immediate concern. Dowerless, scholarly, and detached from woman's "petty desires" (Bardo's phrase in chapter 5; 54), Romola is nonetheless both beautiful and wellborn—a likely candidate for the love interest that Victorian readers expected. The youthful Tito may be the scholar-suitor who will require no dowry but her learning. Readers at the close of part 1 could anticipate a love interest as Romola and her father await his introduction. However, the potential excitement of this love interest is unfulfilled, not only because of the ethereal nature of Tito and Romola's love, but because the course of "true love" runs too smoothly. From the start of installment 2, Bardo is prepared to think of, even hope for, Tito as a suitor. Only Bernardo del Nero's protest momentarily and ineffectually arrests that smooth course.

Part 2 bridges the month's break by immediately re-creating the scene and reintroducing the characters through a single sentence: "When Maso opened the door again, and ushered in the two visitors, Nello, first making a deep reverence to Romola, gently pushed Tito before him, and advanced with him towards her father" (59). The sentence does nothing more than provide stage directions: its presence shows Eliot was aware of the need for bridges between parts. Tito favorably impresses both Romola and Bardo, and by the chapter's end, Bernardo del Nero's warnings produce an effect contrary to his intention. Bardo begins to think of Tito as a match for his daughter. The next chapter, which adds local color but little suspense, is part of the "somewhat unfortunate amplification of Florentine gossip" that Hutton observed in the first volume. That this chapter sets a context for Tito's future actions is irrelevant to its impact on the serial structure, which demands steady forward movement. Like Thackeray's digression to the schoolboy past of Dobbin and George Osborne at the start of *Vanity Fair*'s second installment, the chapter's placement early in the installment minimizes the damage. However, its presence explains the critical reaction that the novel was "*hard* reading" (*Globe and Traveller*, Sept. 21, 1863; 1) and spent too much time on draping the characters in their historical setting (*Spectator*, July 5, 1862; 752). The installment's third chapter renews suspense with the appearance of an unknown monk and the reappearance of Tessa in the crowd on the feast of San Giovanni. Given Tessa's resemblance to Hetty Sorrel in naive and trusting simplicity, Nello's innuendo reminds readers that these women might share the same fate.[32] The last two chapters are arranged so that readers first see Tito rationalizing his choice not to seek his father but to invest his 500 florins, and then reposing with Tessa "Under the Plane-Tree." Taking the metaphorically easy path of investing the money is juxtaposed with his inability to take the uphill walk to Romola and Bardo. His moral and physical lassitude is upset by the shock Fra Luca gives him. Like the Woman in White's blood-stopping touch on the arm of Walter Hartright, "a very thin cold hand [is] laid on his [Tito's]." The "sensation," like Walter's, is both physical and psychological: he is "doubly jarred by the cold touch and the mystery. [Tito] was not apprehensive or timid through his imagination, but through his sensations and perceptions he could easily be made to shrink and turn pale like a maiden" (113). Unlike Collins's novel, however, there is no immediate threat to the safety of speaker or addressee. The problem is psychological: not "What will the hero *do* to shield a defenseless woman from pursuers hard upon her track?" but "How will Tito *react* now that he not only has direct proof that his father is alive but has received an appeal to rescue him, with a witness to that appeal?"

In good serial fashion, Eliot withholds the answer to this question until the next installment, ending the part with a dramatic confrontation between Fra Luca, who assumes that Tito will "go and release [Baldassarre]," and the man whose heart leapt with gladness when he thought momentarily that Baldassarre was dead. The final line, "I am at San Marco; my name is Fra Luca" (114), leaves readers waiting a month to discover whether Tito will rescind his decision to seek his own pleasure or find a way out for his conscience and public appearance.[33] The contrast between Tito's Lethean sleep in Tessa's lap and Fra Luca's death-like touch heightens the drama. Other details stress the moral conflict, self-

sacrifice versus self-indulgence, especially Fra Luca's face "worn by sickness," and the face described in the note, "*a dark, beautiful face, [with]
long dark curls, the brightest smile*" (113).

Echoing the structure of part 2, the third installment also resumes
precisely where the preceding part closed. The opening phrase, "When
Fra Luca had ceased to speak," bridges the two parts. The chapter stresses
Tito's doubleness: his "talent for concealment was being fast developed
into something less neutral" (115). While he "throw[s] extra animation
into the evening" with Romola and Bardo, his mind is forming plans that
are completed by the time he "issued from the grim door in the starlight"
(115–17). To deny Baldassarre's claim, as he intends, is to make a more
deliberate and conscious decision than he has yet done. When he inquires
for Fra Luca the next day, it is not to find out more about his father, but
only to know whether he will need to flee Florence to avoid his duty or
whether fortune will favor him with continued concealment.

This is the critical suspense of part 3 for readers as well as for Tito,
and the installment is structured to make the most of it. Tito's fear abates
when he learns of Fra Luca's illness and departure to Fiesole, and his
hope of winning Romola along with fame and fortune revives. But the
shadow of Fra Luca remains. Ironically, ominously, on the day that Tito
and Romola declare their love, the voluble Monna Brigida lets slip that
Bardo's son is at San Marco and Tito realizes suddenly why the friar's
face had seemed familiar. His contentment in Romola's trustful love and
Bardo's easy consent is tainted anew by fear of disgrace: "There was a
spring of bitterness mingling with that fountain of sweets. Would the
death of Fra Luca arrest it? He hoped it would" (131). Tito's moral
disintegration is signaled by this move from crimes of omission to actively willing harm to another to assure his own safety.

Nemesis is arrested for only two months. Then Tito's cheerful confidence is transformed to fear by two events: the news that Fra Luca has
returned and his meeting with Romola on her way to San Marco to hear
her dying brother's message. These events precipitate Tito to two further
reckless steps in the installment's final chapter: he decides to sell his ring,
and he declines to undeceive Tessa, "his only haven from contempt"
(153), about the mock marriage. From the installment's opening, where
Tito contemplates the "problem" of Fra Luca's message, to its close,
where he entangles himself in new complications, he is shortsighted—
even to his own self-interest. The "hopelessly oblique" moral sight noted
by the *Morning Post* prevents him from seeing consequences for himself

or for others. Unable to confront the consequences of earlier deeds that force him into new deceits, he seeks approval through actions that, paradoxically, put that approval at risk even while he thinks to secure it. In part 4, both the incident with Tessa and the sale of the ring will cause him momentary inconveniences. Tessa accosts him on the Via de' Bardi the day of his betrothal, and he must commission the tabernacle in order to explain to Romola why he sold the ring. More serious consequences become apparent in later installments.[34]

Installment 4 is distinct from 2 and 3 in its relationship with the close of the preceding monthly part. Instead of resuming with Tito at a "lawless" moment of desperation, part 4 opens at San Marco and recalls earlier events through three devices: the title, "The Dying Message"; the opening clause, "When Romola arrived at the entrance of San Marco" (155); and Leighton's drawing opposite the first page. The illustration repeats the chapter's title and pictures Romola grasping a crucifix and kneeling at the bed of a dead monk, while a cowled figure hovers in the background. Readers encounter the scene with a double-consciousness, fearing that Dino's mystical visions will repel his sister and deflect any useful revelation, and yet hoping that the dying man will ask the mundane, human questions that will uncover the specific danger in which Romola stands. But Dino is as blind to human needs as Tito, who is saved once again. The likely consequences for Romola are emphasized by the installment's circular structure: opening with Romola receiving the crucifix, it ends with Tito concealing it within the Bacchus and Ariadne triptych. Readers are left wondering whether the self-centered Tito will fail her, as her brother has.

Between this beginning and end, Tito lingers aimlessly in Nello's barbershop, unaware of his respite and unable either to flee or to face his doom. Hearing that Fra Luca has made a revelation to his sister, he almost gives himself away by claiming his coin and fleeing the city. Nearly half of the installment's second chapter is devoted to the "Florentine Joke" played on the Paduan doctor, an incident that at first seems like filler, more of that "amplification of Florentine gossip" that some critics objected to. While it lengthens Tito's uncertainty, it produces no suspense for readers, who were privy to the scene between Romola and her brother.

However, the "Florentine Joke" is not mere filler to lengthen an installment; part 4, with eight printed pages more than the preceding part, is the third longest of the fourteen parts. In 1871, Eliot recalled the scene as one of the "many parts of 'Romola' [that were] entirely misunderstood." The scene was "a specimen, not of humour as I relish it, but of the practical joking which was the amusement of the gravest old Florentines, and without which no conception of them would be historical" (*Letters* 5: 174). In fact, the scene functions, like some of Shakespeare's comic subplots, as a comic echo of the "grave" matter in the main plot. Surrounding it are events that show Tito's anxiety. Drawn against his will into the circle of acquaintances in Nello's shop, Tito contrives to "look perfectly at his ease . . . [thinking that a] man who let the mere anticipation of discovery choke him was simply a man of weak nerves" (166). Yet Tito's nerves are so weak that the lightest touch of Macchiavelli's hand on his shoulder startles him, foreshadowing the effect of Baldassarre's more vigorous grasp in the next chapter. His misinterpreted solemnity provokes an exchange of glances between Nello and Piero di Cosimo that reminds readers of the Florentine division of opinion about this "much-bepraised Greek" (169), a phrase that also foregrounds Tito as outsider. Monthly readers might recall in the first installment that, like the doctor from Padua in the "joke," Tito the Greek had presented himself for a shave in worn clothing, marking him as a man who had endured misfortune. His reference to Monna Ghita's "fatal seizure" also connects the doctor with Tito. As he had hoped for the deaths of Baldassarre and Fra Luca, Tito, "rous[ing] himself from his abstraction," callously interprets this event to his advantage: "if Monna Ghita *were really taken out of the way*, it would be easier for him to see Tessa again—whenever he wanted to see her" (172; emphasis added). In this context, the practical joke occurs.

The scene demonstrates to Tito the mercilessness of the Florentine crowd. Undertaking to humiliate the imposter and drive him from Florence, Nello stages the very action that Tito fears for himself. Nello's accomplice, Vaiano the conjuror, finds that the trick has had the unexpected consequence of causing his monkey to flee. This event comically underscores the narrator's opening remark on the existence of consequences independent of the will or intention of the actors: "our deeds are like children that are born to us; they live and act apart from our own will" (165). Like the runaway horse with the monkey clinging to its back, the consequences of Tito's deeds are also out of his control.

This pressure of consequences is quickly borne home as Tito learns that Dino has revealed nothing that alters his future. Regretting the sale of the onyx ring, he envisions immediate consequences only: What will

Romola and others think of "the apparent sordidness of parting with a gem he had professedly cherished" (186)? Only later do readers discover the more serious consequence: the ring gives Baldassarre the clue to Tito's whereabouts. But for now, his pliability and moral blindness enable him to brush off this "slight matter" just as he dismisses his fears about the specious marriage ceremony. Tito is sure that it, too, will have "no further consequences" (187).

The end of installment 4 coincides with the end of volume 1 and shows Eliot trying to accommodate the arrangement of individual serial parts and the novel's volume division. Part 4 has no dramatic closure like the preceding installments, but is dominated by a general sense of foreboding. Both the beginning (with Romola at her dying brother's bedside) and the end (with Tito enclosing the crucifix in its "tomb of joy") focus on death, not new life through married love. Tito's oxymoronic phrase signals the futility of his wish that life contain only joy. Knowing his past actions, readers expect that he will be the "tomb of joy" in which Romola buries her chance for happiness. The brief penultimate chapter on the library, Bardo's version of Baldassarre's jewels, forebodes new disappointments. This ominous tone adds general suspense, but does not help readers envision possible outcomes for the next installment. In contrast to the preceding part's dramatic conversation between Tito and Fra Luca, which presented a definite set of possibilities for readers' imaginations, future plot directions are vague at the end of installment 4. A general atmosphere of foreboding is a less powerful inducement to readers to return to the next installment than a definite question such as "Will Fra Luca reveal the truth about Tito?"

Manuscript alterations indicate that Eliot revised the last chapter of installment 4 to emphasize one more specific source of complication for future parts: the mock marriage with Tessa. Page 77/353 of the manuscript shows three titles for chapter 20. "The Hiding of the Crucifix," is given in the left margin and crossed out lightly. Centered below "Chapter XX" is "The Betrothal." Between those two words is the insert: "day of the." "The Hiding of the Crucifix" was probably the original title, although its placement in the margin is peculiar, Eliot's chapter titles almost invariably being centered. Eliot may have rewritten this page (and several subsequent ones) and left the tentative title present to remind herself how to attach the rewriting to the rest of the chapter.

This hypothesis is supported by other manuscript details and by entries in Eliot's journal. First, she records the completion of "P. IV pp. 94" in her journal for July 31, 1862; but notes on August 6, "Having had a new scene to insert in Part IV . . . I have not yet begun Part V." In the interval, Lewes had returned from Spa (on August 2), and either she read him chapters 17 through 20, which she had written in his absence, or—since she does not record reading aloud—perhaps he read the material silently. At this point, they probably discussed changes to heighten the drama. In any case, it is clear from the manuscript that what was added to the final chapter was Tessa's pursuit of Tito and their encounter on the Via de' Bardi and the Ponte Rubaconte. Eliot's pages numbered 77 to 85 appear from their similar handwriting and broad pen strokes to have been written all at one time. On page 85, the writing is smaller and done with a finer pen, starting with the words "Goodby, my little Tessa: I *will* come." As the story line returns to Romola, this handwriting continues onto page 86, which bears the telltale sign of revision—incompleteness. Six words begin at the left margin—"Braccio, but none of the rest," followed by a slanting horizontal line to two key words in the lower right: "of the." These have been added to key into the earlier text; they repeat the first two words at the top of the next page, 87 in Eliot's numbering. This page had clearly been intended to come earlier in the chapter; the "7" in "87" has been written over a "o," in "80." The second numerals on pages 88 and 89 have been written over numbers 81 and 82; and from 90 to 95 (the end of the chapter), the old numbers (83 to 88) have been crossed out and new numbers written just to the right.

It is difficult to be sure precisely what Eliot referred to in the notation "pp 94" on July 31. The completed manuscript has ninety-seven pages, not ninety-four—or ninety-five, as given in the final numbering in her hand. This final 95 was originally an 88. Her manuscript numbering for this part includes, as usual, several revised pages on which she duplicated numbers by adding an "a" or "b," so that the numeral 88 does not indicate the total number of pages. It is possible that Eliot originally had Tessa lying in wait for Tito, but that she later added the actual encounter, "a new scene" that constitutes about three-and-a-half pages of the manuscript (82 to 85 in her revised numbers). To integrate the scene, however, Eliot had to rework the text as far as manuscript page 86, where she picked up the material that ends the chapter. She also had to rewrite, though not substantially, the material in the first part of the chapter to integrate the new scene. This would explain the alteration of the title. The very specific "Hiding of the Crucifix" relates only to the last part of the published chapter, and "The Betrothal" applies only to the Romola-

Tito plot; "The *Day of the* Betrothal" (emphasis added), however, is inclusive enough to cover the scene between Tito and Tessa. This encounter, though it "caused no perceptible diminution of [Tito's] happiness" (200), adds to the suspense by highlighting a commonplace threat—a rival in love—that Victorian audiences would easily have recognized and could ponder in the month they awaited part 5.

Suspenseful serial structures often return readers promptly to some question, problem, or danger left unresolved (i.e., "suspended") at the end of the preceding number. In the conclusions to parts 1, 2, and 3 in *Romola*, very little time has passed. With the end of part 4, Eliot adopts a different convention, in which months or years elapse between numbers. Thackeray ends *Vanity Fair*, installment 9, with George Osborne dead on the field at Waterloo and opens number 10 several months later in Brighton with Miss Crawley and her toadies. In the early parts of *A Tale of Two Cities*, Dickens shifts his scene back and forth between England and France and plays freely with the passage of time as well. Installment 10, July 2, 1859, ends sensationally with a knife through the heart of Monsieur the Marquis. The next installment refers to the passage of twelve months—but it is twelve months of the "English" life of Darnay. Not until four installments later, on July 30, do weekly readers of *All the Year Round* find themselves back in France, where Defarge and the several embodiments of "Jacques" pronounce doom on the Marquis's chateau and all his race.

Eliot's close lacks the outward drama of these two death scenes. Her images of death in part 4 are metaphoric, not literal; part 5 opens with apparently cheerful prospects for Romola and for Florence. Romola and Tito were married eighteen months earlier "in the joyous Easter time, and had had a rainbow-tinted shower of comfits thrown over them, after the ancient Greek fashion, in token that the heavens would shower sweets on them through all their double life" (207). The irony is multiple. The marriage's shower of comfits seems a literal version of Trollopian "sugar-plums" of marriage and gifts with which all good novels must end. But this is the beginning, not the end, of a new volume and installment. Readers recall the closing scene of the betrothal from the October installment, in which the couple emerged from Santa Croce to be confronted by Piero di Cosimo's grim procession. The reference to their "double life" also reminds readers of Tito's double life, his father and Tessa both concealed from his wife.

The installment's second paragraph adds weight on the negative side

of ambiguity. It is a time of political change, with which "the fortunes of
Tito and Romola" are closely connected (207), and of personal change;
Romola has begun to see, if not yet to acknowledge, flaws in her idol.[35]
Their estrangement begins with the principal crisis in this installment,
Tito's encounter with Baldassarre on the steps of the Duomo and his
purchase of the chain mail. First, however, the new volume, like the
proem with which the novel began, provides an overview of Florentine
political and historical events: the coming of Charles VIII of France and
the growing influence of Savonarola. In a non-serial novel, these events
might have begun in the first paragraph of the story, with the reference to
Romola and Tito's wedding left for a chapter devoted to them. Serialization, however, required this explicit connection to events of the preceding
installment, after which the narrator can give the historical background.
Readers tolerated such a lull in the action early in an installment, if it was
not sustained for too long, and if more exciting material appeared before
the part concluded.

In part 5, they did not have to wait long. In the installment's second
chapter, "The Prisoners," Tito is suddenly face to face with the consequences of selling his onyx ring. Reinforced by Leighton's drawing at the
beginning of the installment, the scene of Baldassarre's return etches itself
on the reader's memory. Drama is both internal and external. After Tito's
"first palsy of terror" (223), he tries with desperate "inverted reasoning"
to justify the instinctive denial for which his earlier equivocations have
prepared him. Suspense externally centers on the possibility that Baldassarre will reveal his history to two persons unlikely to sympathize
with Tito's point of view. In the Duomo, Romola sees the old man whose
"grey hairs made a peculiar appeal to her" (227), and Piero de Cosimo
follows Baldassarre in hopes of discovering more about Tito. Their observation and interest build the tension and validate Tito's feeling that his
secret is endangered as long as Baldassarre remains in Florence; he also
fears physical danger from a vengeful Baldassarre. Literally and metaphorically, he dons "The Garment of Fear." Focused on this twofold
threat, part 5's closure is especially effective.

Part 6 bridges the month's break with the same technique Eliot employed at the beginning of installment 4 of "Janet's Repentance": echoing
the words of the preceding part's close. The final sentence of part 5 reads,
"He folded the armour under his mantle, and hastened across the Ponte
Rubaconte" (244). Part 6 opens, "While Tito was hastening across the
bridge with the new-bought armour under his mantle, Romola was pac-

ing up and down the old library, thinking of him and longing for his return" (245). This transition also resembles *Romola*'s transitions from 1 to 2 and 2 to 3 in that the new part begins precisely where the story ended the month before. Just as part 5 opened with a dramatic bridge, and then gave background information, so does part 6: after this transition, the narrative flashes back to a night three months earlier when Romola and her father together awaited Tito's return. The old man hoped for information about the preservation of his library and for Tito's renewed assistance with his work. Bardo waited in vain. Before Tito appeared, Bardo was dead. Although Romola had been disappointed by Tito's diminishing fidelity to her father, her self-doubt leads her to wish that with her father's death, their married life will be "'more perfect now'" (247). This hope, too, is in vain. By first describing the scene of Bardo's death, the narrator introduces general reasons for Romola's disappointment. Then readers witness the first explicit scene of estrangement.

Whereas installments 1, 2, 3, and 5 closed with significant expectations that focused on the next part, installment 6 contains the discreteness that Hughes and Lund identify as typical (81). The image of the chain mail coming at both beginning and end reinforces the sense of roundedness also found in part 4. Any idyllic illusions that readers have retained about the marriage are shattered as Romola faces the truth. For months, her submissiveness and self-doubt had led her to deny obvious signs of Tito's shortcomings. She "felt equal to any self-infliction that would save her from ceasing to love" (251). But Baldassarre's appearance alters Tito's behavior too thoroughly to permit her continued self-deception. "The terrible resurrection of secret fears, which, if Romola had known them, would have alienated her from him for ever, caused him to feel an alienation already begun between them," and when he returns home wearing chain armor,[36] he behaves with a coldness new to their relationship (254).[37] In the final chapter, his coldness contrasts with Romola's passionate, heated defiance when Tito announces that he has sold Bardo's library to the French. Inside the frame of these domestic scenes are other events that continue the tension. Romola suspects "something unpleasant, something disadvantageous" (261) to Tito in Piero's portrait, and Tito's political success is clouded by the sight of Baldassarre in the crowd, looking more like his former respectable and rational self. Again Tito "think[s] that flight was his only resource" (268). The narrator's revelation that the onyx ring led Baldassarre to Florence reminds readers of its rash sale when Tito earlier considered flight. This crime against his father anticipates the crime Tito is about to commit in selling his father-in-law's jewel, the library, to the French to finance this second anticipated flight from Florence.

The installment closes with a confrontation between Romola and Tito. She rejects his reasoning, and he abandons his usual benevolent manipulation and asserts his power as a husband. Her accusation, "'You are a treacherous man!'" (291) leads her, unwittingly, to the truth about Tito's armor: she asks, "with gathered passion, 'Have you robbed somebody else, who is *not* dead? Is that the reason you wear armour?'" (292). With Grandcourtian coldness Tito masters her, "'The event is irrevocable, the library is sold, and you are my wife'" (294). This contest of wills, which ends only with her second departure from Florence near the end of the novel, introduces a dramatic conflict absent heretofore, except in Tito's encounter with Baldassarre on the steps of the Duomo. Because Baldassarre is able only twice—and at long intervals—to follow up that brief, chance encounter with a deliberate confrontation, its effect is seen chiefly in the fear that he engenders in Tito. Much more promising for the dramatic conflict important to a serial story is the domestic struggle with which this December number of the *Cornhill* ends.

Part 7, January 1863, opens with a change of scene and the return of Tessa, who has almost disappeared from the story since the bogus marriage in part 3, September 1862. Just as Tito apparently forgets about her amidst more pressing problems, so the monthly reader has had little reason to remark her absence. Her brief encounter with Tito on "The Day of the Betrothal" in the October number momentarily reminds readers more of Tito's inability to deal with the consequences of his selfish actions than of Tessa herself. There, as with Romola at the end of installment 6, she is the victim of his ruthless assertion of masculine domination. Tessa's fate is then in abeyance until installment 7, where readers find he has been unfaithful to Romola from early in their marriage; by withholding this information, Eliot forces it to take second place after the more important breach of faith—selling the library. This arrangement lays primary emphasis on the larger flaws of his disloyalty, instead of on his bigamy, a popular sensation novel theme. Tito's relationship with Tessa illustrates the complex motives and rationalizations in his character. The Tito who is so brutal when desperate is paradoxically unable to face the negative opinion of a peasant woman; with his usual flexibility, he reasons that "in ultimately leaving Tessa under her illusion, and providing a home for her, he had been overcome by his own kindness." Through this "self-justifying argument" (305), he again chooses the least unpleasant path. Tito's "secret offence against his wedded love" adds to reader interest and excitement, already at a high pitch because of a new secret offense against Baldassarre, whose situation appeals to readers' love of pathos.

While the *Examiner*'s final review suggests that "except in a few passages towards the close, there is nothing to fetch tears" (820), the scene of Baldassarre at Tessa's is an exception. The scene contrasts Baldassarre's poverty with Tito's growing power and wealth. It is a version of the Dives and Lazarus theme in industrial novels like *Mary Barton*, transferred to fifteenth-century Florence. The installment division emphasizes this contrast. For a month, readers were left to contemplate Tito's treachery to his father-in-law, which has supplied him with another large store of money. Part 7 opens with his adoptive father, whose jewels he sold, "wandering about Florence in search of a spare outhouse where he might have the cheapest of sheltered beds" (295). When Tessa invites him to eat a bowl of macaroni, "The invitation was not a disagreeable one, for he had been gnawing a remnant of dried bread" (299). Readers sensitive to the pathetic might also recall his poverty when, in the next installment, they encounter the supper in the Rucellai gardens. A peacock is served only for show, and a wealthy man like Tito "disperse[s] his slice in small particles over his plate" (346). Lest one imagine the contrast to be mere coincidence, the narrative points the moral by connecting the inedible peacock with Fra Girolamo's "teaching the disturbing doctrine that it was not the duty of the rich to be luxurious for the sake of the poor." Again Baldassarre is outside in the "chill obscurity" of a garden (346).

But this is to anticipate. In part 7, Tito has no scruples in ordering Monna Lisa to turn Baldassarre out into the cold, another step in his moral descent. Cruel action has replaced cruel inaction. A brief intervening chapter shows Tito's political duplicity; his enjoyment of life as "a game in which there was an agreeable mingling of skill and chance" has replaced "the freshness of young passion" (317). These signs of moral decay in his public and private behaviors prepare for Romola's reappearance in the final two chapters. "It was more than three weeks before the contents of the library were all packed and carried away. And Romola, instead of shutting her eyes and ears, had watched the process" (320). Her open eyes and ears are metaphoric; she sees the truth and flees, and the installment concludes.

This ending only superficially suggests closure in Romola's "turn[ing] her back on Florence" (334). A closer look shows that instead of the vague expectations that indicate an ending more closed than open, the part offers quite precise possibilities—and dangers—for Romola. If Victorian readers had little precedent on which to base expectations about what Romola could do away from Florence, a more specific danger of recognition and enforced return to Florence, is obvious. Earlier, the narrator had noted "that something else besides the mere garb would perhaps be necessary to enable her to pass as a Pinzochera," nor does Romola realize that her whole posture belies the humility of that sisterhood (327). Yet she senses her risk as she lifts her eyes to see two monks walking in the opposite direction and immediately regrets the action: "Her disguise made her especially dislike to encounter monks: they might expect some pious passwords of which she knew nothing, and she walked along with a careful appearance of unconsciousness till she had seen the skirts of the black mantles pass by her" (334). The narrative's attention to this incident marks its significance for the coming part. If these monks intervene, and the reader is certain they will, what can be expected in the next part? Will Romola abandon her flight? Will she face further brutality from her husband? Will she reveal her griefs to Bernardo del Nero? Is there disgrace for Tito? For the month of January, readers could speculate on possible ways in which the installment's concluding sentence, "She was free and alone" (334), might prove to be ironic.

It is not surprising that the next part marks a positive turn in critical opinion. At twenty-seven published pages, it was the shortest installment to date, but also one of the most exciting. The conflict between Tito and Romola is latent throughout, but the drama centers on parallel encounters in which Tito and Romola are tested. Each is called to assume responsibility for human bonds that have become a burden. Challenged by Baldassarre in a public forum, Tito denies him, and his adopted father is imprisoned. Savonarola recalls Romola to her duty to Florence and to a husband to whom she is pledged, even though she no longer respects or trusts him. She struggles against Savonarola's words and her own sense of duty, but returns. The juxtaposition of these events in this installment highlights the thematic and dramatic parallel.

Like the preceding number, installment 8 opens by leaving in abeyance the mystery of who the monks are and whether they recognized Romola's imposture. Only a passing reference in a subordinate clause notes that Tito's journey "had removed many difficulties from Romola's departure" (335). Instead, the chapter shows Baldassarre shadowing Tito through the dark streets of Florence and gaining admission to the private supper in the Rucellai Gardens by claiming to be a "scholar" accompanying him. His mental faculties partially restored and aware of the futility of matching physical strength with his enemy, Baldassarre hopes to expose Tito's treachery to his friends. Once readers are "hooked" by the excitement of this incipient conflict, the narrative flashes back to the restoration of Baldassarre's memory, which has renewed his hope for vengeance. Chapter 38 ends with a forward look: "now on this evening, he felt that his occasion was come" (342).

Chapter 39 opens with the politicians assembled for the supper. Their discussion of duplicity in Florentine politics is especially ironic because readers know who waits in the garden to prove Tito's falseness. Just before Baldassarre appears among them, the narrative shifts to his vantage point "look[ing] in at the windows, which made brilliant pictures against the gloom." He "had a savage satisfaction in the sight of Tito's easy gaiety, which seemed to be preparing the unconscious victim for more effective torture" (346). This dramatic contrast is heightened by readers' conflicting hope that Baldassarre will unmask the villain and fear lest his "highly strung" mind falter again. Physical contrasts add to the tension: "the men seated among the branching tapers and the flashing cups could know nothing of the pale fierce face that watched them from without. The light can be a curtain as well as the darkness" (346). Baldassarre emerges from the darkness to strike fear in Tito's political co-conspirators by announcing, "'There is a traitor among you'" (354). The political and the private merge, and Tito's desperation prompts him to new moral compromises. "He had never yet done an act of murderous cruelty even to the smallest animal that could utter a cry, but at that moment he would have been capable of treading the breath from a smiling child for the sake of his own safety" (355). In this "fearful crisis for Tito" (357), his cool resourcefulness in lying proves more effective than Baldassarre's fierce intensity; Baldassarre is imprisoned, and Tito is again "master." He has put to good personal use Tournaboni's earlier advice to play his political game well, and "the future belongs to [him]" (351). Questions of how long this will remain so and how whisperings of the event might affect him are suspended as the narrative shifts to Romola in chapter 40.

In installment 8's final two chapters, the stakes in the conflict between Savonarola and Romola are less external. For Romola, the loser, prison is metaphorical not literal. This counterpointed triumphant domination by Tito and dutiful submission by Romola leaves several paths for readers' speculations about the future. Tito has vanquished Baldassarre and expects to rule his wife. What shape will that rule take? How will Romola bear submission? What role will Savonarola play? Since her husband is not of the Frate's party, will her new allegiance produce new conflict between them? Will Baldassarre's claim be revealed to her and give her power over her husband? What will her new duties to Florence mean? How will she reconcile her relationship with San Marco to the memory of her father's vehement anticlericalism? Will she follow in her brother's footsteps? The possible directions of the plot are numerous and somewhat indefinite; in this sense, volume 2 closes as volume 1 had. The last sentences of the final chapter look backward rather than ahead: "Nothing broke the outward monotony of [Romola's] solitary home, till the night came like a white ghost at the windows. Yet it was the most memorable Christmas-eve in her life to Romola, this of 1494" (370). The date is a milestone for what has passed, rather than a marker for what is ahead.

Installment 9, which opens volume 3 of the novel, begins a sequence of suspenseful parts, 9 to 12, that together unite the threads of Tito's private and public treachery in a series of climaxes especially effective in a serial format. Characterization and historical context are already established, and events follow swiftly upon each other. Eliot's manuscript marks the new volume as well as the new part, suggesting that she was aware of structuring both. Like volume 2, volume 3 begins after a lapse of time, from Christmas 1494 to October 1496. Political and religious events are linked to the personal. Part 8's drama of the two vanquished figures, Romola and Baldassarre, is recalled when, ministering to the famine-stricken in Florence, Romola sees again the escaped prisoner "whom she had seen in the Duomo the day when Tito first wore the armour—at whose grasp Tito was paled [sic] with terror in the strange sketch she had seen in Piero's studio" (375). Such reminders are useful for readers who had encountered these events months before. "A wretched tremor and palpitation seized her. Now at last, perhaps, she was going to know some secret which might be more bitter than all that had gone before" (375). Readers await with her a revelation, but Baldassarre does not recognize the "Wife who lived in the Via de' Bardi" whom he had sought in vain, and now confronts—in vain. The revelation is suspended as the narrative shifts to Tito (376).

The part also includes the first faint suggestion of danger to Bernardo del Nero, and, although Tito seems fortune's favorite, his companions remember the "'nasty story a year or two ago about the man who said he had stolen jewels'" (398). Dangerous political games and irreconcilable differences between Romola and Tito merge in the installment's concluding conflict. Overhearing Dolfo Spini and her husband plot to lure Savonarola to his assassination, Romola threatens exposure. As in their confrontation over the library, Tito exerts his "masculine force": both physically, "seizing her wrists," and verbally, "'I am master of you. You shall not set yourself in opposition to me'" (407). Despite her "momentary shuddering horror at this form of contest with him" (408) and her wavering doubts about Tito's guilt, she defies him: "'if the Frate is betrayed, I will denounce you'" (408). Her struggle to believe in Tito against all reason, experience, and evidence ends with his opening the door for her with sycophantic politeness, leaving multiple exciting possibilities for the next installment.

Unanswered questions are more specific than those posed by the preceding part. What will Tito do to thwart this defiant wife? How much physical force will he use? Might his suave behavior at the end of the part, opening the door for her, be a trick to lock her in as he had before? He had had few scruples, after all, in conniving in Baldassarre's imprisonment. How will he balance the conflicting dangers of Romola's threat and Spini's anger if he is thwarted? Will his attempt to resolve this dilemma involve him in danger to himself?

These are not the questions with which part 9 was originally to have ended. Instead, Eliot's original design included chapter 47 in this part, but alterations in parts 10 and 11 left the former too brief even for the brevity that characterizes parts 9 to 12. At twenty-nine, twenty-four, twenty-four, and twenty-five published pages, they are the shortest group in the novel. In chapter 47, Tito ponders the questions that readers would have posed at the end of part 9. He is annoyed at the "air-blown chances" that have interfered with his "devices of skill" (411) in playing his triple game. Though he has mastered his wife, her threat involves him in considerable difficulty and some danger. The latter is increased when Romola visits Nello's barbershop to demand assurance that the Frate has not "'gone beyond the gates'" (413). In giving it, Tito attracts the scrutiny of another double agent, Ser Ceccone, who "was not learned, not handsome, not successful. . . . He was a traitor without charm. It followed that he was not fond of Tito Melema" (414).[38]

With this hint of future threat, chapter 47 would have made an excellent conclusion. In fact, pagination and other manuscript markings show that Eliot originally intended it to end part 9 instead of opening part 10. The two installments completed before she signed her agreement with George Smith in May 1862 and the third written in June are numbered consecutively in her hand, from Roman numerals I to XIV (proem), and then Arabic 1 through 254. Each installment begins on a new page, but there is no indication of the number or month of the part. However, with part 4, the manuscript shows two changes. First, she began to include the numbers for the installments as well as for the chapters. Hence the first page of installment 4 is headed "Part IV." under which is written "Chapter XV"; below that, the chapter title. She also alters her method of paginating. Instead of using continuous pagination, as in parts 1 to 3, she starts the numbering of each new part with "1." With installment 6, yet another change occurs. She begins to add the month in the left-hand margin along with the installment number. These practices continue through part 9, are disrupted with part 10, and then resumed in parts 11 through 14.

The manuscript for installment 10, the only exception to these practices, contains no indication that chapter 47 begins a new part; nor does the word "April" appear, though installments 6 through 9 were marked December through March respectively. With part 11, she resumes these markings. In addition, part 10 is the only installment from 4 to 14 for which she does not restart her page numbering; chapter 47 begins with a 67. Nor does chapter 47 begin on a separate page. Eliot concludes chapter 46 with two lines of text on the top of manuscript page 67. Three lines are left blank, and on a fourth is written "Chapter 47." Another blank line follows as if for the chapter title, but no title is given. After this blank, the text of chapter 47 begins and continues to page 72 in Eliot's pagination; here, the second bound volume of the manuscript also ends. Chapter 47 is not the only chapter that begins mid-page (though the practice is rare), but part 10 is the only installment that begins mid-page. Obviously, the division of part 10 was an afterthought.

The manuscript of chapter 48 provides additional evidence. Although it is the second chapter of part 10, its pagination begins with 1. Centered at the top of the page is the usual indication of chapter number and title: "Chapter XLVIII/Counter Check." The title is in a lighter ink and is underlined twice in a broader pen stroke than the surrounding text, indicating that it may have been added later. Perhaps Eliot thought of the title "Counter Check" when she decided to put chapters 47 and 48 together in the same installment; but chapter 47, prepared as the conclusion to part 9, may already have been at the printer. Hence she could not insert its title in the manuscript as she did the title for 48, "Counter Check." That chapter 47 had passed out of her hands is also suggested by a reminder in Eliot's hand that is inserted in the left-hand margin of chapter 48's first page: "'Cont' of Part X / beginning at Ch 47 / *April.*'" Apparently, chapter 47 was not with the other chapters (48 to 51) in installment 10 when she sent them to the printer, and she needed to explain how this material related to what the printer already had.

The reason for this change of plan probably lies in the problems she had writing enough copy during the winter of 1863. Even as it stands, part 10 is the shortest installment at twenty-four published pages. In the *Cornhill*, chapter 47 occupies the first three pages of installment 10.[39] If Eliot had left it in part 9, she would then have had only twenty-one pages in part 10, well below the thirty-six pages she had contracted for; whereas with chapter 47 removed, part 9 still contains twenty-nine published pages, slightly more than parts 5 and 8. Moving a chapter into the new part was better than following a thirty-two-page part 9 with a twenty-one-page part 10.

The originally planned installment break at the end of chapter 47 would have highlighted Tito's future peril rather than the marital conflict. Readers would have been left for a month to ponder the narrator's last words about Ser Ceccone's enmity. However, instead of pausing for a month to contemplate Ceccone's potential as a threat, the story hastens forward into chapter 48, which again foregrounds the Romola-Tito conflict and a new danger to someone Romola loves. Tito is no longer the pleasant, easygoing figure of the early installments. "The husband's determination to mastery, which lay deep below all blandness and beseechingness, had risen permanently to the surface now, and seemed to alter his face, as a face is altered by a hidden muscular tension with which a man is secretly throttling or stamping out the life from something feeble, yet dangerous" (415). Tito's most effective countercheck is the threat of Bernardo del Nero's "arrest and ruin." "Tito had meditated a decisive move, and he had made it" (416). Powerless, Romola "felt as if her mind were held in a vice by Tito's: the possibilities he had indicated were rising before her with terrible clearness" (417). While this chapter directs suspense forward to the threat to Bernardo and Tito's renewed fear of Baldassarre,[40] the rest of part 10 dissipates these tensions by turning attention to Tessa and Monna Brigida.

This was not what Eliot had first intended. In her journal for January

30, she records, "Having deferred a portion of what I have written [in part 10] I am thrown back a little in my part." Repagination in the manuscript suggests that the portion she deferred was Romola's interview with Camilla Rucellai. She originally planned to follow the short "Pyramid of Vanities" chapter (49) with the drama of this interview (chapter 52). Chapter 49 ends on Eliot's manuscript page 22, and part of chapter 52 was originally numbered 23 to 27 (from "Camilla had a vision to communicate" to "If Romola's intellect had been less capable"). When she deferred this Camilla material until chapter 52, following the reference to "jarring notes" in Savonarola's last preaching in the Duomo (445), Eliot no longer needed a sentence on her original page 23 and therefore cancelled it: "But in this visit of hers to Camilla Rucellai she was brought dangerously near to a point of repulsion, at which she might be driven even from her trust in Savonarola." The rearrangement gives Romola a chance meeting with Piero di Cosimo in chapter 49, prior to her visit to Camilla.[41] In their conversation, Piero reminds her of her father's classical learning and reasoning, which are contrasted with the excesses of Savonarola's Piagnone boys. Camilla's mad or malicious prophecies, which follow this conversation, then become only one additional reason for Romola's disillusionment with Savonarola.

After the return to Tessa and Monna Brigida, Eliot could still have ended her installment with the high drama of Romola's confrontation with Camilla and the sudden appearance of Baldassarre. Although this ending is one that Wilkie Collins or Mary Elizabeth Braddon could have been proud of, it is a measure of Eliot's distance from the sensation school that she chose *not* to make a break here, but instead ended the installment more contemplatively.[42] The critical points for readers to ponder in the interval between installments are the conflict and characterization of Tito and Romola, not Baldassarre's sensational appearance. As the *Guardian* observed of the whole: "There is . . . no lack of exciting incidents, but they are all subordinate to the moral and mental development" of the characters (Sept. 16, 1863; 876).

Eliot's decision to end with the undramatic scene of Monna Brigida's accepting old age was probably a deliberate one. If she wrote the Camilla material on January 30 and then decided to postpone it, she would have had left only twenty-two manuscript pages—making it unlikely that she could have been at page 39 on February 1 and page 43 on February 2, as her journal records. More probably, she had already written the material by the January 30 decision. She decided then not to leave it at a later point in part 10 but, as she says, to "defer" it to the next part. Perhaps the pathos of the final scene appealed to Lewes, or perhaps Eliot noted her slow pace and was unwilling to risk using too much material in part 10 and running short for part 11 as a consequence.

Supporting the idea that she wanted to stress the pathos—and perhaps the value of Savonarola's unworldly teaching—is evidence that during the first two days of February she reorganized her chapters. Monna Brigida's story is placed in a separate one from Tessa's encounter with the Piagnone boys. In the manuscript for part 10, page 40 is followed by 40ª, containing only the final four lines of chapter 50. Then there are nine lines of space and a new heading, "Chapter 51, Monna Brigida's Conversion." The page appears to have been recopied, the writing being broader than on the preceding pages and insufficient space having been left at the bottom, so that the last four words "I will not go" are written below the last line on the page, a common indication of recopying. Eliot also altered her title for chapter 50 from "A Carnival Scene" ("Scene" is likely; this word is somewhat obscured in being crossed out) to "Tessa abroad and at home." The first title would obviously have been more inclusive. Pages 40ª and 40ᵇ include the published text from "hatred and triumphant vengeance" in chapter 50's final paragraph to "Every woman who was not a Piagnone would give a shrug at the sign of her, and the men would" in paragraph 2 of chapter 51. If Eliot wrote up to page 43 on February 2, she may have realized that (since she was going to end the part with Monna Brigida) she could emphasize Baldassarre's seeing the two wives together by breaking the long chapter, "A Carnival Scene," at that point. Then she added two transitional pages between the chapters to introduce Monna Brigida more thoroughly, emphasized her in the new title, and moved her from a comic role to a more sympathetic, even pathetic, one.

Eliot makes the transition from installment 10 to 11 with care. The first half of part 11's opening sentence reminds readers of the preceding close: "The incidents of that Carnival day seemed to Romola to carry no other personal consequences to her than the new care of supporting poor cousin Brigida in her fluctuating resignation to age and grey hairs." Then the plot moves in a new direction: "but they introduced a Lenten time in which [Romola] was kept at a high pitch of mental excitement and active effort" (443). Her constant "haunting fear" (443) for Bernardo del Nero, stimulated by Tito's hints in the preceding installment, outweighs her concern about a revelation from Baldassarre—which would "she thought [refer] only to the past" (446). But the opening chapter skillfully links the two. After hearing Camilla Rucellai's threats to Bernardo, Romola emerges from the church of the Badia where she sought solace, to find herself "face to face with a man who was standing only two yards off her. The man was Baldassarre" (451).

The intrigues of Florentine politics that confounded readers in the early numbers now have a clarity and drama that accounts for the improving critical reception. Baldassarre reveals not only Tito's betrayal of filial love and allegiance, but marital betrayal as well. The shock of this revelation is described by the *Daily News*. Her earlier hopes and love, her gradual "suspicion of [Tito's] truth, scornfully rejected yet returning again with fresh proofs and irrepressible importunity, the irrevocable conviction of his baseness coming at last like an earthquake to divide them by a bottomless abyss, all this is worked out with consummate art" (Aug. 3, 1863; 2). The interview in San Mineato reveals to Romola the extent of her husband's disloyalty.

"The Other Wife," the final chapter in part 11, brings Romola and Tessa together, but the last two and a half pages continue the focus on Florentine politics. Expecting that when Tito says "You have heard it all," he refers to his other family, Romola is horrified to learn that Tito has guaranteed his own safety by betraying her godfather. The installment ends, "They turned away from each other in silence" (476). For Romola as for readers, several unanswered questions remain, the most central being that toward which the installment has been building—the fate of Bernardo del Nero. Installment 11 begins and ends with this "haunting fear," and perhaps Eliot sacrificed a more dramatic closure in the preceding part to achieve this roundedness.

The final three installments that appear in June, July, and August are thematically linked: each focuses on the death of a man on whom Romola had depended, and each death is closely intertwined with the others. The *Cornhill's* June number features a striking illustration of the initial letter. The "T" in the first sentence, "Tito had good reasons for saying that he was safe," resembles a sharp double-headed axe. It is next to the campanile of the Palazzo Vecchio, opposite a full-page drawing of Romola in a small boat, captioned with the concluding chapter's title, "Drifting Away." The contrast between the narrator's assurance of Tito's safety and the axe adjacent to the hall where Florentine political destinies are decided prepares readers for a chapter in which Tito (once again) is master of all situations. Dramatic events and characterization draw readers into the story. Tito's old compatriots are imprisoned and likely to be executed, but his chief regret is that he has opened himself to disdain—to hissing instead of the applause he has always sought—because he could not keep his political treacheries hidden as well as his private ones. "[H]is conduct to his father had been hidden by successful lying: his present act did not admit of total concealment—in its very nature it was a revelation. And Tito winced under his new liability to disesteem" (483). But, like Rosamond Vincy, he accepts no blame. His wrongs to Baldassarre and Romola stem from "mistakes" because he married "the wrong woman" and because of "incalculable circumstances" (483).

By the end of installment 12, suspense arises not only from Bernardo's possible fate, but from Tito's as well. Baldassarre's efforts have been ineffectual, and Romola is unlikely to help him deliberately to revenge. But she has helped inadvertently. In chapter 57, the first in part 12, Tito does not notice Ser Ceccone as he departs from the council chambers; but Ser Ceccone, who is "also willing to serve the State by giving information against unsuccessful employers," notices him (484). This hint would have greater impact had the original mention of Ser Ceccone's dislike for Tito received the emphasis Eliot intended for it, at the conclusion of part 9. But observant readers will still recall Ser Ceccone's envy and know that chapter 57 bodes ill for Tito. The rest of the installment centers on Tito and Romola's continuing conflict. His attempt to placate Romola by recommending that she seek mitigation of Bernardo del Nero's sentence from Savonarola results in further discovery: reference to a "second plot," which enables Savonarola to refuse her request, confirms "that Tito had won his safety by foul means" (496). After Romola tells him she has heard Baldassarre's story, Tito, with "calculated caution . . . stimulated by alarm," again asserts his male dominance to prevent her leaving him. Romola is his property: "'And supposing I do not submit to part with what the law gives me some security for retaining?'" The encounter ends with Romola, like Baldassarre, vanquished, and Tito's "mastery" prevailing (489).

Eliot never has Romola use her information about Tito's "other wife," an element of the story that would have appealed to readers of 1860s sensation fiction, where bigamy was a common feature. Instead, Tessa and the children are almost forgotten in the concentrated interest in Bernardo's fate and Romola's crisis of trust in Savonarola. Drama and pathos combine in the next chapter, when Romola speaks with Bernardo for the last time and attends his execution. Superficially, this seems like an ideal installment ending, with its highly charged emotional content.

[handwritten margin note: CM didn't carry on sensation fiction]

[178]

However, it looks backward rather than forward, closing out a part of Romola's life while not opening up any clear possibilities for readers' speculations in the month's interval. Perhaps for this reason, Eliot concludes the installment with a sudden shift of scene, to Viareggia and Romola "Drifting Away"—the title of the installment's final chapter. Bernardo being dead, what will be Romola's fate as she drifts in a small boat and covers her face in despair? Is this passive, if not active, suicide? The questions avoided earlier when Savonarola called Romola back to Florence recur. What will Romola do in a life outside Florence? Apart from a religious life that her disillusionment with Savonarola seems to preclude, what options were open to a woman like Romola in fifteenth-century Italy? Not only were these questions difficult for readers to answer with anything like a set of probable outcomes; but on this second occasion of Romola's flight, Eliot herself cannot answer them except in the parablelike story of the plague. From the standpoint of installment plotting, this conclusion removes Romola from the scene while the final drama of Tito's life is enacted. Her part in the plot is adrift for two months: she is omitted entirely from installment 13. Other loose ends are tied up, and time is allowed to pass to prepare for Romola's return to the scene of the action, Florence.

Installment 13 does not offer even a verbal bridge to remind readers where part 12 ended. The conflict between Tito and Romola had produced a fast-moving set of installments in numbers 9 to 12. The couple now are separate. The six chapters of installment 13 depict the drama of Savonarola's claims and Tito's duplicity in a Florence without Romola. All that readers heard of her fate in July 1863 was Tito's falsehood to Savonarola regarding his "'wife's unhappy alienation from a Florentine residence'" after Bernardo's death, and his claim that he wishes "'to join her'" elsewhere (535). Bringing to fruition Baldassarre's and Ser Ceccone's hatred and vows of vengeance, the installment ends with the wagon carrying the intertwined bodies of Tito and Baldassarre, moving slowly through Florence, leaving the truth about Tito as much a mystery to the town's inhabitants as it was when he first arrived. As in the last parts of many serial novels, this ending is more closed than open and completes Tito's story. Readers awaiting the final installment in August would have centered their expectations on unanswered questions about Romola, giving a thought now and then to Tessa too. Part 14 resumes precisely where part 12 left off, almost as if 13 had not interrupted the progress of the story. The opening paragraph is arranged to remind readers of events from two months earlier. "Romola in her boat passed from dreaming into long deep sleep, and then again from deep sleep into busy dreaming." One dream recalls Bernardo's death scene: "she felt herself stretching out her arms in the court of the Bargello, where the flickering flames of the tapers seemed to get stronger and stronger till the dark scene was blotted out with light" (557). This link with installment 12 enables a smooth resumption of Romola's story, with closure for her, Monna Brigida, Tessa and the children, and Savonarola as well. Each of the final three installments brings a death that is either tragedy or deliverance for Romola. Arranged thus, the serial structure highlights each individually, with its effect on Romola, more sharply than the volume publication does. The pathos of Bernardo's death, in part 12, is heightened by his regret that he is leaving Romola with no one to depend on or trust. Installment 13 delivers her from a legal tyranny that she has long wished to escape, and installment 14, from a spiritual dependency in which obedience superseded self-determination. The final installment illustrates her new independence as she assumes responsibility for Monna Brigida, Tessa, and the children.

In this second serial work, Eliot continues to shape the devices of successful serialization to achieve her own ends. She structures each installment for maximum plot effect, while also dissecting Tito's moral disintegration. Plot and character can work at cross-purposes in serial publication, and critics felt this was so in the early parts of the novel. The slow, meticulous development of characters in their historical context obscured the care that Eliot took to end her installments with dramatic events. Later, when Tito's moral reasoning has been delineated, Eliot begins to highlight plot development in her serial conclusions, but never diminishes the attention to Tito's characterization or the story's moral thrust.

The effort was not without costs. Once again, she encountered the special problems that serialization involved. Her letters indicate the pressure she felt when her deadlines loomed. Though she preferred the longer installments in George Smith's second offer, even sacrificing £3,000 to gain this advantage, she was able in only five of her installments to supply the stipulated thirty-two pages. Only by writing fourteen instead of the originally planned twelve numbers could she meet her commitment. For her next novel, *Felix Holt*, she returned to volume publication without prior magazine serialization; but with her last two works, the vagaries of the Victorian publishing and library systems led her to try a new publication format, which had its own drawbacks and its own re-wards. Despite not having achieved the agreed-upon length for most parts of *Romola*, Eliot may have realized from the initially negative reaction that *Cornhill*'s installments did not provide ample room for readers to comprehend her gradually developing characters. With *Middlemarch* and *Daniel Deronda*, she wrote eight half-volume installments for each; the manuscript pages of each part averaged more than twice the number of pages in the individual installments of her *Romola* manuscript. These two works were more extensively reviewed than either *Romola* or *Scenes of Clerical Life*; their publication history and readers' reception as they were published will be the focus of the next three chapters.

5

A "Greater Trial of Readers'
Faith and Patience":
Middlemarch, a Bimonthly Serial

Apart from the Liggins authorship controversy following the publication of *Adam Bede*, the publishing circumstances best known to George
Eliot scholars are probably those connected with Eliot and Lewes's decision to issue *Middlemarch* in eight half-volumes in 1871–72. This format
allowed Eliot sufficient room to develop long installments and, ultimately, to publish four volumes instead of the standard three. It also
allowed her to circumvent Mudie's library, which was increasingly an
annoyance to publishers and authors. The idea's origin is disputed. A
letter from Lewes to John Blackwood on May 7, 1871, indicates that he
devised the plan himself, based on the example of Victor Hugo's "long
Misérables" (*Letters* 5: 146). However, in 1849, Bulwer Lytton had discussed with Blackwood a similar plan in which *My Novel* would be
published first in *Blackwood's Magazine*; and then, the author suggested,
in parts costing 2s. or 2s. 6d., containing two numbers each from Maga.
Blackwood in turn proposed 5s. numbers of four magazine parts each. As
J. A. Sutherland points out, "After some months [Bulwer Lytton] came
more and more to the publisher's way of thinking: in June 1850 when he
sent the first four numbers for inspection he was on the brink of accepting Blackwood's scheme." However, Sutherland claims, "the publisher's
nerve was not up to the experiment and the 5s. venture was quietly
shelved" (*Victorian Novelists* 195), or Blackwood was "too prudent to
risk the experiment." Later, given the sales of *My Novel*, "Blackwood
may well have regretted not trying the experimental form of issue" ("Lytton, John Blackwood and the serialisation of 'Middlemarch'" 99–100).

More than twenty years afterward, on October 29, 1871, Bulwer Lytton wrote to Blackwood of his "chagrin" at seeing the announcements for the forthcoming *Middlemarch*: "Of course . . . it is annoying to see the design I had conceived to be my own, forestalled and appropriated by another novelist. The chance of success in such an experiment is in favour of the author who first starts it. . . . And of course it would not become me to imitate any other writer" (qtd. in Sutherland, *Victorian Novelists* 203 and "Lytton, John Blackwood and the serialisation of 'Middlemarch'" 103). John Blackwood reacted to this in a letter to his nephew William on November 2: "Lord Lytton I can put straight, as the plan of G. Eliot's novel was entirely their proposition. I remember something of a discussion about form for some of his [Lytton's] Novels and I was in favour of trying the French system but Simpson was afraid of the paper covers" (*Letters* 5: 211). Sutherland argues that the similarity between details of Lewes's proposal and the earlier conversations between Blackwood and Bulwer Lytton

> can hardly be entirely co-incidental. Presumably in one of the conversations about library monopoly Blackwood mentioned his scheme for the 5/-number and Lewes is either playing up to the publisher by feeding him one of his own bright ideas—or perhaps it had simply slipped his mind who had thought of the new form of serialisation first. ("Lytton, John Blackwood and the serialisation of 'Middlemarch'" 103)

The former seems unlikely. Blackwood himself calls the plan "entirely their proposition," and Lewes had no reason to "play up to" Blackwood at this point. Even as a tactic, it would surely have been more useful to remind Blackwood explicitly of his own good idea, had Lewes believed it to be the publisher's. It is equally likely that a man with Lewes's sharp eye for publication possibilities would have drawn his own conclusions from Victor Hugo's example in *Les Misérables*, published ten years earlier. Lewes had reviewed the work for Maga in August 1862, and although he did not discuss its publication format, he was clearly aware of it. He envisioned the first parts tempting readers to return for the later volumes. Mentioning that "it has excited a great 'sensation' in France," he added, "we will lay before our readers a tolerably full analysis of 'Fantine,' which forms the first part of the work, leaving it to them to seek for the eight succeeding volumes, if they are tempted by these two" (175). Lewes probably recalled Hugo's experiment when he and Eliot contemplated a publishing plan for *Middlemarch*. They were, in fact, reading Hugo's novel aloud nearly every evening in the second half of May and early June 1871, just when Eliot was engaged with her early parts of *Middlemarch* (GHL Diary). Whether his suggestion to Blackwood on May 7 reminded him of the book and inspired the rereading—or whether he and Eliot planned the rereading and this reminded him of the format—is unknown. The reading proved a disappointment, and on June 9 "we were forced to give it up, so dreary and wordy" (GHL Diary).[1] But the publication plan remained.

One did not have to be a genius at reading the publishing climate to discern the need for a change. Blackwood had referred generally to the need for a new format in a letter to Eliot dated March 20, 1867, which referred to the 12-shilling edition of *Felix Holt*, which has "done very little. Our next adventure, I think, we must try some innovation in form of publication" (*Letters* 4: 352). In proposing the format for *Middlemarch*, Lewes reminded Blackwood that he had "more than once spoken of the desirability of inventing some mode of circumventing the Libraries and making the public buy instead of borrowing." When the first set of serial reviews appeared, the *Nonconformist* reviewer, despite not "having any liking for instalments," called readers' attention to this benefit:

> The publishers, in giving us a new novel of George Eliot's, have had the courage to strike out a new form for the novel, and if by doing so they help to bring to an end the old fashion of publishing novels in three volumes at a guinea and a half, they will have done a veritable public service. The fashion belongs to other times, and would have ceased long since, but that the interests of second and third-class authors, and a tribe belonging to an inferior grade, still are promoted by it, and that the libraries, for obvious reasons of their own, also help to maintain it. (Dec. 13, 1871; 1226)

The three-volume novel was to decline and fall more slowly than Silas Wegg's reading of Gibbon; it lasted another twenty years. But this new format, the half-volume scheme adopted for *Middlemarch*, nonetheless proved such a success that Blackwood and Eliot used it again in 1876 with *Daniel Deronda*. This half-volume plan—initially with two-month intervals between parts—gave Eliot the leisure to work out her installments without the unsettling deadline pressure of monthly serialization. It also meant, at least in theory, that she did not have to worry about the length of installments: "ten or twelve pages either way would not matter" (Sutherland, *Victorian Novelists* 196). Eliot alluded to this flexibility in discussing arrangements for publishing *Daniel Deronda* just before its appearance. She wrote to Mrs. Peter Alfred Taylor that since *Adam Bede*, she has declined many offers for magazine serialization "except in the case of 'Romola,' which appeared in the 'Cornhill,' and was allowed to take up a varying and unusual number of pages" (*Letters* 6: 179). With *Middlemarch*, the length of the eight parts also varied, with the longest at 212 pages (book 1, not including the prelude) and the shortest at 174 pages (book 7).[2] Still, the length of individual parts was not a matter of indifference. On September 17, 1871, for example, Lewes wrote to Blackwood suggesting advertisements such as Dickens and Thackeray had used. "By the way a thought strikes me. Would it not be well to have an advertisement sheet bound up with each part—as Dickens and Thackeray had with their parts? (though not of course on the *covers*). This would not only bring in some hard cash, it would help to make the volume look bigger for the 5/- which in British eyes is a consideration not to be neglected" (*Letters* 5: 184). The 174 to 212 pages do not include the end pages of advertisement for gardening books, wine merchants, and the Mutual Life Assurance Society's Scottish Widows' Fund that ultimately helped to pad out the volumes. Blackwood "was concerned primarily with the outward bulk of the parts rather than with having a uniform number of pages in each." Later, when book 3 (175 published pages) proved shorter than the two earlier books, Blackwood advised Eliot and Lewes not to worry about its actual length, noting that they could use thicker paper for that part (Beaty 47). As usual, Blackwood attempted to reassure the worry-prone author, and downplay matters that might distract her from writing. As a result, their "correspondence presents the rather peculiar but pleasant picture of the author concerned over the practical matter of the length of the parts and the publisher discounting this consideration" (Beaty 47). Eliot calculated the number of pages periodically and discussed the size of individual parts up to the last (see her letter to Blackwood, Aug. 4, 1872, regarding books 7 and 8, for example; 5: 296).

The half-volume form had other advantages. Its unusual length allowed Eliot more space than either *Blackwood's* or the *Cornhill* in which to develop characters and plot, and her readers had the solace of knowing that if they had to receive the book in installments at least these were substantial ones. Their length also meant that the parts provided sufficient material for reviewers to treat each one almost as a novel in itself. As a consequence of this, and probably of Eliot's reputation in the 1870s—

when reviewers frequently referred to her as England's greatest living novelist—many newspapers noticed each individual part of her final two novels. Magazines and newspapers had given relatively brief notices of *Scenes of Clerical Life* and *Romola*, but the number and length of the serial reviews were unprecedented for *Middlemarch* and *Daniel Deronda*. I have uncovered eight newspapers that published individual reviews of at least seven of the eight installments of *Middlemarch*, and five more that published reviews for at least half. For *Daniel Deronda*, the number is even higher. (See Appendix 1 for details.) These reviews often ran to several hundred words and included lengthy quotations from the book being noticed; they provide a rare opportunity to examine the effect of reviewer comments on an author's work-in-progress, and to discover the interaction between readers and a text that they can encounter only one part at a time.

Middlemarch needed the larger scope of four volumes that Lewes described in his May 7 letter to Blackwood because it resulted from the fusion of two separate novels that Eliot was working on in the early 1870s. One, tentatively titled "Miss Brooke," focused on Dorothea and her milieu, the county families of the Brookes, Chettams, Cadwalladers, and Casaubon-Ladislaw. The other, "Middlemarch," was the story of the middle-class townsfolk from Middlemarch itself. Recognizing the thematic links between Dorothea's and Lydgate's stories, Eliot decided to fuse the two. The history of these separate books and their fusion is fully detailed in Jerome Beaty's seminal study.[3] Of special interest here is the way in which Eliot arranged her installments, especially her serial conclusions and the openings of new parts, to consider the several necessities of a serial story: a wholeness to each part as well as cohesiveness of the entire work; attention in each installment of a multi-plot novel to all of the several plot lines; and installment conclusions that bring readers back to buy the next part. Anna Kitchel describes Eliot's outlines of the eight books of *Middlemarch* in her *Quarry II* as demonstrating "the novelist as architect. With such a mass of heterogeneous material as she had in hand, each part of the building had to be planned (1) to do its own work and (2) to fit in with the rest of the structure" (14). Some of the work of each part was to entice readers to buy the next part, an especially critical matter when the installments would be two months apart instead of one. The *Nonconformist* might have been articulating Lewes's greatest fears in its notice of book 2, pointing to the hazards of this new mode of publication:

The issue of a story in half volumes with the long interval of two months between each, is one of the severest tests to which a novelist could submit himself. The monthly instalments of serial stories, which have come to form so large a part of our magazines, are read rapidly, and then dismissed until the next month brings its new portion. But a separate publication makes more pretension, and is not to be thus cavalierly treated; and if a work so published is to secure for itself a favourable reception, it must have great intrinsic merit. (Feb. 21, 1872; 202)

Serial reviewers of *Middlemarch*, book 1, had been nearly unanimous in affirming that Eliot's work had such intrinsic merit. That their judgment was important to Lewes and Eliot is indicated by a rearrangement of the plan for book 2 shortly after these notices appeared. Eliot is often believed to have been "above" the influence of newspaper criticism, but the evidence of seven early reviews (most unindexed and unreprinted) suggests that the alterations recorded in Lewes's correspondence and traced in the manuscript by Beaty were made in direct response to public opinion.

The stipulation for wholeness of the individual parts is in some ways at variance with the need for serial endings that are open-ended enough to keep readers in suspense. Installment 1, "Miss Brooke," handles the matter rather curiously. This book combines the two originally separate works with less actual integration of the "Middlemarch" and the county stories than anywhere else in the novel. Disproportionately, its first nine-and-a-half chapters are devoted to Dorothea's courtship; the second half of chapter 10 brings Lydgate to Tipton for the prenuptial dinner along with some other men from Middlemarch, and the final two chapters develop the character of Lydgate and introduce the Vincys and old Featherstone.

Eliot herself was troubled about this arrangement, as her vacillations about where to place the installment break show. In her second *Quarry* for *Middlemarch*, "chapters 11 and 12 are first listed in Part I, then transferred (with changed chapter headings) to Part II. Yet, when Part I was published, the chapters in question had been put back into it" (Kitchel 14). The final arrangement of books 1 and 2 in this regard was not determined until the summer of 1871. Kitchel correctly attributes this final arrangement to the internal requirements of a serial story as much as to length, though the circumstances are much more specific than she records. Considering the length of the *Middlemarch* parts overall, installment 1 is (even without the prelude) a dozen pages longer than the next longest part, and three dozen pages longer than the two shortest. (See Appendix 3.) Of course, when she went to publish book 1, Eliot could not have known the length of parts she had not yet written. In addition, before readers were fully engaged with her story she was perhaps more worried about giving them a "full" part for their five shillings. Nonetheless, as Kitchel suggests, Eliot needed to present more of the town of Middlemarch in her first part. "George Eliot is presenting a picture of life in a small, provincial city and wishes her readers to get in the very first monthly part of her novel a glimpse of the townspeople who are to play such influential parts in the drama" (14). As a result, readers are introduced to Lydgate, who is "almost, if not quite, as important" as Dorothea. Readers meet Rosamond and Fred, as well, before the part ends. True, Kitchel argues, the "story of [Fred's] troubles, his debts, and his love for Mary could have waited till Part II. But that would have denied the very thing George Eliot was bound to stress, the importance of the unimportant, the relation of comparatively trivial people to the lives of the chief actors in her drama of life as it really is" (15). It was not, however, so much this abstract relation of character to character as Blackwood's responses to the first two parts that led Eliot and Lewes to settle on the structure for book 1.

On July 14, 1871, when Lewes sent Blackwood the second part of *Middlemarch*, the first part included only the story of Dorothea. Blackwood had received that part on May 31, and his letter of June 2 responds enthusiastically to "the old twaddle Brooke"; the "excellent Baronet"; Casaubon, who makes him "angry"; and Dorothea: "How she will fare when she wakens to real life is a source of great anxiety to me" (*Letters* 5: 148–49). His failure to mention the Middlemarchers was matched by newspaper reviewers in December 1871, but he and they were not talking about the same book 1. The evidence of this letter is not sufficient by itself to indicate how much book 1 then contained, but later correspondence clarifies the situation. On July 20, Blackwood anticipates early reviewers by being the first to express regret that Dorothea and family were not included in book 2: "It was a disappointment at first not to find any of my old friends of the former part, all except Lydgate [from Dorothea's prenuptial dinner in chapter 10] apparently entirely strangers" (*Letters* 5: 167). The last phrase makes it clear that Blackwood had not read chapters 11 and 12 in part 1.

This correspondence dates the alterations of arrangement shown in

Eliot's *Quarry II*. Blackwood's letter prompted Lewes to suggest that part of book 2 on the Middlemarchers go into book 1. That way, they could be new friends in book 1 and become "old friends" by book 2. Eliot describes the plan on July 24: "Mr. Lewes has been saying that it may perhaps be well to take in a portion of Part II at the end of Part I" (5: 168). On September 7, Lewes affirmed the new plan: "We have added on to the end of part I that portion of part II which closes with the scene at the miserly uncle's—a capital bit to end with; and this new arrangement pitches the interest forward into part II and prepares the way for the people and for Dodo's absence from part II" (5: 184). She was not to reappear until April in book 3, which Lewes had called "Dorothea Married" in a letter to a Boston publisher, J R Osgood & Co., dated July 17 (5: 166).

Lewes's arrangement seems to have been fixed until early December. Langford objected to the arrangement after he read "Miss Brooke," but his letter of October 28 (5: 207) seems not to have instigated any alteration in the plan. The "capital bit," Fred's dilemma regarding the conditions Featherstone places on a promised gift of money, is the close of the book and should have been the readers' focal point for the coming two months. Contemporary reviews demonstrate that this was not the case. Neither Blackwood nor Eliot nor Lewes seems to have realized in September that they had solved one problem only to leave part of Blackwood's July complaint unheeded—readers might still be dissatisfied with a book 2 that omitted Dorothea, no matter how many other old friends it contained. In fact, few readers cared much about Rosamond and Lydgate, old Featherstone, or Fred, Mary, and his debt. They had had too little time to become interested in Fred's problems. What they wanted was more of Dorothea's story—which in book 1 has the wholeness of the conventional Victorian courtship-plus-marriage plot, while the obvious incompatibility of Dorothea and Casaubon provides the suspense to carry readers forward.

Reviewers and Eliot's personal friends shared Blackwood's anxiety. They were so interested in Dorothea that most barely acknowledged the final sixth of book 1. Barbara Bodichon's punctuation may (on a minor scale) resemble Flora Finching's, but her enthusiasm was widely shared: "I hear people say it is so witty amusing and lively so it is but all is shadowed by the coming misery to me. I can't help feeling it desperately. I am very sorry for the poor thing just as if she were alive and I want to stop her. She is like a child dancing into a quick sand on a sunny morning and I feel a sort of horror at your story as if it were all real and going on at this moment" (*Letters* 9: 33–34). Although Bodichon writes that some readers "only see wit character and liveliness, and call it light reading" (9: 34), the several reviews that were published before her letter of December 10 were, in fact, likewise attracted by Dorothea. Eliot and Lewes realized that the original plan to leave her out of book 2 and, hence, out of readers' sight for four months would be a mistake.

The idea that Eliot was unaffected by reviews is a commonplace. Gordon S. Haight notes that serial publication offered writers like Trollope and Dickens the opportunity to respond to criticism from the public while their novels were under way. "[W]ith George Eliot morbid diffidence deprived her of what might often have been helpful criticism. Knowing their disastrous effect, Lewes rarely let her see unfavourable comments" (*Biography* 366). His observation is supported by numerous letters. Two weeks before part 1 of *Middlemarch* appeared, Eliot tells Sara Hennell that she does not wish to hear reactions: "you will be one of the three exceptional people to whom we order 'Middlem[arc]h' to be sent. But do not write to me about it, because until a book has quite gone away from me and become entirely of the non-ego—gone thoroughly from the wine-press into the casks—I would rather not hear or see anything that is said about it" (*Letters* 5: 214–15). Lewes describes his "censorship" to John Blackwood in a letter about *Daniel Deronda* on February 1, 1876: "I take good care that nothing comes to her ears or eyes that would sound or read like objection, being so well aware of how she would lay hold of it as proof of her forebodings being justified." He does not "let her see even the enthusiastic criticisms" (6: 219; see also a letter to William Blackwood, 6: 218).

Eliot's and Lewes's journals, as well as other correspondence, modify these assertions by showing how Eliot valued and needed positive responses. For instance, the passages just quoted regarding *Daniel Deronda* are preceded by Lewes's statement that her spirits were "revived" by "Willie's [William Blackwood's] cheering news and assurances and the Times and other voices." Before *Middlemarch* appeared, Lewes on October 12 had described to John Blackwood "the stimulating effect of your letter yesterday respecting 'Miss Brooke.' She who needs encouragement so much . . . *relies* on you, and takes comfort from you to an extent you can hardly imagine" (*Letters* 5: 201). Another letter during *Middlemarch*'s serialization shows Eliot still thinking of Blackwood's preferences, as well as reviewer comments: "Since Mr. Lewes tells me that the Spectator

considers me the most melancholy of authors, it will perhaps be a welcome assurance to you that there is no unredeemed tragedy in the solution of the story" (*Letters* 5: 296). When George Simpson wrote Lewes
about the reception of book 1, Lewes asked William Blackwood on December 7 to "tell [Simpson] that although Mrs. Lewes is well pleased to
hear what he says of the reception from the press, she has seen *nothing* of
it—her practice being not to look at what is written about her. I have
only seen the Athenaeum and Daily News" (5: 224–25). She might not
have *read* reviews but she knew what they said.

This December 7 letter proposes a change in plan for the second half-
volume of the novel, specifically a rearrangement of books 2 and 3 to
allow material on Dorothea's wedding trip to be introduced in book 2
rather than holding it until book 3: "By this post I send you a batch of
m.s. which we should like set up in *slips* AT ONCE. We think that the
absence of Dodo and her husband from Part II will be felt injuriously and
that the part would be greatly strengthened in interest if some of her story
be introduced, and to make way for it some scenes must be transposed to
Part III" (*Letters* 5: 224). This is an alteration of Eliot's original plan "to
deal with the separate plots in long sections" (Beaty 53). Eliot had modified that plan to meet with Blackwood's objection that he found no old
friends in book 2; she introduced some of those friends into book 1. But
until December, she still planned to devote book 2 entirely to Lydgate-
Vincy-Garth matters; in book 3, she would return to the Casaubon wedding trip to Rome. Between Lewes's description of books 1 and 2, on
September 7, and this rearrangement on December 7, Lewes has other
correspondence about the publication of *Middlemarch*. An undated letter
in November asks William Blackwood about inserting a slip in book 1
stating, "Middlemarch Book II Old and Young will be published on the 1
February" (5: 219), but the December 7 plan seems to have been arrived
at suddenly.

Although George Eliot was no novice at serial publication, *Middlemarch* was her first multi-plot serial novel. Her plan to "deal with the
separate plots in long sections" is at variance with the established method
of Dickens and Thackeray. For instance, in such long multi-plot works as
Vanity Fair, *Bleak House*, and *Our Mutual Friend*, there is seldom an
entire part devoted to just one of the plot lines, especially in the first half
of the novel when characters and plot are still emerging. In *Scenes of
Clerical Life*, each novella-length story contains a single plot line and a
limited number of characters. In *Romola*, Tito and Romola are together

much less often than they are with others; yet despite chapters devoted to one or the other, their story does not break down into entirely separate plots until Romola's second departure from Florence. With *Middlemarch*, however, the separateness begins with the existence of two originally distinct novels. Even after they merged, Eliot evidently still thought of them as distinct entities and did not want to work with the small units of one or two chapters per plot that characterize many multi-plot works. Eliot attached two chapters of the "Middlemarch" story to the end of book 1 to prepare—she thought—for the single focus of book 2 and Dorothea's absence; her attention was on the wholeness of large segments rather than on the requirement of keeping parts of everyone's plot line in readers' sights from month to month.

Lewes had several commercial necessities in mind. Attaching the two "Middlemarch" chapters to book 1 introduces other plots and helps make up an independent half-volume of sufficient length: it "equalizes quantities better, though making part I rather longer than II which however is desirable" (*Letters* 5: 184). Consideration of length also led to a suggestion to William Blackwood: "Before setting up in type it will be well to have pages of the closely printed, less closely printed, and still less closely printed m.s. set up in order to form a calculation of quantity. The part must not *look thin* for 5/- and we must therefore see how many handsome pages it will make" (5: 185). Attempting to balance the conflicting demands of serial structure, artistry, and commercialism almost resulted in a major miscalculation that would have left Dorothea unobserved on her honeymoon for far too long. Lewes rectified this miscalculation in his December 7 letter, whose underlining and capitalization indicate his sense of urgency.

Before this letter, seven serial reviews of book 1 had already been published in England; their content makes this sudden, urgent desire for change intelligible.[4] These reviews were enthusiastic about Dorothea and almost entirely ignored the other plot strands that conclude the first installment. As a measure of readers' expectations (and hence of probable sales for subsequent books), reviews of part 1 were particularly important, especially given Mudie's attempt to "burke" the book (Haight, *Biography* 443). Lewes's sudden letter to John Blackwood requesting that the Dorothea material be set in type for book 2—just a few days after critics expressed their eagerness to hear more of Dorothea—can hardly be sheer coincidence.

Lewes had seen two of the seven published notices by that date, in the

Athenaeum and the *Daily News*. Three appeared in London dailies, the *Daily News* and the *Echo* (both Nov. 28), and the *Standard* (Dec. 2; this last was alluded to in a letter from Langford to John Blackwood on the day the review appeared [*Letters* 5: 224]). The *Manchester Examiner and Times* published a notice on November 29; and two influential weekly magazines, the *Athenaeum* and the *Examiner*, both covered book 1 on December 2, as did the fashionable *Illustrated London News*. Six of these seven reviews were so strongly interested in Dorothea that they ignored almost entirely the last two chapters portraying the Vincy family and other Middlemarchers. Neither the *Echo* nor the *Standard* even mentions the "Middlemarch" plot.[5]

Even if Lewes had not actually seen all of these reviews of book 1, it is likely that with his keen eye for business and proverbial "ear to the ground," he knew the content of some of them.[6] He could extrapolate from the ones he read or heard of that both public and press would not be content to wait until April for Dorothea's reappearance. To exclude her from the February half-volume would risk exasperating, if not losing, the audience for the novel—a loss that could be disastrous for any serial novel and was particularly problematic when the mode of publishing was an experiment.[7]

Three of the unindexed, unreprinted reviews (in the *Echo*, the *Standard*, and the *Illustrated London News*) concentrate on Dorothea and those close to her, to the exclusion or near-exclusion of the last part of book 1. The *Echo*'s focus is not surprising when one observes that the day before its review of book 1, it devoted nearly a half-column simply to quoting the prelude (Nov. 27, 1871; 5). The next day's review makes no mention at all of the last two-and-a-half chapters—nothing of the Middlemarchers who attend Dorothea's prenuptial party, which bridges the two main plots. The review opens by connecting the prelude with the incomplete state of the work: "Whether Miss Brooke will be a 'foundress of nothing' we do not yet know, for only the first volume of the work which treats of her is now before us." The reviewer expects to see Dorothea and Casaubon in the next installment: "the reader is allowed to see that the *next volume* is to work out the results of a marriage between a young woman in want of a mission, and a man with no heart but only conscientiousness, and of twice his wife's age" (emphasis added). The review is also prescient about future trouble from Will Ladislaw (a "young, untameable fellow, half artist, half Bohemian," about whom "our novel-reading instinct smells unmistakable mischief") in book 2—not the book

2 of the original plan, but book 2 as revised according to Lewes's directions on December 7. "The disturber of our peace is packed off to 'the Continent' before the volume closes, but then Casaubon and his wife will be at Rome in the honeymoon, and Casaubon will go studying and leave his wife at home. Our mind misgives on this point" (Nov. 28; 2). The "Middlemarch" plot is unremarked.

The *Standard* is equally uninterested in Rosamond and her family, never mentioning them at all. Its review of book 1 opens with Dorothea: "This volume is the portrait of a woman. Other persons revolve about her, but, so far, Miss Brooke is the central and sustaining figure of the story." And the review concludes with her. Near the end, the reviewer does mention that the novel gives a sketch of the "peculiar social life led in the Midland [*sic*]" and of "sundry incidental characters which, though their figures are only thrown for a moment upon the page, start into life instantly." But from the one illustrative example that follows, it is clear that the reviewer is still contemplating the story of Miss Brooke: "Such is young Ladislaw, a great relief from that awful Casaubon, who extends his honeymoon to Rome." The reviewer concludes with a none-too-subtle message to the author: "we here leave them to the reader, *to meet again* in the Italian capital, let us hope, *before long*" (emphasis added). Neither the *Echo* nor the *Standard* was reticent about dictating its expectations.

Sharing the *Echo* reviewer's dim view of Dorothea's future happiness, the *Illustrated London News* fears the outcome of her "rash union with an egotistical pedant and prig of twice her own age," when this "intense, enthusiastic, aspiring soul" discovers her "fatal mistake." The sensation-novel diction and expectations indicate a reviewer whose emotional involvement will demand more news of Dorothea—soon: "It will be a special mercy of Heaven if she then escape the peril of driving along upon a stream of passion to shipwreck of all that is good in her character; and this danger we expect to see exemplified in the future 'Books' of the Middlemarch story." Though acknowledging the whole "sober and decorous middle-class society of Tipton, Freshitt, and Lowick, neighbouring villages, and in the small manufacturing town of Middlemarch," the notice concentrates on "Mrs. Casaubon, as she must be called when next we meet her." The only mention of the Middlemarch plot comes in a list of characters about whom the two-month interval provides

> ample leisure . . . for critical essayists and conversational talkers to form a
> distinct conception of Dorothea and her sister Celia; of Mr. Brooke . . . , of

the Rev. Edward Casaubon, Sir James Chettam, Mrs. Cadwallader, the Vincy family, and Mr. Lydgate. . . . This task of applying ethical and psychological reflection, under the author's guidance, to the imagination of a set of persons as substantial as those met in real life, must be performed by a steady effort of thought. (534)

The *Illustrated London News* commented that the two-month interval was "a greater trial of the readers' faith and patience than the custom of giving successive portions of a tale in the monthly numbers of an ordinary magazine"—an articulation of Lewes's fear about this mode of publication. The reviewer's qualification only reemphasizes the need to include Dorothea in book 2: the method of publication "would be dangerous to the popular success of a story depending for its effect upon an artful combination of incidents and startling turns of fortune. But the interest of 'Miss Brooke,' and so far as we can yet perceive of 'Middlemarch,' is derived from a thorough study of individual characters." In this case, publication with long intervals between parts can be an advantage. The author "may have thought fit to allow an opportunity for the reader to obtain a deliberate comprehension of each of the characters before involving them in a fully-developed plot." After she and Lewes decided to modify the original plan and publish books 7 and 8 at monthly intervals, Eliot referred more modestly to the effect of the longer intervals: "the slow plan of publication has been of immense advantage . . . in deepening the impression" (*Letters* 5: 297).

Reviews in the *Daily News* and the *Athenaeum*, which Lewes read, are just as explicit in expecting Dorothea and Casaubon in the next installment. Taking a cue from the prelude, the *Daily News* discusses Dorothea's religious intensity, concluding that "the Miss Brooke who will hereafter spring out of the actions and speeches accredited to her by the subtle skill of the author . . . will be a far more vigorous, definite, and lifelike character, with all its humorous lights and whimsical failings, than could have been brought to accord with that first sketch in the poetic prelude" (5). Except for a final paragraph of "quiet epigrams and shrewd sayings" such as often appear in notices of Eliot's novels, the review ends as if Lewes's "capital bit" were Dorothea and Casaubon's departure: "We leave them, in this volume, just as they have started for Rome, to study MSS. in the Vatican; and, until February next, shall hear no more of them" (5). "February next" must have been an ominous phrase to the ears of the shrewd man of business who knew that Dorothea was not scheduled to appear until April. The only reference to the "Middle-march" story is among the epigrams: Rosamond Vincy "acted her own character so well 'that she did not know it to be precisely her own.'"

Like their counterparts in the dailies, the weekly periodicals view *Middlemarch* as the story of "Miss Brooke." The *Athenaeum* thinks "The tale is to centre round a woman's life, as did 'Romola,'" and wonders, "What will come of this sad sacrifice, it is not for us to even attempt to guess; but that no good can come of it, is only too clear." The review continues: "And so Dorothea and Mr. Casaubon start for a wedding tour to Rome; and the rest of the volume is taken up with the doings of the chief families in Middlemarch,—the Vincys, the Waules, the Bulstrodes, the Featherstones, and other *dramatis personae*, such as a country town affords." The placement of these other *dramatis personae* in the second clause of the sentence suggests they are an afterthought, something the reviewer mentions in order to be thorough (713). Almost another full page of anxiety about Dorothea contains only a brief return to the Middlemarchers: "But of the future of Rosamond Vincy, of Mr. Lydgate, of Fred, and of Mary Garth, all is at present uncertain, and we are left looking and waiting for the second part of 'Middlemarch' as eagerly as we waited and looked for the first" (714).

The other important weekly, the *Examiner*, is likewise preoccupied with Miss Brooke and ignores book 1's final chapters. "The main purpose of the work is indicated in its prelude. It is to set forth the temper and the fortunes of a modern Saint Theresa" (1192). A lengthy quotation from the prelude and a column-and-a-half discussion of Dorothea conclude as if the Middlemarchers were not part of the installment. Even Mr. Brooke, Celia, and Sir James are dismissed as "strictly subordinate to Miss Brooke, though each has a distinct and very lifelike individuality of his and her own" (1193). Like the *Illustrated London News*, this review comments that Eliot "is unkind in issuing her new novel . . . in parts," but adds that "her writings, and perhaps 'Middlemarch' especially, will bear this treatment better than most works" and readers can even profit from it:

> Every one who reads this first volume of her new book will close it with something like a feeling of irritation that he must wait two months for the next instalment; but he will gain by the delay if it causes him to look more carefully into the chapters he has at hand, and to get out of them all the meaning that he can. . . . George Eliot gives us just such insight into the

lifelike characters of the people of her story as, if we were clever enough, we might obtain for ourselves during a short stay in the mid-England district in which her scene is laid. . . . She will take us there again in good time. (1192)

The *Examiner*'s patience was no doubt gratifying, but whether that patience would have carried through until April for more insight on Dorothea is another question.

The lone dissenting voice among the notices published before December 7, and the one least likely to have reached Lewes, is in the *Manchester Examiner and Times*. This review begins with the writer's happy expectations derived from the announcement of the novel's subtitle, anticipating "Visions of old delights . . . the glorious landscapes of the midland counties; halls and cottages, with their stories of human passion, their tragedies and comedies; the contrasts of town and country" (3). But the serialization is a disappointment: "We had been counting on a four-volume novel, and we had not sufficient warrant for this hope." Comparing the novel's lack of plot with "Mrs. Gaskell's delightful picture of Cranford," the reviewer from Gaskell's hometown fills three finely-printed columns with commentary on and quotations about Miss Brooke. However, coming to the last chapters of the installment, he notes that "In this part of the book also we first hear of another pair of prospective lovers, in whom we are beginning to feel an interest, when the book comes to an end. Rosamond Vincy will interest the reader more than Miss Brooke, in spite of her weakness for old families, and her regret that her mother was an innkeeper's daughter" (3). Unfortunately, the reviewer does not explain precisely why readers will be more interested in Rosamond.[8] One can infer that his interest stems from a desire for the broad provincial canvas implied in the subtitle and an avowed affection for *Adam Bede* and *Silas Marner*, which gave sympathetic attention to a level of society below the county family.

With this vocal majority declaring for Dorothea, Lewes and Eliot must have realized that they could not ignore the wishes of her public. Obviously, the division they had planned would at best be a disappointment and, at worst, could result in a serious decline in sales. Lewes hastened to communicate to Blackwood the modification of their plan; and on December 31, Blackwood acknowledged the change as "an immense improvement" which "makes [book 2] most attractive" (5: 230). The change meant that the second book conformed to the established practice that a serial story provide readers with a bit of all the plot lines in each installment.

Book 2 demonstrates Eliot's awareness of the serial format's other requirements as well. Its opening connects it with the close of book 1, where Fred Vincy decides to tell his father of his debts in order to obtain a disclaimer from Bulstrode.[9] The first phrase makes the linkage, "In consequence of what he had heard from Fred"; the main clause carries the action forward, "Mr Vincy determined to speak with Mr Bulstrode in his private room at the Bank." The first six chapters develop the Middlemarch plot, with its own dramatic conclusion within the installment: at the end of chapter 18, Lydgate votes with the Bulstrode party for Mr. Tyke, presaging for the young doctor the very "pitiable infirmity of will" that he sees in Mr. Farebrother in the chapter's final sentence.

The final four chapters of book 2 are the ones originally planned for book 3. This alteration not only brought the heroine before the readers without the commercially risky interval of four months, but it also introduced a favorable (to reader interest) kind of danger: possible illicit love. Nothing could be further, so most reviewers said, from the titillation of the sensation novel than the discreet way in which Will Ladislaw's fascination with his cousin's wife is introduced—but at the same time, the fascination remains. If the honeymoon reveals to readers as well as to Dorothea that something is already amiss, Will provides a diversion; and readers were quick to anticipate that the aging and ill Casaubon could be removed from the plot with no disturbance to verisimilitude. Even before Casaubon's fit in book 3, the *Echo* notes book 2's visit by "the young, the handsome, the ardent Will Ladislaw" to "this ill-assorted couple" and asks, "Will the benevolently-disposed reader wish that Providence should remove Mr. Casaubon?" (Jan. 30: 2). The fact that the subtitle of the next book, "Waiting for Death," was announced in advance meant that Victorian readers could and did speculate hopefully that the death would be Casaubon's. Once again, Blackwood is Eliot's typical reader reacting to parts as he receives them: in his first, enthusiastic response to book 3 he told Eliot, "The General will swear at you for not disposing of Casaubon in that fit" (*Letters* 5: 235).[10] These hopes are premature, but the conclusion is satisfying nonetheless because it heightens the pathos of Dorothea's plight and offers a hint of love in her future.

Book 3 opens with a shift from Dorothea-Ladislaw to an entirely different plot line. The reminder to readers, "Fred Vincy, *we have seen*, had a debt on his mind" (emphasis added), marks the shift from book 2 to book 3, but it originated as a transition within book 2. Before the sudden rearrangement of books 2 and 3, the Lydgate material up to Tyke's election would have been followed immediately by a return to Fred and his debt in chapter 19 (see Kitchel 47). When the chapters on Dorothea's life in Rome were shifted to book 2, the transition came to serve as a bridge between books instead of between different subplots within a book. Book 3's first five and final three chapters develop the Middlemarch plot, with only three central chapters on Dorothea and Casaubon. They are an eventful three, however, in extending readers' understanding of Dorothea's disillusionment and their expectation of, or hope for, her release through Casaubon's death. The ending focuses expectations more precisely than did either of the first two closures. At the end of book 1, readers are only mildly interested in the fortunes of Fred Vincy, and the Ladislaw-Dorothea connection is but a vague hint at the end of book 2. Book 3, however, concludes with a vivid picture of the miser Featherstone dead in his bed, clutching the key to his moneybox. The image is dramatic, and the mystery posed for book 4 to resolve is definite. Who will get old Featherstone's money? More subtly, the narrative asks readers to ponder for two months what difference Mary Garth's refusal to compromise her principles will make in the fortunes of Fred Vincy. Victorian readers were as interested in money as in love, and other serialized novels of the period, such as *Our Mutual Friend*, had dramatized to appreciative audiences the theme of the miser and his several wills. Eliot and Lewes were reading one of them, Trollope's *Eustace Diamonds*, as it appeared in the *Fortnightly* from July 1871 to February 1873.[11] In addition, contemporary newspapers often recounted stories of wills discovered. And the most notable inheritance case of the period, perhaps of the century, coincided with the composition and publication of *Middlemarch*.

Thousands of column inches in newspapers of the early 1870s were devoted to a real-life drama centering on inheritance: the two trials and the intervening peregrinations of the "Tichborne Claimant." The civil trial of the man who claimed to be Sir Roger Charles Tichborne, heir to a Hampshire estate and baronetcy, was under way in the very months that readers received their first two installments of *Middlemarch*. Readers thus encountered *Middlemarch* not only in the literary context provided by treatments of inheritance in Dickens, Trollope, and others, but a highly publicized case from the courts. Like many of their contemporaries, Eliot and Lewes were fascinated by the Tichborne trial. In her correspondence, she discusses it side by side with her decisions about the structure of books 3 and 4.

The Tichborne Claimant's civil trial had begun in May 1871, increasing the extraordinary public interest that started when he first appeared in England in 1866. Lewes recorded his interest in the trial in his diary as early as autumn 1871, while Eliot was writing and revising part 3. In the abbreviated fashion common to his diaries, he notes either "Tichborne" or "Tichborne Case" on November 21, 22, and 24; the November 22 entry is part of a list of items worked on, which also includes "Middlemarch proofs" (GHL Diary). Eliot, too, followed it in the press,[12] despite the demands of writing *Middlemarch* and worrying about her health.[13] She and Lewes even attended the January 17 session. Lewes records this and the trial's abrupt termination alongside entries on *Middlemarch*: "Tichborne case suddenly decided by the jury declaring itself satisfied. Read proofs of 'Middlemarch' Book IV" (GHL Diary, Mar. 6, 1872). Eliot's correspondence contains a similar juxtaposition. The "experience [of attending on January 17 was] of great interest to me," she wrote Blackwood, but "Unhappily Mr. Lewes got ill with the bad air, and we had to come away after the third hour of Coleridge's speaking [against the Claimant]." She begins this letter by thanking him for "your encouraging impressions on reading the Third Book."

Just before the paragraph on the Tichborne trial, she discusses the serial structure of books 3 and 4: "Mr. Lewes is much satisfied with the Fourth Book, which opens with the continuation of the Featherstone drama. I wanted for the sake of quantity, to add a chapter to the Third Book, instead of opening the Fourth with it. But Mr. Lewes objects on the ground of effectiveness" (5: 236–37). Her apprehensions regarding length recur on February 21: "It has caused me some uneasiness that the Third Part is two sheets less than the First. But Mr. Lewes insisted that the death of old Featherstone was the right point to pause at" (5: 249). Not all readers agreed. Even four years later, the reviewer for the *Athenaeum* remembers this pause as artificial in contrast to book 1 of *Daniel Deronda*: "whether we were right or no in thinking that in 'Middlemarch' the third part ended with a doubt specially raised in order to end the part with an excitement, there is no such artifice in 'The Spoiled Child'" (Jan. 29, 1876; 160). If the question of Featherstone's wills was not *introduced* solely as an enticement to readers, its placement at the end of book 3 occurred because Lewes recognized an effective serial break.

Blackwood, on March 13, connects Featherstone's surprise legatee, Joshua Rigg (in book 4) with the Tichborne Claimant: "The Frog-faced gentleman becomes at once a thing of flesh and blood as much as the Tichborne Claimant" (5: 255). Eliot responds the next day, "I hope you were as glad as I was at the ending of the Tichborne case" (5: 257). The "serial" drama of the Tichborne matter was to last even longer than the serialization of *Middlemarch*. Eliot and Blackwood's correspondence continues to allude to it until it was more or less settled with the Claimant's conviction for perjury in 1874 and his sentence to fourteen years' imprisonment.[14]

Whether Eliot also saw a link between the Claimant and Joshua Rigg, book 3's timing could not have coincided better with public interest in inheritance, which was stirred up daily by the final events of Tichborne's civil trial. The trial had been broken off in early March when the jury declared it had heard enough evidence to come to a conclusion. In April, "a Grand Jury returned a true bill against the Claimant" for perjury (Woodruff 215–17). He was imprisoned in Newgate from March 7 to April 26. Press coverage kept public interest at a high pitch: "The news that the jury had spoken and that the judge had committed the Claimant to prison was the signal for leading articles in almost every paper, rejoicing at the verdict and denouncing the Claimant. A number of the dailies, such as *The Times*, the *Morning Post* and the *Pall Mall Gazette*, called for the prosecution of the Claimant's fellow conspirators" (Woodruff 218). The Claimant continued his story from prison. On March 23, the *Daily Telegraph* published an interview with him detailing his grim prison life. The *Standard* published a letter on March 25.[15] By the appearance of book 4 of *Middlemarch*, the Claimant had been released on bail and was touring the countryside enlisting support from tenants on the Tichborne estate as well as from the working classes in the large cities—who identified with him whether he was the man he claimed to be or a Wapping butcher named Arthur Orton. For many, the civil trial failed to resolve the question as decisively as it seems to have done for Blackwood and Eliot.[16]

The ending of *Middlemarch*, book 3, left exciting questions of inheritance poised for two months in readers' minds side by side with the question of the true identification of the Tichborne Claimant. The opening of book 4 returns to the inheritance question by placing readers as onlookers at Featherstone's funeral, first with the narrator, then with Dorothea and the other county personages viewing it from a window at Lowick Manor. Finally, the viewpoint joins the "Christian Carnivora" who attend the church service and the reading of the will. Earlier, there had been minor points of contiguity like the prenuptial dinner party and Lydgate's medical attendance on Casaubon; but Featherstone's funeral combines in a more extended way the "Miss Brooke" and the "Middlemarch" plots. As readers view the scene with Mrs. Cadwallader, the Chettams, and Dorothea, and share the potential legatees' suspense about Featherstone's will, their attention is divided: concern for Dorothea increases in the first chapter with Mr. Brooke's news that Will Ladislaw has arrived at Tipton Grange, while suspense over the reading of the will is held for the second chapter.

Even though she had three parts written before book 1 was issued, with book 4 Eliot began to feel again the pressures of serialization. A letter dated November 16, 1871, from Lewes to John H. Balfour Browne, suggests the stress from an extended illness that put Eliot behind schedule: "Mrs. Lewes is just now so absorbed and exhausted by work that I relieve her of all correspondence when practicable" (*Letters* 9: 31). Writing to Alexander Main on November 29, Lewes is more optimistic: "Mrs. Lewes continues well and is vigorously at work again" (5: 218). But her journal for December 1 records: "I ought by this time to have finished the fourth part, but an illness which began sometime after our return from Haslemere [in early September] has robbed me of two months." Her next entry suggests little improvement: "My health has been very troublesome during the last three weeks, and I can get on but tardily. Even now, I am only at p. 227 of my fourth Part. But I have been also retarded by construction which, once done, serves as good wheels to progress" (GE Journal, Dec. 20). She wrote a little more rapidly in December and January, but "at a pace which would scarcely keep her up with the printers if bimonthly parts were to appear" (Beaty 60). Her next entries, January 30 and May 8, show her continuing consciousness of deadlines. In the latter, she records her "life having been a swamp of illness" lately. "In consequence of this incessant interruption almost every week having been half-nullified for me so far as my work has been concerned, I have only finished the Fifth Book, and have still three Books to write—equal to a large volume and a half" (GE Journal). Fortunately, her pace quickened after she detailed the plan for the whole novel in May and June, and she was prepared not only to meet the bimonthly deadline but to conclude with three monthly parts. On July 13, Lewes asked Blackwood, "What think you of publishing VII and VIII at monthly intervals so as to have the whole work completed for December?" (*Letters* 5: 290).

Jerome Beaty's examination of the manuscript shows that she originally planned to end book 4 with chapter 41's foreboding, as Raffles wedges the paper bearing Bulstrode's name between his flask and its cover. However, in order to equalize the parts better (Beaty 49), Eliot decided to make chapter 42 the final one in book 4. Its transitional devices are characteristic of a new installment (Beaty 62), but they can also be used to bridge two plots within an installment. Without Beaty's manuscript evidence and the fact that this one chapter sits rather "alone" at the end of book 4, the transition could be perceived simply as internal—like chapter 37's long opening narrative passage, which effects the transition from the affairs of the Vincys to those of Mr. Brooke and his kin. In the early books particularly, shifts from one plot line to a distinct and separate other one resemble the start of a separate book. Hence, chapter 37 uses the reference to Mr. Vincy, carried over from chapter 36, to segue into references to the death of George IV and other national events. These lead in turn to Mr. Brooke's plans to stand in the coming election. In chapter 42, the preceding passage of time is marked by a reference to Lydgate's wedding-journey, before Casaubon's fears for his health become the focal point.

The inclusion of chapter 42 in book 4 has other advantages, too. It returns readers' attention to the Dorothea-Casaubon plot, especially to Casaubon's illness, and creates new sympathy for him, as he seems to care about his young wife, however tardily and momentarily. Placing their moment of reconciliation at a point of emphasis—the conclusion of an installment—leaves readers with a more positive image of Casaubon, adds complexity to his character, and helps distance him from the stereotype of the jealous elderly husband whose cuckolding had entertained readers since Chaucer's time.[17] This arrangement also gives symmetry and wholeness to the part, the reconciliation resolving their estrangement in the opening of book 4.

One of the strengths of the serial endings in *Middlemarch* is the way in which they, in turn, emphasize the several plots. The originally planned ending to book 4 offered exciting possibilities for future installments. Raffles' possession of Bulstrode's letter bodes ill for the puritanical banker, and the final scene in chapter 41 stimulates readers' interest in further developments. But Eliot also closes book 5 with the Raffles-Bulstrode connection; to have devoted two consecutive endings to it would have placed undue emphasis on that one plot among the several that are fully under way at this point.[18] Since, as Beaty shows (68–69), Eliot had planned book 5 by the time she decided to include chapter 42 in book 4, it is possible that she weighed considerations of structure as well as length to determine the altered arrangement.

Though originally the second chapter in an installment that began with chapter 42, the new opening to book 5—chapter 43—effectively bridges the parts. Like most *Middlemarch* openings, it begins with the narrator's voice; the second sentence places the new chapter in time: "Two days after that scene in the Yew-Tree walk." The obliqueness of this reference to the scene between Dorothea and Casaubon midway through chapter 42 may have made it difficult for some readers two months later to recall instantly what had occurred "in the Yew-Tree walk." But the long opening paragraph brings the general situation, particularly Casaubon's deteriorating health and Dorothea's internal struggle, fully into view once again. The original plan for chapter 42 to open the new installment may have been part of Eliot's continued attempt to develop relatively long sections on a single plot; but with chapter 42's detachment from book 5, the Dorothea section there includes only two chapters as the plots begin to be more fully interwoven. When Dorothea finds Will at the Lydgates, the personal is added to the professional intermingling of their lives. The plot lines are further interwoven when Mr. Farebrother accepts the Lowick living.

With so many plot lines under way by book 5, Eliot could no longer devote long segments to a single one. The Lydgate-Rosamond plot is advanced in only one portentous chapter (45) in which Lydgate is increasingly in conflict with the prejudices of the townspeople, as well as those of his wife, who suggests that his profession is not a "nice" one. In the Dorothea-Casaubon plot, to the undoubted satisfaction of readers who had expressed their wishes on the matter, this installment releases Dorothea from her loveless marriage. Its conclusion establishes further links, when Ladislaw's heritage is connected with both Raffles and Bulstrode. The ending offers both symmetry and suspense. Raffles' exclamation, "Ladislaw!", recalls the latter's presence in Lydgate's house at the beginning of the part, and it introduces a new mystery about him at the very time others seek to blacken his name and Dorothea begins to understand her feelings.

The opening to book 6, chapter 54, consciously connects the preceding book and the present one more than any other installment opening in *Middlemarch*. "By that delightful morning when the hayricks at Stone Court were scenting the air quite impartially, as if Mr Raffles had been a guest worthy of finest incense, Dorothea had again taken up her abode at Lowick Manor" (523). The reference is made only to remind readers of the conclusion to the preceding part—Raffles' return to Stone Court and a mysterious connection between Ladislaw and Bulstrode's unsavory past. After the first sentence, the chapter concentrates entirely on Dorothea's widowhood and does not mention Raffles and Bulstrode. As Dorothea defies the Chettams and Cadwalladers and returns to Lowick alone, her independence promises new developments for her relationship with Ladislaw despite his departure at the end.

By book 6, the several plot lines are thoroughly interwoven. Not only do Will and Mr. Brooke frequent the homes and public places of *Middlemarch*, but Mr. Farebrother lives at Lowick Parsonage and Lydgate is Dorothea's medical attendant. Farebrother receives Mary Garth and Fred Vincy as visitors, and Mr. Garth supervises repairs at Lowick, Freshitt, and Tipton. The contrast is apparent if one compares the chapter-by-chapter contents of book 2 with those of book 6.

Book 2.

Chapter 13. Bulstrode confers with Lydgate on medical matters and with Mr. Vincy on Fred's letter for Featherstone.

Chapter 14. Fred takes the letter to Featherstone, tries to get encouragement from Mary Garth; Lydgate arrives.

Chapter 15. Flashback to Lydgate's background.

Chapter 16. Lydgate at the Vincys, romantic beginnings with Rosamond, question of Tyke's or Farebrother's appointment.

Chapter 17. Lydgate visits Farebrother.

Chapter 18. Lydgate votes for Tyke.

Chapter 19. Will sees Dorothea at the Vatican.

Chapter 20. Dorothea and Casaubon in Rome apartments, miserable.

Chapter 21. Will visits Dorothea.

Chapter 22. Will takes Dorothea and Casaubon on tour of artists' studios. Casaubon jealous.

Book 6.

Chapter 54. Dorothea returns to Lowick. Will bids farewell.

Chapter 55. Dorothea visits Freshitt. Her friends discuss possible suitors.

Chapter 56. Opens with mention of Dorothea's confidence in Caleb Garth. Shifts to Garth's encounter with railway opponents, and his hiring of Fred.

Chapter 57. Fred calls on Mrs. Garth. Surprised to hear of Farebrother's interest in Mary. Calls at Lowick Parsonage.

What is striking is not only the intermingling, which Victorian readers expected by the later parts of a multi-plot novel, but the way in which, by book 6, Eliot has become skilled in framing her story as a whole. In book 2, reversing the order in book 1, one large section is entirely devoted to the Middlemarchers, then one section is devoted to the Casaubons. The ponderous historical framework at the beginning of chapter 19 reveals Eliot's effort to bridge these two plots. Once she has joined the two novels and begins to write them as one, the characters' lives become linked and her "bridges" are more natural. She now pays more attention to the wholeness of each installment. Starting with her alteration of book 4, which meant that both opening and closing focused on the Casaubon estrangement, she moves in a circular pattern wherein the last chapter recalls the first. In book 6, Will begins by taking leave of Dorothea; at the end he comes again to say good-bye, and this time he actually leaves Middlemarch.

This closure represents a change from her original plan. Eliot describes her plan for the ending of book 6 on page 31 of her *Middlemarch Quarry II*: "Part VI ends with the Farebrothers telling Dorothea of Will's sudden departure" (Kitchel 58). As Kitchel notes, Eliot altered this so that "Will's departure . . . is dramatically presented, not narrated by the Farebrother family" (17). The published arrangement is not only more dramatic, it also increases the pathos of Will's lot in life and the sense of futility in their love; the reader, from the perspective of Dorothea in the carriage, first sees Will trudging along the road with his portfolio under his arm, and then, with Will, watches "the carriage [grow] smaller in the distance." The physical distance of Will and Dorothea at Book 6's close is dramatic and suspenseful and also functions as a metaphor for the social distance between them.

With the Dorothea-Ladislaw plot suspended for the moment, book 7 opens with two issues that occupy most of it: Bulstrode's past misdeeds and Lydgate's failing medical practice. The shift is abrupt and bears no sign of any transition recalling the close of book 6. Furthermore, book 7's opening is the only one not in the narrator's voice. The speaker is Mr. Toller, a minor character, whose subject is the fortunes of Lydgate and his wife. Why Eliot introduced their difficulties through this lengthy dinner-party dialogue is difficult to say. There is no evidence that this chapter was originally intended to be an "internal" one in the installment, nor does the fact that this is the first installment to appear at less than a two-month interval provide a rationale. In book 8, a month later, her usual technique of narrative summary resumes. Whatever the reason, the dramatic opening sets Lydgate's troubles in the context of Middlemarch gossip, which provides much of the drama in the installment. Neither malefactor, Rosamond nor Bulstrode, fears legal punishment. Their diminished stature in the eyes of their fellow townspeople is what motivates them; and it is gossip, not the law, that destroys Bulstrode and Lydgate.[19] Dramatically, then, the book's opening and its close, which also uses the unusual feature of dialogue, point to a central theme—the role of speech in the fortunes of the characters. As with books 4 to 6, the part achieves internal wholeness. Not only is the dialogic structure repeated at book 7's beginning and end, but the subject of the dialogue is also echoed. Toller's opening statement intimates, with ill-concealed pleasure, the decline in Lydgate's practice. Dorothea's closing words enthusiastically urge Lydgate's friends to "'find out the truth and clear him!'" The speakers' attitudes sharply contrast, but their subject is the same: Lydgate's medical/scientific, and apparently also moral, failure.

Here, too, Eliot altered the plan noted in her *Quarry II*, which records under "How to End the Parts": "VII. Ends with Lydgate's bribe [*written in above*: outpouring] to Dorothea" (Kitchel 58). This ending depended on other differences, described on the preceding page of the *Quarry*. Apparently, Eliot's original plan was to depict the Dorothea-Will-Rosamond triangle's difficulty and resolution *before* Lydgate borrows from Bulstrode and Raffles returns:

14 Scene of anger & jealousy between Will & Dorothea, ending in her avowal of love & resolve not to marry him[.]

15 Will goes to Rosamond & reproaches her with having ruined his happiness.

16 Dorothea, wrought on by compassion, goes to Rosamond, & so moves her that R. tells D. how Will has been true.

17 Meeting & final reconciliation of Will & Dorothea.
18 Dorothea declares to Sir James her intention to marry Will[.]
19 Lydgate in difficulties has half made up his mind to ask Dorothea for aid, & learns that she is going to marry Will.
20 Raffles comes back. Terror of Bulstrode. Disclosures.
21 Raffles' death. Bulstrode gives Lydgate £1000.
22 Scandal in Middlemarch. Blight on Lydgate & Bulstrode[.] (Kitchel 58)

To resolve the Dorothea plot with so much remaining in Lydgate's story would have reduced interest in book 8 and defied the custom of keeping the various plots interwoven and proceeding at a similar pace. The published arrangement reserves the Will-Dorothea reconciliation for book 8, where it comes about through Dorothea's compassionate attempts to help first Lydgate and then Rosamond. The ending also puts greater emphasis on Dorothea's active role in prompting Lydgate's outpouring about the circumstances surrounding the bribe. Nemesis has already come to Bulstrode, and the happy resolution of Fred and Mary's affairs is hinted strongly in chapter 68. The suspense at the end of book 7 centers, then, on how Dorothea will accomplish her plan to clear Lydgate and how she will reconcile with Will.

Book 8 opens with a link to the prelude as well as to the preceding installment. Since this is the final installment, its wholeness as a part gives way to the wholeness of the entire work. "Dorothea's impetuous generosity," which receives a rapid and "melancholy check," resembles the enthusiasm of the Saint Theresa of the prelude who sets out to do great things, albeit a little prematurely. Dorothea's enthusiastic belief in Lydgate in book 8 also reminds readers of her tendency (in book 1) to credit Casaubon with virtues he does not have. Her generosity is, however, better placed this time, and she triumphs over the worldly sagacity of her counselors. She also defies her own pride and her friends' wisdom by reaching out to Will and abandoning her fortune in favor of happiness. The opening reference to "impetuous generosity" is appropriate thematically for both the book and the entire novel. And the finale carries readers back both to the prelude and to chapter 72, with which book 8 begins.

Although he momentarily suggested opening book 8 with the start of chapter 74, Blackwood agreed. In sending his enthusiastic reaction to book 8, which he read the morning after it arrived "instead of going to Church with the rest of the family," Blackwood recalls that "Lewes said something about changing the division of the Books."[20] He suggests, "There might be a break at page 194, which would make Book 8 begin with 'In Middlemarch a wife could not remain long'" (chapter 74). By the time he arrived at his postscript, however, Blackwood had changed his mind: "On thinking over the division of the Books I feel that Dorothea's declaration of standing by Lydgate is so good an opening for what is to be expected in the last book that it is the most appropriate finish for Book 7, so I would not mind making the one Book thin and the other thick" (*Letters* 5: 307). Including the two short chapters (72 and 73) in book 7 would have equalized the quantity better; as they were published, book 7 has 174 pages and book 8, 193. However, the end of chapter 73 would have been a dull and anticlimactic installment conclusion, and Blackwood apparently saw this even as he wrote his letter.

Once Eliot had combined the two initially separate novels, she was able to use the length provided by half-volumes to shape her installments carefully. Her contemporaries had three or four chapters to work with in each installment of the twenty-part serial, and often fewer in magazine installments, but the nine to fifteen chapters in each book of *Middlemarch* allowed Eliot more latitude to interconnect her plots to achieve wholeness. At the same time, the suspense of her endings pitched the plot forward and enticed readers to purchase the next part.

This experiment was an artistic tour de force in the structuring of serial parts and a major financial and critical success as well. After book 6 appeared, the *Leeds Mercury* reported in its "Literary Arts Gossip" column that "This mode of publication has been recommended to the acceptance of the noble [Lord Lyttelton, who was working on a 'new romance'] by the success attending the experiment made by George Elliot [*sic*]." This newspaper also denied that the change to monthly publication meant "that the new mode of publication has not realised expectations." This is a mistaken notion, the paper declares:

> The alteration decided upon with respect to the issue of the concluding parts, has been dictated by simple expediency. Had the original conditions been strictly carried out, the book would not have been completed till February, which as far as the literary market is concerned, may be regarded as the middle of the publishing season. By accelerating the issue of the last two parts, however, the publishers will be able to sell the book in its complete form at Christmas. (Oct. 10, 1872: 3)

Lewes had the season in mind in proposing monthly publication to Blackwood as early as July 17, 1872: "Christmas would then have the whole world of Middlemarch to enjoy" (*Letters* 5: 290).

The whole world was not only reading *Middlemarch*, but talking and writing about it to each other, to Eliot, and to the rest of the world in newspaper critiques. Eliot's own letters recount humorous incidents like one response to Bulstrode: "Mrs Merridew, having lain awake all night from compassion for Bulstrode, said, 'Poor, dear creature, after he had done so much for that wretch, sitting up at night and attending on him! and I don't believe it was the brandy that killed him: and what is to become of Bulstrode now,—he has nobody left but Christ!'" (5: 343; also related by Lewes to Alexander Main, 5: 337). Lewes also told Blackwood of the West End clergyman who saw in Bulstrode "the awful dissection of a guilty conscience" (5: 333). Whatever their individual conclusions, "'Everybody,'" Lewes wrote on November 25, 1872, "seems greatly agog as to how *Middlemarch* will end and Mrs. Lewes feels perfectly sure that everybody will be disappointed" (5: 333). Readers were not, however, disappointed. During the twelve months of serialization, they had become involved in the several strands of the plot, as this attention to Bulstrode demonstrates. Most welcomed the generally optimistic ending, even if there were a few who held out for a marriage between Dorothea and Lydgate as the best way to bring the two major plot lines—the county families and the Middlemarchers—together.

Eliot's admiring public had to wait more than three years for her next novel, also an eight half-volume serial, *Daniel Deronda*; instead of two main plots gradually drawn together, many saw it as a single plot that gradually broke into two.

6

Daniel Deronda, "No Ordinary Love Story or Mechanical Web": The Tale of Two Plots

Iꜰ *MIDDLEMARCH* BEGAN as two books later unified into one that exhibits traces of its dual origin, *Daniel Deronda*'s serial development led some of its first readers to regard it as one book that becomes two. The serial structure, of course, is not solely responsible for this perception; F. R. Leavis's famous division of *Deronda* into "good" and "bad" halves was not based on installment reading. But the perception of dualism began during the novel's serial publication when, after initial enthusiasm, serial readers found their attention gradually removed from Gwendolen's story by the increasingly prominent "Jewish plot." Many were disappointed that the concluding installment failed to unite Gwendolen and Deronda. Furthermore, Deronda's story, especially in the last four books, was not the story of English life that prepublication advertisements and earlier parts had encouraged readers to anticipate.

With Lewes's approval, Blackwood had advertised the novel as a tale of modern English life. On November 17, 1875, he asked Lewes whether they "should let loose any gossiping paragraphs." Such paragraphs were particularly desirable because "the name Daniel Deronda does not give the idea of such a thorough picture of English life [and so] we had better put [the public] on the right and most popular scent" (*Letters* 6: 186).[1] For Blackwood and for many other readers, *English* life was the *most popular* scent, and he could not know in November that it was not exactly the *right* one. Fearing that the title would obscure this desirable feature in the early books, he was not aware how much the unwritten second half would turn on the "Jewish" plot. By the time he received the later books, Blackwood had no option but to encourage Eliot to follow her own design and hope she would carry her readers with her.

English readers, however, were not entirely ready to be carried away by a strong Jewish interest, which many did not regard as part of "modern English life." As installments began to devote more time to Deronda's search for Mirah's family and his own heritage, contemporary reviews record the public's growing disillusionment. As the serial parts of *Middlemarch* progressed, Eliot intermingled plots and characters more skillfully. But in *Daniel Deronda*, she is not as successful in developing both stories in order to make them, in later installments, increasingly interconnected. Gwendolen disappears from large segments of the last four books, and even in books 7 and 8, where her life is most dramatically intertwined with Deronda's, their individual stories are still dominant. Unlike the world of *Middlemarch*, in which merchants, bankers, wealthy farmers, and county families are part of a single community, the worlds of the Jewish inhabitants of London and of the minor aristocracy are bridged only tenuously and momentarily by the figure of Deronda. The two social groups are hardly aware of each other's existence. Real readers seem to have been similarly separate. The portions of the later books devoted to the development of the Jewish story evoked some decidedly negative responses, betraying reader indifference and even outright hostility to Jews.[2]

Division of the novel into two distinct halves was contrary to Eliot's intention. On October 2, 1876, with serialization completed, she wrote Barbara Bodichon: "I meant everything in the novel to be related to everything else there" (6: 290). But long before that, she had feared that readers would not agree, and even Lewes shared her doubts. On December 1, 1875, he gave Blackwood one of his customary hints: "Your admiration is very cheering to her, and I must add that your taking so heartily to the Jewish scenes is particularly gratifying to me, for I have sometimes shared her doubts on whether people would sufficiently sympathize with that element in the story" (6: 196).

Apart from the general diffidence that always plagued her, this anxiety about the reception of the Jewish plot seems to have been the chief problem Eliot faced in the course of serialization. Lewes and Blackwood quickly agreed about how to present the work, and the parts were completed well in advance of publication. Since *Adam Bede*, she had "been continually having proposals from the proprietors or editors of periodicals but . . . always declined them, except in the case of 'Romola,'" Eliot writes on October 20, 1875, to Mrs. Peter Alfred Taylor, whose husband had just become editor of the *Examiner*. However, even if she "could gain more by splitting my writing into small parts, I would not do it, because the effect would be injurious as a matter of art" (6: 179 and 179n2). Two days before, Blackwood had written to confirm the start of *Deronda* in February, using the *Middlemarch* format: "As to form I do not think we can do better than follow *Middlemarch* only making the publication monthly as the audience are more ready" (*Letters* 6: 178).[3]

More than half the book was written before publication began. On November 15, Eliot "read the Mordecai Chapter of Deronda" to Lewes, and three days later they "Walked on Blackfriars Bridge watching [the] sunset" (GHL Diary, Nov. 15 and 18). (The entire book 5 is called "Mordecai," but Lewes's "Mordecai Chapter" probably refers only to the final chapter, 40, in which Mordecai is the principal focus.) On the same day book 1 appeared, February 1, Lewes sent "Part 6 for printers to begin on; part 7 [he adds] will follow in a few days" (6: 219). Illness and a busy social life combined to render this prediction slightly premature. Book 7 was mailed to Blackwood on April 10 (*Letters* 6: 237), and book 8 was completed June 8 (GHL Diary). Even so, Eliot's early start meant that deadline pressures were never as formidable with *Deronda* as with her prior serials.

Having more than half the work written before publication allowed Eliot to spend more time pondering the serial breaks, a mixed blessing at best. Letters record her uncertainty about how to divide the parts, and Blackwood and Lewes were more obviously involved, the letters suggest, than with the division of her other serial novels.[4] As with *Middlemarch*, size was one consideration, especially in the division of the early books. When the "four first monthly parts [were] ready for travelling," Eliot told Blackwood, "I am still a little uncertain about the way the quantities will turn out, but I have divided these two volumes to the best of my calculation. I found that the first volume—i.e. the first two parts—would turn out enormously thick on my first plan of division, and have therefore revised the arrangement" (*Letters* 6: 172). By the date of this letter, October 10, she had already altered her plans for dividing books 1 and 2. Her original plan had "made the two first parts considerably longer— Pt. I ending at the end of the Archery Ball, and Part II at the end of Mirah's story," she wrote Blackwood on November 10. However, "I found that by this arrangement, the first part would be more than 220 pp. and the second at least 190—making the 1st vol. tremendously thick" (*Letters* 6: 181). Under the discarded plan, book 1 would have concluded at the end of chapter 11 (as published); in fact, the chapters that were published as 10 and 11 were originally a single chapter. In the manuscript, the last lines of chapter 10 read "The incident had no suddenness for Gwendolen; she was prepared for it to happen at any moment; in fact it was already stale in her imagination. But"; the word "But" is at the end of the page, and the next page continues with Grandcourt's introduction. The decision to interrupt the narrative flow and start a new chapter and book was obviously made after the text on these pages had been written. When Eliot decided to introduce chapter and installment breaks at this point, she added at the top of the second of these pages the heading, "Chapter XI," and the notation in the upper left-hand corner, "For motto, See Back." She was able to squeeze the chapter number into the unruled space at the top of the page, but there was no room for the motto, which had to be entered on the back of the sheet, which was usually left blank.

The manuscript also shows alterations that help readers of book 2 pick up the story line again after a month's hiatus.[5] The top ruled line of the manuscript originally read, "But when Lord Brackenshaw moved aside a little for Grandcourt to come forward and she felt herself face to face." This would have been sufficient to continue the flow of the story within a chapter but, as the start of a new chapter and new installment, it provided too little context and none of those important reminders to readers of "where we were,"—necessary after a month's break. To supply the transition, in the space above the ruled lines, Eliot repeats the phrase "Mr. Grandcourt's wish to be introduced" above "But when Lord Brackenshaw." In addition, she drew a line through "for Grandcourt to come forward" on the first two ruled lines of the page, and wrote over them "for the prefigured stranger to come forward," which reminds book 2's readers that they, as well as Gwendolen, are meeting the stranger Grandcourt for the first time. She also repeats the phrase "had no suddenness for Gwendolen," which was part of a sentence at the end of book 1 in the manuscript (already quoted) but later deleted. But she repeats only the first clause in the new part; she did not transfer the second, with the narrator looking into Gwendolen's mind, and deleted it from the end of chapter 10 before publication. By the end of book 1, Gwendolen already struck some reviewers as a trifle too blasé and self-centered, and this phrase, in the book's final line, would have increased that impression. Instead, readers and Gwendolen are both left with the question, "Will you allow me to introduce Mr Mallinger Grandcourt?" There is no hint that either will find the introduction "stale," as dramatic plot supersedes characterization at the end of book 1.

Dramatically, the decision to close book 1 just before Gwendolen's long-anticipated introduction to Grandcourt was an excellent one. Readers have *heard* much, but *seen* nothing of this object of marital speculation by the families at Quetcham and Offendene. Nonetheless, when the proofs arrived, Eliot's anxieties about the division returned. In her November 10 letter to Blackwood, she explained her original plan and asked for his "opinion about the length of the four first Parts of D. D." She notes that on the proofs "Pts. III and IV make respectively 170 and 175 pp. Pts. I and II being 191 and 180." Books 1 and 2 are still longer than 3 and 4, but now she fears there is not enough "psychological" weight in part 1; readers may not feel there is enough story. "I fear that the present division [in the proofs] may make the two first parts—the impression of which is of course supremely important—rather poverty-stricken in point of matter" (*Letters* 6: 181).

Did Eliot worry, with the Archery Ball gone from book 1 and Mirah's confession deferred to book 3, that there was not enough forward-looking incident in the first two books? Yet the first books of *Middlemarch* and *Daniel Deronda* are similar in amount of incident, and even in the nature of the main "matter": the daily life of a headstrong, marriageable young woman. True, Dorothea Brooke is married by the end of the first book, and perhaps Eliot worried that in *Deronda*, book 1, her heroine had not even met the man who would be her successful suitor. Recalling the size of *Middlemarch*,[6] she asks Blackwood:

> What do you think? As to the III and IV Parts—there are two Books of *Middlemarch* which are 175 and 176 respectively, but they don't come together. The question of course is rather of matter in relation to interest than in relation to quantity.
>
> If you are for the larger size of Parts I and II and Mr. Lewes concurs, (he is this morning at Cambridge) I could throw the same amount into Parts III and IV—not less, I fear, because of the difficulty as to properly dividing the subject matter. Unhappily I cannot drill myself into writing according to set lengths. (6: 181–82)

Blackwood demurs on the decision-making, beginning his letter of November 17 with "you are by far the best judge" (6: 185). His comment is equivocal: "As it stands the first part ends very well with the introduction of Grandcourt to Gwendolen but is of course more complete after the Archery Ball" (6: 185). Eliot, in turn, leaves the decision to Lewes, telling

Blackwood to anticipate a letter: "As to the division Mr. Lewes has made up his mind decidedly" (6: 187).

Lewes used the occasion to comment on several publication questions. In October, Blackwood had proposed monthly serialization, but his November 17 letter mentions "a difference of opinion among us" regarding the interval between parts.

> Mr. Simpson holds strongly, and my nephew inclines for an interval of two months between the four first parts at any rate, as it takes the public a long time to digest and fully appreciate the value of such food and talk to their neighbours about it as we found with Middlemarch. I on the contrary am in favour of only one month's interval as our audience is much more ready than it was for Middlemarch and I am afraid of the two months giving the Librarians a better opportunity of starving their supplies. (6: 186)

Lewes responds to this first issue by affirming monthly publication. As for the division, he wisely does not alter book 1. "I have read and reread the parts with a view to decide as to their divisions and come to the decided conviction that the present arrangement is on the whole the best" (6: 189). To have included the whole of the Archery Ball would not only have produced an especially long installment, but would have given too great a sense of closure to the book. Ending before the introduction leaves readers in the same state of anticipation as Gwendolen herself. As the London *Globe and Traveller* observes, "Patience is sorely tried" in readers who must wait "a whole month for [their] introduction to Mr. Mallinger Grandcourt" (Jan. 31, 1876; 6). The *Academy* notes that book 1 "leaves the reader's mind in an admirable state of suspense" (Feb. 5; 120). Lewes knew that the impatience that heightens the event for Gwendolen would not hurt readers either.

Lewes did propose one slight alteration regarding book 2, also in the interest of suspense. On November 17, Blackwood had voted for a return to the discarded original arrangement for its close rather than the division found in the proofs. "I lean to what you now propose which would make the first volume [book 2] end with the close of Mirah's story and the explanation of Deronda's being at Leubrunn [*sic*] which draws this whole tale and dramatis personae together" (6: 185). He suggests that "as a wind up to the second part Mirah's most touching narrative to dear old Mrs. Meyrick is necessary to waken up the full interest in the little wanderer." He also tries to allay Eliot's concern about length: "Practically if there is to be a difference in the thickness of the volumes it is well that the two first should have the preponderance, and . . . by the time the public have reached the third volume they will be too happy to take and pay for whatever you give. Divide as you think best without regard to the outward aspect of the volumes" (*Letters* 6: 185–86). Eliot originally had altered books 1 and 2 because they were too long; Blackwood's new suggestions support the old plan, but for different reasons. He failed, however, to see that this plan would have altered the serial effect. Blackwood liked pathos, as his responses to "Amos Barton" show, and certainly, readers' attention for the intervening month would have been focused on the pathos rather than on the suspense of Mirah's unrevealed background. But this would have come at too great a cost to suspense, which, as the proofs stood, is emphasized by withholding Mirah's narrative until book 3. Eliot, however, had diminished its effect by appending a final meditative chapter for Deronda after he leaves the Meyricks.

Lewes saw this chapter's effect immediately and rejected both Blackwood's advice and Eliot's revised plan. Instead, he told Blackwood to "throw the last five pages of volume I on to the opening of volume II," that is, from book 2 to book 3 (6: 189).[7] This arrangement, along with his affirmation that book 1 end just before Grandcourt's introduction, preserves the most effective serial structure for both books—1 and 2. "At each close there is strong *expectation* excited—the best of all closes," Lewes wrote. "The end of the scene in Mrs. Meyrick's moves me so that I can't patiently read the few pages which follow—they come as anticlimax but would open volume 2 quite pleasantly" (6: 189). By moving this material to book 3,[8] and ignoring Blackwood's wish to close with Mirah's "touching narrative," Lewes ends book 2 with only a hint, and a rather melodramatic one, of Mirah's past. Readers are left to speculate on the potentially titillating facts behind her simple speech, "I am come a long way, all the way from Prague by myself. I made my escape, I ran away from dreadful things. I came to find my mother and brother in London" (242). For the month of March, then, readers could ponder questions like, Why and whom did she have to escape? What were the "dreadful things"? Where are her mother and brother? Mirah's short, simple sentences, contrasting with the narrator's long periods, emphasize her narrative's potential for breathless excitement when it resumes in April. In contrast, chapter 19 would have been a ponderous distraction from the drama of Mirah's rescue and anticipated tale, a dull note for a serial ending.

In reducing the size of the first book, Eliot had ended book 1 with chapter 10's question by Lord Brackenshaw, instead of chapter 11's general speculation in the narrator's voice. With book 2, considerations of size led her again to the fortuitous suspenseful close, and Lewes kept her from spoiling it when he detached the meditative ending and moved it to book 3 as chapter 19. Book 2 is only 173 pages as a result, but it is surrounded by two longer books—book 1 at 189 pages and book 3 at 186—thus allaying Eliot's earlier fear about two adjacent short installments.[9]

This correspondence also indicates their awareness of the role that reviews played in advertising a serial novel, and they took this into account in planning the publication schedule. Because Victorian newspapers did not vary their size according to the availability of news as much as modern papers do, the opening of Parliament often dominated the periodicals to the exclusion of other subjects. Blackwood worried that the late winter Parliamentary session might push reviews of book 1 off the newspaper pages and suggested that "the first part should be published about the 15th of January so as to give the Newspapers time to speak out before the meeting of Parliament" (*Letters* 6: 186). Mid-month was a curious time to publish, however; readers were accustomed to obtaining separate-part serials on the first day of the month.[10] Lewes's rather rambling response in his November 18 letter shows him pondering this problem even as he writes. The book would have to be announced for February 1, even if it came out on January 15 or a few days later, but the American rights—worth £1,500—complicate the matter. But then, he decides, January 15 is "too early since it will make six weeks between [books] 1 and 2" (*Letters* 6: 188–89). Publication on February 1 was included in the tickler Lewes proposed on November 22 (*Letters* 6: 192), although continuing problems with *Harper's* American arrangement almost caused publication to be delayed until March 1.[11]

These problems were finally resolved, and the extensiveness of the newspaper reception in late January and early February was unprecedented in Eliot's serial publication experience. Twenty-nine newspapers in the United Kingdom published reviews, many of them quite lengthy, within the first two weeks, from January 29 to February 9. Two more were published later in February. (See Appendix 1 for details.) Both their number and their content demonstrate again Lewes's understanding of the reading public and the most effective publication and division for a serial. There were complaints that the novel was serialized, but the

Weekly Scotsman was, like others, glad at least for monthly publication instead of the two-month "wearisome intervals" of *Middlemarch* (Feb. 5, 1876; 6). Some reviews emphasized the novel's exciting, even sensational, plot devices. For example, the *Sunday Times* refers to "a savour of the sensation novel" in the opening chapters of book 1, even though it "disappears immediately" (Feb. 20; 7). The *Figaro* describes book 1 as leaving Gwendolen "on the brink of an introduction" (Feb. 9; 10). Book 1 is a "tantalizing fragment" whose readers will have to wait a month for "the solution of its mysteries" said the London *Times* (Jan. 31; 6). The *Manchester Examiner and Times* refers to its "exciting introductory chapters" and the "melodramatic" incident of the hidden panel (Jan. 29; 5–6). "At first . . . not much impressed" by book 1, the *Glasgow News* "found ourselves very much in the position of poor Oliver Twist in our demand for more" by the end. While arguing that "George Eliot never condescends to be flippant, any more than she condescends to be sensational," the notice centers its speculation about book 2 on the sensation novel's device of mixed identity: Gwendolen "is introduced (on the last page) to a certain Mr. Mallinger Grandcourt, whom we shrewdly suspect will turn out to be identical with Daniel Deronda" (Jan. 29; 2). After these expectations are disappointed in book 2, the *News* review excuses itself by pointing out that book 1 had given readers the "merest glimpse of the hero, and our curiosity was therefore baffled to a great extent" (Feb. 28; 2). The London *Globe and Traveller* notes that the book is very different from Eliot's usual work. Gwendolen is already a "vigorously original creation," whereas Deronda "is at present only the name of a somewhat mysterious young man whom we just saw at Baden without hearing him speak a word" (Jan. 31; 6).

By book 2, the difference between this and Eliot's previous work grows even more noticeable. As the *Globe* predicts, the novel "is likely to differ in a very marked way from any form of novel to which George Eliot has hitherto accustomed us. The effects aimed at appear to be of a much broader and more markedly dramatic order." It anticipates "a romance and a mystery" in Mirah's story, and uses the word "mystery" again to refer to Deronda. Altogether, the novel "can hardly fail to obtain a dramatic interest of a sharper and intenser kind than any of her former works, with the possible exception of 'Romola.' . . . 'Middlemarch' was a picture; 'Daniel Deronda' bids fair to be a drama" (Feb. 29; 6). While the *Glasgow News* recalls in its second notice that the action of book 1 "did not move very rapidly," with Mirah's appearance at the end of book 2,

"There are evidently stirring things in store for all concerned. . . . no one who has once begun 'Daniel Deronda' will be satisfied until he has read it all" (Feb. 28; 2). The *Examiner*'s second review also singles out Mirah: "Of all the new characters introduced in this book . . . the most interesting is the last comer, a poor Jewish girl" (Mar. 4; 265). Noting that a new character "threatens to play a distinguished part in the drama of Deronda's life," the *Glasgow News* predicts that Mirah "is likely to obliterate from Daniel's brain the memory of Gwendolen" or at least, "she will loom largely in his mind" (Feb. 28; 2). The *Manchester Examiner and Times* laments that after Deronda's "exciting adventure" in "sav[ing] a beautiful girl from suicide," we are "cruelly pulled up and informed that 'Daniel Deronda, Book III., Maidens Choosing,' will be published on 1st April" (Feb. 28; 3). The *Figaro* quotes Mirah's phrase "dreadful things," remarking that readers await book 3 "with great eagerness" (Mar. 22; 10). *John Bull* calls Mirah "exquisitely drawn" with "pathetic grace . . . but we know little of her as yet, and await the next chapter anxiously" (Mar. 11; 178–79). The Edinburgh *Daily Review* judges book 2 "more clever, more fascinating, in the true sense of the word than anything perhaps George Eliot has ever written except the hypocrite scene in 'Middlemarch'"; nonetheless, it must be distinguished from "an ordinary love story or mechanical web of the Wilkie Collins order" (Feb. 28; 5). Summarizing what many felt at the end of book 2, the Liverpool *Daily (Evening) Albion* writes: "The reader . . . is left considerably mystified by the story, and deeply interested in its development. It is trying to the patience to have to read any story serially, especially if the curtain is brought down just as our curiosity has become most eager" (Feb. 28; 2). This, of course, was precisely the effect Lewes desired.

Only the *Aberdeen Journal* and the *Athenaeum* find the first book tame. The former is disappointed that book 1 has "little incident. Gwendolen, her mother, and some half-sisters, came to stay in a house near the rectory of the heroine's uncle. . . . The rector's son comes home from the University, and falls violently in love with his pretty cousin. He is somewhat heartlessly rejected, and in his despair resolves to emigrate to Canada." This seems to summarize the plot for this reviewer. The overall atmosphere is "even less tender than of old"; the book is too worldly, it omits the "action of higher powers, and the validity of higher hopes." The reviewer makes "these remarks under protest, and shall be too glad to retract them if justified by the subsequent course of the story" (Feb. 9; 6). While the next *Aberdeen Journal* notice becomes much more positive, the *Athenaeum* holds fast to its initial negative judgment throughout the serialization of *Deronda*. The latter's first review points to the novel's similarity to *Middlemarch*, "Again does George Eliot's tale centre round a woman's life." But here the likeness ends. Whereas book 1 of the earlier novel is a "complete fragment, perfect in itself," book 1 of *Deronda* contains "nothing that satisfies . . . nothing that indicates what the future of the story is to be," and the part "concludes more tamely than it began" (Jan. 29; 160). The *Edinburgh Courant* adopts the metaphor of book 2's title, "Meeting Streams": "we are still by the side of the maiden stream, which is the more sparkling and impetuous of the two, and it is almost a relief to be led to the deeper, calmer waters of Deronda's early life." In this arrangement, there is "true art." Having seen him only briefly in book 1, readers nonetheless "know by all the rules of art that he is certain to exercise a powerful influence for good or evil on the wilful heroine" (Feb. 28; 6). In this new book, Deronda's story is "narrated with a simplicity and power which most people will probably prefer even to the gayer scenes of the earlier chapters" (Feb. 28; 6).[12] By the end of book 2, most readers were engaged and enthusiastic, whether they preferred Deronda or Gwendolen.

Chapter 19, with five paragraphs in the narrator's voice, opens book 3 undramatically—"very pleasantly," Lewes suggested—with a narrative summary. Lewes could recommend this arrangement because he knew that Eliot's readers would recognize the chapter as a familiar "warm-up" before the drama resumes—a technique used by other serial writers, but especially favored by Eliot in the openings of most *Middlemarch* installments. Despite the pathos of Mirah's narrative, the drama continues to center on Gwendolen. Unlike the first three books of *Middlemarch*, installments 1 to 3 of *Deronda* could not be rearranged to provide proportionate attention to each of the story lines. There was simply not enough "Deronda" matter in them for rearrangement to balance the plots. In book 1, he figures only in the first two chapters—a brief, enigmatic presence. Book 2 is more evenly divided. Deronda's history is presented in the three final chapters, following five chapters on Gwendolen. If Eliot's plan to include Mirah's story in book 2 had been followed, the Deronda and Gwendolen portions would each have occupied five chapters. However, this gain in book 2 would have been offset by his being nearly eliminated from book 3, which contains only three appearances by Deronda: his meditations in the short chapter 19; the end of chapter 20, where he returns briefly after Mirah confides in Mrs. Meyrick; and chapter 25, where he makes a minor appearance in connection with Grand-court's arrival at Leubronn in desultory pursuit of Gwendolen. Only the last would have been included in book 3 under the discarded first plan; only the second and third were included in book 3 at proof stage, before Lewes's direction to Blackwood to move the final five pages of book 2 into book 3. Even with these three appearances, the *Manchester Examiner and Times* notes that we "hear but little of Deronda," although Mirah's "autobiographical sketch is not only one of the most charming in the book, but as an example of pathetic and poetical narrative, it has never been excelled by the accomplished author" (Mar. 29; 3). The serial reader/reviewer observes what is less evident to readers who encounter the whole work at once: it is Mirah rather than Deronda who appears when Gwendolen is offstage. The *Athenaeum* begins its third notice by observing that "the hero, who gives his name to the story, has not yet become the chief character" (Apr. 1; 461). Book 3 soon returns to Gwendolen, and the conclusion affirms her preeminence by making the proposal scene the final incident readers encounter before the story halts for a month.

Manuscript alterations in this section again demonstrate Eliot's attention to the effect of the chapter sequence on the installment overall. Cancelled page numbers show that published chapters 22 and 23 were to have been in reverse order,[13] so that Gwendolen's sending for Klesmer would have been followed immediately by their interview and *then* by the chapter recounting Miss Arrowpoint's confrontation with her parents. The original sequence would have been (using the published chapter numbers):

Chapter 21   Davilows prepare for Sawyer's Cottage and Gwendolen writes to Klesmer.
Chapter 23   Gwendolen's interview with Klesmer.
Chapter 22   Klesmer and Catherine defy the Arrowpoints and Klesmer leaves Quetcham.

After Chapter 23, the movement of the Gwendolen plot is direct: from her resignation to the move to Sawyer's Cottage and the necessity of becoming a governess, to Grandcourt's return, his proposal, and Gwendolen's acceptance. Not only does the new arrangement make stronger the contrast between Klesmer's altruism and Gwendolen's egoism (Handley, "Manuscript" 64–65), but in the original sequence, the Arrowpoint family conflict would have been anticlimactic after the downfall of Gwendolen's last hope. Thus, the movement of her story would be disrupted. By reversing the order, Eliot produced greater suspense; readers await (with Gwendolen) Klesmer's visit, then see her hopes dashed and her doubtful rescue by Grandcourt.

After her engagement, readers recognize that Gwendolen's prediction that "everything is to be as I like" is as unlikely as Dorothea's expectations of great gains in learning in her marriage to Casaubon. Gwendolen and Grandcourt both being "spoiled," the *Globe and Traveller* anticipates that the story of their union is "likely to be of peculiar dramatic intensity" (Apr. 10; 6). The *Nonconformist* predicts: "a very deep vein of tragedy is to be touched on in the issues that spring out of this union that in all outward . . . respects seems so suitable and fortunate" (Apr. 12; 363). From "the resolution [Gwendolen] takes at the end of the book . . . some very bitter fruit will come" predicts the *Edinburgh Courant* (Mar. 30; 4).

Book 4 begins precisely where 3 left off. Events leading up to the marriage occupy the first four chapters, after which Deronda's story develops as he searches for Mirah's mother and brother among the Jewish neighborhoods of London. The amount of attention given this new subject surprised readers, of whom Blackwood was the first to register a guarded hesitation. Having already received the usual hints about Eliot's self-doubt, Blackwood catches himself up in a letter dated November 30: "It seemed hard to be torn away from Gwendolen after she read that 'horrible' letter and Grandcourt came down 'dressed for dinner,' but so exquisitely do you work the other chain of your story that one is speedily as engrossed as ever. Where did you get your knowledge of the Jews? But indeed one might say that of all your characters, so life-like and human are they" (6: 195). That he protests a bit too much is suggested not only by his vague praise but also by a comparison of this letter with another four months later in which a slip in memory reveals what caught his attention most. Sales are "most satisfactory," Blackwood writes on April 10, 1876, although "I expected more of a spirt in sale [with book 3] but I think the closing scene of Book Four, I mean the Jewel scene, will set all the world talking. There is immense puzzlement as to what the author is going to make of Gwendolen, which is a good thing and none are more sorely baffled than the Newspaper critics" (6: 238).

Other readers also confused the Jewel scene with the close of book 4. The *York Herald* calls book 4 "more fascinating" than earlier books. It "creates a strong desire for those which are to follow" (May 11; 3). The source of this fascination is clear in the next month's review, which begins as if book 4 *had* ended with the Jewel scene. "The last book of this fascinating story left us where Gwendolen and her husband arrive at Ryelands, and the former receives Mrs. Glasher's letters [*sic*] and the diamonds" (June 7; 3). The *Tablet* laments the change of focus as a failure of artistry: "The catastrophe is strongly and shortly told; but the sudden break and total change of interest in this volume is either an error in art or an unworthy device; we are obliged to leave Gwendolen with Lydia Glasher's diamonds at her feet, receiving her bridegroom with scream upon scream, and to interest ourselves through three long chapters in Deronda's search among the Jews" (May 27; 683). The *Manchester Examiner and Times* recognizes the power of the Jewel scene, but expects a closer connection among the various plots and characters. Arguing that this new book shows "the superiority of the ordinary method of publication," the reviewer laments the dearth of "incidents"; "we are permitted to hope [however] that in the earlier chapters the author is beginning to weave the diverse threads of interest into a compactly united narrative." This does not happen. "After renewing our interest in Gwendolen, [Eliot] abruptly turns from that young lady's story at a very exciting moment and condemns us to wonder for a whole month" about the outcome. "Leaving Gwendolen's fortune, we are compelled to follow Deronda in his very unwilling search for relatives of Mirah." "Compelled" suggests that the reviewer is as unwilling as Deronda to follow the search. After the sentence just quoted, the review returns to the Gwendolen plot and Lydia Glasher, whose story "is full of tragic pathos." Readers "must wait [a month] before we can estimate the effect of her cunning but cruel revenge" (Apr. 27; 7). The review mitigates slightly this attention to the Gwendolen plot by ending with two excerpts on Mirah and one on Deronda's first meeting with Mordecai.

The Jewel scene, with the high drama of Gwendolen's hysterics, would have made a splendid installment close: "He had expected to see her dressed and smiling, ready to be led down. He saw her pallid, shrieking as it seemed with terror, the jewels scattered around her on the floor. Was it a fit of madness? In some form or other the Furies had crossed his threshold" (331). This is a closing scene any sensation novelist would have been pleased to create, and it is no wonder some confounded it with the actual ending of the book. By book 4, however, Eliot needed to devote more space to her title character, and so the Jewel scene simply closes Gwendolen's part of the installment. Three lengthy chapters follow in which Deronda searches for Mirah's brother, and the book ends with vague suspense as Deronda determines to learn more about Mordecai and "the reason why it was forbidden to ask Mrs Cohen the elder whether she had a daughter" (371). One of Eliot's few red herrings, this reference appears to have no other function than to increase suspense. Nothing is ever made of Mrs. Cohen's daughter, even though she is referred to thrice later in the novel: briefly in chapter 40 near the close of book 5; again in book 6, chapter 46; and in book 7, chapter 50. The reference near the end of book 5 focuses the concerns around which the suspense of its conclusion is built. In book 6, Mordecai asks Deronda not to "dwell on my sister more than is needful" in announcing to the Cohens that Mirah has been found (533). This reference is unnecessary to add to the already intense drama and the pathos of chapter 46, but it does show Mordecai in his complexity. His grand, if seemingly fanciful, vision does not preclude human compassion. In the first chapter of book 7, when Mordecai admits that he "undervalued [Mrs. Cohen's] heart. . . . She is capable of rejoicing that another's plant blooms though her own be withered" (576), the attempt seems to be to increase sympathy for the Cohen family. From this point on, readers neither learn, nor, contemporary reviews suggest, care to learn the daughter's fate. The final notice in the *Manchester Examiner and Times*, speculating on the unrevealed future of several minor characters, mentions this lacuna, "Of the lost daughter of the Cohens, about whose story Mordecai was reticent even to Deronda, we hear nothing whatever" (Aug. 31; 7).

With seven of the eight books completed before book 4 was published, Blackwood's Jewel scene *faux pas* would have been especially troubling to the author. The day after she received his letter, Eliot records her fears about the later books: "The success of the work at present is greater than that of Middlemarch up to the corresponding point of publication. What will be the feeling of the public as the story advances I am entirely doubtful. The Jewish element seems to me likely to satisfy nobody" (GE Journal, Apr. 12, 1876, qtd. in *Letters* 6: 238). While this fear was not new, it was probably exacerbated by Blackwood's confusion about the end of book 4, which suggested how much more compelling he found Gwendolen's story. On April 12, Eliot would also have been especially aware of the future predominance of the Jewish story because she had just sent off book 7, as the same journal entry notes.

Since she was so far ahead of schedule at this point, Eliot had no deadline worries. The plan for books 5 and 6 passes without remark in her letters and journal, except for a comment that "the third volume (which I have not yet finished) would be regarded as the difficult bridge" (*Letters* 6: 199). While Eliot does not elaborate, clearly books 5 and 6 bridge the novel in more than one way. First, these books lead to the climactic scenes in both of the main plot lines. Deronda's search for Mirah's relatives foregrounds the mystery of his own heritage and a destiny connected with Mordecai's Zionist vision. In contrast, Gwendolen's life disintegrates, as Lydia Glasher's curse accompanying the diamonds is fulfilled and Gwendolen finds herself powerless to change or control her life. She begins to fear the temptation that confronts her in her hatred for Grandcourt. This volume, then, moves the two plot lines toward the climactic events of book 7.

Volume 3 is also the place in a multi-plot serial where we might expect bridges to be formed, if they haven't already, *among* the various plots and characters. By this point in *Middlemarch*, the lives of the characters fully converge. But in *Deronda*, the plots threaten to diverge more and more as Deronda moves away from the narrow life of the English upper classes around Grosvenor Square and Park Lane and into the lives of poor Jews in London's East End. Gwendolen's desperate hold on his sympathy forces occasional connections, but the divergence of his life is clear, its inevitability tenuously balanced with the serial form's need for plots to be interconnected. Retrospectively, one can argue that Deronda remains an unseen moral presence in Gwendolen's life. But some of the original, serial readers found it difficult to see, or to accept, this connection.

Deronda's appearance during the prenuptial festivities of Gwendolen and Grandcourt had reestablished their connection made wordlessly at Leubronn three books earlier, but by the end of book 4, each plot is again distinct. Gwendolen's closes with the Jewel scene, and Deronda's at the Cohens' flat above the bookshop. Book 5 opens upon the luxurious Christmas festivities at Topping Abbey, where Gwendolen takes precedence as the bride of the heir apparent. Two long chapters, in which Deronda and Gwendolen's relationship draws the attention of both Grandcourt and Sir Hugo, end with Sir Hugo's hope that Deronda is "not playing with fire," and his observation that "between ourselves, I fancy there may be some hidden gunpowder in [the Grandcourts'] establishment" (510). Readers also detected this gunpowder. The *York Herald*, for example, noted the "dangerous interest" between Gwendolen and Deronda that "has to be kept within reasonable bounds, and there is just the possibility that Deronda may fail to restrain it" (June 7; 3). Readers seem to have anticipated the conventional seduction or elopement.

Four final chapters, approximately equal in length to the first two, center on Deronda, Mirah, Klesmer, and Mordecai. Deronda fits in at Topping Abbey, but Gwendolen has no place among London Jews, except as a potential wealthy patron for Mirah. Once again, the installment ends by emphasizing the Deronda-Mordecai connection, though this may not have been Eliot's original intention for book 5. Manuscript pagination shows that the final chapter, published as chapter 40, originally followed published chapter 38: chapter 38 ended on Eliot's page 116, and the first page of chapter 40 was 117—later altered to 131, when she wrote published chapter 39 to go between the already written two chapters. Either she meant book 5 to be one chapter shorter, or she intended to end with Klesmer's visit to Mirah.[14] If the latter, she must have changed her mind before actually writing chapter 39, since its pagination shows only one set of numbers in Eliot's hand.[15]

Visiting Blackfriars Bridge helped her with the lighting effects she needed to dramatize the scene in chapter 40 in which Deronda rows out of the sunset toward Mordecai, and the latter's face is "brought out by the western light into startling distinctness and brilliancy—an illuminated type of bodily emaciation and spiritual eagerness" (459). Changes in the manuscript made as a result of her observations include extensive corrections on the first and third pages in this chapter. Eliot's original motto was only two lines long; as far as decipherable under the heavy strokes of the cancellation, it was not attributed to Wordsworth's *Excursion*, as is the longer published motto. She moved the original opening of a description of the time and the sunset to the third manuscript page (119/133/137) after "where Deronda meant to land." She moved a passage from the opening paragraph, "It was nearly half past four . . . luminous movement," along with a section written on the back of the first folio in the chapter (117/131/135), "the alternate flash of ripples or currents . . . brooding glory." (The motto from the *Excursion* is also on the back of this folio.) When she decided to insert a new chapter 39 and make 40 the last in book 5, placing Deronda's visit to the Meyricks before the Blackfriars Bridge scene meant that she needed a transition; hence, the extensive blotting and correction on page 117/131/135.

The decision to end with chapter 40 was a wise one from the point of view of serialization. Reviewers had already focused on Mirah rather than on Deronda; ending the installment with Klesmer's visit would have emphasized her role even more. The hint of love is also rather conventional and would have made too prominent Hans Meyrick's hopes. In fact, the manuscript indicates that Eliot added a sentence to the end of published chapter 39 to diminish this effect. One short sentence was probably her original close: "In this way Hans got food for his hopes." However, the manuscript shows that the published closing sentence—"How could the rose help it when several bees in succession took its sweet odour as a sign of personal attachment?"—was added in a different pen stroke and squeezed in below the last line. Thus, Eliot diminishes the impact of Hans's love and returns readers to Deronda, who can be perceived as one of the "several bees," but whose relationship with Mordecai remains the center of his story in this installment.

These alterations and Eliot's visit to Blackfriars Bridge indicate the care she took to set the scene of Mordecai's prophetic vision of Deronda as his "new self" (461). As an installment ending, though, his expectation that "the rest will come" to pass and Deronda's promise to return (472) provide only a general direction for readers' expectations. Perhaps for that reason, their conversation concludes with a reminder of the reason Deronda is in the Jewish quarter of the East End—his search for Mirah's relatives. A brief allusion to the Cohens' daughter and the question of Mirah's mother and brother provide more definite subjects for suspense when the installment closes.

Book 6 opens precisely where 5 had left off,[16] with the narrator's comment to the reader, "Imagine the conflict in a mind like Deronda's, given not only to feeling strongly but to question actively, on the evening after that interview with Mordecai" (473). The first three chapters center on the Philosophers' Club's conversation on change, progress, development, nationhood, and a host of other topics related to the Zionist plot— a conversation that some reviewers greeted with impatience. Chapter 43, which reveals Mirah's connection with Mordecai, aroused more interest, but many readers were relieved when the narrator opened chapter 44 with the question they, too, had been asking, "And Gwendolen?" (508).

From here in book 6, Deronda touches Gwendolen's life more in her thoughts than in her actions. "She was thinking of Deronda much more than he was thinking of her—often wondering what were his ideas 'about things,' and how his life was occupied" (508). Despite Gwendolen's limited frame of reference—her "lap-dog" perception (508)—she recognizes the bitter ironies in her situation. Visiting her family during Grandcourt's absence at Gadsmere, she is solicited by her Uncle Gascoigne to use "a wife['s] great influence with her husband" to urge Grandcourt to run for Parliament. His "whole speech had the flavour of bitter comedy" to Gwendolen (512), bitterness compounded by Mrs. Gascoigne's assumptions about a wife's influence and her tendency, like the women of Milby, to blame the victim. She "felt Grandcourt's haughtiness as something a little blameable in Gwendolen" (513). The irony of powerlessness in the woman who had once determined to do as she liked gives way to pathos as Gwendolen, with feelings she hardly understands, gives her mother thirty pounds for her sisters.

Gwendolen and Deronda meet only twice in book 6. On both occasions, the flirtation and elopement that Sir Hugo and reviewers earlier feared or predicted plays no part in the explosive potential of their relationship. Their first conversation in book 6 occurs at Lady Mallinger's party, where Hans Meyrick alarms Deronda by his question about an "interesting quarrel" with the "young duchess" (525). Gwendolen fears that she has "not kept up the perfect air of equability in public which was her own ideal" (525) and which Grandcourt demands. However, with a calculated reticence that reveals how completely Gwendolen is under his control, Grandcourt saves his rebuke (545). And when Grandcourt announces, "Lush will dine with us. . . . You will treat him civilly," Gwendolen "dared not" protest. "She was as frightened at a quarrel as if she had foreseen that it would end with throttling fingers on her neck" (525–26). The menace in their relationship builds suspense for serial readers, but the installment does not end here. Instead, chapters 46 and 47 return to Deronda, Mordecai, and Mirah. The pathos and drama of Mordecai and Mirah's reunion is succeeded by a scene in which Mrs. Meyrick's narration of the finding of Mirah's brother evokes a response that articulates the stereotypes of anti-Semitic thought. Hans fears Mirah's recovered brother might be "'a fellow all smiles and jewellery—a Crystal Palace Assyrian with a hat on.'" And he imagines sarcastically having "'this prophet Elijah to tea with us'" (539). Hans's objections and earlier comments by otherwise sympathetic characters like Amy, Mrs. Meyrick, and Lady Mallinger point to Eliot's awareness of contemporary attitudes.[17]

Deronda's deliberate role in effecting this reunion contrasts with his inadvertent, reluctant part in the Grandcourt-Gwendolen drama. His second meeting with Gwendolen in book 6 is a result of Gwendolen's command, given with "royal permissiveness": "'I wish you would come and see me tomorrow between five and six'" (564–65). Their meeting is brief. A suspicious Grandcourt discovers them and orders Gwendolen to go yachting with him in the Mediterranean. The menace in Grandcourt's "No; you will go with me" (568) would have made it an excellent speech for the serial close. There is no evidence, however, in the manuscript, letters, or journals that Eliot considered transposing the two final chapters in order to present events in chronological sequence or to highlight this feature of the Gwendolen plot by placing it at the end of the part. Perhaps she saw that the brief final chapter is significant both dramatically and thematically: Deronda's emotionally-wrought interview with Sir Hugo reiterates the themes of inheritance and legitimacy. Although readers learn that he will be "going away" for some time (674–75), serial reviews show no expectation that the unnamed site at which Deronda will meet his mother might bring him near the Grandcourts' yachting—even though hindsight leads one to wonder if the chapter was placed at the end to promote that expectation.[18] In any case, placing the revelation to Deronda at the end of the installment indicates the importance of the Jewish plot. While some readers continued to regard Gwendolen as the main character, Eliot signals here the equal, or even preeminent, role of Deronda, whose story had ended parts 4 and 5 as well.

Given the brevity and infrequency of Deronda and Gwendolen's actual meetings, it is a tribute to Eliot's skill in dramatizing Gwendolen's thoughts and fears that there still seems considerable contact between them in book 6. Even so, some reviewers objected to the Deronda plot, while others personally applauded it, but assumed that most readers would not be enthusiastic. The *Examiner* notes that

> George Eliot has a keen sense of humour. It is, perhaps, the least deniable of her many great gifts. And therefore, we venture to think, she must have derived not a little amusement from thinking of the bewilderment she has caused among the 20,000 readers of 'Daniel Deronda,' some of whom must be simple folk who read her as a social duty, by giving them such a nut to crack as the wonderful Jew Mordecai. (Review of books 6 and 7, Aug. 5; 885)

The *Figaro* begins by citing public expectations, "There is a great deal about Mordecai in this part and, perhaps, some will think, too little about Gwendolen"; nevertheless, the Philosophers' Club discussions are "extremely interesting" (July 29; 11). *John Bull* notes the problem of disappointed expectation: "The chapters relating to Gwendolen and her husband are not more nobly or truly written than those which tell of the grand visions of Mordecai, but they strike a chord which the other entirely fails to touch, and awaken an interest which few, if any, feel for the more original and poetical conception" (July 1; 433). Neither the *Globe* nor the *Guardian* are as sympathetic. For the former, Gwendolen "still holds . . . the predominant interest that she took at the outset" (July 18; 6), and the latter asserts that "when we have discussed Gwendolen we have discussed the book" (Oct. 4; 1312). The *Athenaeum* is the most negative: the first third of book 6 is "even more completely wanting in interest to the general reader than were [the Jewish scenes] which have gone before them; but when we come again to the story, [the] interest becomes more marked." The review continues with four excerpts, all focusing on the heroine (July 1; 14–15).

Book 7 opens with a brief, explicit transitional sentence: "This was the letter which Sir Hugo put into Deronda's hands" (575). The first chapter portrays his departure for Genoa, while the second depicts his first meeting with his mother. These chapters, 50 and 51, appear to have been planned from the start to open the book, but reorganization thereafter increases the dramatic effect and intermingles the two plot lines. Chapters 50 and 51 occupy pages 1 to 36 of the manuscript. The original order then placed published chapters 53 to 55 in the sequence 54, 53, and 55, but numbered from 52 to 54 because published chapter 52 was written while she was working on book 8, during or just after she completed published chapter 61. The original narrative structure was thus (using published chapter numbers):

Chapter 50   Deronda reads the letter and leaves for Genoa.
Chapter 51   Deronda meets the Princess Halm-Eberstein.
Chapter 54   Gwendolen and Grandcourt arrive at Genoa and go boating in the harbor.
Chapter 53   Deronda has a second interview with his mother.
Chapter 55   Grandcourt drowns.

The original plan is evident in the manuscript because the numbers for published chapters 54 and 55 remain as originally given, numbers 52 and 54. Manuscript pagination also confirms the earlier arrangement.[19]

Eliot's decision to write a new chapter 52, in which Hans sends Deronda news from home, and readers learn of Mirah's fear that her father has reappeared, occurred late in the revision process—during or after the composition of published chapter 61 in book 8.[20] Since chapter 61 returns to the Meyricks, the subject may have reminded her that she had omitted them—and Hans's love for Mirah—from part 7. The new chapter 52 serves several purposes. It is a comic interlude and a reminder of the "normal," in the midst of coincidence and sensation: the simultaneous appearance of Deronda and the Grandcourts at Genoa, and Deronda's emotion at meeting his mother followed by Grandcourt's drowning and Gwendolen's remorse. The *Manchester Examiner and Times* called the interviews between Deronda and his mother "almost too remarkable—violent we had almost called them—and the whole scene is only saved from being what is customary to call melodramatic by the consummate literary skill of the author." The reviewer welcomes chapter 52 and the letter from Hans, which "interrupts the successive interviews between the mother and son": "It is almost a relief to meet the Meyricks again" (July 27; 7). The *York Herald* is explicit about this chapter's function: the mother-son interviews are "the most powerful pages in the story, and we follow Daniel's responsive feelings with as much interest as if the whole thing were going on before our eyes. A comical letter from Hans Meyrick, with glimpses of new feeling in Mirah, comes in as an interlude between the two interviews, but only serve [*sic*] to heighten their force" (Aug. 8; 3).

The new chapter 52 is also useful in introducing Mirah more fully into book 7. The original plan allowed her one brief appearance only. In the opening pages, her sense of "belonging" to the Cohens quietly rebukes Deronda's elitism in fearing that this working-class Jewish family is too vulgar for her and reminds readers again to look beyond stereotypes. But originally, after this chapter, Mirah returns in book 7 only in Deronda's conversation with his mother. Despite readers' early expectations of a union between Gwendolen and Deronda, Eliot planned a different outcome. Therefore, it was critical that sympathy and interest in Mirah be maintained in an installment that demonstrated Gwendolen's compelling emotional need for Deronda. Hans's letter tantalizes readers with the possibility of a new love interest for Mirah, while her father's reappearance shows her need for Deronda's protection. Keeping her in sight as a rival to Gwendolen heightens the dramatic tension of the closure. When Gwendolen begs Deronda not to forsake her and collapses, weeping, upon the floor, readers have Mirah's claims in view as well.

With Deronda now welcoming his Jewish heritage, the two plots threaten to diverge more than ever. "When Deronda met Gwendolen and Grandcourt on the staircase, his mind was seriously preoccupied. He had just been summoned to the second interview with his mother" (636). This surprise encounter leads to another kind of mental preoccupation as Gwendolen and Grandcourt ponder his presence. She hopes for a private conversation, while Grandcourt suspects collusion and knows that his wife is "now counting on an interview with Deronda whenever her husband's back [is] turned" (631). Thus, while Deronda meets his mother, his presence dominates the minds and conversation of Gwendolen and Grandcourt. Grandcourt, fatefully, fatally, determines not to go boating without his wife. The structure of chapter 55 reflects Deronda's own dividedness. In the first half, he meditates on the Princess Halm-Eberstein's information; in the second half, he learns that Grandcourt has drowned.

Eliot's initial arrangement presented Deronda's first interview, then Gwendolen and Grandcourt's boating, and then Deronda's second interview. The Gwendolen-Grandcourt chapter begins with an analogue from Dante that increases sympathy for Gwendolen and marks the extremity of their marital discord. It was to have closed with Grandcourt's punctilious consultation of Gwendolen's wishes in superficial matters, "'If you like, we can go to Spezia in the morning, and let them take us up there,'" and her ironic response, "'No; I shall like nothing better than this'" (635). Beneath the quiet surface of this exchange is the tension between Grandcourt's mastery and Gwendolen's despair, self-repression, and murderous hatred. However, this is not the way the published chapter ends. In the manuscript, below the line and in slightly darker ink, are three additional sentences spoken by Grandcourt: "Very well; we'll do the same to-morrow. But we must be turning in soon. I shall put about" (635). These words were probably added when the original chapters 52, 53, and 54 became chapters 54, 53, and 55. More precisely than did the original close, they prepare for the accident, which is only partially reported later in Gwendolen's confession and in eyewitness accounts, filtered through Deronda. Eyewitnesses see only the surface text, and the installment closes with the narrator's ironic assumption of the popular voice, "Such grief seemed natural in a poor lady whose husband had been drowned in her presence" (653). The installment concludes with ambiguity about Gwendolen's role in the drowning and the direction of her future relationship with Deronda.

Another effect of the rearrangement of book 7 is to establish more firmly Deronda's commitment to Judaism before he is forced into a new connection with the Grandcourts. The lately added chapter 52, focusing on Mirah, comes between the two meetings of Deronda and his mother. Before readers' or Deronda's attention turns to the Grandcourts, these three chapters establish his intention to welcome his newfound heritage and recover his grandfather's papers. In the final three chapters, 55 to 57, then, Deronda is divided between his desire to pursue this new information and his feeling of duty to Gwendolen. The direction that book 8 will take is clear for all readers to see—although not all readers were so disposed, as the reviews demonstrate.

The effect of the reworking of published chapters 52 to 55 in book 7 is paradoxical. It emphasizes the separateness of the plots even as its ending is the first to bring them together. The new arrangement increases their discreteness, as the two plots are presented in two large blocks—chapters 50–53 on Deronda's Jewish connection and chapters 54–57 on Gwendolen's marriage. In contrast, the original order of chapters 53–55 would have alternated the plot lines, moving from Deronda to Gwendolen to Deronda to Gwendolen. Despite the ending, however, no rearrangement could produce a thorough integration of plots similar to that of later *Middlemarch* books, because the worlds of Deronda and Gwendolen have increasingly diverged in the last four books. That is precisely the point, but a point that readers resisted. Just when Gwendolen most needs Deronda's help and most strongly appeals to his sympathetic nature— just when the ending seems about to move in the direction readers as well as characters like Hans have anticipated (794–95), the other forces in Deronda's life—his heritage and his connection with Mordecai and Mirah— turn him away from Gwendolen. Eliot signals this divergence in the structuring of book 7: Deronda's destiny as a Jewish leader is firmly established before Gwendolen desperately pulls him into her life, and the book closes with his departure and Gwendolen's collapse. In emotional and dramatic power, the final scene rivals the Jewel scene in book 4, and this time Eliot does use it to close an installment.

The addition of a new chapter 52 also added more matter to book 7, which is the shortest of the eight. Commenting on the proofs of book 7 on April 18, Eliot is "concerned to see that the part is nearly a sheet smaller than any of the other parts." Lewes "insists that B. VII is thick *enough*," she tells Blackwood, and she seems to hope for the same verdict from him. "It seemed inadmissible to add anything after the scene with Gwendolen, and to stick anything in, not necessary to development, between the foregoing chapters, is a form of 'matter in the wrong place' particularly repulsive to my authorship's sensibility" (*Letters* 6: 240).

Blackwood makes no suggestion for alteration and book 7, at 160 published pages, is some dozen pages shorter than any other.[21]

Despite—or perhaps because of—the marked direction book 7 had given the Deronda plot, Eliot remained anxious about the conclusion. And Blackwood, who resembled his reading public in disliking unhappy or open-ended conclusions, continued both to encourage and to worry, as he had from the time of *Scenes of Clerical Life*. On May 9, Lewes wrote of their pleasure in the reception of book 4: "The Jewish element has been more generally popular than we expected," and "I am curious to see how volume 3 will be received." His next paragraph explains that Eliot is "feeble, despondent and incredulous of being able to finish effectively. She gets on slowly with part VIII" (*Letters* 6: 247). Altogether, the letter demonstrates conflicting hope and doubt that book 4's enthusiastic reception will continue for future books. Blackwood writes back with encouraging sales, "I never recollect a case in which the sale of a work published in a serial form kept so closely up to the first start." He discounts their fears about the Jewish portion, although certain expressions in his postscript suggest unease: "*I am puzzling* greatly as to how Mrs. Lewes is to wind up in one more book and *I am certain the public after reading book 7 will sympathize* with me in wishing that there were to be more. Indeed I see symptoms already that the public would gladly have it prolonged to any length she wished" (*Letters* 6: 250; emphasis added). Was Blackwood hinting, as late as May 11, that he hoped she would not give the public the unsatisfactory conclusion that book 7 seems to presage? If so, he received his answer when he visited Eliot on May 18, a meeting he describes to William Blackwood:

> She says she never reads any review, but she certainly hears plentifully all that is said or written in London on the subject of Deronda. She remarked that it was hard upon her that people should be angry with her for not doing what they expected with her characters, and if people were no wiser in their speculations about more serious subjects such as theories of creation and the world than they were about the characters one poor woman was creating it did not say much for human wisdom. (*Letters* 6: 253–54)

Blackwood's share of human wisdom led him to know that anything more than a hint was too much, although his letters reveal continuing uncertainty. He wrote to William on June 6 that the early chapters of part 8, just in proof, "certainly made me weep" (6: 261); in writing to Lewes, he praised the conclusion as "Grand, glorious, and touching" (6: 262). At the same time, he seems to anticipate objections when he adds, to the latter, "In fact criticism and eulogism are out of place. I feel more than ever what I have often said to critics: 'Bow and accept with gratitude whatever George Eliot writes'" (6: 262). He had made the same argument to quell Langford's doubts about book 5, "she is so great a giant that there is nothing for it but to accept her inspirations and leave criticism alone" (6: 262n4a).

After book 6 appeared in July, he again remarks on speculation about the conclusion.

> The public continue all abroad as to what your finale is going to be, and it was great sport to me in London that I could decline all discussion of the Book because I knew so much more than the rest of the world that I would be arguing at an unfair advantage. . . . Delane said at Ascot, 'If I proclaim in the Strand here is the one man who has read the whole of Daniel Deronda, the ladies will tear you in pieces unless you tell them some lies or make a clean breast of it.' (6: 271–72)

The next paragraph, less jocular, betrays his unease. "There will I know be disappointment at not hearing more of the failure of Gwendolen and the mysterious destiny of Deronda, but *I am sure you were right* to leave all grand and vague, and the real disappointment of your public will be that their monthly food for interesting thought and speculation is stopped" (6: 272; emphasis added). His "I am sure you were right" and "*real* disappointment" hint at uncertainty, rather than unequivocal affirmation.

Blackwood's unease with the conclusion—to which only he and others in the firm were privy at the date of this letter, July 12—comes just as reviews begin to manifest English readers' failure to sympathize with the Jewish part of the novel. Lewes and Blackwood's original advertisement of "George Eliot's New Story of English Life" fitted the content of the early parts, but misled readers about what was coming later. Since he was privy to Eliot's research into Jewish life and history long before she began to write *Daniel Deronda*, Lewes knew the general direction the plot would take. When he suggested that "gossiping paragraphs" preceding the first installment "may as well say that the new book like 'Middlemarch,' is a story of English life but of our own day, and dealing for the most part in a higher sphere of Society" (6: 192–93), he probably had no intention to deceive. For him and for Eliot, the Jewish story was as significant a manifestation of modern English life as Bulstrode's Evangelicalism or Dinah's Methodism. As Lewes commented to Blackwood on December 1, 1875, "I have reflected that [as] she formerly contrived to make one love Methodists, there was no reason why she should not conquer the prejudice against the Jews" (*Letters* 6: 196). One advantage of the serial structure was its ability to draw the audience into the plot slowly. Even resistant readers might come to accept the new direction almost unawares. Some did, but many did not, and the dual thrust of the plot has been debated ever since.

7

Filling in the Blanks: Readers Respond to the Serialization of *Middlemarch* and *Daniel Deronda*

IN THE LATE TWENTIETH CENTURY serialized novels are rather rare. When casual readers pick up a copy of *Bonfire of the Vanities*, for example, they are often unaware that it first appeared in twenty-seven installments in *Rolling Stone* magazine. But for Victorian readers, the serial was everywhere—a powerful competitor or, frequently, a herald of the three-decker novel. Periodical reviewers—that special class of Victorian readers who were called upon to speculate publicly on directions and outcomes for novels not yet completed—were as aware, probably, as the novelists of the special demands of the serial form. They compared different serial writers' techniques and often lamented the delayed gratification involved in reading serially.

George Eliot had, of course, been a reviewer for the *Westminster Review*, the *Leader*, and other periodicals before becoming a novelist. From her first installment of "The Sad Fortunes of the Reverend Amos Barton," her narrators comment on the characters, plot, and purpose of fiction. It is perhaps a case of turnabout being fair play that finds her, in the 1870s, hailed as England's "greatest living novelist"; and her last two novels subject to an unusual outpouring of critical comment, including discussion of the theory and practice of serialization.

The London *Globe and Traveller*, which published one of the first reviews of book 1 of *Daniel Deronda*, distinguishes the artistic structure of Eliot's work from that of other famous contemporary serial novelists:

> George Eliot may be published in parts, but she writes with a view to the
> effect of the whole. Dickens made every part a little whole in itself; he

always introduced every character, carried on every portion of his story, gave each an equal climax, and duly balanced pathos with humour. The result is, that he reads better piece-meal. Thackeray's characters were like our acquaintances—we were anxious to know from time to time what they were actually doing, but we had no means of taking a complete view of their lives, and cared for their society more than for their history. But every novel of George Eliot is an elaborately consistent drama which rouses continuous attention, and gains in direct effect when the beginning, middle, and end are grasped together. (Jan. 31, 1876; 6)

The argument of the *Globe and Traveller*, that one should be able to perceive a literary work as a whole, with beginning, middle, and end, is countered by others who marvelled at the way in which the serial work unfolded, seeing the novel as process rather than product.

For Victorian novels published first as three-deckers, little record exists of their readers' reactions while the work was in progress. But with serials, publishers, friends of the author, and the general public recorded their reactions to individual parts as the reading process was under way, and they were forced to pause and contemplate the novel in its incomplete form.

The most formal reaction to the incomplete work was the serial review. Despite some critics' objections to serialization, dozens of reviews were published while the installments of *Middlemarch* and *Daniel Deronda* appeared. Many papers in Britain published a full set of reviews, sometimes coinciding to the day with the publication of a new part of the novel. Others published occasional reviews, which covered two or more half-volumes in a single review or simply reviewed some installments and omitted others. The number of reviews varies significantly for the two novels, with *Middlemarch* being reviewed in fewer papers and also having fewer full sets of reviews published. (See Appendix 1.) One can only speculate on the reason for the difference. *Middlemarch* reviews occasionally complain about the long intervals between bimonthly parts and later about the confusion occasioned by the switch from bimonthly to monthly serialization. *Deronda* reviewers who dislike serialization consoled themselves that at least the intervals are only one month instead of two. *Middlemarch* was also Eliot's first novel to use the half-volume installment; by the publication of *Daniel Deronda*, reviewers had a better idea of what to expect.

Victorian critics examined serial novels with many of the same questions that the three-volume works evoked. But in addition, these serial works prompted special discussion of issues such as the temporal dimension of literature, the problem of wholeness in a work seen initially only in parts, the pauses or blanks that this special publication format imposes on a text, and the nature of readers' interaction or entanglement with the serial text.

The temporal dimension involved in reading a long work is unavoidably apparent in a serialized novel. Reader-response theorist Wolfgang Iser posits this dimension for all texts:

> In every text there is a potential time sequence which the reader must inevitably realize, as it is impossible to absorb even a short text in a single moment. Thus the reading process always involves viewing the text through a perspective that is continually on the move, linking up the different phases, and so constructing what we have called the virtual dimension. (*Implied Reader* 280)

Existing in any literary work, this dimension is more noticeable in long works and especially in serialized novels. With enforced intervals for contemplation and the necessity of putting impressions to paper before the work could be seen in its completeness, serial reviewers register their awareness of this temporal dimension. Metaphors in reviews of *Middlemarch* and *Daniel Deronda*, particularly the metaphor of the journey, highlight this dimension. For example, the *Edinburgh Courant* responds to *Deronda*, book 3: "We shall be glad, and expect to find, that 'Maidens Choosing' is only the stretch of bleak country which in most journeys you have to pass ere you can get from one rich valley to another. But as our range of vision is for the moment limited to this comparatively small bit of the landscape, bleak we must not hesitate to declare it" (Mar. 30, 1876; 4). The *Glasgow News*, at book 4, is glad to see that now "the narrative is carried on straightforwardly." Serial publication and the structure of the opening parts caused confusion, but finally "we are on the high road of the story; indeed, at the conclusion of the present part, we may be said to be at Half-Way House, and to be in the centre of what plot there is" (June 6, 1876; 2). The London *Standard*'s concluding review combines the issue of wholeness with the journey metaphor: *Deronda* is "not more disappointing in parts than it is unsatisfactory as a whole. . . . We have travelled for eight wearisome months with a company of persons not one of whom has endeared himself or herself to us on the journey, and it is a positive pleasure to know that we shall never meet any of them again, for George Eliot, at any rate, has the decency to bury her dead out of sight" (Sept. 25, 1876; 2).

Early reviewers of *Middlemarch* had used a similar image: the introduction has "at first sight a cold and formal air [and] the strangers [are] more or less strangers to us at the close of the book [but] the reader must wait for some further traveling in their company before he finds that he and they have been shaken well together, and understand each other" (*Daily News*, Nov. 28, 1871; 5). And the *Westminster Review* describes the chapter headings as "finger-posts showing us the road we are to travel" (Jan. 1872; 277). The *Examiner*'s metaphor is a variation on that theme: Eliot "gives us just such insight into the lifelike characters of the people of her story as, if we were clever enough, we might obtain for ourselves during a short stay in the mid-England district in which her scene is laid" (Dec. 2, 1871; 1192).

Eliot was aware of the relationship between a reader's journey through a text and a person's journey through life. She inverts the figure in chapter 54 of *Adam Bede*, making the journey literal and the reading metaphorical. On Adam's second journey to Snowfield, he recalls his first: "What keen memories went along the road with him! He had often been to Oakbourne and back since that first journey to Snowfield, but beyond Oakbourne, the grey stone walls, the broken country, the meagre trees, seemed to be telling him afresh the story of that painful past which he knew so well by heart." Adam is identified with a reader journeying through a text; both text and reader alter in time: "But no story is the same to us after a lapse of time; or rather, we who *read* it are no longer the same interpreters" (573; emphasis added). Eliot expressed this same view in her own voice, thanking George Smith for a copy of *Henry Esmond*, which he sent her in March 1863: "I suppose it is ten years since I read it, and in ten years one gets a different person and finds new qualities in everything" (*Letters* 4: 79). Victorian serialization brought readers to a special awareness of this time axis. The serial story reinforced the illusion of time passing and events receding because of the actual passage of time in the weekly, monthly, or bimonthly pauses between installments.[1]

While reviewers like the *Athenaeum*'s critic argued that part publication was "a mistake when applied to works of imagination which are neither sensational nor humorous" (Jan. 29, 1876; 160), others link the experience of reading in parts favorably with mid-Victorian realism. The

Spectator's final review of *Middlemarch* entered the debate ongoing during that novel's appearance as to whether serial publication was good for either the novel's artistry or for the readers' apprehension of it. There is "no sign of a half-completed or altered design anywhere" to suggest that the novel was published before it was completed,[2] but "whether the reader should study the instalments as they are doled out" is another matter:

> We are disposed to maintain that no story gets so well apprehended, so completely mastered in all its aspects, as one which, written as a whole, is published in parts. There is, at all events, this to be said in its favour,—that it is the only way in which human life itself, of which fiction is supposed to be the mirror, can be studied. There you are not allowed to see the beginning, middle, and end at a sitting . . . but must usually become perfectly familiar with the human elements of a story before you see them even begin to combine into a plot. (Dec. 7, 1872; 1554)

The disagreement between this critic and the reviewer for the *Globe and Traveller* was part of a larger debate on the nature and purpose of the serial reading experience. Some readers preferred their novels "whole" and refused to read them until they were issued in volume form. But others felt this course was barely possible for a social human being. In its first review of *Daniel Deronda*, the *Manchester Examiner and Times* disputed the idea that one could simply wait; recalling the publication of *Middlemarch* four years earlier, the reviewer asked: "Was it possible to meet one's friends during that long winter without hearing the infatuation of Dorothy [*sic*], and her subsequent awakening, with all its consequences, the subject of general conversation?" (Jan. 29, 1876; 5).

Reviewers recognized that the decision to serialize involved more than the inclinations of either reader or author. They shared Lewes and Blackwood's dislike for the constraints imposed by Mudie's adherence to the three-decker. The *Nonconformist* praises serial publication in its review of *Middlemarch*: independent half-volumes are a laudable way "to help bring to an end the old fashion of publishing novels in three volumes at a guinea and a half." The reviewer places this new format in the context of other kinds of serials: "We have not any great liking for instalments, . . . [but] it is better to have one of this magnitude than the small portions with which we are often tantalised in the monthly magazines" (Dec. 13, 1871; 1226–27). The London *Guardian*, aware that serial parts may be *too* apt to recede into the past, argues against it in a novelist like Eliot:

Serial publication is suitable enough to a good many modern tales. They are meant only to amuse for a spare half-hour; they are forgotten as soon as thrown aside, and just sufficiently remembered, when taken up again, to save the trouble of a fresh introduction. But it is not a satisfactory way of reading a new novel by George Eliot. For this is a work of art, which suffers a good deal by being broken into fragments. There is a purpose and completeness about the whole which is very much impaired by being taken in only at successive and distant intervals. (Jan. 3, 1872; 23)

The work-of-art-as-object image underlies objections to the serialization of *Daniel Deronda* four years later. Arguing from a product rather than process metaphor, the *Glasgow News* compares part publication to the partial viewing of a sculpture: "There is something particularly unsatisfactory in criticising the first portion of a novel. . . . It is like passing judgment upon a statue of which only a fragment is before us. The fragment may be beautiful in itself, but it is impossible to judge of its relation to the other parts, or to conceive the fine proportions of the perfect work" (Jan. 29, 1876; 2). Both the *Aberdeen Journal* and the *Examiner* use architectural metaphors. Reviewing the first installment of *Deronda*, the former complained, is "like criticising a single brick of a stately edifice." But that is the author's fault in publishing in parts: "We cannot read the book without forming an opinion" (Feb. 9, 1876; 6). The *Examiner* began with a different metaphor. Its first notice compares *Daniel Deronda* with *Middlemarch*, which bore serialization well because it was like a "Greek trilogy; you might as well begin at the fourth [*sic*] and extend backwards and forwards, as begin at the first and read straight through; you might read one 'book,' and leave off without a painful sense of incompleteness" (Jan. 29, 1876; 124). By its third notice, however, Greek drama gives way to an architectural image: "The foundations of 'George Eliot's' story are at length completed, and the walls begin to rise with considerable rapidity" (Apr. 1, 1876; 381). Seeing the novel as a sculpture in process, *John Bull* concludes that the first seven books present "a wonderful marble group, in which the sculpture, though far advanced, does not yet represent the whole design" (Nov. 23, 1872; 806).

Daniel Deronda's narrator sees a difference between the plastic and narrative arts in terms of stability and change. Describing Gwendolen, the narrator suggests that "Sir Joshua [Reynolds] would have been glad to take her portrait; and he would have had an easier task than the historian at least in this, that he would not have had to represent the truth of change—only to give stability to one beautiful moment" (102). Serial reading highlighted the "truth of change" by forcing readers to pause for a month and contemplate what had occurred before they encountered a new situation in a new part.

Reviewers sometimes described the effect of the incompleteness in terms of the contemplation allowed readers. The *Westminster Review*'s brief notice of the first book of *Middlemarch* acknowledges that serialization "taxes" the reader and the critic, but at the same time "Eliot's novels bear publishing piecemeal better than any other writer's. Like all great masters, she makes those pauses and gives us those breaks which are so necessary for repose in the enjoyment of a work of art." The metaphor from the visual arts with which this review continues derives from the concept of process: *Middlemarch* "is very like looking at some newly begun picture by a great artist. He explains to you that where you see a few blurred lines there will be some saint's face, and that here, where all is blank, will be the cross which she will bear, and that there . . . will lie the shattered crown of glory which she should have worn" (Jan. 1872; 276–77). Iser notes that these pauses for "repose" are different in the serial story.

> The interruptions are more deliberate and calculated than those occasioned by random reasons. . . . they arise from a strategic purpose. The reader is forced by the pauses imposed on him to imagine more than he could have if his reading were continuous, and so, if the text of a serial makes a different impression from the text in book-form, this is principally because it introduces additional blanks, or alternatively accentuates existing blanks by means of a break until the next installment. This does not mean that its quality is in any way higher. The pauses simply bring out a different kind of realization in which the reader is compelled to take a more active part by filling in these additional blanks. (*Act* 192)

The ubiquitous reviews of *Middlemarch* and *Daniel Deronda* stimulated the creative use of those blanks by initiating a dialogue between reader and reviewer, to add to the dialogue between reader and text or between reader and reader.

Some reviewers regarded this active role in filling the blanks as part of the pleasure of serial reading. According to the *Examiner*'s review of *Daniel Deronda*, book 2, the "fragmentary" mode of publishing gives ample time . . . for the study and free social discussion of the characters, for speculation as to their unrevealed past and their unreached future. It is needless to say that there are few novelists whose work is sufficiently interesting to invite or sufficiently profound and intricate to bear such vivisection; but "George Eliot" is so full of secondary meanings, and has acquired such a reputation for meaning more than she says, in spite of her unremitting care to explain her chief points, that every prominent incident in an uncompleted novel is surrounded, in addition to its intrinsic effect, with all the interest of a puzzle. Opinions during the last month have been much divided as to what she intends to make of her heroine; bets have been freely laid, and if the gifted authoress were open to secret negtciations [*sic*], she might add indefinitely to the profits, if not to the artistic unity, of her work, by consenting to accept suggestions from interested parties.

If authors, including George Eliot, were not impervious to such suggestions, this reviewer's tongue-in-cheek solution would have required a significant change in their habit of beginning to publish a work before they completed it: "If this method of publication should extend, and if a kind providence were to send us a cluster of 'George Eliots,' it would be necessary for the protection of Her Majesty's subjects to pass an Act of Parliament requiring all the MSS. to be lodged in trustworthy hands before the issue of the first instalment" (*Examiner*, Mar. 4, 1876; 265). Assuming that the blank spaces give rise to thoughtful consideration of the complexities of the work (Eliot's "secondary meanings") rather than mere excited speculation about the superficial aspects of the plot, this review counters one of Iser's points about serial production. The appeal to readers' "norms and values," Iser says, is characteristic of modern serial stories which strive for commercial success (*Act* 191). The *Examiner* argues that Eliot challenges her readers rather than making this appeal.

Four years earlier, in reviewing *Middlemarch* book 3, the *Examiner* relates the anecdote of a couple for whom the pauses between installments were reinforced by many more of their own creation:

We heard the other day of a husband and wife who find in each two-monthly instalment as much as they can read in the two months, two or three pages affording the text for a whole evening's thought and discussion, and we can both understand and admire their state of mind. There is hardly a page of 'Middlemarch' in which there is not enough condensed wisdom to furnish an hour's profitable reflection, and they who have time thus thoroughly to master the teacher's lessons are much to be envied. (Mar. 30, 1872; 333)

This reviewer understands the complex nature of the interaction between reader and serial text. The pauses between parts not only add to the period of reflection, but create an opportunity for extended interaction among readers.

Not all readers were as concerned with secondary meanings and profitable reflection as the couple described in the *Examiner*. For some, the breaks simply provided a safe outlet for the human desire for gossip. According to the *Daily News*, *Daniel Deronda* offers "a field for personal gossip without any harm in it, and we can speak ill of the heroine, or defend her, praise the characters we like, and utter our minds about those we find antipathetic, with all the zest, and without any of the mischief, of real gossip about real people" (Jan. 29, 1876; 2). Both major and minor characters receive greater focus when the serial breaks occasion the gossiping discussion usually associated with "real" people. The *Spectator*'s initial notice, headed "Gwendolen Harleth," points out that "no young lady with a flesh-and-blood existence is likely to be half as much discussed in English drawing-rooms for the next eight months as she is" (Jan. 29, 1876; 138). Reviewing *Middlemarch*, the *Leeds Mercury* argues that readers' involvement with even minor figures demonstrates Eliot's ability to create characters who "all live and move like real men and women, and even though they flit before us on a single page, they take life and shape directly." To illustrate the point, the review describes one reader's response to Borthrup Trumbull, "who scarcely appears four times from the first page to the last":

Not long ago a reader of the story, wandering in Dreamland through "the footless fancies of the night," found himself sitting at a Barmecide feast by the side of a gentleman who talked volubly in language of the most ornate description. The dreamer felt sure that he had met his companion before; but it was only after a lengthened conversation, in which the peculiar characteristics of his style of talking became more clear, that the idea suddenly flashed upon him that he had at last met Mr. Borthropp [*sic*] Trumbull. With which happy conviction he awoke. Not for some months had he read Trumbull's name, and yet so distinct and vivid was the impression of the auctioneer's individuality upon his mind, that even in his sleep he recognised it. The same sort of thing may sometimes happen after reading Shakspere; but how often does it happen after reading the ordinary work of an ordinary novelist? (Dec. 14, 1872; 12)

Another kind of involvement is recorded in the story of a "young lady" who so disliked Casaubon "that she called the dullest and most sunless spot in her charming fernery 'her Casaubon'" (*Manchester Guardian*, Nov. 1, 1872; 7).

Dreaming about Borthrup Trumbull, gossiping about Gwendolen Harleth, or avenging Dorothea by appropriating her husband's name may seem to violate the line between text and audience, but that is precisely the point. As they became entangled with the characters, serial readers experienced a mixture of frustration at delayed gratification along with the pleasure and suspense that came from treating the characters as if they were real. Reviews show that they were conscious of this blurring of the line between fact and fiction.[3] The London *Figaro* acknowledges this entanglement in its first review of *Deronda*: "It is characteristic of George Eliot to make the personages who figure in her stories almost live and breathe before us, and it is excusable if one forgets at times that they are fictitious" (Feb. 9, 1876; 10). Another reviewer comes to regard the pleasure of gossiping about the characters during the intervals between parts as compensation for this mode of publication. The *Manchester Examiner and Times* complains initially that the "delightful anticipations" aroused by the announcement of a new story by George Eliot would have been heard "with more unqualified pleasure" had not its serial publication also been announced—so that readers will have "to wait in rebellious misery during the monthly intervals" (Jan. 29, 1876; 5). However, the reviewer has a change of heart by book 3: it is "too early to form an opinion about the merits of 'Daniel Deronda' as a dramatic story, and novel readers may still amuse themselves by speculating about its coming events; and the actual pleasure which many of us experience in doing so should not be forgotten when we object to the annoying intervals between the publication of the parts" (Mar. 29, 1876; 3). The serial review, often published under the pressure of time to match the appearance of a new number, becomes the record of readers' personal gossip and entanglement with the story.

Eliot's readers, like any others, brought their reading history and preconceptions with them when they encountered her text.[4] As Lewes phrased it regarding one of his own works, "the reader brings his views, theories, superstitions to disturb the effect of a proposition" (*Letters* 6: 96). To

See note

Middlemarch and *Daniel Deronda*, Eliot's readers brought expectations derived from her own earlier works and the works of her contemporaries—particularly the sensation novels of the 1860s—as well as from their conception of the genre itself, which in the 1870s was still suspect in the eyes of some Victorians. The "New Books" column in the *Illustrated London News* for October 5, 1872, opens by observing that "The novelists are never allowed to pause, in their desperate attempts to produce fresh combinations of domestic and social adventure for the entertainment of indolent readers, who want to be amused in the easiest manner" (323).[5] The *Leeds Mercury* begins its review of *Middlemarch* with a comment that echoes the narrator in chapter 5 of *Northanger Abbey*: "It is only a book—nay, worse, it is only a novel. In its outward shape there is nothing to distinguish it from a hundred other novels which have been poured from the teeming English press during the last twelve months" (Dec. 14, 1872; 12).

Contemporary critics acknowledge that their own and their readers' expectations derive from other novels. The London *Echo* refers to "our novel-reading instinct" which "smells unmistakable mischief" in the character of Ladislaw as early as the first installment of *Middlemarch* (Nov. 28, 1871; 2). The *Glasgow News* contrasts Eliot's work with the usual structure of the novel: serialization of "lesser" writers than Eliot "would not so much matter. The first chapters of a story by Miss Braddon, for instance, are generally sufficient for all purposes of criticism and insight into the general tendency of the production. Most modern novels are constructed upon well-defined and perfectly well-known principles." This reviewer instances Trollope and "Ouida" as other examples of predictable authors, and adds, "'Guy Livingstone's' romances can be reviewed almost before they are written, so uniformly are they built upon the same old lines" (Jan. 29, 1876; 2). The Edinburgh *Daily Review* likewise draws the distinction between Eliot and the "ordinary love story or mechanical web of the Wilkie Collins order" (Feb. 28, 1876; 5).

Other reviewers use this contrast to humorous effect in setting *Middlemarch* apart from other works. The London *Daily Telegraph* observes that it is the topic of conversation everywhere: "'Have you read the last Book?' is an almost inevitable question in the haunts of men." The reviewer feigns regret that "of late a certain sense of public disappointment has found utterance. There are complaints that the instalments appear at uncertain times; that the story itself is not intensely interesting; and that a certain vein of melancholy runs throughout."

The fault, however, lies in the expectations readers form based on other fiction:

> To understand these complaints one must observe how other writers of the day treat their readers. They supply so many pages every month. Then they manage, as a rule, to leave their heroine in a position of perplexity or peril. Either she has run away from home, or is left on London Bridge with only fourpence-halfpenny and an opera cloak; or her soul has been softened by the charm of a dragoon, who has killed his first wife; or she "breaks off" clasped in the passionate embrace of her brother-in-law, her grandfather, or other prohibited being. Here GEORGE ELIOT entirely fails; she does not consider the necessities of the present day. We want something lively and exciting; something to take up on the road or rail, after a late breakfast, or before a Richmond dinner; something spiced, that will tickle the mental palate and not demand any thought. (June 8, 1872; 6–7)

George Eliot's "failure" is, for this tongue-in-cheek reviewer, a measure of her superior stature as a philosophical, not a sensation, novelist. One would like, though, to know what this reviewer would have said four years later when Deronda discovers the singer Mirah Lapidoth, run away from home, penniless, wrapped in her woolen cloak, about to drown herself below Richmond Bridge. The *Daily Telegraph* was, alas, silent on the subject of *Deronda*.

Overall, contemporaries felt that *Daniel Deronda* had more "incident" than *Middlemarch*. Certain scenes especially evoked the pattern of the sensation novel: the opening scene, with the heroine gambling at a fashionable watering place; the incidents surrounding Mrs. Glasher directly or indirectly, including Gwendolen's receipt of the diamonds with which chapter 31 ends; the drowning of Grandcourt, and Gwendolen's confession to Deronda (reviews of book 1 in the *Sunday Times* [London], Feb. 20, 1876; 7; of book 3 in the Liverpool *Weekly Albion*, May 6, 1876; 7; and of book 7 in the *Edinburgh Courant*, Aug. 7, 1876; 4). To these, reviewers added other sensation-style occurrences, predicting that Deronda and Grandcourt would prove to be the same person and that Daniel and Mirah would be brother and sister (reviews of books 1 and 6 in the *Glasgow News*, Jan. 29, 1876; 2; July 1, 1876; 2). Comments on *Middlemarch*, in contrast, remark the absence of titillating events and express their view of the genre as well. The *Edinburgh Courant* argues on January 6, 1873, that

It would be as untrue as it would be unjust to call "Middlemarch" a novel in the sense in which the word is used now-a-days. The most briefless of barristers who ever perpetrated his three volumes, the most impecunious of penny-a-liners who ever dashed off a tale for a twopenny journal to rescue his only coat from pawn, the most gushing of schoolgirls afflicted with the *cacoethes scribendi*, would blush to offer so tame and uneventful a tale to his or her readers. There is neither a bigamy nor an abduction, neither forbidden banns nor illicit love—nothing even approaching to a literary "header"—in all its light parts. It deals with the commonest incidents of daily life. (7)

John Bull's review covering books 3 to 7 comments that readers who "attack" *Middlemarch* "as children do a stick of barley-sugar . . . will soon turn from the feast unsatisfied, for no mere lover of the purely sensational or the mawkish love tale of the period will find much to desire within these small green books" (Nov. 23, 1872; 806). These last two reviews indicate the power of Eliot's realism to subdue readers' sense of the sensational in events like Raffles' blackmail and Bulstrode's murder. The sensational disappears amidst the complex characterization.

The serial format itself created special expectations for readers. Reviewers were as aware as the authors of the special principles on which serial novels were constructed, particularly what Iser calls the necessity of "break[ing] off at the point of suspense" (*Act* 191).[6] J. Don Vann suggests, however, that although the striking conclusion was part of serial readers' horizon of expectations generally, they did not expect it in George Eliot's work (*Victorian Novels* 12–13; see also Beaty). This may have been true of some readers, but despite Eliot's reputation, mixed expectations arose in part from the fact that she was a woman writer. As Elaine Showalter points out, "the prominence of women, not just as consumers but also as creators of sensation fiction, was one of its most disturbing elements" (3). Though some reviewers make a pro forma disclaimer placing Eliot in a category of her own, these disclaimers only highlight the gender bias. The final London *Globe and Traveller* review, for example, observes that "A new novel by George Eliot is no ordinary literary event. It is not the annual contribution of three volumes of empty immoralities, to which the novel-reading public is, unfortunately, so well accustomed from the prolific pens of many of our most popular authoresses" (Dec. 3, 1872; 6). The *Weekly Dispatch's* initial notice of *Daniel Deronda* avoids the term "authoress," sometimes used for Eliot in reviews of the 1870s, but blames women for the habit of writing in installments:

> The habit of publishing novels in parts . . . cannot be said to be favourable to the production of first-rate fiction. To write a volume, or three volumes, in parts, is a sin worthy of, and, we hope, only committed by, a certain section of authors, *chiefly women, whose fluency largely dilutes their brains.* To publish a novel in parts is, with all due respect to our author, almost equally wrong. A part, by the nature of things, must end with a sensation; it may not be the moment, familiar to "penny dreadfuls," when the dagger is poised over the sleeping man, or the lovely heroine is struggling in the grasp of the villain of the story as her lover breaks on to the scene; but it is, and in truth must be, a "situation." (emphasis added)

The review adds that the results are disastrous for artistic effect, because the "reader loses the frame of mind necessary for the contemplation of the writer's skill, and merely waits, more or less excited, for a month, passing his time in futile guesses whether the young man to whom the heroine is introduced as we part with her, is the right one, or the one destined to stand in the right one's way" (Feb. 13, 1876; 6). This writer is one of many who object that such a technique did not produce "first-rate fiction."[7] This review also points out that overinvolvement in the excitement of the story works against the distance necessary for aesthetic response. The contemplative effect—reader watching his or her own responses—is gone. Plot interest takes precedence.

Serial reviews of *Middlemarch* frequently comment that the plot is slow and the chief interest is in the characters, and some defend serialization on this account. Though Eliot is "unkind in issuing her new novel . . . in parts," her work "will bear this treatment better than most works. By her the ordinary method of plot-making is but slightly regarded" (*Examiner*, Dec. 2, 1871; 1192). Instead of employing the plot techniques of Collins, who "could by working the story up to a certain definite point in each number, sustain the interest throughout," Eliot appeals through "Original conceptions of character worked out with consummate art, philosophic views . . . wise apophthegms . . . felicities of style, [and] bits of poetic description" (*Nonconformist*, Feb. 21, 1872; 202). The story in *Middlemarch* is so mild that by book 3, there has been "nothing more exciting than the death of a disagreeable old gentleman" (*Nonconformist*, Apr. 10, 1872; 376). The Roman Catholic *Tablet*'s reviewer "rather tremble[s] for the contents of the third volume [book]," but not because of a suspenseful plot. The tremor is moral; an illicit liaison between Dorothea and Will "would oblige us to judge unfavourably" of the book (Mar. 2, 1872; 264). The *Tablet*, however, was delighted by their legal union at the end. "Of course, she offends her whole family; but the mistake, if mistake it were, ensured the lifelong happiness of two great and noble natures" (Dec. 21, 1872; 780).

Not all readers shared this sentiment. Some expected the deaths of both Casaubon and Rosamond and the union of Dorothea and Lydgate. As early as its second notice, the *Echo* asks, "Will the benevolently-disposed reader wish that Providence should remove Mr. Casaubon?" (Jan. 30, 1872; 2). And Providence does. (Providence, however, was not so obliging with Rosamond—and quite equivocal with Raffles.) Noting the relationship of Will Ladislaw and Dorothea in book 2, the *Examiner* fears and hopes:

> But if we were to attempt to forecast Dorothea's future, we should be inclined, we confess, to attach more significance to what we are told about Mr Lydgate, a young doctor, who has come to settle in Middlemarch for a time, than to anything we learn relating directly to herself. There is obviously an artistic relationship already in course of being established between the two characters, and we fear this bodes no good to Dorethea [*sic*]. (Feb. 3, 1872; 125)

By book 6, the *Examiner* prefers Lydgate to Ladislaw and is glad that "we close the book with no fast assurance that she will marry [Will] in the end." Hope centers on a catastrophe that will remove Rosamond.

> Lydgate, who finds that in marrying Rosamond he has committed nearly as great a blunder as was Dorothea's wedding with Mr Casaubon, though he is not yet brought any nearer to the widow, still appears as a possible alternative to Ladislaw. And, though Lydgate's silly little wife is admirably drawn, and all her movements must be followed with interest, by reason of the skill with which they are recounted, no reader of the book would very much regret her death, if thereby the clever man and the refined woman of the novel were to be brought into closer relations.

The reviewer even wonders, "is there to be any serious issue to the at present harmless flirtations between Ladislaw and Rosamond?" (Oct. 5, 1872; 985). If not death, the divorce court? Certainly the idea is bold for a proper literary magazine, but the juxtaposition of the hope for Rosamond's death and the hint that her flirtation with Will may become more significant, suggests the reviewer was open to Rosamond's removal by any means. Eliot offers neither death nor divorce, and to the last, the *Examiner* wishes for another outcome:

> It is not easy to like young Ladislaw; one is tempted to think that, in marrying him, Dorothea makes nearly as great a blunder as she did in marrying Mr Casaubon. How much pleasanter it would have been for Lydgate to be her husband? But, unfortunately, things do not always go pleasantly in real life, and the fate that befals Dorothea is very natural, though not very welcome. (Dec. 7, 1872; 1204)

Also regretting that Dorothea and Lydgate are not joined in novelistic bliss, the *Leeds Mercury* saw it as a feature of Eliot's realism:

> We suppose that hardly any one has read the story without feeling disappointed that it did not end in the marriage of Lydgate and Dorothea. Certainly two human beings better suited for each other it would have been difficult to find. But all through the book they are kept apart until their fates have been decided for them, and they are bound to other and less fitting mates. Is not this, again, a wonderful touch of reality? How often in real life do people marry those whom all the world, except themselves, see to be best suited for them? (Dec. 14, 1872; 12)

Eliot recognized this from the start; Jerome Beaty demonstrates that the union of Dorothea and Will "had been decided upon from the time the very earliest plans for *Middlemarch* were entered in the notebook: 'Dorothea's second marriage' appears in the list of 'Private dates' on *Quarry II*, 4" (Beaty 88).

When *Daniel Deronda* appeared four years later, reviewers expected the slow-paced plots of *Adam Bede* and *Middlemarch*, but quickly perceived that this novel was very different. The *Weekly Dispatch* contrasts *Deronda* with *Middlemarch*:

> In "Middlemarch" we had a story which might have appeared in almost any form without suffering from it, so the evil of part-publishing remained almost unheeded. With "Daniel Deronda" this is not the case. We venture to say that when the remainder of the book is published, the first impulse of many readers will be to rush to the end to see what becomes of Gwendolen Harleth. Study of the gradual development of character gives way to the impulse of mere curiosity, and the work of George Eliot sinks at once to the level of the three-volume novel of mediocre missishness, which inspires

the reader with no other thought than a languid wish to know which particular commandment the *dramatis personae* are to set at naught. (Feb. 13,
1876; 6)

One notes both the association of simple curiosity about the plot with
women's writing and reading ("missishness") and the implied accusation
of sensationalism ("which particular commandment" is to be "set at
naught"). This perception of much greater curiosity about *Deronda* continues and even increases with the subsequent installments—which, ironically, may explain in part why *Deronda* was reviewed during its serialization more frequently than *Middlemarch* had been.

Forming expectations based on prior reading is a process in which all
readers engage. But serial readers go further. Knowing that an author can
alter a text not yet published, they sometimes articulate their expectations without the detachment or the understanding of realism that the
Examiner and the *Leeds Mercury* demonstrate. Reviewers of *Daniel Deronda*, in particular, were quick to blame the author for not taking their
suggestions, which locate Mary Elizabeth Braddon's sensation heroines
in Trollope's "sugarplum" endings.[8] Eliot both exploits and undercuts
these expectations. She uses the characteristics of such texts, but alters
them—challenging her readers to accept the alterations. In *Middlemarch*,
she had broken with the "happily-ever-after" marriage pattern by focusing on the miserable marriages of the Casaubons and the Lydgates; and
although she "rewards" Dorothea with a happy second marriage, its
equivocal nature is acknowledged in the finale. For Lydgate, however,
there is no reprieve, while the undeserving Rosamond makes a comfortable, wealthy second marriage (which she regards as her reward). In
Deronda, Eliot breaks the pattern further by giving Gwendolen Harleth
a first marriage even more miserable than that of either *Middlemarch*
couple and then, no happy second marriage.

The *Edinburgh Courant* comments on this disposition of events in its
final notice of *Daniel Deronda*, which opens with a touch of humor at
the expense of young female readers: "'How does it end?' is a crucial
question with all novel-readers, solved by young ladies in a summary
fashion peculiarly their own, and entering deeply into the judgment of
even the more orthodox and patient among us, who are content to read
the chapters in their natural order." *Deronda*, however, does not end
with sensational incidents nor "in the ancient and approved manner
which Scott conformed to with a smile at its tyranny, and which Thackeray

openly derided without ever wholly rejecting it." Its author declines to follow "this time-honoured custom" of "marshall[ing] in" her characters "before the curtain falls, in pairs as far as lawfully may be. . . . What is to become, matrimonially or otherwise, of most of her characters is left entirely to the reader's imagination. Only one marriage ceremony is provided in this last book; and it is open to any one to speculate" what will become of the other characters, Rex, Hans, Anna, the Meyrick sisters—and especially "the dashing heroine herself" (Sept. 4, 1876; 3).

Eliot was aware of readers' resistance. "People in their eagerness about my characters are quite angry, it appears, when their own expectations are not fulfilled—angry, for example, that Gwendolen accepts Grandcourt etc. etc.," she wrote Blackwood on April 18, 1876, as she was working on proofs of book 7. "One reader is sure that Mirah is going to die very soon and I suppose will be disgusted at her remaining alive. Such are the reproaches to which I make myself liable." These examples of reader expectations caused her to ponder apprehensively the novel's final disposition, but Blackwood's approbation reassured her: "that you seem to share Mr. Lewes's strong feeling of Book VII being no falling off in intensity, makes me brave" (*Letters* 6: 241).[9]

Two sets of reviews serve to contrast reviewer-readers' attempts to dictate the story and their reactions when Eliot does not cooperate. The initial review of *Daniel Deronda* in the *Manchester Examiner and Times*, which thought the introductory chapters "exciting," argues that Eliot's novel does not work well as a serial: she is "too great an artist to modify the plan of her work to the necessary conditions of a serial story." In particular, the review objects to the book's opening in one time and place, and then shifting almost immediately to another (Jan. 29, 1876; 5). The next review, however, is "even grateful to the author for not having begun her novel at the beginning of the story during the narrative of Grandcourt's lovemaking and Gwendolen's indecision, since it gives us the assurance of her escape from a man who is utterly unworthy of her" (Feb. 28, 1876; 3).

This confidence in Gwendolen's escape is, of course, premature. The next notice opens with regret, even disapproval, of the self-centered heroine:

When the excellent Mr. Gascoyne endeavoured to console his niece . . . by reminding her of the benefits of chastisement to all who adjust their minds to it, even he (with all his shrewdness) could have had no suspicion of the inappositeness of his remark. To Gwendolen there was neither sweetness nor use in adversity, and so far was she from adjusting her mind to the discipline of sorrow that the prospects of hardship and drudgery only intensified her selfishness and enfeebled all her more generous instincts. (Mar. 29, 1876; 3)

Apparently forgetting his own earlier remarks, the reviewer congratulates those readers "who have been bitterly rebuking the infatuated admirers of the heroine, who predicted from the first that she would pass triumphantly through her trial" (Mar. 29, 1876; 3).

Among readers who envisioned a marriage between Deronda and Gwendolen, none is more vehement in objecting to the final disposition of events than the reviewer for the London *Figaro*, who blames the author angrily for his disappointment. This disappointment is perhaps greater because expectation was so high. Reviewing book 1, the *Figaro* recalls *Middlemarch*, which "we have always regarded . . . as the greatest novel of the present century" and one that "could never be equalled." But now, it seems that "'Daniel Deronda' will be a very formidable rival." Though arguing that George Eliot "disdains to resort to the ordinary devices of the novel-writer," the reviewer's conventional expectations include the prediction that both Grandcourt and Deronda will fall in love with Gwendolen and that Klesmer is already "rapidly" doing so! (Feb. 9, 1876; 10).

By book 4, "That [Gwendolen] will marry Grandcourt is a certainty; it remains to be seen whether, from some cause or other, she will subsequently marry Deronda. The author created them for each other; she is almost in duty bound to bring them together at last" (May 24, 1876; 11). By the next number, it is clear that Gwendolen and Deronda will "be more than they are to each other. . . . It is possible danger will be averted, but it lies ahead." Like so many reviewers who saw (usually with dismay, though that does not seem so with the *Figaro* writer) connections between *Daniel Deronda* and sensation fiction, *Figaro*'s reviewer sees Gwendolen's coming rebellion in terms of an elopement: "If she is saved from a more unhappy fate—if, indeed, it could be more unhappy—than the perpetual presence of a man she abhors, it will be because Deronda himself will refuse to be tempted of the devil—Gwendolen, and not only Gwendolen, might demur to the description, but Society makes no distinction" (June 28, 1876; 5).

By book 6, the reviewer has rewritten the novel to his satisfaction. If Gwendolen had been "content with poverty for a short time, she might have escaped it eventually and been satisfied with her life. For Deronda, who, it is manifest, has really loved her from the outset, would surely have married her." This speculation concludes with a scenario from novels like *Aurora Floyd* and *East Lynne*: "It depends upon him, more than upon her, whether she makes the plunge which women, even better than her, have done in all times—a plunge never to be justified, but how often capable of extenuation?" (July 29, 1876; 11). The moral ambivalence with which the sentence concludes was a frequent complaint against the attractions of the sensation novel.[10] Discussing book 7 two weeks later, the reviewer again resists the direction of the text: the "disappointment that seems to be in store for the reader . . . is very bitter. If, after all, Deronda and [Gwendolen] are not to come together, some people will wish they had never perused the book. The catastrophe which takes place in the part before us will then have occurred in vain" (Aug. 12, 1876; 11). The idea of a change in character rather than in situation is clearly not part of the context of expectations for this writer; Grandcourt's drowning is regarded simply as a device for freeing Gwendolen for a second, happy marriage.

This plot twist may remind readers of the sensation novel, including *Aurora Floyd*, whose independent heroine resembles Gwendolen Harleth and whose repellent first husband meets a violent death suspected to be at the hand of his wife. Reviewers, however, just as often cite *Middlemarch* as contributing to such expectations. The Edinburgh *Daily Review* notes Deronda's reappearance in book 4 in connection with Gwendolen and adds: "George Eliot almost challenges us to speculate how she will work out his fate in connection with the new wife's, so as to recall Dorothea and her husband's nephew in 'Middlemarch' by the care with which the intercourse between the two is described" (Apr. 27, 1876; 5). Of course, with *Middlemarch* there were reviewers, like the *Tablet*'s, who feared sensational outcomes from the Will-Dorothea friendship too.

At *Deronda*'s conclusion, the *Morning Post* acknowledges "a feeling, not actually of disappointment, but of unsatisfied expectation. . . . The real living interest of the romance centres around the two principal figures . . . and from the manner in which both characters first appear on the scene the reader is naturally brought to imagine that upon the relations between them in after life will depend the informing spirit of the book" (Oct. 17, 1876; 3). The *Figaro* is less detached: "We had thought Deronda loved [Gwendolen]—the author is to blame if we are mistaken," but Eliot and Deronda may still change their minds: "there is still sufficient uncertainty concerning what may happen to hold one in suspense.

. . . [Gwendolen] is, by far, the more suitable wife for Deronda. We shall be angry with him if he does not see that himself" (Aug. 12, 1876; 11). When neither Deronda nor Eliot obliges, the critic is indignant:

> We shall not seek to conceal that the concluding instalment of 'Daniel Deronda' is exceedingly disappointing. Although we feared from the incidents in the preceding part that the author would make the mistake of marrying Deronda to Mirah Lapidoth, we did not give up hope that it might be otherwise. If no other way out of the difficulty could have been found, we thought that an accident might happen by which Deronda's marriage with the young Jewess would have been rendered impossible. It is quite certain that if he could not have married Mirah he would have been only too glad to have had Gwendolen.

The reviewer finishes the novel "with a sense of absolute annoyance. . . . We take leave of [Deronda] gladly, wondering at our folly in ever enthroning him as a model of well-nigh unapproachable excellence. But it is George Eliot who is responsible for our repentance, and it is George Eliot whose latest book is stamped with a grievous flaw" (Sept. 27, 1876; 12). Published four days earlier, the *Manchester Examiner and Times*'s final review on August 31, 1876, is a prescient response to the *Figaro*'s charges that Eliot led her readers astray:

> "Fruit and Seed," as would be anticipated by all experienced readers of the two previous books, contains scarcely any new revelations, and if we had not actually heard of one or two individual examples, ordinarily supposed to be far-seeing persons, who professed to hold a contrary opinion, we should have supposed that the author's intention to marry Daniel and Mirah would have been generally recognised. And certainly it is not her fault if any readers of the previous chapters complain of a surprise about this climax. (7)

Readers like the *Manchester Examiner and Times*'s ordinarily "far-seeing" ones or reviewers like the *Figaro*'s are writing the novel to their own expectations and refuse to accept the directions that Eliot embeds in her text.

Particularly vigorous, but not atypical, the *Figaro*'s response points to the problem of combining commercial and popular success with aesthetic quality. Some reviewers saw popular success as the raison d'être for fiction. The London *Observer* posits that the object of the novel "is to please, and to please the many. Indeed, we might say that the novel is strictly utilitarian in origin and end, its aim being the greatest happiness of the greatest number of readers." It laments many deficiencies in *Daniel Deronda*'s failure to fulfill readers' expectations, but most of all, that Gwendolen, "when she has once been very distinctly presented to our minds . . . acts in a totally different way from that upon which we had a right to count" (Sept. 3, 1876; 7).

Other readers and reviewers disagreed, acknowledging that readers were disappointed with *Deronda* because it failed to conform to familiar patterns, but arguing that this is part of its value. In its April review of book 3, the *Globe and Traveller* calls *Deronda* "more conventional in form than any of George Eliot's previous novels" (Apr. 10, 1876; 6). In its final review it argues that "the reasons [for the readers' disappointment] are not hard to find. It deals with people and with things of a very different order, in every respect, from those we expect to meet with in George Eliot's novels, and it is hard to distinguish all at once between genuine disappointment and the very natural feeling that arises from looking eagerly for one thing and finding another, though the two may be of equal value. We are taken away from our familiar homesteads" (Sept. 12, 1876; 6).

If she had read this review, Eliot would have been pleased, for her goal in *Daniel Deronda* was to take readers away from these homesteads. After affirming the positive features of Eliot's "disappointing" novel, the *Figaro*'s final words, "What a glorious conclusion there might have been!" (Sept. 27, 1876; 12), may even be read not as a lament, but as a tribute to the success of Eliot's refusal to conform in *Daniel Deronda*.

Conclusion

By 1876, George Eliot was referred to regularly in reviews as "England's greatest living novelist," and many placed her with Scott and Dickens as the foremost novelists of the century. As the culminating work of her career, *Daniel Deronda* would have attracted attention no matter what publication format it adopted. But for *Deronda*, as for any work, the serial format meant a difference in the kind and amount of that attention. Serialization extended the period during which readers were actively discussing a popular work and during which nonreaders could not avoid hearing of it. A serial's plot and characters were likely to be on the lips even of nonreaders, just as a modern television series may be known in some detail to those who have never seen it. An amusing account of the familiarity of *Deronda*, even in the "mouths of babes," is recounted in the *Manchester Critic and National Reform Union Gazette*. Citing—it's not clear how seriously—the "pernicious effect of George Eliot's latest novel on the minds of the community," the writer describes a scene in "one of our High Schools [where] a little maid was being examined in 'Religious Knowledge.'" The girl "went on swimmingly to Daniel, then stopped." When the teacher asked her to continue, there was silence until she "proved equal to the occasion, exclaiming triumphantly— Deronda!" (June 30, 1876; 22).

In the 1870s, when Eliot's fame was at its height and when two of her four serial works appeared, newspapers often featured accounts like this one that testified to the way in which Eliot's serial novels became part of popular lore. The period between installments created a distinctive relationship between the public and the author and text. Serialization gave readers more time than they had with the usual three-volume novel to contemplate and discuss a new work, and each period of contemplation reinforced their expectations for coming events and character developments. In turn, these expectations were reinforced or reshaped as readers discussed the installment with friends and acquaintances. Such a relationship became the norm rather than the exception for writers who, like Dickens, published most of their works serially. But for George Eliot, this special reader-author-text relationship was always perilous. It exacerbated her diffidence. Instead of the single concentrated moment of public reaction accompanying three- or four-volume publication, serialization produced "too many [of these] momenti," to borrow Eliot's own phrase about *Middlemarch*. Public response stretched over many months of publication. Even when Eliot would have preferred to ignore it, her journals and letters, and those of Lewes, show how unequal she was to this stoic effort.

With *Scenes of Clerical Life*, *Adam Bede* and *The Mill on the Floss*, her fears about public reaction to her personal life increased her usual diffidence about her powers of creativity—and contributed to her reluctance to serialize the latter two works. Her pride in her reputation as a writer and her fear and anger about public and private response to her reputation as a woman led to the misunderstanding with Blackwood, which contributed to her decision not to publish *The Mill on the Floss* in parts. With *Scenes of Clerical Life*, the anonymity of the magazine serial had provided a welcome screen behind which she could conceal her identity. Although she decided not to risk serialization, she maintained that concealment in publishing *Adam Bede* in three volumes, with well-known consequences in the Liggins imposture. By the time she was writing *Romola*, however, she was ambivalent about anonymity. It would give her shelter when, well known as the author of the popular *Adam Bede*, she wished to try her hand at historical fiction. At the same time, she wanted her name to be recognized, and she disliked being "credited" with the works of other anonymous authors whose style or subject bore some general affinity to her own.

With *Daniel Deronda* and *Middlemarch*, the many reviews occasioned by each part added a public dimension to the debate and discussion of their merits beyond any that Eliot experienced with her first two serials, *Scenes of Clerical Life* and *Romola*. These hundreds of reviews in daily, weekly, and semiweekly newspapers throughout England and Scotland testify to Eliot's importance, as they both registered public expectations and also helped to create them. Such public discussion benefited and handicapped the novelist. Financially, extended discussion helped create an audience of buyers for a serial and for the volume editions that followed. Furthermore, as Eliot, Lewes, and the reviewers all noted, the extended period of contemplation between installments helped readers grasp a difficult character or become comfortable with an unfamiliar place, such as the Florence of *Romola*. Serialization also led people to read a novel twice, once during its serialization and again when the volumes appeared.

how do you know this -- maybe people took up novels more when here!

The public reaction could also provide an author with sound advice—in addition to much that was not sound. If Eliot did not alter her fiction to conform to the conventions of the day, she did respond to commercial necessity where it did not affect the essence of her work—attempting to equalize the length of the parts of *Daniel Deronda*, for example. And she considered the actual and probable responses of her public, restructuring books 2 and 3 of *Middlemarch* or rearranging chapters in *Daniel Deronda*. She was conscious of her readers and reshaped her installments with them in mind; or decided, in the case of *Adam Bede* and *The Mill on the Floss*, not to publish serially at all.

The financial considerations involved in serialization were complicated. Eliot could reject it for *The Mill on the Floss* because she feared it would diminish volume sales and then adopt it for *Middlemarch* and *Daniel Deronda* for the equally sound reasons that their four-volume length required an innovative format to encourage sales—and that the economic power of the circulating libraries, especially Mudie's, needed to be challenged. For these last two novels, serial installment sales were strong but did not adversely affect volume sales. As reviewers pointed out, many of those who did not want to read serially, but preferred to await volume publication, could not ignore a novel that was discussed wherever they went. Even when the plot of *Deronda* took an unexpected turn, its sales remained strong, as Blackwood pointed out in several letters while publication was under way (see 6: 271–73, 279n2, 295).[1]

Paradoxically, while *Deronda*'s Jewish plot may have seemed unsuitable to the serial format, serialization probably helped maintain sales of the later parts. Readers in the course of the spring of 1876 had become so thoroughly involved in the narrative of Gwendolen Harleth's troubles that, by the summer, they were committed to buying the new installments regardless of the change of direction. With initial four-volume publication, the conversation of those who had rapidly completed the whole book might have been equivocal enough to discourage potential new buyers and borrowers from ever beginning it.

In other ways, *Deronda* was the best suited of Eliot's four serial works for this form of publication. It combined her usual psychological characterization with spectacular incidents of plot to provide strong reasons for readers to return to buy subsequent installments. Gwendolen's character—vivid, complex, even disagreeable to many readers—nonetheless invited further attention. Like Becky Sharp, she both attracts and repels. She is a less predictable figure than either Dorothea Brooke or Rosamond Vincy and much more complex than Romola, Hetty Sorrel, and Dinah Morris. Gwendolen's own indecisiveness gives the touch of unpredictability that is valuable to a serial. Though some reviewers hastened to note that Eliot was not writing in the sensation mode, others observed the unusual presence of sensation-style incidents—the melodrama of Mirah's past and her attempted suicide, the threat that the presence of Mirah's father brings, and Gwendolen's temptation to murder as she grows more desperate under Grandcourt's tyranny. Reviewers' predictions of sensational outcomes were not so farfetched in *Deronda* as they had been for *Middlemarch*. Predictions, for instance, that Will Ladislaw might provide an illicit connection for Dorothea are hardly justified by her characterization, whereas the idea that Gwendolen might engage in a desperate, illicit relationship is more plausible, just as it is plausible that she might be driven to murder Grandcourt. Other features of the sensation novel include the hint of bigamy in the concealed "other wife" and Lydia Glasher's revenge with the "poisoned" diamonds.

While Eliot's handling of the sensation potential gradually became more sophisticated, she rarely exploits the dramatic ending in a way that interferes with her focus on character and theme. Thus, she ends Gwendolen's story in book 4 with the dramatic event of Lydia's revenge in the Jewel scene; however, needing to emphasize the Deronda-Jewish plot, she ignores the scene's potential as a serial ending and focuses instead on her new subject. Sometimes, of course, her plans for a dramatic closure were modified by the internally conflicting requirements of serialization. In *Romola*, she had to abandon her powerful dramatic ending in part 9 to lengthen part 10. This is loss without perceptible gain. Other alterations had their compensations. When she moved chapter 42 of *Middlemarch* to the close of book 4 from its original place at the opening of book 5, the part lost a dramatic, mysterious conclusion (the Raffles-Bulstrode connection), but it gained an internal symmetry and a new depth and subtlety in Casaubon's characterization. In *Deronda*, she signals the importance of the Deronda-Jewish plot by ending book 6 with Deronda on the brink of learning about his heritage rather than with the conflict between Gwendolen and Grandcourt when the latter interrupts her tête-à-tête with Deronda.

Study of Eliot's serial work also provides us with a view of her growing ability as a writer. While Blackwood and reviewers recognized, from the first clerical scene, a writer far beyond the ordinary novelist of the 1850s, her handling of the special demands of the serial became increasingly skillful in the course of her composition of those three narratives. Blackwood's advice might have been repugnant at times, but his sound commercial instincts, added to those of George Henry Lewes, reminded George Eliot of the need to observe the conventions of the serial even while she held fast to her advocacy of realism. If "Amos Barton" was a "scene"—a sketch of place and character—her next two stories, equally powerful in evoking person and place, exhibit a dramatic quality missing in the first. She becomes more adept in pacing her plot, in generating suspense, and in producing a climax that is effective in the individual part and yet does not disturb the flow of the work in the volume form or unduly call attention to the fact that it was first published as a serial.

These qualities are characteristic of all her later serial work. She retains her own vision and yet benefits from the reactions of publisher and public. In *Romola*, she combines her own requirement for precise historical delineation with the public's demand for drama, especially in the later installments. And in *Middlemarch* and *Daniel Deronda*, with their longer, half-volume installments, she has the leisure to develop her characters and still respond to the serial format's demand for plot devices to maintain reader interest. In fact, unlike novels of the sensation school in which character may be subordinate to plot, *Daniel Deronda* makes Gwendolen's character so intriguing that it worked together with plot to bring readers back.

Many reviewers used the image of the journey to characterize the experience of serial reading. This is also an appropriate metaphor for the experience of serial writing. Eliot's serial fiction spans the entire journey of her fiction-writing career, from *Scenes of Clerical Life* to *Daniel Deronda*. It was a perilous, discouraging journey at times, one that she sometimes longed to abandon. But it was a journey on which she learned from those who accompanied her—her reading public.

APPENDIX I

Reviewing History of George Eliot's Novels

This list is a selective one. Reviews collected in Carroll or in Holstrom and Lerner have been omitted where they do not bear upon the serialization of Eliot's fiction. Some reviews listed here are brief notices appearing in magazine columns in 1857 and 1862–63 when *Scenes of Clerical Life* and *Romola* were being serialized. Reviews of the serially published works are listed first. At the end of this appendix are reviews of the two novels that Eliot intended to serialize, *Adam Bede* and *The Mill on the Floss*, and one cited review of *Silas Marner*.

SCENES OF CLERICAL LIFE

Atlas (London)
    Anon. (Feb. 6, 1858): 89–90.
British Quarterly Review (London)
    [Bayne, Peter]. 45 (Jan. 1867): 141–78 [includes *SCL, AB, MF, SM, R, FH*].
Church of England Monthly Review
    Anon. "Clerical Novels." 8 (Apr. 1860): 271–81.
Daily News (London)
    Anon. (Feb. 5, 1858): 2.
Edinburgh Courant
    Anon. "The Magazines." (Apr. 7, 1857): [3].
    Anon. "The Magazines for June." (June 4, 1857): [3].
    Anon. "The Magazines and Serials." (Aug. 18, 1857): [3].
    Anon. (Jan. 26, 1858): [3].
Edinburgh Review (London)
    [Norton, Caroline E. S.]. 110 (July 1859): 223–46 [includes *SCL* and *AB*].
Examiner (London)
    Anon. (Apr. 11, 1857): 229.
    Anon. (Jan. 23, 1858): 52–53.
Guardian (London)
    Anon. (Mar. 3, 1858): 192.

Illustrated Times (London)
  Anon. (Jan. 17, 1857): 43.
  Anon. (Feb. 7, 1857): 91.
  Anon. (Mar. 7, 1857): 155.
  Anon. (Apr. 4, 1857): 218.
  Anon. (May 16, 1857): 310.
  Anon. (June 13, 1857): 375.
  Anon. (July 4, 1857): 11.
  Anon. (Aug. 15, 1857): 123.
  Anon. (Oct. 10, 1857): 250.
  Anon. (Nov. 14, 1857): 327.
John Bull and Britannia (London). "Magazines and Serials."
  Anon. (Jan. 3, 1857): 12.
  Anon. (Feb. 7, 1857): 92.
  Anon. (Mar. 14, 1857): 171.
  Anon. (Apr. 4, 1857): 220.
  Anon. (May 2, 1857): 284.
  Anon. (June 6, 1857): 363.
  Anon. (July 4, 1857): 427.
  Anon. (Aug. 8, 1857): 507.
  Anon. (Sept. 5, 1857): 572.
  Anon. (Oct. 3, 1857): 636.
  Anon. (Nov. 7, 1857): 715.
  Anon. (Feb. 8, 1858): 91.
Leader (London). "Literature."
  Anon. no. 354 (Jan. 3, 1857): 16.
  Anon. no. 359 (Feb. 7, 1857): 134–35.
  Anon. no. 363 (Mar. 7, 1857): 231.
  Anon. no. 367 (Apr. 4, 1857): 329.
  Anon. no. 372 (May 9, 1857): 448.
  Anon. no. 376 (June 6, 1857): 544.
  Anon. no. 380 (July 4, 1857): 639.
  Anon. no. 389 (Sept. 5, 1857): 857.
  Anon. no. 398 (Nov. 7, 1857): 1072.
  Anon. no. 407 (Jan. 9, 1858): 43.
Literary Gazette, and Journal of Belles Lettres, Science, and Art
  Anon. (Jan. 23, 1858): 82–83.
Morning Advertiser (London)
  Anon. (Jan. 8, 1858): 3.
Morning Chronicle (London)
  Anon. (Jan. 15, 1858): 6.

Morning Post (London)
  Anon. (Feb. 25, 1858): 3.
National Review (London)
  [Martineau, James]. "Professional religion." 7 (Oct. 1858): 487–515.
  [Hutton, R. H.]. "The novels of George Eliot." 11 (July 1860): 191–219.
Nonconformist (London)
  Anon. (Feb. 10, 1858): 115–16.
North British Review (Edinburgh)
  [Lancaster, H. H.]. 45 (Sept. 1866): 197–228 [includes *SCL, AB, MF, SM, R, FH*].
Press
  Anon. (Jan. 3, 1857): 19.
  Anon. (Feb. 7, 1857): 138.
  Anon. (Mar. 7, 1857): 240.
  Anon. (Apr. 4, 1857): 342.
  Anon. (May 9, 1857): 462.
  Anon. (June 6, 1857): 562.
  Anon. (July 4, 1857): 658.
  Anon. (Aug. 1, 1857): 754.
  Anon. (Jan. 16, 1858): 68.
Quarterly Review (London)
  [Robertson, James Craigie]. 108 (Oct. 1860): 469–99 [includes *SCL, AB, MF*].
Revue des deux Mondes (Paris)
  Forgues, E.-D. "La vie cléricale en Angleterre." (May 15, 1858): 305–31.
Saturday Review (London)
  Anon. "A New Novelist." (May 29, 1858): 566–67.
Statesman (London)
  Anon. (Jan. 23, 1858): 378.
Times (London)
  Anon. "Recent Novels.—Scenes of Clerical Life and White Lies." (Jan. 2, 1858): 9.

ROMOLA

Athenaeum (London)
  Anon. no. 1862 (July 11, 1863): 46.
British Quarterly Review (London)
  Anon. 38 (Oct. 1863): 448–65.
  [Bayne, Peter]. 45 (Jan. 1867): 141–78 [includes *SCL, AB, MF, SM, R, FH*].
Christian Remembrancer (London)
  Anon. 52 n.s. (Oct. 1866): 445–79 [includes *FH*].

Critic
   Anon. "Periodicals and Magazines." 25 (July 15, 1862): 20.
   Anon. "Periodical Literature." 25 (July 1, 1863): 399.
Daily News (London)
   Anon. (Aug. 3, 1863): 2.
Edinburgh Evening Courant. "The Magazines."
   Anon. (July 7, 1863): 6.
   Anon. (Aug. 4, 1863): 6.
Englishman (London) [with which is incorporated the *Atlas*].
   Anon. "The Magazines of the Month." (Aug. 15, 1863): 1.
Englishwoman's Domestic Magazine
   Anon. 7 n.s. (Aug. 1863): 187–88.
Examiner (London)
   Anon. (Dec. 6, 1862): 775.
   Anon. (Dec. 26, 1863): 820–21.
Globe and Traveller (London)
   Anon. (Sept. 21, 1863): 1.
Guardian (London)
   Anon. (Aug. 6, 1862): 763.
   Anon. (Dec. 31, 1862): 1247.
   Anon. (Apr. 1, 1863): 315.
   Anon. (Sept. 16, 1863): 875–76.
Illustrated Review (London)
   Anon. 3 (Jan. 15, 1862): 423–26 [article mainly on Savonarola].
Illustrated Times (London). "The Literary Lounger. The Magazines."
   Anon. (July 5, 1862): 159.
   Anon. (Aug. 9, 1862): 239.
   Anon. (Dec. 13, 1862): 535.
   Anon. (Feb. 7, 1863): 87.
   Anon. (May 2, 1863): 314.
   Anon. (June 6, 1863): 398.
   Anon. (July 25, 1863): 58 [column now called "Literature"].
John Bull and Britannia (London)
   Anon. (July 5, 1862): 428.
   Anon. (Aug. 5, 1862): 492.
   Anon. (Sept. 6, 1862): 571.
   Anon. (Oct. 4, 1862): 635.
   Anon. (July 4, 1863): 427.
   Anon. (Aug. 1, 1863): 491.

London Review
   Anon. (Aug. 1, 1863): 124–25.
Manchester Examiner and Times
   Anon. "Art and Literary Gossip." (July 7, 1863): 3.
Morning Advertiser (London)
   Anon. (July 10, 1863): 3.
Morning Post (London)
   Anon. (Aug. 25, 1863): 3.
Nonconformist (London)
   Anon. "Periodicals for March." (Mar. 4, 1863): 176–77.
   Anon. "Periodicals." (Apr. 1, 1863): 258–59.
   Anon. "The Magazines." (July 8, 1863): 553–54.
   Anon. "The Magazines." (Aug. 12, 1863): 654.
North British Review (Edinburgh)
   [Lancaster, H. H.]. 45 (Sept. 1866): 197–228 [includes *SCL, AB, MF, R, SM, FH*].
Observer (London)
   Anon. (July 19, 1863): 7.
Press (London)
   Anon. (Aug. 1, 1863): 738.
Reader (London)
   Anon. 1 (Feb. 7, 1863): 152.
   Anon. 2 (July 11, 1863): 28–29.
Spectator (London)
   [Hutton, R. H.]. (July 5, 1862): 752.
   [Hutton, R. H.]. (Aug. 2, 1862): 864.
   [Hutton, R. H.]. (Oct. 4, 1862): 1117.
   [Hutton, R. H.]. (Nov. 29, 1862): 1339.
   [Hutton, R. H.]. (Feb. 7, 1863): 1616.
   [Hutton, R. H.]. (Mar. 7, 1863): 1729.
   [Hutton, R. H.]. (July 18, 1863): 2265–67.
Standard (London)
   Anon. "The Magazines." (Jan. 2, 1863): 3.
Sunday Times (London)
   Anon. "The Magazines." (June 7, 1863): 2.
   Anon. "The Magazines." (July 5, 1863): 2.
   Anon. "The Magazines." (Aug. 2, 1863): 2.
Times (London)
   Anon. (Sept. 5, 1863): 11.

Weekly Dispatch (London)
    Anon. (July 26, 1863): 6.

MIDDLEMARCH

Aberdeen Journal
    Anon. (Jan. 24, 1872): 6.
    Anon. (May 1, 1872): 9.
    Anon. (June 19, 1872): 6.
    Anon. (Aug. 21, 1872): 6.
    Anon. (Oct. 9, 1872): 6.
    Anon. (Nov. 6, 1872): 6.
    Anon. (Jan. 22, 1873): 6.
Academy (London)
    Lawrenny, H. [pseud. of Edith Simcox]. 44, no. 63 (Jan. 1, 1873): 1–4.
Athenaeum (London)
    Anon. no. 2301 (Dec. 2, 1871): 713–14.
    Anon. no. 2310 (Feb. 3, 1872): 137–38.
    Anon. no. 2318 (Mar. 30, 1872): 393.
    Anon. no. 2327 (June 1, 1872): 681.
    Anon. no. 2335 (July 27, 1872): 112.
    Anon. no. 2354 (Dec. 7, 1872): 725–26.
British Quarterly Review (London)
    Anon. 55 (Jan. 1, 1872): 267.
    [Hutton, R. H.]. 57 (Apr. 1, 1873): 407–29.
Daily News (London)
    Anon. (Nov. 28, 1871): 5.
    Anon. (Jan. 29, 1872): 5.
Daily Telegraph (London)
    [Stark, Herbert]. (June 18, 1872): 6–7.
    Anon. (Dec. 27, 1872): 7.
Echo (London)
    Anon. (Nov. 27, 1871): 5.
    Anon. (Nov. 28, 1871): 2.
    Anon. (Jan. 30, 1872): 2.
    Anon. (Mar. 25, 1872): 2.
    Anon. (May 28, 1872): 2.
    Anon. (July 25, 1872): 2.
    Anon. (Sept. 30, 1872): 2.
    Anon. (Oct. 30, 1872): 2.

Edinburgh Courant
  Anon. (Jan. 6, 1873): 7.
Edinburgh Review (London)
  [Milnes, Richard Monckton]. 137 (Jan. 1873): 246–63.
Examiner (London)
  Anon. (Dec. 2, 1871): 1192–93.
  Anon. (Feb. 3, 1872): 125–26.
  Anon. (Mar. 30, 1872): 333–34.
  Anon. (June 8, 1872): 575–76.
  Anon. (July 27, 1872): 743–44.
  Anon. (Oct. 5, 1872): 985–86.
  Anon. (Dec. 7, 1872): 1204–05.
Figaro (London)
  Anon. (July 20, 1872): 455.
  Anon. (Aug. 24, 1872): 535.
  Anon. (Feb. 15, 1873): 7.
Globe and Traveller (London)
  Anon. (Dec. 14, 1871): 6.
  Anon. (Feb. 22, 1872): 1–2.
  Anon. (July 27, 1872): 4.
  Anon. (Dec. 3, 1872): 6.
Guardian (London)
  Anon. (Jan. 3, 1872): 23.
  Anon. (Feb. 21, 1872): 262.
  Anon. (Apr. 10, 1872): 490.
  Anon. (Aug. 7, 1872): 1021.
  Anon. (Oct. 23, 1872): 1340.
  Anon. (Feb. 12, 1873): 206.
Illustrated London News
  Anon. (Dec. 2, 1871): 534.
  Anon. (Oct. 5, 1872): 323.
John Bull and Britannia (London)
  Anon. (Mar. 2, 1872): 163.
  Anon. (Sept. 7, 1872): 621.
  Anon. (Nov. 23, 1872): 806.
Leeds Mercury
  Anon. (Oct. 10, 1872): 3.
  Anon. (Dec. 14, 1872): 12.
London Quarterly Review
  [Forman, H. Buxton]. 40 (Apr. 1873): 99–110.

Manchester Examiner and Times
  Anon. (Nov. 29, 1871): 3.
  Anon. (Feb. 28, 1873): 3.
Manchester Guardian
  Anon. (Dec. 21, 1871): 7.
  Anon. (Feb. 7, 1872): 7.
  Anon. (Mar. 30, 1872): 5.
  Anon. (June 7, 1872): 7.
  Anon. (July 31, 1872): 7.
  Anon. (Oct. 4, 1872): 7.
  Anon. (Nov. 1, 1872): 7.
  Anon. (Dec. 6, 1872): 7.
Nonconformist (London)
  Anon. (Dec. 13, 1871): 1226–27.
  Anon. (Feb. 21, 1872): 202.
  Anon. (Apr. 10, 1872): 376.
  Anon. (June 12, 1872): 624–25.
  Anon. (July 31, 1872): 797.
  Anon. (Oct. 9, 1872): 1037.
  Anon. (Nov. 6, 1872): 1132–33.
  Anon. (Dec. 11, 1872): 1268.
Observer (London)
  Anon. (Dec. 17, 1871): 2.
Quarterly Review (London)
  [Laing, Robert]. "Middlemarch, a Study of Provincial Life." 134 (Apr.
    1873): 336–69.
Saturday Review (London)
  Anon. (Dec. 7, 1872): 733–34.
  Anon. (Dec. 21, 1872): 794–96.
Spectator (London)
  [Hutton, R. H.]. (Dec. 2, 1871): 1458–60 [comparison of Eliot and Tenny-
    son, followed by comments on her idealism by A. Creed on Dec. 9,
    pp. 1494–95].
  Anon. (Dec. 16, 1871): 1528–29.
  Anon. (Feb. 3, 1872): 147–48.
  Anon. (Mar. 30, 1872): 404–06.
  Anon. (June 1, 1872): 685–87.
  Anon. (Aug. 3, 1872): 975–76.
  Anon. (Oct. 5, 1872): 1262–64.
  Anon. (Dec. 7, 1872): 1554–56.
  Anon. (Dec. 14, 1872): 1582–83.

St. Paul's Magazine
  Smith, George Barnett. 12 (May 1873): 592–616.
Standard (London)
  Anon. (Dec. 2, 1871): [5].
  Anon. (June 3, 1872): 2.
  Anon. (Aug. 8, 1872): 5.
  Anon. (Nov. 13, 1872): 5.
  Anon. (Dec. 4, 1872): 5.
Tablet (London)
  Anon. (Jan. 6, 1872): 12.
  Anon. (Mar. 2, 1872): 263–64.
  Anon. (May 18, 1872): 616.
  Anon. (June 15, 1872): 744–45.
  Anon. (Aug. 17, 1872): 202–03.
  Anon. (Oct. 26, 1872): 523–24.
  Anon. (Nov. 16, 1872): 620.
  Anon. (Dec. 21, 1872): 779–80.
Times (London)
  [Broome, Frederick Napier]. (Mar. 7, 1873): 3–4.
Tinsley's Magazine (London)
  Anon. "The Theory of Fiction." 43 (1873): 88–92.
Vanity Fair (London)
  Anon. (Dec. 9, 1871): 184.
  Anon. (Apr. 13, 1872): 115.
  Anon. (June 15, 1872): 188.
  Anon. (Aug. 10, 1872): 43.
  Anon. (Jan. 4, 1873): 4.
Westminster Review
  [Wise, J. R.]. 97 o.s./41 n.s. (Jan. 1872): 276–77.
  [Wise]. 99 o.s./43 n.s. (Jan. 1873): 325–26.
Yorkshire Gazette (York)
  Anon. (Dec. 9, 1871): 2.
  Anon. (Feb. 3, 1872): 5.
  Anon. (Apr. 6, 1872): 5.
  Anon. (June 15, 1872): 5.
  Anon. (Aug. 17, 1872): 8.
  Anon. (Oct. 12, 1872): 2.
  Anon. (Nov. 16, 1872): 2.
  Anon. (Dec. 7, 1872): 2.

DANIEL DERONDA

Aberdeen Journal
   Anon. (Feb. 9, 1876): 6.
   Anon. (Mar. 8, 1876): 6.
   Anon. (June 28, 1876): 6.
   Anon. (Aug. 16, 1876): 6.
Academy (London)
   Anon. (Feb. 5, 1876): 120.
   Saintsbury, George. (Sept. 9, 1876): 253–54.
Athenaeum (London)
   Anon. no. 2518 (Jan. 29, 1876): 160.
   Anon. no. 2523 (Mar. 4, 1876): 327.
   Anon. no. 2527 (Apr. 1, 1876): 461–62.
   Anon. no. 2531 (Apr. 29, 1876): 593–94.
   Anon. no. 2536 (June 3, 1876): 762.
   Anon. no. 2540 (July 1, 1876): 14–15.
   Anon. no. 2544 (July 29, 1876): 143.
   Anon. no. 2549 (Sept. 2, 1876): 303.
Birmingham Daily Mail
   Anon. (Feb. 2, 1876): 4 [from the *World*].
British Quarterly Review (London)
   Anon. 63 (Apr., 1876): 583.
   Anon. 64 (Oct., 1876): 472–92.
Daily News (London)
   Anon. (Jan. 29, 1876): 2.
   Anon. (June 6, 1876): [2].
   Anon. (Aug. 31, 1876): 3.
Daily Review (Edinburgh)
   Anon. (Jan. 29, 1876): 6.
   Anon. (Feb. 28, 1876): 5.
   Anon. (Mar. 28, 1876): 5.
   Anon. (Apr. 27, 1876): 5.
   Anon. "Daniel Deronda and Mordecai." (May 30, 1876): 3.
   Anon. (June 27, 1876): 5.
   Anon. (July 28, 1876): 5.
   Anon. "'Daniel Deronda' and the Comtists." (Sept. 5, 1876): 2.
Echo (London)
   Anon. (Jan. 29, 1876): 4.
   Anon. (Mar. 2, 1876): 4.
   Anon. (Apr. 3, 1876): 2.
   Anon. (June 16, 1876): 4.

Anon. (June 30, 1876): 4.
Anon. (July 26, 1876): 4.
Anon. (Aug. 28, 1876): 4.
Anon. (Sept. 13, 1876): 4.
Eclectic Magazine
Anon. 14 n.s. (Dec. 1876): 657–67 [reprint from *British Quarterly Review* 24 n.s./64 o.s.].
Edinburgh Courant
Anon. (Jan. 29, 1876): 6.
Anon. (Feb. 28, 1876): 6.
Anon. (Mar. 30, 1876): 4.
Anon. (Apr. 29, 1876): 4.
Anon. (June 7, 1876): 6.
Anon. (July 6, 1876): 2.
Anon. (Aug. 7, 1876): 4.
Anon. (Sept. 4, 1876): 3.
Edinburgh Review
Anon. 144 (Oct. 1876): 442–70.
Examiner (London)
Anon. (Jan. 29, 1876): 124–25.
Anon. (Mar. 4, 1876): 265–66.
Anon. (Apr. 1, 1876): 381.
Anon. (June 3, 1876): 632–33.
Anon. (Aug. 5, 1876): 885–86.
Anon. (Sept. 2, 1876): 993–94.
Figaro (London)
Anon. (Feb. 9, 1876): 10.
Anon. (Mar. 22, 1876): 10.
Anon. (Apr. 19, 1876): 11.
Anon. (May 24, 1876): 11.
Anon. (June 28, 1876): 5.
Anon. (July 29, 1876): 11.
Anon. (Aug. 12, 1876): 11.
Anon. (Sept. 27, 1876): 12–13.
Fortnightly Review (London)
Colvin, Sidney. 26 n.s. (Nov. 1, 1876): 601–16.
Gentleman's Magazine (London)
Francillon, R. E. "George Eliot's First Romance." 239 (Oct. 1876): 411–27.
Glasgow News
Anon. (Jan. 29, 1876): 2.
Anon. (Feb. 28, 1876): 2.
Anon. (Mar. 30, 1876): 2.

Anon. (June 6, 1876): 2.
Anon. (June 15, 1876): 2.
Anon. (July 1, 1876): 2.
Anon. (July 18, 1876): 2.
Globe and Traveller (London)
Anon. (Jan. 31, 1876): 6.
Anon. (Feb. 29, 1876): 6.
Anon. (Apr. 10, 1876): 6.
Anon. (May 15, 1876): 6.
Anon. (July 18, 1876): 6.
Anon. (Sept. 12, 1876): 6.
Guardian (London)
Anon. (Feb. 2, 1876): 153–54.
Anon. (Mar. 15, 1876): 357.
Anon. (June 21, 1876): 825.
Anon. (Oct. 4, 1876): 1312.
Illustrated London News
Anon. (June 24, 1876): 610.
Anon. (Aug. 5, 1876): 127.
Anon. (Sept. 9, 1876): 246.
Jewish Chronicle (London)
Anon. (July 21, 1876): 251 [2 sentences on books 1–5].
Anon. (Sept. 8, 1876): 357 ["First Notice"].
Anon. (Sept. 22, 1876): 390 [about the prototype of Mirah].
Anon. (Sept. 22, 1876): 394 ["Second Notice"].
Anon. (Sept. 29, 1876): 407 [about translation].
Anon. (Oct. 13, 1876): 437 [in "Town and Table Talk" section; paragraph from the *Public Leader*].
Anon. (Nov. 17, 1876): 516 [paragraph from *Vanity Fair*: why Eliot wrote *DD*; GHL of Jewish descent].
Anon. (Nov. 24, 1876): 539 [in "Town and Table Talk" section].
Anon. "Conversationists Unmasked." (Dec. 8, 1876): 565.
Anon. "'Daniel Deronda' First of Two Articles" and "The Rev. Dr. Hermann Adler on 'Daniel Deronda'" (Dec. 15, 1876): 585–86.
Anon. (Dec. 22, 1876): 601–02 ["Second and Concluded Article"].
John Bull and Britannia (London)
Anon. (Feb. 5, 1876): 91.
Anon. (Mar. 11, 1876): 178–79.
Anon. (Apr. 1, 1876): 227.
Anon. (May 6, 1876): 307.
Anon. (June 3, 1876): 369.
Anon. (July 1, 1876): 433.

Anon. (Aug. 5, 1876): 513–14.
Anon. (Sept. 16, 1876): 609–10.
Leeds Mercury
Anon. (Jan. 29, 1876): 12.
Anon. (Mar. 1, 1876): 6.
Anon. (Apr. 26, 1876): 6 [extracts].
Anon. (May 31, 1876): 6.
Anon. (June 28, 1876): 6.
Anon. (Aug. 2, 1876): 6 [extracts].
Anon. (Aug. 31, 1876): 8 [extracts].
Liverpool Daily Post
Anon. (Sept. 8, 1876): 4.
Liverpool Weekly Albion [reviews, often shortened, reprinted in *Liverpool Daily (Evening) Albion*]
Anon. (Jan. 29, 1876): 7 [Jan. 29: 3].
Anon. (Mar. 4, 1876): 7 [Feb. 28: 2].
Anon. (Apr. 1, 1876): 7 [extracts].
Anon. (Apr. 29, 1876): 7 [extracts].
Anon. (May 6, 1876): 7 [May 11: 4].
Anon. (July 1, 1876): 7 [extracts].
Anon. (July 29, 1876): 7 [Aug. 18: 4].
Anon. (Sept. 2, 1876): 7.
London Quarterly Review
[Marzials, Frank T.]. 47 (Jan. 1877): 446–71.
Mail (Dublin)
Anon. (Feb. 2, 1876): 2 ["a republication from the substance of *The Times*"].
Anon. (June 5, 1876): 2.
Manchester Critic and National Reform Union Gazette
Anon. 6 n.s. (June 30, 1876): 22.
Manchester Examiner and Times
Anon. (Jan. 29, 1876): 5–6.
Anon. (Feb. 28, 1876): 3.
Anon. (Mar. 29, 1876): 3.
Anon. (Apr. 27, 1876): 7.
Anon. (May 29, 1876): 4.
Anon. (June 28, 1876): 7.
Anon. (July 27, 1876): 7.
Anon. (Aug. 31, 1876): 7.
Manchester Guardian
Anon. (Jan. 29, 1876): 8.
Anon. (Feb. 28, 1876): 7.

Anon. (Apr. 28, 1876): 7.

Anon. (May 30, 1876): 6.

Anon. (Sept. 4, 1876): 6.

Midland Counties Herald: Birmingham and General Advertiser

Anon. (Feb. 3, 1876): 18 [mostly extracts].

Morning Mail (Dublin)

Anon. (Feb. 1, 1876): [4] [reprint of *Daily News*].

Anon. (Mar. 28, 1876): 4 [extracts only].

Morning Post (London)

Anon. (Oct. 17, 1876): 3.

Nation (Dublin)

Anon. no. 555 (Feb. 17, 1876): 115, 117.

Anon. no. 556 (Feb. 24, 1876): 131.

Anon. no. 558 (Mar. 9, 1876): 160–61.

Anon. no. 584 (Sept. 7, 1876): 153 [one sentence deferring comment].

Anon. no. 589 (Oct. 12, 1876): 230–31.

Anon. no. 590 (Oct. 19, 1876): 245–46.

New Quarterly Magazine (London). "Current Literature and Current Criticism" [pages recorded for Eliot's work].

Anon. 6 (Apr. 1876): 269–78.

Anon. 6 (July 1876): 514–26.

Anon. 7 (Oct. 1876): 240–51.

Nonconformist (London)

Anon. (Feb. 2, 1876): 110–11.

Anon. (Mar. 29, 1876): 312.

Anon. (Apr. 12, 1876): 363.

Anon. (May 31, 1876): 555.

Anon. (Aug. 16, 1876): 823–24.

Anon. (Sept. 13, 1876): 919–20.

North American Review

Whipple, Edwin P. 124 (Jan. 1877): 31–52.

Observer (London)

Anon. (Jan. 30, 1876): 7.

Anon. (Mar. 12, 1876): 2.

Anon. (Apr. 16, 1876): 2.

Anon. (Sept. 3, 1876): 7.

Pall Mall Gazette (London)

Anon. (Aug. 24, 1876): 10 [alludes to *DD*].

Anon. (Sept. 30, 1876): 12.

Anon. (Oct. 4, 1876): 10.

Quarterly Review (London)

[Courthope, W. J.]. 63, no. 293 (Jan. 1879): 81–112.

Saturday Review (London)
    Anon. 42 (Sept. 16, 1876): 356–58.
    Anon. 42 (Sept. 23, 1876): 390–92.
Spectator (London)
    Anon. "Gwendolen Harleth." (Jan. 29, 1876): 138–39.
    Anon. "George Eliot's Heroines." (Feb. 12, 1876): 207–08.
    Anon. (Apr. 8, 1876): 463–64.
    Anon. "The Hero of 'Daniel Deronda.'" (June 10, 1876): 733–34.
    Anon. "The Strong Side of 'Daniel Deronda.'" (July 29, 1876): 948.
    Anon. (Sept. 9, 1876): 1131–33.
Standard (London)
    Anon. (Feb. 7, 1876): 6.
    Anon. (Mar. 6, 1876): 6.
    Anon. (Apr. 3, 1876): 3.
    Anon. (June 12, 1876): 3.
    Anon. (July 10, 1876): 2.
    Anon. (Aug. 14, 1876): 2.
    Anon. "George Eliot's Later Manner." (Sept. 15, 1876): 2 [20 years of novels].
    Anon. (Sept. 25, 1876): 2.
Sunday Times (London)
    Anon. (Feb. 20, 1876): 7.
    Anon. (Mar. 19, 1876): 7.
    Anon. (Apr. 23, 1876): 7.
    Anon. (May 14, 1876): 7.
    Anon. (June 18, 1876): 7.
    Anon. (July 23, 1876): 7.
    Anon. (Aug. 20, 1876): 7.
Tablet (London)
    Anon. (Feb. 19, 1876): 234.
    Anon. (Mar. 11, 1876): 329–30.
    Anon. (Apr. 15, 1876): 490–91.
    Anon. (May 27, 1876): 683.
    Anon. (July 1, 1876): 9–10.
    Anon. (July 29, 1876): 138.
    Anon. (Aug. 26, 1876): 266.
    Anon. (Nov. 4, 1876): 587.
Times (London)
    Anon. (Jan. 31, 1876): 6.
    Anon. (June 5, 1876): 5.
Vanity Fair (London)
    Anon. (Oct. 14, 1876): 239–40.

Victoria (London)
  Richardson, Abby Sage. 28 (1876): 227–31.
Weekly Dispatch (London)
  Anon. (Feb. 13, 1876): 6.
  Anon. (Aug. 13, 1876): 6.
Weekly Review and Reformer (Edinburgh)
  Anon. (Feb. 5, 1876): 7 [same as *Daily Review*, Jan. 29].
  Anon. (Mar. 4, 1876): 7 [shorter version of *Daily Review*, Feb. 28].
  Anon. (Aug. 5, 1876): 1.
  Anon. "George Eliot on Human Life." (Nov. 4, 1876): 8 [from *Edinburgh Review*].
Weekly Scotsman and Caledonian Mercury (Edinburgh)
  Anon. (Feb. 5, 1876): 6.
Westminster Review (London)
  [J. R. Wise]. 105 o.s. 49 n.s. (Apr. 1876): 578–79.
  [J. R. Wise]. 106 o.s. 50 n.s. (July 1876): 281–82.
  [J. R. Wise]. 106 o.s. 50 n.s. (Oct. 1876): 575.
World (London)
  Anon. "George Eliot." (Feb. 2, 1876): 10–12.
  Anon. (Sept. 6, 1876): 19–20.
York Herald
  Anon. (Feb. 1, 1876): 3.
  Anon. (Mar. 1, 1876): 3.
  Anon. (Apr. 5, 1876): 3.
  Anon. (May 11, 1876): 3.
  Anon. (June 7, 1876): 3.
  Anon. (July 5, 1876): 3.
  Anon. (Aug. 8, 1876): 3.
  Anon. (Sept. 4, 1876): 6.
Yorkshire Gazette (York)
  Anon. (Feb. 5, 1876): 5.
  Anon. (Mar. 18, 1876): 8.
  Anon. (Apr. 22, 1876): 8.
  Anon. (May 13, 1876): 8.
  Anon. (June 10, 1876): 8.
  Anon. (July 15, 1876): 4.
  Anon. (Aug. 5, 1876): 8.
  Anon. (Sept. 23, 1876): 8.

· *Appendix 1* ·

ADAM BEDE

Athenaeum (London)
  Anon. no. 1635 (Feb. 26, 1859): 284.
Blackwood's Magazine (Edinburgh)
  [Collins, W. Lucas]. 85 (Apr. 1859): 490–504.
British Quarterly Review (London)
  [Bayne, Peter]. 45 (Jan. 1867): 141–78 [includes *SCL, AB, MF, SM, R, FH*].
Christian Observer (London)
  Anon. "Recent Semi-Religious Works of Fiction." (Jan. 1860): 21–29 [pages
  for *AB* only].
Church of England Monthly Review
  Anon. 7 (Oct. 1859): 244–53.
Critic
  Anon. 18 (Apr. 9, 1859): 347.
  Anon. 18 (Apr. 23, 1859): 387.
Daily News (London)
  Anon. (Feb. 24, 1859): 2.
Dublin Review
  [Taylor, Frances M.]. 47 (Sept. 1859): 33–42.
Edinburgh Evening Courant
  Anon. (Feb. 15, 1859): 3.
Edinburgh Review
  [Norton, Caroline E. S.]. 110 (July 1859): 223–46.
Examiner (London)
  Anon. (Mar. 5, 1859): 149.
Guardian (London)
  Anon. (Mar. 2, 1859): 207.
Illustrated Times (London)
  Anon. (Feb. 19, 1859): 123.
Leader (London)
  Anon. no. 466 (Feb. 26, 1859): 270.
  Anon. no. 474 (Apr. 23, 1859): 524.
Literary Gazette
  Anon. no. 35 (Feb. 26, 1859): 281–83.
Morning Chronicle (London)
  Anon. (Feb. 28, 1859): 6.
Morning Post (London)
  Anon. (Mar. 16, 1859): 3.
National Review (London)
  [Hutton, R. H.]. "The Novels of George Eliot." 11 (July 1860): 191–219.

North British Review (Edinburgh)
Anon. 30 (May 1859): 562–64.
Anon. "Imaginative Literature. The Author of Adam Bede and Nathaniel Hawthorne." 33 (Aug. 1860): 165–85.
[Lancaster, H. H.]. 45 (Sept. 1866): 197–228 [includes *SCL, AB, MF, SM, R, FH*].
Press (London)
Anon. (Feb. 12, 1859): 169–70.
Quarterly Review (London)
[Robertson, James Craigie]. 108 (Oct. 1860): 469–99 [*SCL, AB, MF*].
Statesman (London)
Anon. (Feb. 12, 1859): 70–71.
Westminster Review
[Chapman, John]. 15 n.s. (Apr. 1859): 486–512.

THE MILL ON THE FLOSS

Athenaeum (London)
Anon. no. 1693 (Apr. 7, 1860): 467–68.
Atlas (London)
Anon. no. 1693 (Apr. 14, 1860): 291–92.
Blackwood's Magazine (Edinburgh)
[Collins, W. Lucas]. 87 (May 1860): 611–23.
British Quarterly Review (London)
[Bayne, Peter]. 45 (Jan. 1867): 141–78 [includes *SCL, AB, MF, SM, R,* and *FH*].
Church of England Monthly Review
Anon. 8 (June 1860): 431–39.
Critic
Anon. 20 n.s. (Apr. 14, 1860): 458–59.
Daily News (London)
Anon. (Apr. 17, 1860): 5.
Dublin University Magazine
Anon. "Recent Popular Novels." 57 (Feb. 1861): 192–208 [includes *MF, The Woman in White,* and *Lavinia*].
Eclectic Review
Anon. 112 (Aug. 1860): 222–24.
Edinburgh Evening Courant
Anon. (Apr. 20, 1860): 3.
Englishwoman's Domestic Magazine
Anon. 1 n.s. (May 1860): 44–45.

Examiner (London)
  [Ware, L. G.]. (June 16, 1860): 372–73.
Illustrated Times (London)
  Anon. (June 2, 1860): 345.
John Bull and Britannia (London)
  Anon. (Apr. 14, 1860): 235.
Lady's Newspaper
  Anon. (Apr. 21, 1860): 310–11.
Leader and Saturday Analyst (London)
  Anon. "George Eliot's New Romance." (Apr. 14, 1860): 355–56.
Manchester Examiner and Times
  Anon. (Apr. 10, 1860): 3.
Morning Advertiser
  Anon. (Apr. 26, 1860): 3.
Morning Chronicle (London)
  Anon. (Apr. 10, 1860): 6.
Morning Post (London)
  Anon. (Apr. 19, 1860): 6.
National Review (London)
  [Hutton, R. H.]. "The Novels of George Eliot." 11 (July 1860): 191–219.
North British Review (Edinburgh)
  Anon. "Imaginative Literature." 33 (Aug. 1860): 165–85.
  [Lancaster, H. H.]. 45 (Sept. 1866): 197–228 [includes *SCL, AB, MF, SM, R,*
    and *FH*].
Press (London)
  Anon. (Apr. 7, 1860): 335–36.
Quarterly Review (London)
  [Robertson, James Craigie]. 108 (Oct. 1860): 469–99.
Sun (London)
  Anon. "Literature." (Apr. 23, 1860): 2.
Tait's Edinburgh Magazine
  Anon. 27 (May 1860): 308–11.
Weekly Scotsman and Caledonian Mercury (Edinburgh)
  Anon. "Notes on Books." (Apr. 7, 1860): 6.
  Anon. (Apr. 21, 1860): 6.

SILAS MARNER

Morning Post (London)
  Anon. (Apr. 4, 1861): 2.

APPENDIX 2

Romola Manuscript and *Cornhill* Pagination

Installment	MS Pagination	Total	Cornhill *Pages*	Total
1	GE: [I]-XIV, 1–82 (68ª, 79ª)[1] BL: 2–99	98	July 1862 1–43	43
2	GE: 83–182 (121ª) BL: 100–200	101	Aug. 1862 145–186	42
3	GE: 183–254 (226ª, 237ª) BL: 201–274	74	Sept. 1862 289–318	30
4	GE: 1–95 (57ª, 69ª)[2] BL: 275–371	97	Oct. 1862 433–470	38
5	GE: 1–60[3] BL: 1–68	68	Nov. 1862 577–604	28
6	GE: 1–92 (22ª, 44ª) BL: 69–162	94	Dec. 1862 721–757	37
7	GE: 1–74[4] BL: 163–236	74	Jan. 1863 1–30	30
8	GE: 1–65 (10ª, 22ª, 53ª)[5] BL: 237–303	67	Feb. 1863 145–171	27
9	GE: 1–67 (5ª, 36ª, 36ᵇ) BL: 304–373	70	Mar. 1863 281–309	29
10	GE: 67–72, 1–47[6] (40ª, 40ᵇ, 46ª) BL: 373–378, 1–50[7]	56	Apr. 1863 417–440	24
11	GE: 1–56 (51ª) BL: 51–107	57	May 1863 553–576	24
12	GE: 1–57 (12ª, 21ª, 38ª, 49ª) BL: 108–168	61	June 1863 681–705	25
13	GE: 1–81 (30ª, 61ª) BL: 169–251	83	July 1863 1–34	34
14	GE: 1–61 (24ª, 39ª, 48ª, 53ª) BL: 252–316	65	Aug. 1863 129–153	25
Total Pages:		1065		436

APPENDIX 3

Middlemarch and *Daniel Deronda* Pagination

George Eliot worried about the unequal length of her separately published parts of *Middlemarch* and *Daniel Deronda*, but she was unable to write to a set length. The following table shows the variation in page length of the text over the eight parts of each novel. Each volume was paginated anew.[1]

PAGINATION IN *MIDDLEMARCH*

Book	Page Numbers in Parts	Total Pages
1	1–212[2]	212
2	215–410	196
3	3–175	173
4	179–377	199
5	3–191	189
6	195–384	190
7	3–176	174
8	179–371	193

PAGINATION IN *DANIEL DERONDA*

Book	Page Numbers in Parts	Total Pages
1	3–191	189
2	195–367	173
3	3–188	186
4	191–364	174
5	3–196	194
6	199–393	195
7	3–162	160
8	165–367	203

NOTES

INTRODUCTION

1. "*Wise, Witty, and Tender Sayings* was published on 6 January 1872 as a small octavo volume with gilt-edged leaves, costing 5 shillings" (Hawes), a month after the first installment of *Middlemarch* appeared. Eliot received her copy on December 28, 1871 (entry from GHL Diary, qtd. in *Letters* 5: 229).

2. J. Don Vann lists thirty-five Trollope works published in serial; one, however, is *Harry Heathcote of Gangoil*, which appeared in a single installment in the Christmas issue of the *Graphic* in 1873 (*Victorian Novels*, 141-69).

3. *Mr. Scarborough's Family* could also be described as "posthumous," although its publication was more advanced, thirty-six of its fifty-six installments having appeared by the date of Trollope's death on December 6, 1882. Only three parts of *The Landleaguers* had appeared by then.

CHAPTER I

1. The original readers of *Cranford*, who encountered the novel in *Household Words* in nine sporadically issued installments between December 1851 and May 1853, read a slightly different version of the debate between the Captain and Miss Jenkyns over the relative merits of established and new writers. As editor of *Household Words*, Dickens felt it would be inappropriate for him to allow the reference to *Pickwick* in his own magazine, and he changed Captain Brown's initial question to "Have you seen any numbers of 'Hood's Own?'" [*sic*], to which Miss Jenkyns replied in the next column, "'Now allow me to read you a scene, and then the present company can judge between your favourite, Mr. Hood, or Dr. Johnson'" (*Household Words*, Dec. 13, 1851: 268). While the comparison is now patently absurd, even in 1851 it would not have had the same effect as a reference to *Pickwick*. Though Gaskell's letter is not extant, she must have complained to Dickens about the substitution, because he wrote to her "in great haste" on Dec. 5, 1851, that he "was so delighted with" her tale that he "put it first in the No. (not hearing of any objection to my proposed alteration by return of Post) and the No. is now made up and in the Printer's hands." (It appeared Dec. 13.) After asking her not to blame him "for what I have done in

perfect good faith," he adds that though he is gratified by her reference to him, "with my name on every page of *Household Words* there would be—or at least I should feel—an impropriety in so mentioning myself" (Dickens, *Letters* 6: 548–49). He also altered a reference to himself in installment 7, published April 2, 1853. The original *Household Words* text refers to "a passage in Hood, which spoke of a chorus in which every man took the tune he knew best, and sang it to his own satisfaction." When *Cranford* appeared in book form in 1853, Gaskell restored "Dickens" to the passage, and with it, the meaning. The Hood reference in the serial does not eliminate Gaskell's close paraphrase of the narrator in chapter 32 of *Pickwick Papers:* "The chorus was the essence of the song; and as each gentleman sang it to the tune he knew best, the effect was very striking indeed."

2. For a sample of the variety of titles serialized in this period, one might look to R. M. Wiles's list for the daily paper, *All-Alive and Merry; or, The London Morning Post.* This paper sold for a farthing, evaded the stamp duty, and from 1739 to 1743 included histories of England and of the Inquisition, of "Tarquinius, Lucretia, and Brutus," the "History of the Adventures of Joseph Andrews," a version of Robinson Crusoe, and letters "from a beautiful young Damsel to her Parents" as a part of the readers' fare (Wiles 46).

3. Harland S. Nelson points out that this break at the end of chapter 37 "magnifies this 'coming event' in two ways: directly, by labeling it explicitly, and indirectly, by making clear that it does not concern Estella. Considering how important she has been to him, this coming event must have a quite unlooked-for gravity" (82–83).

4. Readers who preferred something more elegant could get a copy "Whole bound, morocco, gilt edges" for *6s. 6d.*, and those who opted for the middle ground could get half-bound, morocco, with marble leaves at *4s. 6d.*

5. Lever had explained that he worked "just as I live—from hand to mouth. I can do nothing continuously—that is, without seeing the printed part close behind me. This has been my practice for five-and-twenty years, and I don't think I could change it—at least I should deem it a rash experiment" (Porter 3: 226).

6. J. Don Vann explores the mutually unsatisfactory connection between Dickens and Gaskell, and the difference between their relationship and Dickens's later one with Charles Lever, in "Dickens, Charles Lever and Mrs. Gaskell."

7. This last appeared from May 27, 1882, to June 16, 1883, in the continuation of *All the Year Round*, twelve years after Dickens's death. In the midst of its publication, Trollope himself died (Dec. 6, 1882).

8. The conference is called "Completeness is All," and experts are also examining other incomplete works such as Schubert's 8th symphony and Puccini's *Turandot.*

9. "Tickler" returned in the form of a new dog, Tickler II, in two later

installments: "Tickler II among the Thieves" in October 1860, and "Tickler II Again" in October 1862 (*Blackwood's*, vols. 88 and 92).

10. *Annals of a Publishing House* was published in three volumes, not in installments, but its appearance too was affected by the author's health. Oliphant died after finishing volume 2, and John Blackwood's daughter, Mrs. Gerald Porter, had to complete the story in volume 3.

11. The lapse can be partially accounted for by the hiatus in the appearance of the Miss Brownings as well as by Gaskell's use of the honorific appellation, "Miss Browning," for the eldest daughter and Miss Phoebe Browning's habit of referring to her as "sister" rather than by name. As a consequence, Miss Browning's given name appears infrequently.

12. The altered ending hints at a reconciliation between Pip and a chastened Estella. I think, however, that in the serialization Dickens moved too markedly toward the original ending for the alteration to work well. The novel's serial parts point toward the separation of Pip and Estella more decidedly than toward their unity; and Dickens never edited his text to bring it into greater consistency with even an ambiguous, to say nothing of an optimistic, reading of the conclusion.

13. Jerome Beaty originally suggested that the dating of the letter that Eliot enclosed with the manuscript of part 5 is in error, citing her journal entry of May 8 for the book's completion (64, 64n5). In the "Addenda and Corrigenda" that accompany volumes 8 and 9 of the *George Eliot Letters*, a corrected date—May 6—is supplied (*Letters* 9: 353).

14. I am grateful to members of my 1987 NEH Seminar for School Teachers for pointing out Howells's novel to me.

15. Captain Crowe, for instance, "unsheathed his hanger [a kind of short sword but clearly also a phallic symbol]." Along with the novel's reference to his mistaken notion that "they should be instantly boarded," these instances signal to the reader that neither man nor incident is to be taken seriously. Likewise, there is suspense-breaking humor when Mr. Fillet takes up a poker—which, the narrator adds, "happened to be red-hot," and the ostler pulls down a rusty firelock that had hung "by the roof, over a flitch of bacon."

16. John Vladimir Price suggests another explanation: that Smollett attempts to make the readers complicitous with the narrator, through "early appeals and addresses to the reader, within the body of the novel," and in greater frequency than in his other novels. The reason for this is the novel's serialization. Smollett realizes "that he was attempting something unique in the history of English fiction, that is, extended and prolonged serial publication, accompanied by illustrations. The reader needed to be reminded of his importance as well as the effort that would be expected of him in keeping up with the story" (Bold 202).

Victorian serial authors were writing within a well-established tradition and, though a few worked within an episodic structure, they generally had recourse to other devices to keep their readers returning for the next installment.

CHAPTER 2

1. Installment 1 of *Scenes of Clerical Life* appeared in *Blackwood's* as the lead article for January 1857; Lewes was the author of the fourth article in the same issue, "New facts and old fancies about sea anemones." Lewes became a regular *Blackwood's* contributor in 1856 with "Metamorphoses," May to July; and the first series of "Sea-Side Studies," August to October.

2. This at first glance appears to be the letter with proofs for "Amos" that arrive just as Lewes was writing for them (*Letters* 2: 281). As recorded in Blackwood's letter book, however, the letter makes no reference to the "Great Unknown," but it does contain a paragraph describing Mrs. Blackwood's response to the story: "being a Nottinghamshire Rectors daughter she could appreciate the descriptions of the people in an English Country Parish" (Blackwood's Private Letter Book July 1852 through January 1857; National Library of Scotland). To this, Lewes's postscript replied: "Mrs. Blackwood's testimony is better than our's—certainly than mine, who know nothing of country parsons" (2: 281). Perhaps the letter, dated December 10, was not sent immediately and another note was added along with the rest of the proofs. Or, perhaps Haight's dating is incorrect, and instead of December 18, Lewes's letter should be dated December 11. Both were on a Thursday. In fact, Eliot's journal reference on Friday, December 19, to a letter from Blackwood may have caused Haight to date Lewes's letter December 18, since only the day is given in the heading.

If Lewes's published letter *is* dated incorrectly in the collected *Letters*, it is possible that there was a second letter from Blackwood, no longer extant, containing the references to the "Great Unknown" and the "keel of other stories." Her one journal entry between December 10 and 19—on December 13—makes no reference to any letter. It is possible, though not likely, that she would have made an entry on the 13th but waited until the 19th to refer to Blackwood's letter.

3. A note to "How I Came to Write Fiction" in the collected letters suggests, however, that she may actually have begun on September 23, misdating her journal as Tuesday, September 22—when Tuesday that year was the 23rd (*Letters* 2: 407n3).

4. More than a year earlier, Eliot's journal records that, since February's "discouraging news" that *Scenes* was selling "very slowly" (GE Journal, Feb. 4, 1858), "several encouraging fragments of news about the 'Scenes' have come to my ears—especially that Mrs. Owen Jones and her husband—two very different people—are equally enthusiastic about the book. But both have detected the woman" (GE Journal, Apr. 3, 1858). By June 1859, they had detected the particular woman, based on evidence that included a change in "the Lewes style of living." She "tried to make Mrs. OJ say that she would like to know you (not that you would like to know her)," Bodichon wrote, "but she seemed to feel fear! I do not think she would call even if she knew you were George Eliot. I said a great

deal about my pleasant visits. I was trying experiments on her for my own satisfaction not on your account at all." It is these remarks that precede Bodichon's exclamation on "what cowards people are!" (*Letters* 3: 103).

5. Lewes received a letter with the same sentiments when he submitted "Metamorphoses" to *Blackwood's* earlier in 1856. John Blackwood wrote about Lewes's second installment:

> I do not like to accept any Series long or short for the Magazine without having seen the whole, as you may readily imagine I would get into no End of Scrapes if I did so. At least in the case of Authors with whose powers and mode of working I was not thoroughly acquainted. I shall put the first part into type but before positively accepting the Metamorphoses and publishing the tale in the Magazine I should like to see the completion which I think you must have pretty well reached by this time. (Blackwood's Private Letter Book July 1852 through January 1857; National Library of Scotland)

6. As Lewes and Eliot both became involved in writing for Maga, Blackwood came to appreciate Lewes's editorial judgment. On November 18, 1856, Blackwood agreed to look at a scientific paper from another friend of Lewes, the Reverend George Tugwell, unless it is one "which you think will hardly do" (2: 275). Tugwell had not sent the paper to Lewes by February 15, 1857, when Lewes assured Blackwood that if Tugwell does write the promised paper, he will not forward it "unless I think it probable you will accept it" (*Letters* 2: 296–97). Blackwood had just written Lewes two days earlier about the positive reception of "Amos Barton," adding, "Generally contributors introducing friends' M.S.S. to Editors assume the character of bores, but you are a noble and memorable exception" (*Letters* 2: 296).

7. Mary Hamer discusses Trollope's dislike of the common practice, and his decision with *Framley Parsonage*, his first serialized novel, "to write a novel that would be designed as a serial but would not be written from month to month as it came out" (70). *Framley Parsonage* was composed between November 1859 and June 1860, and published in the *Cornhill* from January 1860 to April 1861. Hamer also notes: "His practice, although his position was so much less favoured than hers, is closer to George Eliot's than to that of Thackeray or Dickens" (70). This last statement is certainly not true for *Scenes of Clerical Life*, and only somewhat more accurate for Eliot's last serial novel, *Daniel Deronda*.

8. Redating her letter June 30 does not explain this paradox. Perhaps she was so harried at this time by the combination of Blackwood's criticism and the crisis in her personal affairs that she did not see the impossibility of waiting to print. Or perhaps the letter is still misdated.

9. Eliot originally intended the story of *Adam Bede* to be part of *Scenes*, but Blackwood's objections, especially to "Janet," deterred her. The history of her plans for *Adam Bede*'s serialization is traced in chapter 3.

10. Many years later, she remembered their origin as "*one* paper in 'House-

hold Words'; and I never meant to write more, so killed Capt Brown very much against my will" (*Letters* 748). However, "because of the immediate popularity of the first 'Cranford' paper and the writer's increasing ability to pull in readers . . . Dickens gave her the freedom of his columns for as many 'Cranford' papers as she cared to write" (Dorothy Collins 59–60). The first letter, to Eliza Fox, is dated December 1851 and is probably the more accurate of the two in representing the situation. The first installments of *Cranford* appeared December 13, 1851, and January 3, 1852. The letter stating her intention to write one installment was written to John Ruskin on March 5, 1865, when she might be expected to recall her intentions a little less precisely than in a letter written the month the first installment of *Cranford* appeared.

11. Dickens might not have felt that parts were so discrete, or he might simply have wanted more of a popular story. A postscript to his letter to Gaskell dated December 1, 1852, asks "Cranford???" The editors of the new Dickens letters observe in a note that "The last instalment, 'Visiting at Cranford', had appeared on 3 Apr (*HW*,V,55); CD was obviously worried by the long delay before the next" (Dickens, *Letters* 6: 812 and 812n1). Much earlier in the year, he had jokingly chided Gaskell for not sending an installment of *Cranford*, "O what a lazy woman you are, and where IS that article!" (Dickens, *Letters* 6: 609).

12. On March 18, she describes spending "the evening pleasantly in spite of ailing bodies, reading Mrs. Gaskell's pretty *Cranford*." The next evening, they were reading chapter 6, "Poor Peter" (GE Journal). This chapter incorporates particularly well the humor and pathos that Eliot herself combined so effectively in *Scenes of Clerical Life*.

13. Wilkie Collins in *The Woman in White* in 1860 has Walter Hartright exclaim on the inability of Victorians to imagine the wild and dangerous in the midst of "civilised London": attempting to avoid his pursuers, Walter concludes that "I had first learnt to use this stratagem against suspected treachery in the wilds of Central America—and now I was practising it again, with the same purpose and with even greater caution, in the heart of civilised London!" (418).

14. *Lady Lee's Widowhood* by Edward Bruce Hamley was serialized in *Blackwood's* from January to October 1853.

15. E. E. Kellett is one of many writers to point out the role of the family reading aloud as an influence on the nineteenth-century novel: "No one can read certain novels of the time without perceiving that they were intended . . . for a public not so much of individuals as of 'household'" (2: 49).

16. For the full text of this letter, see my forthcoming article in *Publishing History* (scheduled for fall 1994).

17. Blackwood's letters of January 30 and February 10 both record positive responses to Amos, though it is not always clear whether he means Amos the story or Amos the character. Despite what "startled" Blackwood—i.e., two "familiars—about the best men going—declaring dead against Amos"—opinions

were generally favorable. Blackwood noted Thackeray's positive response to a small portion of the story that he shared with him while Thackeray was staying at the publisher's house (*Letters* 2: 290–91; 293).

18. Other novels return precisely to the point at which the previous install-ment broke off, sometimes even repeating the final words of the earlier episode as a reminder to readers of the action of the last week or the last month. Thus, Dickens ends installment 16 of *Nicholas Nickleby* with Newman Noggs calling out after Nicholas "Stop thief! Stop thief!" (2: 512). The first sentence in install-ment 17 recalls the action of the preceding number by repeating this phrase: "Finding that Newman was determined to arrest his progress at any hazard, and apprehensive that some well-intentioned passenger attracted by the cry of 'stop thief,' might really lay violent hands upon his person, . . . Nicholas soon slack-ened his pace" (2: 513). Wilkie Collins returns readers of *The Woman in White* instantly to the dramatic action in installment 2 by repeating the closing words of the first part, "'She has escaped from my Asylum'" (22). Other examples from *The Woman in White* include the transitions from installments 5 to 6, 10 to 11, and 14 to 15. The author of a single-plot novel could use flashbacks or shift to other characters to avoid beginning at the place at which the preceding installment left off. However, to do so carelessly would be to risk losing the reader.

19. Anthony Wybrow is not Sir Christopher's actual son, but his nephew and chosen heir, and the stories also differ in that most of the conflict in "Gilfil" takes place in the second generation, whereas the conflicting triangles in "Hester Ben-field" are among members of the first generation.

20. This study of George Eliot's serial fiction attempts only to suggest the context of the periodicals in which her first two serials, *Scenes* and *Romola*, appeared. It does not reiterate the obvious—the superiority of *Scenes* to "Hester Benfield" or *The Athelings*. While Eliot's earliest readers often recognized her superior talent, they were not always as cognizant of the shortcomings of other works published alongside hers. But even when they were aware, these works still formed part of the reading context from which they approached Eliot's fiction. Nor does this study attempt the exhaustive look at *Blackwood's* or the *Cornhill* that Louis James calls for and models in "The Trouble with Betsy: Periodicals and the Common Reader in Mid-Nineteenth-Century England."

21. The one manifestation of Hester's pride is her refusal to accept a gift of money from Lady Helen Maldon, who then gives Hester her card so that she can return the "loan." This effects the happy ending, when Frank Benfield, seeing on the card the maiden name, Maldon, comes to Lady Helen Allenby to ask her help in finding his father, whose inscription in the book of Milton's poetry reads George Maldon Asleigh. The tragedy in Hester's situation results from love, not pride. She comes to love George Asleigh and so accepts his suit. When she finds out her second marriage is bigamous, her love for her daughter by Dr. Thornton causes her to conceal her first marriage, rather than reveal her daughter's illegitimacy.

22. A strong controlling voice minimizes the melodramatic potential in "Hester Benfield."

23. Thomas Noble calls Caterina a "piece of apprentice work" (134) for later figures like Hetty Sorrel and Maggie Tulliver, and suggests that "[o]ne might almost consider Wybrow a rough sketch for Arthur [Donnithorne] if he had any of Arthur's good qualities" (132). One of the most thorough and perceptive studies of these connections is Felicia Bonaparte's *Will and Destiny*, which sees more than a slight resemblance between Anthony and Arthur as well as other complacent young men, such as Fred Vincy, who rely on Providence instead of on their own consciences and efforts.

24. "Hester Benfield" anticipates *Adam Bede* in some striking ways, particularly in the pregnant, forlorn Hester's journey to find her husband. Even her name—Hester—is the same as the full name of Hetty Sorrel (and, of course, of Hester Prynne in *The Scarlet Letter*).

25. Mary Barton, in Gaskell's novel of that name (1848), has another reaction when she learns that Harry Carson has not intended to marry her and only proposes when he is "desperate." Escaping from him and the pandering Sally Leadbitter, Mary discovers her real feelings and thereafter avoids Carson's advances, though not before the damage has been done that leads to Jem Wilson's trial for Carson's murder.

26. Like Dickens altering *Great Expectations*'s ending, Thomas Hardy claimed to have changed the ending of *The Return of the Native* to meet "certain circumstances of serial publication." In his note to the Wessex edition of 1912, Hardy says he had not originally planned a marriage between Thomasin and Venn, but altered his ending, so that "Readers can therefore choose between the endings, and those with an austere artistic code can assume the more consistent conclusion to be the true one." However, Michael Millgate contends that the "evolution is so successfully handled in the novel as it stands as to prompt certain doubts about the footnote" (142).

27. For readers in the 1850s, Caterina's foreign origin placed her among significant actual and literary antecedents. In 1849, Maria Manning, called the "foreign temptress" by Thomas Boyle (62), murdered her lover. In *Bleak House*, serialized from March 1852 to September 1853, Tulkinghorn's murder is found to be the crime of Lady Dedlock's passionate, vengeful French maid, who had been discharged. The British narrow view of foreigners is humorously presented by the narrator's comment that Sir Christopher and Lady Cheveral had no intention of adopting Caterina "as their daughter," but thought it "a Christian work to train this little Papist into a good Protestant, and graft as much English fruit as possible on the Italian stem" (104, 103). Their benevolent chauvinism could easily turn to outright hostility in English readers who followed the Manning case or the trouble caused by Lady Dedlock's wholly unsympathetic former maid. While his reference is to a male victim of murder, much of what Richard Altick says about

xenophobic, anti-Papist sentiment in the 1850s in connection with the Madeleine Smith trial in Edinburgh is also pertinent here (*Scarlet* 178–79).

28. Experienced and sophisticated readers did not disdain pathos. George Henry Lewes recognized it as a key to success in fiction in his well-known assessment of Eliot's potential as a fiction writer, recorded in "How I Came to Write Fiction," in which he considered how well she could write both comedy and pathos (*Letters* 2: 408). Dickens, as an editor as well as a successful author who frequently employed pathos, was susceptible to its effect. At the beginning of his *Household Words* editorship, he wrote to Elizabeth Gaskell that her story for the first number, "'Lizzie Leigh,'" had "interested me greatly, as I read it. And it made me cry—which I mention because I take that to be indisputable proof of its effect" (Dickens, *Letters* 6: 48). Thomas A. Noble discusses the pathos in *Scenes of Clerical Life*, particularly in reference to "Amos Barton" (109–22).

29. Knowing Charles Edward Mudie's personal stance toward the "moral" novel, publishers sometimes precensored books. Readers like Geraldine Jewsbury for *Bentley's* anticipated Mudie's objections and rejected works for their supposed immorality (Griest 123–25).

30. Just before Eliot began "Janet's Repentance," Blackwood and Lewes exchanged letters concerning the difficulty posed by "lady readers" of Lewes's "Seaside Studies," which was to begin its second series in *Blackwood's* in June 1857. Regarding the "analysis of the faeces of the Actiniae," Blackwood observed, "The quotation from your clinical authority is painfully minute and could not be otherwise than distasteful, especially to ladies who form a large section of the readers of such papers" (*Letters* 2: 322). Lewes replied, "I shall cut out the objectionable faeces altogether. But you must confess it is an awful wet blanket on a writer's shoulders, that terror of lady readers, and what they will exclaim against" (*Letters* 2: 325).

31. Roland F. Anderson argues that Blackwood's inability to grasp Eliot's pleas for realism during publication of *Scenes of Clerical Life* led to her famous pronouncement in chapter 17 of *Adam Bede* (39–47).

32. In keeping with her greater realism, George Eliot's delirium tremens scene treats its subject unsparingly instead of softening it as Dickens did in the interpolated story in chapter 3 of *Pickwick Papers*. There the impact is diminished by two facts: it is a story told by and about persons with whom neither the Pickwickians nor the readers have developed special sympathy or interest, and it depicts few of the horrible and fantastic imaginings of the alcoholic. Instead it shows more of the sick man's imaginative return to the stage and the pub, as if these were simply the mental wanderings of anyone near death.

In its realistic, vivid portrayal of alcoholism and wife abuse, Eliot's story may be more meritorious for the modern reader than for the reader of *Blackwood's* in 1857—when Victorian self-satisfaction expressed in the Exposition of 1851 had only begun to be challenged by the realities of the Crimean War and the Indian

Mutiny. The horrors of the latter were reported in great detail in British newspapers (including an article on the "Bengal Mutiny" in *Blackwood's* September 1857 issue), but these horrors were at a distance, both literally and figuratively. What Blackwood termed Eliot's "bold choice of a plot" was too close to home (*Letters* 2: 386), even though Eliot claimed to have "softened" her picture. "The real town was more vicious than my Milby; the real Dempster was far more disgusting than mine; the real Janet alas! had a far sadder end than mine" (*Letters* 2: 347). Despite this basis in fact, Eliot did make a few minor changes in the first installment (see Noble's edition of *Scenes*), but she refused to compromise on the delirium tremens scene or the scene of Janet's encounter with the hidden brandy bottle.

33. George Henry Lewes used the same word—"finest"—in writing to Blackwood about the latter's initial objections:

> I was in raptures with 'Janet's Repentance' when Eliot first read it to me and declared it would be the finest thing he had written. Your letter therefore considerably staggered me, as I have much confidence in your judgement; accordingly I reread the part with a critical eye to detect the objections you spoke of. In vain! Two readings have left me in the dark. Either you or I must be under a profound misconception of the effect likely to be produced. (*Letters* 2: 351)

Although one is tempted to interpret Lewes as admonishing Blackwood to show enthusiasm, Lewes apparently had expressed these views to Eliot herself two weeks earlier. Her letter to Blackwood accompanying the first installment of "Janet" notes that "Lewes seems to have higher expectations from the third story than from either of the preceding" (*Letters* 2: 335).

34. Robertson's quotations come from the *Quarterly*'s notice of *Jane Eyre* (Dec. 1848, vol. 84, pp. 153–85). The Eliot notice seems to suggest that both were written by Robertson. However, both the Brontë *Critical Heritage* and the *Wellesley Index to Victorian Periodicals* attribute the Brontë review to Elizabeth Rigby. Like other Victorian reviews, the reviews of both *Jane Eyre* and *Scenes* were published anonymously; Robertson is obviously using the general "we," referring to the periodical, not the individual author.

35. Realism is no excuse, according to Robertson. In fact, "this conscientious fidelity has very serious drawbacks," including dullness and tediousness. Quoting Eliot's discussion from chapter 17 of *Adam Bede*, beginning "It is for this rare, precious quality of truthfulness that I delight in many Dutch paintings . . . ," Robertson argues, "If some Dutch painters bestowed their skill on homely old women and boozy boors, there is no evidence that they were capable of better things, and their choice of subjects is no justification for one who certainly can do better" (484–85). The purpose of fiction is moral uplift, but here "there is a love for exploring what would be better left in obscurity; for portraying the wildness of passion and the narrowing miseries of mental conflict; for dark pictures of sin and remorse and punishment; for the discussion of questions which it is painful

and revolting to think of." It is particularly dangerous "to familiarize the minds of our young women in the middle and higher ranks with matters on which their fathers and brothers would never venture to speak in their presence" (498). Eliot had told Blackwood, "I can hardly believe that the public will regard my pictures as exceptionally coarse" (*Letters* 2: 348), a word that Robertson uses to condemn the portrayal of alcoholism in a woman character.

36. The Roman Catholic *Tablet* would have provided another dimension of religious opinion, but, though it reviewed even the individual installments of Eliot's last two novels, it failed to notice *Scenes of Clerical Life* in serial or book form.

37. Haight reprints the first part of this journal entry in *Letters* 2: 411n3, but does not include this sentence. For a record of these clerical reactions in Lewes and Blackwood's correspondence, see *Letters* 2: 406 and 8: 186.

38. It would also have taken her drinking outside the private domain and might erroneously have identified her with the class of alcoholics that the narrator treats less sympathetically in chapter 2. As Peter Fenves points out, this "social dimension" to alcoholism is replaced in the narrative by Janet's "personal, intrapsychic struggle" (428).

39. This incident convinced Dickens that the author was a woman: "I have not the faintest doubt that a woman described her being shut out into the street by her husband, and conceived and executed the whole idea of her following of that clergyman" (qtd. in Eliot, *Letters* 2: 428).

40. There is, of course, the obvious irony of the "heartless" Wybrow dying from a heart attack.

41. Others who have recently treated the connection between newspaper accounts and fiction include Thomas Boyle, whose *Black Swine in the Sewers of Hampstead* is built on the clippings of criminal trials made by one William Bell Macdonald, who retired as a naval surgeon to his Scotland estate, Rammerscales, in 1837. The collection gives testimony to one Victorian's fascination with crime reports in the popular press. Beth Kalikoff, in *Murder and Moral Decay in Victorian Popular Literature*, also discusses the interest in "public and private murder" in the Victorian period. She cites newspaper accounts of several kinds of domestic murder, but no particular cases parallel to Dempster's violence and murderous potential.

42. Dickens presents a grotesque image of these crimes—and, of course, a foreshadowing of later developments—in his description of the coverings in Dombey's house after his first wife's death: "Bell-handles, window-blinds, and looking-glasses, being papered up in journals, daily and weekly, obtruded fragmentary accounts of deaths and dreadful murders" (*Dombey and Son* 75).

43. I am indebted to Virginia Morris's book for pointing me to Keith Thomas's essay.

44. Eliot treats this Victorian justification for abuse briefly in *Felix Holt*.

Dredge, a workman who frequents Chubb's public house in Sproxton, where Felix attempts to convert the men to the virtues of education, proclaims that "I've been aforced to give my wife a black eye to hinder her fron going to the preachin'." When Mike Brindle asks "with some disgust" why he can't leave her alone, Dredge responds: "no more I did beat her afore, not if she scrat' me . . . but if she jabbers at me, I can't abide it" (224).

45. Nancy L. Paxton traces Spencer's growing conservatism, which separated more and more his views from Eliot's, but she does not discuss "Janet's Repentance."

46. At the time he read the manuscript for this part, even Blackwood did not know how many installments Eliot would require to complete the story. In the letter redated by Haight as June 30, she had written that the story "will require at least three—possibly four—numbers of the Magazine. I mean, that the whole story will be in three or four parts" (*Letters* 2: 300; redated in 9: 342). He already had installment 3 in hand when Eliot wrote on August 9 that "The story, I expect, will be completed in two more numbers" (2: 373). She confirmed this September 5 (2: 381).

47. *The George Eliot Letters* include none from John Blackwood to either Eliot or Lewes between August 15 and October 15, 1857, though both wrote to the publisher, sending, among other things, parts 4 and 5 of "Janet's Repentance." Haight footnotes one reference that indicates a lost letter from Blackwood, but there were probably others as well (*Letters* 2: 378n9). All the letters printed in volumes 2 and 8 of the collected letters are "outgoing" letters, from Eliot or Lewes to someone else, with the exception of one from Thornton Lewes to his father, dated Hofwyl, 2 October. The blank suggests some consistent loss of correspondence that the couple received during that period. None of the extant correspondence from Eliot and Lewes to Blackwood refers to any comment the publisher might have made on the conclusion to part 4.

48. The ending to "Janet's Repentance" is, of course, more conventional than that of *Daniel Deronda*, affirming Divine support for Janet and adding a final brief chapter that summarizes her life and the story's moral.

49. Mrs. Raynor is visiting a dying sister-in-law; Mrs. Pettifer and Mrs. Crewe are out for the day.

CHAPTER 3

1. The extant correspondence does not explain why Eliot thought Blackwood might have objected to her portrayal of the Church's treatment of Methodism. Perhaps she was recalling her experience with "Janet's Repentance" and Blackwood's objection to her Bishop. When *Adam Bede* appeared, nothing in the reviews indicated an objection by the established Church. The Church of England's weekly, the *Guardian*, and the *Church of England Monthly Review* were

both enthusiastic. Though disliking the melodrama of Arthur's last-minute reprieve for Hetty and objecting to the marriage at the end, the *Guardian* found the
novel exemplary and on the way to being a classic. The *Church of England
Monthly Review* praised the honest portrayal of Mr. Irwine as a man with faults
and virtues.

2. After publication, reviewers for the *Daily News* and the Edinburgh *Evening
Courant* declined to give the plot summary common in newspaper reviews: "Indeed, [the story] is so simple, and its interest so dependent upon the associations
which insensibly accumulate in the course of the narrative, that its charm would
entirely evaporate under any summary treatment" (*Daily News* 2). The *Courant*'s
argument could have come from Eliot herself: "A few lines . . . would suffice for
an outline, but they would at the same time prevent a just appreciation of the
wonderful tact and truth to nature with which the author preserves his secret
until the inevitable moment brings it to light. The reader, indeed, is almost made
an actor in the tale. He feels himself, as it were, one of the rural community of
Hayslope, and he shares with the rest the general unconsciousness of what is
about to befall" (Feb. 15, 1859; 3).

3. See *George Eliot Letters* 8: 203–04.

4. *George Eliot Letters* 2: 448.

5. *George Eliot Letters* 2: 448–49.

6. Several other letters from this letter book are included in *The George Eliot
Letters*, but not this one. Haight included excerpts from these letters in volume 2,
but did not reproduce the entire texts until volume 8. For example, compare 2:
449n8, an excerpt from the 1857–58 letter book, with the whole text of this letter
to Lewes on April 30, 1858, reproduced in 8: 203–04.

7. The letter-book letter also explains the definiteness of two journal entries in
which she takes responsibility for the decision. On May 4, she records a "Letter
from Blackwood today, in which he appears to fall in rather with the idea of
separate publication for *Adam Bede* than of publication in the Magazine" (GE
Journal). Another entry six months later reinforces the idea that it was her decision not to serialize: "I proposed that the notion of publication in Maga should
be given up" and Blackwood "assented" (rpt. in *Letters* 2: 502–05).

8. The *Saturday Review*'s comments are well known: "Hetty's feelings and
changes are indicated with a punctual sequence that makes the account of her
misfortunes read like the rough notes of a man-midwife's conversations with a
bride. This is intolerable. Let us copy the old masters of the art, who, if they gave
us a baby, gave it us all at once. A decent author and a decent public may surely
take the premonitory symptoms for granted" (*Critical Heritage* 76). Lewes called
these comments "priggish and disgusting," but noted that "they will give a *tone* to
opinion and they prove that the book produces a deep and peculiar impression"
(GHL Journal, Feb. 26, 1859). The *North British Review* also objected that
Hetty's sin is "given too prominent a place in the tale," and the *Examiner* disliked

the delineation of Hetty's sufferings as unnecessary, even counter to the moral lesson. The naivete of the period can only be suggested by the unintentional humor in Vera Brittain's experience half a century later of adolescent girls "searching for obstetrical details through the Bible and such school-library novels as . . . *Adam Bede*" (48).

9. *Adam Bede* was, in fact, serialized fewer than ten years later as the first in a series of her works to be issued in parts between 1867 and 1869. The back cover for the opening numbers reads: "This Edition will be published in Monthly Numbers, price SIX-PENCE. Each Number will contain a highly-finished engraving, executed under the direction of Mr J. D. Cooper, by a selection of able Artists." *Adam Bede* was the first in the series, numbered 1–7; followed by *The Mill on the Floss*, 8–16; *Silas Marner*, 17–18; *Scenes of Clerical Life*, 19–23; and *Felix Holt*, 24–30. This publication is another form of cheap, fascicle issue described in chapter 1. The breaks were determined by signatures and not by the structure of the narrative.

In 1876, contemplating the increased public interest in her fiction and the firm's long-range plans, John Blackwood wrote to his nephew William about the possibility of issuing Eliot's works "in three-penny numbers, 'for which Adam Bede, Middlemarch, and at least three of the others are admirably adapted'" (qtd. in *Letters* 6: 297n5).

10. These numbers are continuous throughout the volume and appear in the upper right-hand corner of each page. In contrast, Eliot repeats or skips numbers as she revises and then has to alter her numbering scheme; the British Library numbers are therefore simpler and more reliable to use in counting pages for comparative purposes.

11. Her dedication on page 1 of the bound manuscript states, "A large portion of [this work] was written twice, though often scarcely at all altered in the copying, but other parts only once." The appearance of the manuscript supports this claim. In only a few places in the manuscript are emendations visible, such as those appearing on the final manuscript page of chapter 9.

12. By now the numbering has been adjusted for chapters 1 to 13. However, since chapter 14 *ends* with the Poysers, Hetty, and Dinah all going to bed, this reference to writing chapter 14 up to the "going to bed" is mystifying—until one notes that the manuscript does not begin chapter 15 on a new page. Instead, its number and heading, "The Two Bedchambers," have been squeezed in on half a line above the beginning of a new paragraph: "Hetty and Dinah both slept on the second story in rooms adjoining each other." The chapter break here was evidently a second thought, formed sometime after Eliot began to write the material that appears in chapter 15.

13. There is one confusing piece of evidence: Blackwood's reference on March 31 to "the two other parts you mention" (2: 446). This may have resulted from

the fact that Eliot marked only the end of part 1 in the manuscript, and Black-wood may not have realized that he already had three, and not two, parts.

14. In his correspondence about *Scenes of Clerical Life*, there is no evidence that Blackwood and Eliot ever "fixed upon" a particular length of pages, nor that he suggested she strive for installments equal in length. In fact, her installments vary by several published pages.

15. The fact that Eliot avoids such repetition in *Middlemarch*, by closing book 4 with Casaubon and Dorothea instead of the Raffles–Bulstrode plot with which book 5 ends, does not diminish the likelihood of deliberate repetition here. *Middlemarch* had several plot lines under way, in contrast to *Adam Bede*, and many more characters whose lives could provide the requisite suspense.

16. Her statement regarding her desire not to become like so many serial novel-ists who produced two or three books a year for the sake of the income is well known: "I don't want the world to give me anything for my books except money enough to save me from the temptation to write *only* for money" (*Letters* 3: 152).

17. Five are given in volume 3 and one in volume 8 of the *Letters*. In several more letters in late September and early October, Eliot or Lewes wrote to the Brays to clarify the matter. Other allusions to Bracebridge's actions in letters to correspondents who were not involved indicate how distressed Eliot was.

18. Haight makes a similar judgment in his biography, citing an unpublished letter of September 18 from John to William Blackwood: the former "would rather give up £4000 than lose the book for the Mag. if it keeps up to sample" (307). John followed William's advice, however, when he offered Eliot £3,000 on September 21.

19. R. F. Anderson may be partially correct in attributing Eliot's coolness during negotiations for *The Mill on the Floss* to her chagrin at not having retained the copyright to *Adam Bede*. However, he does not sufficiently credit Eliot's sensitivity about her anonymity and the Liggins controversy, especially in such a gender-biased and critical publishing climate. As a result, he overemphasizes Blackwood's magnanimity to Eliot's detriment ("Negotiating for *The Mill on the Floss*" 30).

20. Eliot's tone betrays none of the ungraciousness that the Blackwoods later attributed to her: "I *do* feel more than I ought about outside sayings and doings, such as Mr. Bracebridge's," she writes, and

> If you were living in London instead of at Edinburgh, I should ask you to read the first volume of "Sister Maggie" at once, for the sake of having your impressions; but it is inconvenient to me to part with the M.S. The great success of "Adam" makes my writing a matter of more anxiety than ever: I suppose there is a little sense of responsibility mixed up with a great deal of pride. (*Letters* 3: 184–85)

21. Since late spring, members of the firm had feared that the authorship was becoming known. John Blackwood wrote to his brother from London on May

30, "I saw Dallas yesterday and was shocked to find that he had heard who the real author of Adam Bede was and Thackeray today said he had heard it was Lewes and Miss Evans. I put them off the scent pretty neatly. So long as it is merely a rumour it does not much matter." William responded the next day, "I am not surprised at G.E.'s secret having leaked out but as long as he does not let on himself rumours are not of much consequence." Langford wrote June 13: "Mr Crawley heard a curious story in the City about the authorship—that these books were written by a lady who lives with Mr Lewes 'a very clever woman.' I should be sorry for such a notion to get about." And William wrote to John on June 16, "I hope the secret of the authorship will be kept—I have great misgivings that it can however" (Letters in the National Library of Scotland).

22. The March notice also saw the competition bringing renewed vitality to the periodical market: "Magazine literature was generally considered to have been long declining, and in several instances to have reached its last gasp, when, a very few months ago, two new competitors entered the field, and, by their wealth of talent and resources, either asserted or understood, seemed determined to prove to the world that the belief was falsely based."

23. Lewes's choice of words was perhaps unfortunate, but the apparently unusual naivete here may indicate his and Eliot's assumption that their relationship was a marriage in all but the formalities bestowed by Church and State.

24. The exchange began with a forthright letter from Eliot asking Blackwood "whether you still wish to remain my publishers, or whether the removal of my incognito has caused a change in your views on that point" (3: 215). Several long letters that follow can be read in Haight's edition, 3: 216–24.

25. Mudie's control of publishing generally and his censorship in particular were issues that recurred periodically in the columns of Victorian newspapers. One year later, throughout the autumn of 1860, newspapers and periodicals carried letters about Mudie's alleged bias against Church of England books. High Church works, including the novel *Miriam May*, were at the center of correspondence to several newspapers. In response to earlier criticisms, Mudie wrote to the Church of England *Guardian* that, adhering to the principle of running a "select" library, he rejected this novel because of its distortions of truth and its poor quality. The *Guardian* responded in a parenthetical note in the same column: "We did not make our accusation without having personal knowledge of the difficulty that has been experienced in obtaining High Church books from Mr. Mudie's." After enumerating instances of the editor's own futile application, it cites the experience of correspondents, adding that

> we do not know a single instance of difficulty in obtaining other books, but have
> often admired the apparent lavishness with which a new copy of a book has been
> obtained, when there was not one in the library at the time of application. . . . And
> supposing *Miriam May* to be as bad as Mr. Mudie thinks it—and we plead guilty to

ignorance of its contents—we do not see why he should be allowed to make it a stalking horse on which he may escape from the other charges, which are authenticated. (Oct. 17, 1860; 899)

Other quite diverse periodicals not aligned with the established church were also critical. The *Saturday Review* noted that the servility of certain publishers' letters "written to exonerate him [Mudie] from the charges" leads to the conclusion "that Mr. Mudie is in a position to make himself the dictator of literature" (Nov. 3, 1860; 550). The *Plymouth Mail* headlined a column on the controversy, "THE BOOK-DESPOT," and offered the inflammatory statement "We do not want to see the Republic of *Letters* turned into an empire under a literary Bonaparte" (Nov. 7; 4). Guinevere Griest discusses the subject of Mudie's influence on books' content at length (140–55). Gaye Tuchman analyzes Mudie's influence in the larger context of women writers and the Victorian publishing industry.

26. Blackwood wrote Eliot that she knew "how much I have been opposed" to removal of the incognito. "It may prove a disadvantage and in the eyes of many it will, but my opinion of your genius and confidence in the truly good, honest, religious, and moral tone of all you have written or will write is such that I think you will overcome any possible detriment from the withdrawal of the mystery which has so far taken place" (*Letters* 3: 217). His correspondence with his brother shows that he was sounding more optimistic here than either of them really felt.

27. Blackwood carefully concealed these views in his letters to Lewes and Eliot. Only after the novel appeared did he remark in one letter to Lewes that "Langford does not say much of the opinions of The Garrick about The Mill but I rather gather that the verdict there is not so universally favourable as about Adam. The knowledge of the secret would make them more critical I daresay" (*Letters* 3: 290). The members of this dramatic and literary club would have been more likely to know the gossip about Eliot's personal life than would the general public.

To Eliot herself, Blackwood wrote cautiously, "I have heard a good deal of sort of ex post facto wisdom proceeding from the knowledge of who the book is written by, especially among the small deer of criticism" (3: 305). By then Eliot was able to treat the matter with humor and responded that she was "in repose" about the *Mill*, and that it would have to be judged later, "when the judgment upon it is no longer influenced by the recent enthusiasm about 'Adam,' and by the fact that it has the misfortune to be written by me instead of by Mr. Liggins" (3: 307). She used Blackwood's own phrase in a letter to Charles Bray, explaining that she has seen no reviews, "It was certain that in the notices of my first book after the removal of my incognito there would be much *ex poste facto* wisdom, which could hardly profit me, since *I* certainly knew who I was beforehand" (3: 324).

28. The brothers seem to have temporized about putting her name on "The Lifted Veil." John wrote to William on June 15, 1859, that the story

is not pleasant but it is very powerful and will be read with interest. Looking at the experiment again I did not dislike it so much as at first. I proposed to put George Eliot to it but I said I thought it better not to fritter away the prestige which should be kept fresh for the new novel. In this I am sure you will agree with me altho [*sic*] I daresay I am the only Editor who would have objected to the name in the present furor. I suppose the other Magazines would give any money for a scrap with George Eliot's name attached. I forget whether I mentioned that Delane told me that enlightened Gentleman Mr Reeve the Editor of the Edinburgh has applied to Liggins for an article. (NLS)

William's response the next day suggests that the Blackwoods, knowing the truth of authorship, did *not* want what the other magazines might have given any money for: "I quite agree with you about not putting G.E.'s name to the Lifted Veil. Tho' I dont like the story and cant think it fulfils the promise which the finely written opening holds out yet I have no doubt it is one which will catch much attention. . . . I hope the secret of the authorship will be kept" (NLS).

29. The metaphor was, coincidentally, echoed twelve years later in a review of a novel she did publish serially, *Middlemarch*. In an otherwise favorable notice of installment 2 on February 3, 1872, the *Athenaeum* objected to "the present manner of appearance [which] spoils much of our enjoyment. Even those who do not like champagne in tumblers, are not bound to prefer their nectar by the drop" (138). The "drop" here was the largest Victorian serial part heretofore published— an entire half-volume!

30. Another source of annoyance at this time was Blackwood's apparent nonchalance about the supposed sequel to *Adam Bede* being advertised by Newby, especially when other friends and would-be publishers were waxing wroth. Lewes's journal entry for November 22 goes on to say that his call upon Dickens was also "about an article on 'Adam Bede Junior' which he wanted me to write [for *All the Year Round*], but I declined, as I could not do it with temper calm enough" (GHL Journal). Eliot writes a longer entry on the same subject:

> We have been much annoyed lately by Newby's advertisement of a book called "Adam Bede, Junior, A Sequel," and today Dickens has written to mention a story of the tricks which are being used to push the book under the pretence of its being mine. One Librarian has been forced to order the book against his wish, because the public have demanded it! Dickens is going to put an article on the subject in Household Words [*sic*], in order to scarify the rascally book sellers. The Blackwoods are slow to act in the matter—hitherto have not acted at all: not being strongly moved, apparently by what is likely to injure me more than them. Several persons have expressed their surprize at the silence of the Blackwoods. (GE Journal, Nov. 22, 1859)

Suspicion of indifference was strong on both sides.

31. Eliot's note has not been found, but probably, given her reluctance to discuss money, she had declined Dickens's offer by talking about artistic consid-

erations in a way that seemed to him inconclusive. His own recollection was that "Mrs. Lewes's note merely asked me, in acknowledging the receipt of the Tale of Two Cities, whether something was not sacrificed, through the necessities of such a plan, to terseness and closeness of construction" (3: 261). Nonetheless, Dickens was gracious; perhaps in appreciation, Eliot asked Blackwood on March 22 to send only one presentation copy of her new novel—to Dickens, "who has behaved with a delicate kindness in a recent matter" (3: 279).

32. Lewes had not published a novel in well over a decade, and it is hard to imagine that his name on a work of fiction would have promoted the circulation of their new magazine. On the other hand, perhaps they were desperate. Lewes records their continued solicitation, with the result that they "made me promise that if I should change my mind, and think of writing one, he [Lucas] should have the refusal of it" (GHL Journal for Mar. 1, 1860, qtd. in *Letters* 3: 268).

CHAPTER 4

1. Gordon Haight's account of the chronology of these negotiations is confusing. He correctly cites the dates for Smith's offer through Lewes as January (an initial inquiry, recorded in Lewes's journal on the 23rd) and February 1862. However, he then notes that "*The Adventures of Philip*, which had started in the January number of the *Cornhill*, was clearly not going to be popular, and Trollope's *Framley Parsonage*, which had been, would conclude in April" (*Biography* 355). This combination of circumstances caused Smith to seek a contribution from George Eliot "to buoy up the declining sale." In fact, *Philip* began in January 1861, and *Framley Parsonage* concluded in April 1861. Trollope's next contribution, "The Struggles of Brown, Jones, and Robinson" began in August 1861 and would conclude in March 1862, just a few days after Smith's meeting with Lewes. This fact, added to the unpopularity of Thackeray's novel, which overlapped *Romola* by only two months, July and August 1862, was problematic for Smith. In addition, the windup of *Agnes of Sorrento* in May 1862 meant that Smith was faced not only with the problem of declining sales, but with the need for a continuing novel—a constant problem of the Victorian journal editor.

2. It did not do so, and instead the slippage continued (see Sutherland, "*Cornhill's* Sales"). On May 25, more than a month before serialization began, Blackwood was prescient and not merely finding the grapes sour when he related the story of her "defection" to Langford: "if the story is the one I suppose, I have no doubt it will be a fine thing but it was doubtful in my mind how far it would bear being given in fragments in the Magazine and certainly it would not suit the readers of the Cornhill. I intended to have decided on the form of publication when I had read the M.S." (*Letters* 4: 38).

3. The two longest installments of *Scenes of Clerical Life* were close to the length of the shorter installments of *Romola*. Part 1 of "Amos Barton" is 58

manuscript pages long, as is part 1 of "Janet's Repentance." The shortest installments of *Romola* are 56 and 57 manuscript pages (parts 10 and 11), but the
longest run to 98 and 101 pages. The total number of manuscript pages is 1,065,
which averages 76 manuscript pages for each of the 14 parts.

4. Smith even sent an advertisement to *Blackwood's Magazine,* an action that
outraged Langford, who called the whole matter a "disgusting transaction, which
certainly does not surprise me on her part, but does rather on the part of Mr.
Smith." He wrote John Blackwood that "in the first flirt of temper I thought you
should refuse insertion [of the advertisement], but it will certainly be more dignified to insert it" (*Letters* 4: 38n2). With characteristic—and shrewd—forbear-
ance, John Blackwood declined to enter the fray and continued to be cordial to
Lewes and Eliot. As a welcome result, Eliot returned to the house of Blackwood
for all her future work except "Brother Jacob" (*Cornhill,* July 1864), which she
made a gift to Smith after the unsatisfactory sales of *Romola.* More than ten years
after *Romola,* Blackwood was able to joke with Eliot about the *Cornhill* rivalry.
In a letter dated November 19, 1874, he "long[s] to see that 'Slice of M.S.' which
has passed into the 'irrevocable'"—an early reference to *Daniel Deronda*; he then
adds general news on his return from the country, which includes a reference to
a new fox terrier. "It is a perfect demon of mischief. Its first act was to tear my
own copy of the monthly Magazine and then it tried to apologise to me by utterly demolishing a Cornhill" (6: 91–92). By then, Blackwood's good humor and
fair treatment had obviated the chance that Eliot would defect to another
publisher.

5. To indicate the dual numbering system, Eliot's numbers will be given first,
followed by a slash and then the British Library numbers, which were added later
and form an unbroken sequence.

6. The British Library manuscript numbering begins with a 1 on the page on
which Eliot dedicated her manuscript to Lewes, a page written after the manuscript's completion; the BL numbering of the actual text begins with Arabic
numeral 2.

The dedication reads:

> To the Husband
> *whose perfect Love has been*
> *the best source of her insight & strength,*
> *this manuscript is given by*
> *his devoted wife, the writer.*

7. The 82 includes two pages marked 68[a] and 79[a].

8. Thackeray was aware of the story's unpopularity as early as May 24, 1861,
when he wrote to Mrs. Baxter, "I think Trollope is much more popular with the
Cornhill Magazine readers than I am: and doubt whether I am not going down
hill considerably in public favor" (Thackeray, *Letters* 4: 236; see also 4: 242–

43n45). His opinion did not change; after he concluded the novel, he wrote to his mother that he had written "Finis to Philip: rather a lame ending" (4: 270).

9. Smith actually did undertake a *6d.* part publication years later with Anthony Trollope's *Last Chronicle of Barset*, but, in Trollope's own assessment, "the enterprise was not altogether successful" (*Autobiography* 229). R. H. Super notes that though reviewers "pointed out, with courteous approval, the innovation of weekly parts," the financial success of the plan is uncertain. "Parts issues brought their publishers profit not only through sales to the public, but also through the pages of advertising bound with each number, and in the later numbers of *Last Chronicle* the advertising pages had almost withered away to Smith, Elder's own announcements" (209).

10. The reference to publishing the whole at *6/* is rather puzzling, since a three-volume novel sold for *31s. 6d.* Even at this early stage, the leisurely unfolding of the plot indicates that Eliot had a long novel in mind. And there is no other mention of longer installments (such as the later *5s.* parts for *Middlemarch* and *Daniel Deronda*) for which Smith and Lewes thought to charge *6s.* The numbers are very clear in his journal.

11. The reference to her fourth chapter actually indicates published chapter 5, "The Blind Scholar and his Daughter." It begins on page 59/74 and was originally numbered IV. When Eliot decided to add a new chapter IV titled "First Impressions" midway on page 53/68, she lightly scratched out the "I" in the heading "Chapter IV" to make it "Chapter V." The new chapter IV ends on page 58/73, so she was beginning page 59/74, or her seventy-third page of writing by actual page count.

12. If she saw the review of the volume publication of *Romola* in the *British Quarterly Review* for October 1863, she might have been amused at the unknowing reinforcement of her opinion regarding her name. After scathing comments on *Salem Chapel*'s treatment of Dissenters, the reviewer comes to *Romola*: "It is with very different feelings we turn to a novel that bears the name of George Eliot on the title-page, sure that it will well repay the reading; for high among our writers of fiction—even among the highest, in right of that fine novel—would we place the author of 'Adam Bede'" (453). The rest of the review would not have amused her as much, however. It applauds "many portions of this fine work" but finds that "as a whole it is very unsatisfactory" and, sharing the sentiments of other reviewers, wishes Eliot had set the scene "in our own land" (464–65).

13. George Smith's recollection of the situation is rather different. Since it was written many years later, it is probably less accurate than the details recorded in Eliot and Lewes's journals and letters. Smith conflates into a two-day period what actually occurred over several months.

> The largest payment made for a novel was 7,000*l.*, to Mrs. Lewes (George Eliot) for 'Romola.' The largest payment made for short articles was 12*l.* 12*s.* a page, to Mr. Thackeray, for his 'Roundabout Papers.' In regard to the payment to Mrs. Lewes, an

incident seems to deserve honourable record as a signal proof of the author's artistic sensibility. Mrs. Lewes read part of 'Romola' to me, and anyone who has heard that lady read and remembers her musical and sympathetic voice will understand that the MS. lost nothing in effect by her reading. On the following day I offered her 10,000*l.* for the book for the CORNHILL MAGAZINE, and for a limited right to subsequent publication. It was stipulated that the book should form sixteen numbers of twenty-four pages each. Before the appearance of the first part Mrs. Lewes said that she found that she could not properly divide the book into as many as sixteen parts. I took exception to this alteration of our arrangement, and pointed out that my offer was based on the book being in sixteen parts, and that my calculations were made with regard to the MAGAZINE being able to afford a payment of so much a number. She said that she quite understood that the alteration would make a difference to me, but that she supposed the amount of the difference could easily be calculated. George Lewes and I did all we possibly could to persuade her to reconsider her decision, but in vain. We pointed out to her that the publication in the MAGAZINE was ephemeral, and that the work would be published in a separate form afterwards and be judged as a whole. However, nothing could move her, and she preferred receiving 7,000*l.* in place of 10,000*l.* for the book. (*Cornhill*, June 1901; 10)

Some details in Smith's recollection do accord with the actual transaction. His monetary figures are correct, and 384 pages (16 x 24) was the length stipulated in the contract signed May 21, but in "twelve monthly portions" (*Letters* 8: 301).

14. How she arrived at this number is unclear. Before she added her new scene and altered the numbers of the final pages of the part, she had given 88 as her last page—but she had in fact written ninety sheets, two more resulting from pagination 57ª and 69ª. Since the original page 88 has only ten lines of writing, there would not have been four more sheets simply left off without page 88 showing evidence of them; unless, of course, the page was later recopied. More likely, there was additional material before the very marked concluding tone of page 88.

15. The rewriting of the first chapter in installment 5 included rearrangements and additions to the beginning of the chapter. The page numbering gives the first clue to this, two sets of numbers appearing through this chapter, 21 as published, and chapters 22 to 24. She obviously rewrote and expanded the original first page, perhaps using material from original pages 5 to 7. The page numbering of chapter 21 is arranged thus:

GE Original Numbering	GE Renumbering	British Lib Numbering
	1	1
	2	2
	3	3
	4	4
	5	5

	6	6
	7	7
2 (overwritten by:)	7ª	8
3 (overwritten by:)	8	9
4 (overwritten by:)	9	10
? & 8 (?)	10	11
9 (crossed out)	11	12
	12	13 (a page added later; originally 9/11/12 fed directly into 10?&12/13/14)
10 (?) & 12	13	14
11 corrected to 14	14	15
12	15	16

The original pages 1, 5, 6, and 7 were reworked but with a few traces left in the manuscript and published text. For example, at the top of original page 3 (later 8/9) is the sentence "Yet at that time, as we have seen, there was a man in Florence who for two years and more had been preaching that a scourge was at hand." This and what follows would make more sense if the material on manuscript pages 5 and 6 had not just appeared. As it stands, "as we have seen" seems an unnecessary reminder. The novel also has a curious verbal repetition and a contradiction on page 6: "And as long as four years ago he had proclaimed from the chief pulpit of Florence that a scourge was about to descend on Italy and that by this scourge the Church was about to be purified." The phrasing is repetitive of what was on original page 3 and is now on 8/9, while the years are given differently, at two and four.

Since it is the chapter opening that has been rewritten, it is possible that Lewes suggested she begin with Romola and Tito to connect readers with the place at which the preceding part left off. The part's opening with the date and the mention of the eighteen months that have passed were clearly not part of the original plan; a cancelled passage at the top of the new page 13 (Orig. GE10?&12/ BL14) reads "And now, on the seventeenth of November, 1494." Written above "And" is "But," which she also cancelled. The "But" was probably added before she cancelled the date, to avoid the repetition of "And," which also began the top of the new page 12. Needing a stronger transition after the date was cancelled, she added in the margin "Fra Girolamo's word was powerful yet now that" to lead into "the new Cyrus had already," the "new Cyrus" being a term already mentioned on page 4 of the revised manuscript.

16. She did not always feel overburdened that fall. A letter two days later to

M. d'Albert-Durade describes her feeling of serenity. She is "enjoying existence more than I ever did before" (4: 68).

17. It is not certain whether she had already decided to hold chapter 46 for part 10 when she read part 9 aloud. There is no question, however, that chapter 46 was originally intended to be included in installment 9. The manuscript shows that the chapter begins partway down a page with no marking or direction for the installment break. For the first time, all the chapters in the part are headed by Arabic rather than Roman numerals. Chapter 46 is also headed by Arabic numerals, but Roman numbering is briefly resumed with chapter 47. Evidently, chapter 47 originally began the new part, and chapter 46 was later moved to become the opening chapter in part 10—perhaps after she read the part to Lewes. Worry over his suggestions may have led to the headache she mentions.

18. George Eliot's well-known dislike for London may have stemmed from her longing for the open country spaces of her Warwickshire youth, but she was undoubtedly correct when she also attributed her illnesses to London's unhealthy air. In *Endangered Lives, Public Health in Victorian Britain*, Anthony S. Wohl details the state of the air that polluted even the London parks, which were supposed to act as "'respirators' to help purify the lungs" (210). One of Eliot's favorite walking places, Regent's Park, was not immune: "The gardeners in Regent's Park claimed they could tell at a glance how many days the sheep had been pastured there by the blackness of their wool" (Wohl 210).

19. One mark of her dissatisfaction with this part is the fact that every chapter seems to have been partly rewritten after the next chapter was under way; each chapter begins with a superscript number "a" added to a repeated page number. The alterations add one page to each chapter.

20. *Agnes of Sorrento* had begun in *Cornhill* in May 1861 and ended in May 1862, just two months before *Romola* began.

21. This quotation, slightly altered, comes from chapter 46 (407).

22. This remark must refer to Thackeray's *Adventures of Philip*, which the reviewer had just mentioned, rather than to *Silas Marner*, Eliot's most recent "tale."

23. Sir Cresswell Cresswell, appointed the first "judge in ordinary" in January 1858 when "the probate and divorce court was created," was especially in the public mind at this time. He suffered serious injuries from a runaway carriage on July 11 and died July 29, 1863 (*DNB* 5: 72–73).

24. In August 1862, the *Critic* changed from a semimonthly to a monthly publication and reduced its review section. Consequently, there is no continuing sequence of *Romola* reviews. After August 1862, the novel was mentioned only twice, in July and August 1863.

25. Eliot made use of the historical parallel differently in the prelude to *Middlemarch*, juxtaposing the opportunities for the nineteenth-century woman of aspiration unfavorably against those of an earlier woman leader, Saint Theresa of

Avila, who sought to reform the Church. In contrast, Romola's training has been in the pagan authors. At the time of her flight, she repudiates all monkish wisdom and learning as superstition.

26. No other study in Eliot's fiction has the same psychological and moral complexity, not even that of Gwendolen Harleth, who comes closest. But as a serially published novel, Gwendolen's story works better not only because the installments are longer but because it includes—and even centers on—love. Gwendolen's several suitors were the focal point of reviews of books 1 and 2. Book 1 left readers waiting a month to meet Henleigh Mallinger Grandcourt, the man Gwendolen herself has come closest to imagining as a potential husband. After their marriage, one possible suitor—Deronda—remains prominent, and another—Rex Gascoigne—hovers unmarried in the background. As will be illustrated in chapters 6 and 7, readers had a familiar context for definite, exciting expectations from each installment.

27. Like Rosamond concealing her actions and making her husband reluctant to ask questions, Tito makes Romola "afraid of any hasty movement, as men are who hold something precious and want to believe that it is not broken" (262). Rosamond defies her husband by countermanding his order to give up their Lowick Gate house; Tito secretly sells Bardo's library. When their transgressions are revealed, both malefactors are defiant and intractable. The major difference is that Tito is the more interesting and sympathetic character because of the Nemesis that he fears and because he has some shame and sense of wrongdoing, however much he tries to conceal it from himself. Rosamond, on the other hand, remains convinced of her correctness to the very end and never comprehends Lydgate's bitter joke about the pot of basil.

28. Felicia Bonaparte (*Triptych*) and Mary Wilson Carpenter both discuss the stoic dimension in Romola's character. Bonaparte's argument for Romola as epic hero explains how and why this heroine defies the conventional novelistic role of loved and loving and takes on a broader poetic, symbolic function.

29. Wolfgang Iser notes that the pauses that readers create for themselves are likely to be at very different places than the ones imposed by the serial format. This point will be discussed more extensively in connection with readers' responses to *Middlemarch* and *Daniel Deronda* in chapter 7.

30. Later Romola's disillusionment grows as she sees Tito's "hopelessly shallow readiness which professed to appropriate the widest sympathies and had no pulse for the nearest" (289).

31. This is not to suggest that Eliot endorses so simplistic a view. The polarizations of classical and Christian early in the novel are resolved in complex ways later on, as Felicia Bonaparte shows (*Triptych*). But one of the effects of serialization is to emphasize elements within a particular installment, because readers have only that partial text on which to meditate and from which to form expectations during the month before the next part appears.

32. Nello's comment on the contadina Tessa as one of Tito's potential "stolen chickens" (92) is a cynical version of the animal imagery associated with Hetty in *Adam Bede*.

33. Linda Hughes and Michael Lund connect *Romola*'s serialization with Victorian concepts of historical development. Their view of the fourteen parts as "discrete units of plot, each advancing the story through a significant phase" (81) emphasizes the wholeness of the parts, but does not acknowledge Eliot's skill in working with the serial format's requirement for dramatic, open endings. The conclusion to part 2 is only one of several in which this skill is manifest.

It is principally at the volume breaks, which occur after installments 4 and 8, that the sense of closure and discreteness is stronger than the dramatic forward movement and openness of one part to the next. Hughes and Lund note these as "two major instances of time's passing between numbers" (81).

34. Recognition of the ring brings Baldassarre to Florence, and the false marriage leads Baldassarre to believe that Romola will feel this injury to her pride and seek vengeance. Subsequently, Baldassarre informs Romola not only of the other wife, but of his own grievances.

35. Romola realizes the full extent of Tito's deceitfulness only after his attempted betrayal of Savonarola, when she acknowledges that "Every one who trusted Tito was in danger" (412). Soon after she observes that their alienation began "the night you first wore that chain armour" (418).

36. At the end of part 5, as noted earlier in this chapter, Tito *folds* the armor under his mantle; the beginning of part 6 uses the phrase, "with the new-bought armour under his mantle." When he arrives home, Romola lays "her arm on his chest," feels the armor, and asks, "'What have you got on under your tunic, Tito?'" (254). The discrepancy is explained by the fact that Tito does not return home immediately, presumably going to Tessa's, where he must have donned the armor that he only carried away from Niccolo's shop. Serial readers cannot, however, easily have guessed this, since information about his household arrangements with Tessa is not given until the next part, installment 7.

37. This state of marital disillusionment was Eliot's focus in "Janet's Repentance" and is the center of her last two novels. Other concerns dominate the three novels between *Scenes* and *Romola*. Marital discord is the chief outward conflict here; it is especially notable in the later installments, for which reader interest became stronger. Serial parts thrive on conflict, and the marital discord universalizes the Romola–Tito relationship, making it seem less "foreign" to readers who wanted a native English novel.

38. Readers find out later that Tito's death results directly from this encounter. Ser Ceccone assists the slow-witted Dolfo Spini in discovering Tito's treachery, thus precipitating his leap into the river—and into the death grip of Baldassarre.

39. Since *Romola* appears first in each number of *Cornhill*, nearly half a page is regularly taken up with the magazine's title and date of issue, as well as the

story's title and capital letter illustration. With chapter 47 in part 9, half of the first page would still be needed for this material, so part 10 would actually have run to twenty-one and a half pages.

40. "Counter Check," chapter 48, ends with Romola asking Tito about the old man in Piero's picture whom she has just seen again; Tito, though he has threatened and alarmed Romola about Bernardo del Nero, is alarmed enough "to put on his coat of chain armour" (420).

41. Manuscript page 20 ends with the word "Virgin" in Piero's statement that "the most holy Virgin herself has always been dressed well," and page 21 repeats the word "Virgin." This suggests that the last two pages may have been recopied—perhaps to accommodate a different transition after Eliot postponed her Camilla chapter.

42. The sudden, startling appearance of a new or missing—perhaps dangerous—character is a technique found in the best serial endings of contemporary sensation novelists.

CHAPTER 5

1. In his essay on *Les Misérables*, Lewes criticizes Hugo for the 165-page description of a "bishop-saint" with which he opens his narrative—never to mention him again. It is tempting to wonder if his own criticism recurred to him when early reviews objected to the prelude (focusing on a foundress-saint) on the grounds that it seemed to have no relevance.

2. Likewise, *Daniel Deronda* was uneven in length, with book 7 the shortest at 160 pages and book 8 the longest at 203 pages.

3. Beaty's study has been amplified in regard to books 1 and 2 by Stanton Millet. Millet's article traces especially the changes between books 1 and 2, which are treated from another perspective in what follows in this chapter.

4. One might also cite two other likely sources of opinion: reactions at two dinners Lewes attended (the first with Eliot) on December 6 and 7, and an eighth essay, "The Idealism of George Eliot and Mr. Tennyson," which appeared in the *Spectator* on December 2. Entries about the dinners were followed in his journal by a comment on December 8, "Good news of the success of 'Middlemarch.'" Though he does not record any conversation about *Middlemarch* (or anything else in particular), it is likely that he heard this "good news" at one or both dinners, and that it reinforced the opinions behind his decision to rearrange books 2 and 3.

Langford wrote to Blackwood that, in the *Spectator*'s article, "Middlemarch is alluded to in the highest terms" (*Letters* 5: 224). However, these terms are reserved for Dorothea, who is the only character mentioned, apart from a brief allusion to Celia as "the sister of little feeling." The essay, which expects even at this early stage that the novel will be "a great one," singles out Dorothea's idealism and concludes that the "new story is intended to paint the misery of the moral chaos into which the highest ideal yearnings naturally lead and plunge her heroine" and "that the heroine is to be the victim of her own idealism, and to founder on the rocks of uncongenial circumstance" (1459). The *Spectator* objected to this conclusion and published a response from A. Creed the following week (December 9). We know that Lewes was aware of the original article, because he mentions Creed's rejoinder in his letter to Barbara Bodichon, "Wasn't Creed's letter striking?" (5: 225). The *Spectator*'s first regular notice of the parts of *Middlemarch* did not appear until December 16.

5. Only one of these reviews is reprinted in Holmstrom and Lerner, and none appears in Carroll's *George Eliot, The Critical Heritage*; four are not found in any index. The only serial reviews reprinted in Carroll are six of the seven published in the *Spectator*; Holmstrom and Lerner include the *Daily News* notice. The most complete bibliographies, Fulmer's and Geibel's, do not refer to the *Echo, Illustrated London News, Manchester Examiner and Times*, or *Standard* reviews.

6. Lewes's attention to public opinion and its impact on sales, as reflected in critical notices, is evident in many letters. For instance, he had evidently scrutinized the reviews of part 2 before he wrote to Blackwood on February 13: "I am disappointed at the Times and some other papers holding back—evidently intending to notice the book when complete—but *then* their advertisement (which is *all* they can give) will be of little use" (*Letters* 5: 247). The cumulative evidence in letters and journals supports Eliot's statement in 1876 that while Lewes "protects me from reading about myself . . . [he] reads everything about me that comes in his way." And as always, the protection had limits, as she adds regarding a recent article: "He read aloud to me two sentences from it" (*Letters* 6: 230). He kept careful watch on newspaper comments, and she heard more and was more interested than some letters would make it seem. For instance, after *The Mill on the Floss* was published she wrote, "From all we can gather the votes are rather on the side of 'The Mill,' as a better book than 'Adam'" (GE Journal, July 1, 1860).

7. Beaty, citing the letter of December 7 and Blackwood's agreement on December 31 to include the Dorothea parts in Book 2, comments: "Had this change not been made, readers of the parts would have heard nothing of Dorothea for four months. . . . This would have been an impossible burden on the memory and patience of the reader. The idea of independent parts had to give way to the practical consideration of the reader of parts which were published only every other month." He does not speculate on the immediate impetus behind Lewes's letter of December 7, nor does he emphasize, except obliquely in his reference to the "impossible burden," the commercial reasons behind the decision (54).

David Carroll attributes the inclusion of the Dorothea material in book 2 to Eliot's growing awareness of "the need to keep the reader in touch with the different strands of the novel over the two-monthly intervals" ("Introduction," *Middlemarch* xli). Citing Beaty, he adds, "One can see the desire for the completeness of the parts giving way to the balancing of elements within each part and the needs of the plot development" (xlii), but he does not mention the influence of reviewers.

8. The reviewer offers a long quotation beginning with Mrs. Vincy's "Knock at Mr. Fred's door again, Pritchard" and continuing through Fred's "eating his toast with the utmost composure" despite Rosamond's aspersions on "grilled bone," but the quotation does not explain the reviewer's preference for Rosamond.

9. The alterations to book 2 which Stanton Millet describes must have taken place before Eliot decided to move chapters 11 and 12 to book 1. Page 6 of her *Quarry II for Middlemarch* shows these chapters as the first two in book 2. The chapter that Millet suggests was originally chapter III in book 2 but became chapter V, and then XV, is in the *Quarry* already given as "XV Lydgate's history and present ambition 160–173" (Kitchel 46–47).

Chapters 11 and 12 also appear on page 5 of the *Quarry* in the list of chapters in book 1 (Kitchel 46). However, their descriptions are briefer (as if repeated); and unlike the other chapters in the list for book 1, they bear no page numbers. Obviously, Eliot added them later to the book 1 list; if she had done so before she made the list for book 2, they would not have appeared as they do in that list as well, with page numbers and fuller descriptions.

10. The "General" is General William George Hamley (*Letters* 5: 207n4).

11. Lewes's diaries record their reading it on these dates: September 30 and December 1, 1871; and January 4, February 2, March 1, July 9, August 31, and November 2, 1872. Undoubtedly, other dates were omitted not because they failed to read the story, but because he didn't happen to record the reading.

12. Eliot and Lewes had a personal interest in the trial because of their friendship with Charles S. C. Bowen, the "junior in the Tichborne case on whom Coleridge mainly relies"—as Eliot described him to Blackwood January 5, mentioning an evening with friends, of whom Bowen was one (*Letters* 5: 234). On January 29, in a letter to Sara Hennell, she calls Coleridge's "addressing the jury . . . a very interesting occasion to me" and hopes to go again "to hear a cross-examination of Ballantyne's" (*Letters* 5: 243).

13. Her letters throughout this period are full of allusions to her ill health. One shows her especially conscious of her mortality. On January 29, 1872, she wrote to François D'Albert-Durade, describing her new book and her state of health as well as her marital happiness, adding "But if I live to see you again, you will be rather startled at the effect of the years upon me" (5: 242). This same letter explains the publication plans for her new book and her concern that her "want of health has retarded me in my work—which would be a matter of no consequence if I had not begun to print." But, she adds, "I am advanced enough to make all things easy if I can keep well now" (5: 241).

14. See *Letters* 5: 462, where Blackwood calls him "that beastly Claimant," and 6: 21–22 and 40. Actually, the Tichborne Claimant was in the public eye until his death. Throughout his imprisonment, his supporters traveled the country decrying what they considered a miscarriage of justice. Sara Hennell wrote to Eliot on April 23, 1874 about a lecture given at Coventry by the Claimant's counsel George Dawson, who was so broken down that it was "quite piteous to see him" (*Letters* 6: 40n6).

15. Press coverage was curtailed later, during the criminal trial in 1873–74, but before then the Tichborne Claimant's story was ubiquitous in newspapers throughout Britain.

16. Even if they had already formed their opinions about the Claimant, Eliot and Lewes followed his criminal trial in 1874 with continuing interest and attended at least three sessions of it:

> Went to the *Tichborne Trial* Bowen having got seats for us; stayed till 1/4 past 3 listening to *Hawkins*—much of it very good and much wearisome in its details and superfluity of proof. (GHL Diary, Jan. 27, 1874)

> Went again to the Tichborne Trial to hear the Lord Chief Justice (Cockburn) open his summing up. Very masterly in exposition, and grave eloquent and dignified in rebuke of Kenealy's conduct of the case. (Jan. 29)

> At breakfast there arrived an order from the Lord Chief Justice to hear the final summing up and verdict in the *Tichborne Trial*. We had to hurry to the court and were fortunate in getting one seat for Polly and standing room for me. The scene very impressive and interesting. The Lord Chief spoke with emotion and dignity. Mellor and Lush also addressed the Jury. The verdict was delivered amid great excitement. (Feb. 28)

17. As George Schlesinger points out, Casaubon is (at most) cuckolded intellectually, not physically (53). Schlesinger reduces to a phrase, "despite some moments of tenderness between them" (56), the positive image of Casaubon, with which chapter 42 concludes. It is not within the purview of his essay to notice the emphatic placement of this chapter at the end of the installment or to reflect on its effect on serial readers.

18. The repetition in Eliot's serial endings to the four installments of *Adam Bede* projected for serialization, three of them focusing on Arthur's feeble attempts to resist temptation, would not have been problematic had that novel actually appeared in parts. *Adam Bede*'s plot is single-minded; Arthur's temptation, Hetty's seduction, and the consequences to Adam and to others are *the* action of the novel.

19. Rosamond is the malefactor, but she is not destroyed. Instead, she is the social phoenix who arises from the ashes of her husband's scientific career. Toller's sarcastic phrase for Lydgate—Farebrother's "scientific phoenix"—is more ironic than he knows.

20. Lewes's suggestion is not recorded in their journals or in published letters.

CHAPTER 6

1. The publishing world had not heard of the Jewish direction for the story, but Blackwood and Lewes needed the gossiping paragraph to squelch an "absurd rumour" that the book was about "American life" (*Letters* 6: 189). This was not the only absurd rumor. On December 15, Eliot wrote Blackwood: "Apparently there are wild reports about the subject-matter of Deronda—among the rest, that it represents French life! But that is hardly more ridiculous than the supposition that after refusing to go to America I should undertake to describe society there" (*Letters* 6: 199).

2. See my article in *Victorian Periodicals Review* (1988) for a detailed assessment of the attitudes to the Jewish plot in *Daniel Deronda*.

3. The proposal to start in February had originated with Lewes and was merely affirmed by Blackwood: "I think Lewes is right about February being the best month to begin publication. The active world of London is then drawing together and although I do not think it greatly matters when such a Ship as yours is launched it is well to have the buzz of talk open at headquarters at once." Judiciously, he adds, however: "The main thing of course is not to hurry or harass you. It would be better to begin publication in the dog days than do that in any degree" (*Letters* 6: 178). His letter was a response to Eliot's on October 10 in which she explained that Lewes's arrangements with the American publishers for simultaneous appearance in *Harper's* had determined the dates: "Mr. Lewes thinks it will not be well to publish the first part till February. December he says will be too soon for the necessary arrangements with America, and January he maintains is a bad month for publishing anything, whereas February is altogether eligible" (6: 172).

4. This is probably illusory, as far as Lewes's role is concerned. Both Eliot's and Lewes's journals record continual reading of all her works in progress, and he commented and advised frequently on the serial structure as he did on other issues.

5. The manuscript evidence for the changes here is complicated. The chapter number for the published chapter 11 is given as "XI" in the manuscript, but the next chapter is also "XI," and the rest of book 2 continues as if chapter 11 had originally been chapter 10. That is, published chapters 12 through 18 are numbered in the manuscript XI through XVII (except for XIV, the first page of which was condensed and recopied as GE 204 and 205). One hypothesis to explain this is that Eliot made the correction to published chapter 11 very late in the writing process. When she wrote the first volume of *Deronda*, she did not intend even to make a chapter division at the start of chapter 11 (as published). Hence, she went on from 10, the final chapter in book 1, to the 11 in the manuscript and so on to manuscript chapter 17. When she decided to break the part at the point of Grandcourt's introduction, she not only had to make a better transition, she had

to create a new chapter break. She had room at the top of the page to write, centered, "Chapter XI," but she had no room for the motto and had to write in the upper left-hand corner of the leaf, "For motto, See Back." The corrections to the first sentence are made in the space above the first ruled line.

6. On the other hand, she felt that *Middlemarch* from the start had had "too many 'momenti'" (GE Journal, qtd. in *Letters* 5: 137).

7. Graham Handley in the "Introduction" to the Clarendon edition notes:

> In the proofs Book II closes with Chapter XIX, which was originally the last five pages of Chapter XVIII, the page numbers being 367–72. The motto for this Chapter XIX is written at the foot of 372. Pages 368–72 are also numbered 4–8 in pencil; these are the page numbers in the final printed version, belonging to Chapter XIX, the opening of Book III which Lewes had advised and then ordered. (xxii)

8. Moving these last pages to book 3 necessitated starting a new chapter, number 19 as published, since the final five proof pages to which Lewes referred were not a separate chapter in the manuscript. As already noted, Eliot had also created an additional chapter when she broke chapter 10 just before Grandcourt's introduction. Consequently, the chapter numbers in the manuscript of book 2 are each lower by one number than the chapters in the serial and subsequent published versions. What the manuscript calls "Chapter XVII" is actually published chapters 18 and 19. The final manuscript chapter in volume I is given as "XVIII" but is actually published chapter 20, the second chapter of book 3.

9. Lewes's November 18 letter sounds like the final word on the question, but apparently he and Eliot reconsidered once more. On November 22, he wrote to Blackwood: "The question of division into parts has greatly 'exercised' us latterly but finally we have come to a decision and abide by that already existing in the proofs. Accordingly I telegraphed this morning to cancel Mrs. Lewes's letter of yesterday." Unfortunately, this letter, as Haight's note says, "has not been found" and so we cannot know what further possibilities Eliot and Lewes explored to close books 1 and 2 (6: 192 and 192n7).

10. In fact, the parts of *Deronda* did at least once come to the hands of readers a few days before the first of the month. The *Manchester Examiner and Times*'s notice of book 4 on April 27, 1876, begins, "we have not had to wait until Mayday for the fourth book of 'Daniel Deronda,' and 'Gwendolen Gets Her Choice' has already been in the hands of thousands of happy readers" (7).

11. Several letters passed hurriedly between Lewes and Blackwood before the matter was settled and the February date finally reconfirmed (see *Letters* 6: 211–13).

12. The *Courant* was not quite accurate in this audience analysis, but it could hardly have anticipated the direction Eliot's novel would take, especially after the fourth or fifth book. Even as early as book 3, however, this reviewer is in the minority in preferring Deronda's story: "It is to the hero and his surroundings that the chief interest attaches, and accordingly the first two chapters, which tell the story of the young Jewess, have most of romance in them" (Mar. 30; 4). By

book 7, although the "whole part is one of high-wrought [*sic*] interest . . . the artistic power of the scenes between Deronda and his mother seem [*sic*] to us greatly superior to that of the scene with Gwendolen." In the former, "there is not a phrase which does not contribute to the dramatic power and vividness of the conception." But the "highly-sensational incident" of Grandcourt's drowning is less satisfactory. "The fact is that 'sensation' is not [George Eliot's] *forte*, and her *forte* is so strong that we cannot help wishing she would content herself with it" (Aug. 7; 4). The accusation of sensationalism appears in reviews throughout *Daniel Deronda*'s publication.

13. Chapter 21 ends on manuscript page 14. Published chapter 23, which was originally numbered in Eliot's hand 15 to 37, would have been next. Published chapter 22, to follow, was originally numbered in Eliot's hand 38 to 55. The numbers are lined through and replaced in her hand thus: chapter 23 becomes published chapter 22, on manuscript pages renumbered 15 to 33, and chapter 22 becomes published chapter 23, manuscript pages numbered 34 to 56. As Graham Handley points out, the result is a "gain in dramatic impact, in artistic and structural coherence" ("Manuscript" 64).

14. Unfortunately, her letters and journals provide no hint as to which of these is more likely.

15. The chapter numbering shows certain alterations at this point, but these are more likely the result of Lewes's decisions about how to divide books 2 and 3 than the result of internal changes in book 5, which was nearing completion in the middle of November, the same time that Lewes wrote to Blackwood (November 18) about the arrangement of books 2 and 3. On November 15, Eliot had read her "Mordecai" chapter to him, and they walked to Blackfriars Bridge on November 18.

The pagination and chapter numbering for book 5 run thus:

Chapter number	GE Pagination	BL Pagination
XXXV (orig. XXXIV)	1–43 (incl. 22ᵃ)	2–45
XXXVI	43ᵃ–78 (incl. 76ᵃ)	46–82
XXXVII	79–101	83–105
XXXVIII	102–116	106–120
XXXIX (orig. XXXVII)	117–130	121–134
XL (orig. XXXVIII)	131–153 (orig. 117–137)	135–157

Published chapters 36 to 38 show no altered original numbers, but that may be because the first pages of 37 and 38 seem to have been recopied, and 36 may have been as well. In any case, to add one number to these requires only a single extra pen stroke, not so easily detected as alterations to numbers like XXXIV and XXXVIII.

What probably happened was that Eliot wrote published chapter 40 as chapter XXXVIII in the old numbering. When she added published chapter 39, she simply gave it the chapter number to precede this, without changing the earlier numbers to account for the extra one. Her altered pagination would have been enough to guide her through her manuscript. She probably also began published chapter 41 in book 6 with this old numbering, since it bears an original XXXIX, later altered to XLI. That chapter, though, seems to have been destined for book 6 from the start, since its pagination begins with 1. At some point after she renumbered the chapters in book 2, she altered the numbers in books 5 and 6.

The fact of the changes doesn't help date precisely the writing of published chapter 39, since she could have written it after the Blackfriars Bridge visit—*if* she did not renumber her chapters precisely when Lewes (November 18) sent his directions to Blackwood to make old chapter 17 into two published chapters 18 and 19. If she was in the throes of writing and revising chapter 40, she might not have bothered with this minor editorial correction until the writing of the book was completed, or even beyond that.

16. Book 6 shows no sign of internal reordering of chapters that occurred with some of the other books, although the manuscript numbering for the first chapter is not the same as in the published text. In the manuscript the first chapter is given as XXXIX, published as chapter 41, an alteration that may be attributable to the renumbering of chapters following Lewes's direction to break chapter 17 into 18 and 19. Subsequent numbers match the published text except for chapter 46, which is given as XLV. This latter may be simple absence of mind, such as occurred occasionally in Eliot's page numbering. The chapter shows no sign of change beyond some minor revisions.

17. Amy, with a little more delicacy than Hans, shares his sentiment that Mirah might have forgotten her religion if her relatives were not found. Much earlier she had suggested that "'Perhaps it [Mirah's religion] would gradually melt away from her, and she would pass into Christianity like the rest of the world, if she got to love us very much, and never found her mother'" (234). And even Mrs. Meyrick says to Mirah (although she repents afterward), "'if Jews and Jewesses went on changing their religion, and making no difference between themselves and Christians, there would come a time when there would be no Jews to be seen'" (347).

18. Reviewing book 7, the Liverpool *Weekly Albion* calls this "one of those coincidences which all novel readers make allowances for" (July 29; 7), but none of the reviewers predicts a chance encounter between Deronda and the Grandcourts in the Mediterranean.

19. Chapter 51 ends on page 36 of Eliot's manuscript. The pagination for the original sequence was then:

Published chapter 54 [52 in MS.]: originally paginated 37 to 58, later altered by GE to 88 to 109.

Published chapter 53 [53 in MS.]: originally paginated 59 to 72, later altered by GE to 74 to 87.

Published chapter 55 [54 in MS.]: originally paginated 73 to 78, later altered by GE to 110 to 115.

Published chapter 56 [55 in MS.]: originally paginated [79], 80 to 100, repaginated 116 to 138.

20. An extra chapter [given as 56 in the manuscript but published as 57] is inserted mid-page on 95/132. A hasty glance might suggest that this insertion accounts for the misnumbering that follows in the first four chapters of book 8, but that cannot be. The number 56 is given in the manuscript; if published chapter 52 had been written by this point, this number would be 57. Instead, the opening chapter of book 8 was originally numbered 57; an 8 has been written over a clearly visible 7. The original chapter number 58 is lined through and a 59 written next to it, the original 59 is lined through and replaced by a 60, and the original 60 is scratched out and a 61 written above. The introduction of published chapter 52 must have occurred at this point, since the final chapters—published as 62 to 70—bear their published numbers with no sign of alteration. This new chapter 52 was paginated after its completion as 37 to 73 to fit in after chapter 51's concluding page, 36.

21. Appendix 3 counts the actual text pages. When Haight (*Letters* 6: 240n1) gives 162 pages for book 7, he is including the two pages before the text actually begins.

CHAPTER 7

1. In *The Victorian Serial*, Linda Hughes and Michael Lund explore the temporal dimension of serial reading, particularly in the context of the historical novel or poem. See chapter 3, "Living in History," 59–108.

2. This, of course, is not actually the fact. As Eliot's and Lewes's letters make clear, and as I have discussed in chapter 5, although the design was planned in advance, the book was written as the installments were appearing.

3. Iser asserts that the latter element is essential to the aesthetic experience (134), though, he argues, "[w]hile we are caught up in a text, we do not at first know what is happening to us. This is why we often feel the need to talk about books we have read—not in order to gain some distance from them so much as to find out just what it is that we were entangled in" (*Act* 131).

4. Both reader-response and reception-aesthetic theorists examine readers' responses in the context of works previously encountered. For example, in the opening chapter in Jauss's *Toward an Aesthetic of Reception*, the literary reader's "horizon of expectations" is a dominant feature in his theses regarding a renewal of literary history. Jauss stresses the idea that a literary work does not "present

itself as something absolutely new in an information vacuum," but appears in the context of all that a reader has previously encountered. The literary work, then,

> predisposes its audience to a very specific kind of reception by announcements, overt and covert signals, familiar characteristics, or implicit allusions. It awakens memories of that which was already read, brings the reader to a specific emotional attitude, and with its beginning arouses expectations for the "middle and end," which can then be maintained intact or altered, reoriented, and even fulfilled ironically in the course of the reading according to specific rules of the genre or type of text. (23; see also Iser, *Implied Reader* 288)

In encountering a text in the temporal dimension that both Iser and Jauss stress as part of the reading process, the reader constantly forms, breaks, and re-forms expectations. The text itself offers signals that shape this process, but the reader also comes predisposed to certain expectations.

5. This is from "New Books," a review of *To the Bitter End*, by M. E. Braddon (J. Maxwell and Co.). Following a half-column on Braddon's book and several others is a brief notice of *Middlemarch*, through book 6.

6. Wilkie Collins put it more concretely in his famous comment, "Make 'em cry, make 'em laugh, make 'em wait." George Meredith claims to have "resisted every temptation to produce great and startling effects" (Vann, *Victorian Novels* 14, 3).

7. Iser makes the point that nineteenth-century readers "often found a novel read in installments to be better than the very same novel in book form" (*Act* 191).

8. Iser sees a literal coauthorship as part of the appeal of the serial: the basic function of the cutting technique used in the serial story is "the interruption and consequent prolongation of tension. . . . The result is that we try to imagine how the story will unfold, and in this way we heighten our own participation in the course of events. Dickens was a master of the technique; his readers became his 'co-authors'" (*Act* 191). The potential hazards of this coauthorship are obvious. As Iser points out, the serial novel needs a wide audience for commercial success and therefore "dare not make too many inroads into the repertoire of norms and values prevalent in that public" (191). At the same time, both Iser and Jauss link the aesthetic value of a work with its making of inroads into the norms and values—the expectations—of readers:

> The way in which a literary work, at the historical moment of its appearance, satisfies, surpasses, disappoints, or refutes the expectations of its first audience obviously provides a criterion for the determination of its aesthetic value. The distance between the horizon of expectations and the work, between the familiarity of previous aesthetic experience and the "horizonal change" demanded by the reception of the new work, determines the artistic character of a literary work, according to an aesthetics of reception: to the degree that this distance decreases, and no turn toward the horizon of yet-unknown experience is demanded of the receiving con-

sciousness, the closer the work comes to the sphere of "culinary" or entertainment art. (Jauss 25)

Iser, too, posits that "expectations are scarcely ever fulfilled in truly literary texts" (*Implied Reader* 73).

9. Abby Sage Richardson in *Victoria* magazine described the popular view of Eliot's imperviousness to readers' pressure:

No desire to spare the feelings of her reader ever induces her to abate one jot or tittle of her purpose. Other novelists have grown to sympathize so much with the characters they had created that they devised for them happier destinies than they first intended. It is said that Charlotte Brontë was swayed from the tragic ending of one of her novels by the letters from readers, which besought her to bring the heroine to a happy close [it's unclear how this occurred, since Brontë's novels were not serialized]; and that even Thackeray sometimes averted the sword of fate from over the heads of his favorites. But this author is as inexorable as life itself. No weak pity for the suffering she depicts swerves her pen, and she does not shrink from putting before us the saddest of problems as persistently as life itself presents them. (228–29)

10. The charge of moral ambivalence (at best) in sensation fiction was one made by numerous reviewers in the 1860s. For instance, one critic noted that "Crime is inseparable from the sensation novel, and so is sympathy with crime, however carefully the author professes, and may even suppose himself, to guard against this danger by periodical disclaimers and protests" ("Our Female Sensation Novelists," qtd. from the *Christian Remembrancer* in *Littell's Living Age*, Aug. 22, 1863; 353).

CONCLUSION

1. He did acknowledge in a letter to Lewes dated October 19, 1876, that "From the outward aspect of opinion I do not think we can calculate upon such a sale of Deronda at 7/6 as for Middlemarch" (*Letters* 6: 298).

APPENDIX 2

1. GE stands for George Eliot's pagination in the manuscript, and BL for the British [Museum] Library pagination. Eliot's pagination cannot be used to calculate the number of pages without taking into account the way she revised. She often made emendations by using the same page number plus a superscript "a" or "b." Very occasionally, she confuses numbers as well. Much more reliable for counting is the BL pagination, which was added when the manuscripts were received there. The BL numbers include whatever prefatory material, such as dedications to G.H. Lewes, Eliot added after she received her manuscript back from the publisher. The ratio of manuscript and printed pages will not always be the same. For instance, there are more manuscript pages but fewer printed pages in installment 2 compared to installment 1 because some pages have only a small amount of writing on them

(e.g., page 114 in installment 2 contains only one-and-three-quarter lines). Eliot's handwriting also varies somewhat as to space it occupies.

2. From installment 4 onward, Eliot began each new part over again with 1, instead of using continuous page numbering as she had for installments one through three. The only exception to this is in installment 10, where she took the last chapter of what she had originally planned for installment 9 and placed it as the first chapter in installment 10. Since she did not renumber her pages, installment 10 begins with final manuscript page numbers from the previous part.

3. Eliot's numbering for this part includes some renumbering too complex to be indicated parenthetically on the table in this appendix. She begins conventionally, running page numbers 1 to 38, with four superscript numbers, 7^a, 15^a, 34^a, and 37^a immediately following the pages with those numbers. Page 38 is followed by pages 39 and 40, and *then* by a 39^a and 40^a. The rest of the pages in the chapter proceed in sequence again with an additional two pages, 43^a and 54^a. Hence, sixty "base" pages plus eight superscript pages gives the installment total of sixty-eight pages. Normally, superscript pages follow immediately the page of the same number without the superscript; but sometimes Eliot left a sequence of old numbers that formed a consecutive unrevised part of her manuscript and simply added superscripts to them, when she had written new pages that preceded them and had the same number. This is what she did with chapter 3 of *Adam Bede*, where she inserted a new chapter and new pages 44 to 53, renumbering the pages at the beginning of the chapter that now became 4, so that pages 44 to 53 are followed by 44^a to 53^a.

4. The notation "58 & 59" appears at the head of a single page, obviously condensed from two pages that were rewritten. In order to avoid renumbering, Eliot simply headed them with this notation to indicate their place in the sequence. There are also two pages numbered 66. The final page was numbered by GE in pen as 72. A penciled notation written over that has the correct number, 74.

5. This installment also includes one page headed "17 & 18," obviously two pages condensed and recopied as one page, probably for the same reasons that the notation "58 & 59" heads a single page in the preceding installment.

6. As chapter 4 discusses in detail, Eliot obviously meant to include pages 67 to 72 in installment 9. At some point she realized that she needed or wanted to place them in installment 10 instead, but probably no longer had the manuscript in hand to renumber the pages or make any marks indicating the division. Her page 1, originally meant to begin installment 10, includes a notation in the upper left corner of the page, "'Cont' of Part X." The revised division of part 9 must have been included in a direction to George Smith, perhaps on the proofs.

7. The reason for the restarted numbering in the British Library pagination is that the first part of this installment is in bound volume 2, and the second (and larger) part in bound volume 3. Each volume starts with new BL pagination.

APPENDIX 3

1. Actual pages of text, not including the title page that began each part. The gaps in pagination between the two books in each volume are accounted for by the fact that the title page (recto and verso) was counted. When a book ended on a right-hand page, as it did whenever the ending number in this table was an uneven one, the back of the last page (although blank) was also counted. This happens with books 3 and 5 of *Middlemarch* and book 1 of *Daniel Deronda*. As this table shows, only "Miss Brooke" began its text with page 1.

2. Not including the prelude, which is three printed pages long, v–vii.

BIBLIOGRAPHY

Contemporary reviews of Eliot's novels are listed separately, in Appendix 1.

Altick, Richard D. *The English Common Reader: A Social History of the Mass Reading Public 1800–1900.* Chicago: U of Chicago P, 1957.
———. *Victorian Studies in Scarlet.* New York: W. W. Norton, 1970.
———. *Writers, Readers, and Occasions: Selected Essays on Victorian Literature and Life.* Columbus: Ohio State UP, 1989.
Anderson, R. F. "Negotiating for *The Mill on the Floss.*" *Publishing History* 2 (1977): 27–39.
———. "Things Wisely Ordered: John Blackwood, George Eliot, and the Publication of *Romola.*" *Publishing History* 11 (1982): 5–39.
Anderson, Roland F. "George Eliot Provoked: John Blackwood and Chapter Seventeen of *Adam Bede.*" *Modern Philology* 71 (1973–74): 39–47.
Ashton, Jean W. *Harriet Beecher Stowe: A Reference Guide.* Reference Guides in Literature. Boston: G. K. Hall: 1977.
Barry, James Donald. *The Literary Reputation of George Eliot.* Diss. Northwestern U, 1955. Ann Arbor: UMI, 1988.
Bauer, Carol, and Lawrence Ritt. "'A Husband Is a Beating Animal': Frances Power Cobbe Confronts the Wife-Abuse Problem in Victorian England." *International Journal of Women's Studies* 6 (1983): 99–108.
Beaty, Jerome. Middlemarch *from Notebook to Novel: A Study of George Eliot's Creative Method.* Illinois Studies in Language and Literature 47. Urbana: U of Illinois P, 1960.
Beer, Gillian. *George Eliot.* Key Women Writers Ser. Bloomington: Indiana UP, 1986.
Bennett, Scott. "Revolutions in Thought: Serial Publication and the Mass Market for Reading." *The Victorian Periodical Press: Samplings and Soundings.* Eds. Joanne Shattock and Michael Wolff. Leicester: Leicester UP; Toronto: U of Toronto P, 1982. 225–57.
Benson, James D. "'Sympathetic' Criticism: George Eliot's Response to Contemporary Reviewing." *Nineteenth-Century Fiction* 29 (1975): 428–440.
Bodenheimer, Rosemarie. *The Politics of Story in Victorian Social Fiction.* Ithaca: Cornell UP, 1988.

Bold, Alan, ed. *Smollett: Author of the First Distinction*. Totowa, NJ: Barnes & Noble, 1982.

Bonaparte, Felicia. *The Triptych and the Cross: The Central Myths of George Eliot's Poetic Imagination*. New York: New York UP, 1979.

——. *Will and Destiny: Morality and Tragedy in George Eliot's Novels*. New York: New York UP, 1975.

Boyle, Thomas. *Black Swine in the Sewers of Hampstead: Beneath the Surface of Victorian Sensationalism*. New York: Viking, 1989.

Brittain, Vera. *Testament of Youth: An Autobiographical Study of the Years 1900–1925*. New York: Penguin, 1989.

Brown, Lucy. *Victorian News and Newspapers*. Oxford: Clarendon P, 1985.

Butt, John, and Kathleen Tillotson. *Dickens at Work*. Fair Lawn, NJ: Essential Books, 1958.

Carpenter, Mary Wilson. *George Eliot and the Landscape of Time: Narrative Form and Protestant Apocalyptic History*. Studies in Religion Ser. Chapel Hill: U of North Carolina P, 1986.

Carroll, David, ed. *George Eliot: The Critical Heritage*. The Critical Heritage Ser. New York: Barnes & Noble, 1971.

——, ed. Introduction. *Middlemarch*. By George Eliot. Oxford: Clarendon P, 1986. xiii–lxxxv.

Chapman, Raymond. *The Sense of the Past in Victorian Literature*. New York: St. Martin's P, 1986.

Clubbe, John, and Jerome Meckier, eds. *Victorian Perspectives: Six Essays*. Newark: U of Delaware P, 1989.

Cobbe, Frances Power. "Wife-Torture in England." *The Contemporary Review* 32 (April 1878): 55–87.

Collin, Dorothy W. "The Composition and Publication of Elizabeth Gaskell's *Cranford*." *Bulletin of the John Rylands University Library* 69 (1986): 59–95.

Collins, William Wilkie. *The Moonstone*. Ed. J. I. M. Stewart. New York: Penguin, 1966.

——. *The Woman in White*. Ed. Harvey Peter Sucksmith. New York: Oxford UP, 1973.

Coolidge Jr., Archibald C. *Charles Dickens as Serial Novelist*. Ames: Iowa State UP, 1967.

"Cresswell, Sir Cresswell." *Dictionary of National Biography* 5: 72–73.

David, Deirdre. *Intellectual Women and Victorian Patriarchy: Harriet Martineau, Elizabeth Barrett Browning, George Eliot*. Ithaca, NY: Cornell UP, 1987.

Dickens, Charles, Carlo Fruttero, and Franco Lucentini. *The D. Case, The Truth about the Mystery of Edwin Drood*. Trans. Gregory Dowling. 1989. New York: Harcourt Brace Jovanovich, 1992.

Dickens, Charles. *Dombey and Son*. Ed. Peter Fairclough. New York: Penguin, 1985.

———. *Great Expectations*. Ed. Angus Calder. New York: Penguin, 1967.

———. *The Letters of Charles Dickens*. Ed. Madeline House, Graham Storey, and Kathleen Tillotson. Pilgrim Edition. 6 vol. to date. Oxford: Clarendon P, 1965– .

———. *The Life and Adventures of Nicholas Nickleby*. Reproduced in facsimile from the original monthly parts of 1838–39. 2 vols. Philadelphia: U of Pennsylvania P, 1982.

———. *Our Mutual Friend*. Ed. Michael Cotsell. World's Classics. New York: Oxford UP, 1989.

———. *Pickwick Papers*. Chicago: New American Library, 1964.

———. "Postscript. In lieu of Preface." *Our Mutual Friend*. Ed. Michael Cotsell. World's Classics. New York: Oxford UP, 1989. 821–22.

———. "Preface to the Original Edition, 1839." *Nicholas Nickleby*. Ed. Michael Slater. New York: Penguin Books, 1978 (rpt 1987). 45–47.

———. *A Tale of Two Cities*. Ed. George Woodcock. New York: Penguin, 1970.

Eco, Umberto. "Interpreting Serials." *The Limits of Interpretation*. Bloomington: Indiana UP, 1990. 83–100.

Eliot, George. *Adam Bede*. Ed. Stephen Gill. New York: Penguin, 1980.

———. *Daniel Deronda*. Ed. Graham Handley. Clarendon Edition of the Novels of George Eliot. Oxford: Clarendon P, 1984.

———. *Essays of George Eliot*. Ed. Thomas Pinney. New York: Columbia UP, 1963.

———. *Felix Holt*. Ed. Peter Coveney. 1866. New York: Penguin, 1979.

———. *The George Eliot Letters*. Ed. Gordon S. Haight. 9 vols. New Haven: Yale UP, 1954, 1978.

———. *Middlemarch*. Ed. David Carroll. Clarendon Edition of the Novels of George Eliot. Oxford: Clarendon P, 1986.

———. *The Mill on the Floss*. Ed. Gordon S. Haight. Clarendon Edition of the Novels of George Eliot. Oxford: Clarendon P, 1980.

———. *Romola*. Ed. Andrew Brown. Clarendon Edition of the Novels of George Eliot. Oxford: Clarendon P, 1993.

———. *Scenes of Clerical Life*. Ed. Thomas A. Noble. Clarendon Edition of the Novels of George Eliot. Oxford: Clarendon P, 1985.

———. *A Writer's Notebook, 1854–1879, and Uncollected Writings*. Ed. Joseph Wiesenfarth. Charlottesville: UP of Virginia, 1981.

Fenves, Peter. "Exiling the Encyclopedia: The Individual in 'Janet's Repentance.'" *Nineteenth-Century Literature* 41 (1987): 419–44.

Ford, George H. *Dickens and His Readers: Aspects of Novel-Criticism since 1836*. Princeton: Princeton UP, 1955.

[Fraser, Louisa Melville]. "Hester Benfield." *Blackwood's Magazine* 81 (March 1857): 339–55.

Fryckstedt, Monica Correa. "Geraldine Jewsbury's *Athenaeum* Reviews: A Mirror of Mid-Victorian Attitudes to Fiction." *Victorian Periodicals Review* 23 (1990): 13–25.

Fulmer, Constance Marie. *George Eliot: A Reference Guide*. Boston: G. K. Hall, 1977.

Gaskell, Elizabeth. *Cranford / Cousin Phillis*. Ed. Peter Keating. New York: Penguin Books, 1986.

———. *The Letters of Mrs Gaskell*. Eds. J. A. V. Chapple and Arthur Pollard. Cambridge: Harvard UP, 1967.

[———]. "Our Society at Cranford." *Household Words. A Weekly Journal*. (Dec. 13, 1851): 265–74.

[———]. "Stopped Payment, at Cranford." *Household Words. A Weekly Journal*. (Apr. 2, 1853): 108–15.

Gatrell, Simon. *Hardy the Creator: A Textual Biography*. Oxford: Clarendon P, 1988.

Geibel, James Wayne. *An Annotated Bibliography of British Criticism of George Eliot, 1858–1900*. Diss. Ohio State U, 1969. Ann Arbor: UMI, 1970. 70–6780.

Graham, Walter. *The Beginnings of English Literary Periodicals: A Study of Periodical Literature, 1665–1715*. Rpt. 1926. New York: Octagon/Farrar, Straus and Giroux, 1972.

———. *English Literary Periodicals*. Rpt. 1930. New York: Octagon Books, 1966.

[Greg, Percy]. "Mr. Trollope's Novels." *National Review* 7 (October 1858): 416–35.

[Greenwood, Frederick]. "Notes on Denis Duval." *Cornhill* 9 (June 1864): 655–65.

Griest, Guinevere L. *Mudie's Circulating Library and the Victorian Novel*. Bloomington: Indiana UP, 1970.

Gussow, Mel. "'Drood' Evokes the Mirth of an English Music Hall." Rev. of *The Mystery of Edwin Drood*, by Charles Dickens and Rupert Holmes. Imperial Theater, New York. *New York Times* Dec. 8, 1985: H3.

Haight, Gordon S. *George Eliot: A Biography*. New York: Oxford UP, 1968.

Hamer, Mary. *Writing by Numbers: Trollope's Serial Fiction*. New York: Cambridge UP, 1987.

Handley, Graham. Introduction. *Daniel Deronda*. Ed. Graham Handley. Clarendon Edition of the Novels of George Eliot. Oxford: Clarendon P, 1984. xiii–xxxii.

———. "The Manuscript of Daniel Deronda: A Change in Sequence?" *George Eliot Fellowship Review* 18 (1987): 61–65.

Harden, Edgar F. *The Emergence of Thackeray's Serial Fiction*. Athens: U of Georgia P, 1979.

Hardy, Barbara, ed. *Middlemarch: Critical Approaches to the Novel*. New York: Oxford UP, 1967.

Hardy, Thomas. *A Pair of Blue Eyes*. Ed. Alan Manford. World's Classics. New York: Oxford UP, 1985.

Hawes, Donald. "George Eliot's 'Sayings.'" *George Eliot— George Henry Lewes Studies*. Nos. 20–21 (1992): 49–57.

Hildreth, Margaret Holbrook. *Harriet Beecher Stowe, A Bibliography*. N.p.: Archon Books, 1976.

Holmstrom, John, and Laurence Lerner, eds. *George Eliot and Her Readers: A Selection of Contemporary Reviews*. New York: Barnes & Noble, 1966.

Howells, W. D. *Fennel and Rue*. New York: Harper and Brothers, 1908.

———. *W. D. Howells. Selected Letters, Volume 3: 1882–1891*. Ed. Robert C. Leitz. Boston: Twayne, 1980. 6 vols.

———. *W. D. Howells. Selected Letters, Volume 5: 1902–1911*. Ed. William C. Fischer. Boston, Twayne, 1983. 6 vols.

Hudson, Derek. Introduction. *Master Humphrey's Clock* and *A Child's History of England*. By Charles Dickens. Oxford Illustrated Dickens. New York: Oxford UP, 1958. v–xi.

Hughes, Linda K., and Michael Lund. *The Victorian Serial*. Charlottesville: UP of Virginia, 1991.

Iser, Wolfgang. *The Act of Reading: A Theory of Aesthetic Response*. Baltimore: Johns Hopkins UP, 1978.

———. *The Implied Reader: Patterns of Communication in Prose Fiction from Bunyan to Beckett*. Baltimore: Johns Hopkins UP, 1974.

Jacobs, Joseph. "Mordecai: A Protest Against the Critics." *Macmillan's Magazine* 36 (June 1877): 101–11.

James, Louis. "The Trouble with Betsy: Periodicals and the Common Reader in Mid-Nineteenth-Century England." *The Victorian Periodical Press: Samplings and Soundings*. Eds. Joanne Shattock and Michael Wolff. Leicester: Leicester UP; Toronto: U of Toronto P, 1982. 349–66.

Jauss, Hans Robert. *Toward an Aesthetic of Reception*. Trans. Timothy Bahti. Minneapolis: U of Minnesota P, 1982.

Johnson, Edgar. *Charles Dickens, His Tragedy and Triumph*. Vol. 1. New York: Simon and Schuster, 1952. 2 vols.

Kalikoff, Beth. *Murder and Moral Decay in Victorian Popular Literature*. Nineteenth-Century Studies. Ann Arbor, MI: UMI Research P, 1986.

Kaplan, Fred. *Dickens, A Biography*. New York: William Morrow, 1988.

Kay, Donald. *Short Fiction in* The Spectator. Studies in the Humanities No. 8. University: U of Alabama P, 1965.

[Kaye, J. W.]. "Outrages on Women." *North British Review* 25 (May 1856): 233–56.

Kellett, E. E. "The Press." *Early Victorian England, 1830–1865*. Ed. G. M. Young. London: Oxford UP, 1934. 2: 3–97.

Kitchel, Anna Theresa, ed. *Quarry for* Middlemarch. Spec. issue *Nineteenth-Century Fiction* 4: (1950): 1–68.

Knapp, Lewis M., ed. *The Letters of Tobias Smollett*. Oxford: Clarendon P, 1970.

————. *Tobias Smollett, Doctor of Men and Manners.* New York: Russell and Russell, 1963.

Knoepflmacher, U. C. *George Eliot's Early Novels: The Limits of Realism.* Berkeley: U of California P, 1968.

Leavis, F. R. *The Great Tradition.* London: Chatto and Windus, 1948.

Lehmann, R. C., ed. *Charles Dickens as Editor: Being Letters Written by Him to William Henry Wills His Sub-Editor.* 1912. New York: Straus Reprint, 1971.

Levine, Philippa. *Victorian Feminism 1850–1900.* Tallahassee: Florida State UP, 1987.

[Lewes, G. H.] "Victor Hugo's Last Romance." *Blackwood's Magazine* 92 (August 1862): 172–82.

Lohrli, Anne, comp. Household Words: *A Weekly Journal, 1850–1859, Conducted by Charles Dickens.* Toronto: U of Toronto P, 1973.

Lund, Michael. "Clocking the Reader in the Long Victorian Novel." *Victorian Newsletter* 59 (1981): 22–25.

————. "Literary Pieces and Whole Audiences: *Denis Duval, Edwin Drood,* and *The Landleaguers.*" *Criticism* 28 (1986): 27–49.

Martin, Carol A. "Contemporary Critics and Judaism in *Daniel Deronda. Victorian Periodicals Review* 21 (1988): 90–107.

————. "Reading *Middlemarch* in Installments as Victorian Readers Did." *Approaches to Teaching* Middlemarch. Ed. Kathleen Blake. New York: MLA, 1990. 85–97.

————. "Revising *Middlemarch.*" *Victorian Periodicals Review* 25 (1992): 72–78.

Mayo, Robert D. *The English Novel in the Magazines, 1740–1815, with a Catalogue of 1375 Magazine Novels and Novelettes.* Evanston: Northwestern UP, 1962.

Miller, D. A. *The Novel and the Police.* Berkeley: U of California P, 1988.

Millet, Stanton. "The Union of 'Miss Brooke' and 'Middlemarch': A Study of the Manuscript." *JEGP* 79 (1980): 32–57.

Millgate, Michael. *Thomas Hardy, His Career as a Novelist.* New York: Random House, 1971.

Morris, Virginia. *Double Jeopardy: Women Who Kill in Victorian Fiction.* Lexington: UP of Kentucky, 1990.

Nelson, Harland S. *Charles Dickens.* TEAS 314. Boston: Twayne, 1981.

Noble, Thomas A. *George Eliot's* Scenes of Clerical Life. Yale Studies in English vol. 159. New Haven: Yale UP, 1965.

Nowell-Smith, Simon. *The House of Cassell, 1848–1958.* London: Cassell & Company Ltd., 1958.

[Oliphant, Mrs.]. "A Christmas Tale." *Blackwood's Magazine* (Jan. 1857): 74–86.

[————]. *The Athelings. Blackwood's Magazine* 79 (June 1856): 625–42; 80 (July 1856): 26–45; (Aug. 1856): 153–75; (Sept. 1856): 290–311; (Oct. 1856): 379–402; (Nov. 1856): 528–47; (Dec. 1856): 660–77; 81 (Jan. 1857): 42–57; (Feb.

1857): 189–204; (Mar. 1857): 282–97; (Apr. 1857): 465–79; (May 1857): 569–87; (June 1857): 719–30.

————. *William Blackwood and His Sons. Annals of a Publishing House.* 3 vols. Edinburgh: William Blackwood and Sons, 1897. Vols. 1 and 2.

Oppenlander, Ella Ann. *Dickens' All the Year Round: Descriptive Index and Contributor List.* Troy, NY: Whitson Publishing Co., 1984.

"Our Female Sensation Novelists," *Littell's Living Age* 78 (Aug. 22, 1863): 352–69. [Reprinted from the *Christian Remembrancer.*]

Paroissien, David, ed. *Selected Letters of Charles Dickens.* Boston: Twayne, 1985.

Patten, Robert L. *Charles Dickens and His Publishers.* Oxford: Clarendon P, 1978.

Paxton, Nancy L. *George Eliot and Herbert Spencer: Feminism, Evolutionism, and the Reconstruction of Gender.* Princeton: Princeton UP, 1991.

Perkin, J. Russell. *A Reception-History of George Eliot's Fiction.* Ann Arbor: UMI Research Press, 1990.

Pollard, Graham. "Serial Fiction." *New Paths in Book Collecting.* Ed. John Carter. 1934. Freeport, NY: Books for Libraries Press, 1967. 247–77.

Porter, Mrs. Gerald. *John Blackwood by His Daughter Mrs. Gerald Porter. Annals of a Publishing House.* 3 vols. Edinburgh: William Blackwood and Sons, 1898. Vol. 3.

Prager, Arthur. *The Mahogany Tree, An Informal History of Punch.* New York: Hawthorn Books, 1979.

Price, John Vladimir. "Smollett and the Reader in *Sir Launcelot Greaves.*" *Smollet: Author of the First Distinction.* Ed. Alan Bold. Totowa, NJ: Barnes & Noble, 1982. 193–208.

Rich, Frank. "State: 'Drood,' a Musical in the Park." Rev. of *The Mystery of Edwin Drood,* by Charles Dickens and Rupert Holmes. Delacorte Theater, New York. *New York Times* Aug. 23, 1985: C3.

Richardson, Abby Sage. "*Daniel Deronda.*" *Victoria* 28 (1876): 227–31.

Richetti, John J. *Popular Fiction Before Richardson, Narrative Patterns, 1700–1739.* Oxford: Clarendon P, 1969.

Rosenberg, Edgar. "A Preface to *Great Expectations*: The Pale Usher Dusts His Lexicons." *Dickens Studies Annual* 2 (1972): 294–335.

Sadleir, Michael. *The Evolution of Publishers' Binding Styles, 1770–1900.* Bibliographia: Studies in Book History and Book Structure. New York: Richard R. Smith, Inc., 1930.

Schlesinger, George. "A Tale of Two Cuckolds." *Durham University Journal* 48 (1986): 51–58.

Showalter, Elaine. "Desperate Remedies: Sensation Novels of the 1860s." *Victorian Newsletter* 49 (Spring 1976): 1–5.

Smith, George M. "Our Birth and Parentage." *Cornhill* 83 o.s. 10 3rd. ser. (June 1901): 4–17.

Smollett, Tobias. *The Life and Adventures of Sir Launcelot Greaves.* Ed. Peter Wagner. New York: Penguin Books, 1988.

Spector, Robert Donald. *Tobias George Smollett.* Updated Edition. Twayne's English Authors Series 75. Boston: Twayne, 1989.

Spencer, Herbert. *An Autobiography.* 1904. Vol. 2 of 2 vols. *The Works of Herbert Spencer.* Vol. 21. Osnabrück: Otto Zeller, 1966.

———. *The Study of Sociology.* 1880. *The Works of Herbert Spencer.* Vol. 12. Osnabrück: Otto Zeller, 1966. 21 vols.

Steig, Michael. *Stories of Reading: Subjectivity and Literary Understanding.* Baltimore: Johns Hopkins UP, 1989.

Stevick, Philip. *The Chapter in Fiction: Theories of Narrative Division.* Syracuse: Syracuse UP, 1970.

Stowe, Harriet Beecher. Anonymous Introductory Note. *Agnes of Sorrento. The Writings of Harriet Beecher Stowe.* Riverside edition. Vol. 7. New York: AMS P, 1967. 16 vols. vii–x.

Super, R. H. *The Chronicler of Barsetshire, A Life of Anthony Trollope.* Ann Arbor: U of Michigan P, 1988.

Sussman, Herbert L. *Victorians and the Machine: The Literary Response to Technology.* Cambridge: Harvard UP, 1968.

Sutherland, J. A. "Lytton, John Blackwood and the serialisation of 'Middlemarch.'" *Bibliotheck: A Scottish Journal of Bibliography and Allied Topics* 7 (1975): 98–104.

———. *Thackeray at Work.* London: Athlone P, 1974.

———. *Victorian Novelists and Publishers.* Chicago: U of Chicago P, 1976.

Sutherland, John. "Chips off the Block: Dickens's Serialising Imitators." *Dickens and Other Victorians.* Ed. Joanne Shattock. New York: St. Martin's, 1988.

———. "*Cornhill's* Sales and Payments: the First Decade." *Victorian Periodicals Review* 19 (Fall 1986): 106–8.

Taylor, Ina. *A Woman of Contradictions: The Life of George Eliot.* New York: Morrow, 1989.

Thackeray, William Makepeace. *Denis Duval. Cornhill* 9 (Mar. 1864): 257–91; (Apr. 1864): 385–409; (May 1864): 513–36; (June 1864): 641–54.

———. *The Letters and Private Papers of William Makepeace Thackeray.* Ed. Gordon N. Ray. 4 vols. New York: Octagon/Farrar, Straus and Giroux, 1946, 1973.

———. *The Newcomes.* 1853–55. Intro. M. R. Ridley. Everyman's Library. London: Dent; New York: Dutton, 1910, 1962.

———. *Vanity Fair: A Novel Without a Hero.* Ed. Geoffrey and Kathleen Tillotson. Boston: Houghton Mifflin Company, 1963.

Thomas, Keith. "The Double Standard." *Journal of the History of Ideas* 20 (1959): 195–216.

Tillotson, Geoffrey, and Kathleen Tillotson. Introduction. *Vanity Fair, A Novel*

Without a Hero. By William Makepeace Thackeray. Boston: Houghton Mifflin, 1963. v–xxxix.

Trollope, Anthony. *An Autobiography.* Intro. Bradford Allen Booth. Berkeley: U of California P, 1947.

———. *Barchester Towers.* New York: New American Library, 1963.

Trollope, T. Adolphus. *La Beata.* London: Chapman and Hall, 1861. 2 vols.

Tuchman, Gaye, with Nina Fortin. *Edging Women Out: Victorian Novelists, Publishers, and Social Change.* New Haven: Yale UP, 1989.

Uphaus, Robert W., ed. *The Idea of the Novel in the Eighteenth Century.* Studies in Literature, 1500–1800, No. 3. East Lansing, MI: Colleagues Press, 1988.

Vann, J. Don. "Dickens, Charles Lever and Mrs. Gaskell." *Victorian Periodicals Review* 22 (1989): 64–71.

———. *Victorian Novels in Serial.* New York: MLA, 1985.

Veeser, H. Aram. *The New Historicism.* New York: Routledge, 1989.

[Warren, Samuel]. "Tickler Among the Thieves! Extract from an Autobiography, with a Prefatory Notice." *Blackwood's Magazine* 79 (Feb. 1856): 200–08; 80 (Aug. 1856): 198–221.

[———]. "Tickler II. Among the Thieves!" *Blackwood's Magazine* 88 (Oct. 1860): 408–21.

[———]. "Tickler II. Again!" *Blackwood's Magazine* 92 (Oct. 1862): 481–502.

Wiesenfarth, Joseph. *Gothic Manners and the Classic English Novel.* Madison: U of Wisconsin P, 1988.

Wiles, R. M. *Serial Publication in England Before 1750.* Cambridge: Cambridge UP, 1957.

Williams, Raymond. *The Long Revolution.* New York: Columbia UP, 1961.

Wohl, Anthony S. *Endangered Lives: Public Health in Victorian Britain.* Cambridge, MA: Harvard UP, 1983.

Woodruff, Douglas. *The Tichborne Claimant: A Victorian Mystery.* New York: Farrar, Straus and Cudahy, 1957.

INDEX

Clerical Life, 32, 44–45, 47, 59–61, 65, 68–72, 77, 78–80, 89, 91, 92; in *Silas Marner*, 120–21
Pendennis, 20
Penny Magazine (S.D.U.K.), 15
Phillips, Samuel (novelist), 23
Pickwick Papers, 1, 5, 8–9, 17, 19–20, 30, 42–43, 50, 287–88n. 1, 295–96n. 32
Press, The (London), 120, 267, 269, 282, 283
Prime Minister, The, 18

Quarterly Review (London), 65, 73–74, 91, 267, 272, 278, 282, 283

Rambler, The, 5, 12
Reader (London), 140–41, 269
Realism, 241–42, 246, 250, 253, 254–55, 264; absence of, in Stowe's *Agnes of Sorrento*, 149; in *Adam Bede*, 96–97, 105, 299n. 2; Blackwood on, in *Scenes*, 38–39, 40, 63–68, 71–72, 295n. 31, 296n. 33; in *Daniel Deronda*, 254–58; and family readership of *Blackwood's*, 64–65, 66, 72–74; GE adherence to, in *Scenes of Clerical Life*, 52, 65–68, 295n. 32; in *Middlemarch*, 253; and reviewers of *Romola*, 139–40, 144–45; and reviewers of *Scenes*, 60–61, 68–76, 296–97n. 35; use of, in *Romola*, 139–40; use of, in *Scenes*, 32, 38–39, 40–41, 43, 45–46, 49–50, 52, 60–61, 79, 82, 90–92
Return of the Native, The, 57, 294n. 26
Revue des deux Mondes (Paris), 267
Robertson, James Craigie (reviewer for the *Quarterly Review*), 65, 73–74, 82, 91–92, 296n. 34, 296–97n. 35
Robinson Crusoe, serial republication of, 7, 288n. 2

Rogue's Life, A, 16
Romola: advantage of serialization for new subject, 125; Blackwood and plans to serialize in *Blackwood's Magazine*, 124–26, 129, 306n. 4; character of Tito improves serial reception of, 139–40, 152–56, 158; compared to other serial fiction, 158, 164; deadline pressures severe, 126–28, 130–37; disadvantages and risks of serializing, 124, 128, 130, 137–38, 141–43, 146–48; fails to improve *Cornhill Magazine* circulation, 305n. 2; GE decides against anonymity, 128–29; historical setting, 125, 137–49, 158, 307n. 12; illustrations for, 124, 130, 133, 134, 138, 160, 165, 177; monetary arrangements with *Cornhill Magazine*, 127, 128, 129, 180, 307n. 10, 307–8n. 13; negotiations to serialize in *Cornhill Magazine*, 123–25, 127–31, 133, 173, 180, 305n. 1, 306n. 4, 307n. 10, 307–8n. 13; prepublication delays in writing, 126–27, 128, 130; responses from friends and acquaintances, 133–34; reviews, 136, 137–44, 146–48, 169, 180, 267–70; serial endings, 148, 154–160, 162–80; serial readers expect love interest, 149–52, 157. *See also* Abuse, of wives; Bigamy; *Cornhill Magazine*; Smith, George
Ruth, 56

St. Paul's Magazine (London), 273
Saturday Review (London), 71–72, 81, 267, 272, 278, 299–300n. 8, 302–3n. 25
Scarlet Letter, The, 294n. 24
Scenes of Clerical Life: advantages of serializing, 33–34, 36, 42; "Amos" as Christmas story, 43, 46; *The Athelings* in *Blackwood's*, 45–46, 53, 56–57, 59–62, 78, 293n. 20; and "A

Christmas Tale" in *Blackwood's,*
43–44, 58, 60; clergy in, 35, 38–39,
44, 48, 62, 67–68, 69–70, 72, 74–
77, 80; early revelation of plot, 33,
59, 61, 62, 79–80, 88–89, 148;
"Hester Benfield" in *Blackwood's,*
53–60, 62, 78, 293nn. 19–21,
294nn. 22, 24; Janet like other
women, 83–87; Janet as victim, 78,
79–83, 86–88, 90; plan for linked
stories, 33, 40–41, 47, 65–66, 191,
298n. 46; propriety of subject matter, 38, 41, 58, 63–68, 72–74, 76,
77, 92, 96; realism in, 38–39, 41,
58, 64–66, 68, 69, 71–72, 79, 81–
82, 92; responses from friends and
acquaintances, 47, 76–77, 292–93n.
17; reviews, 35, 43–45, 55, 60–63,
68–77, 81, 106, 142, 181, 186, 265–
67; risks of serializing, 36–37, 38;
and serial ending in "Amos Barton,"
33, 46–49, 50–52; and serial endings in "Janet's Repentance," 53,
78–80, 82–83, 88–92; and serial
endings in "Mr Gilfil's Love-Story,"
53, 58–59; tradition of linked stories in *Cranford,* 42, 52, 292n. 12;
tradition of linked stories in *Pickwick Papers,* 42–43; and *What Will
He Do with It?* in *Blackwood's,* 63,
70, 115. *See also* Abuse, of wives;
Alcoholism; Anonymity; Blackwood, John; *Blackwood's Magazine;*
Deadlines (GE); Lewes, George
Henry; Serial installments, length of;
Women authors
Scott, Sir Walter, 22, 96–97, 138, 141,
148, 149, 254, 260
S.D.U.K. *See* Society for the Diffusion
of Useful Knowledge
Sensation fiction, 1, 43, 313n. 42,
323n. 10; and *Daniel Deronda,* 219,
224, 248–50, 256–57, 263, 264,
318–19n. 12; and *Middlemarch,* 194,
198, 250–53; and readers' and
reviewers' expectations, 219, 248–51,

254, 256–57, 263, 323n. 10; and
Romola, 148, 151–55, 158, 167, 175,
178, 313n. 4; and *Scenes of Clerical
Life,* 43, 53; and *Silas Marner,* 121;
themes, 56–58, 63–64, 297nn. 41–42
Serial installments, length of: in *Adam
Bede,* 100, 103; in *Daniel Deronda,*
181, 185, 213, 215–18, 234–35, 285
(Appendix 3), 325nn. 1–2; in *Middlemarch,* 181, 182, 184–85, 209,
285 (Appendix 3), 313n. 2, 325nn.
1–2; in *Romola,* 129–32, 133–37,
174, 180–81, 185, 284 (Appendix 2),
305–6n. 3, 307n. 10, 312–13n. 39,
323–24nn. 1–7; in *Scenes of Clerical
Life,* 120, 130, 301n. 14
Serialization: advantages of, 9–10, 12–
14, 15–16, 33–34, 36, 42, 125, 184–
86, 194–95, 196–97, 209, 222, 237,
244–46, 260–62; author-reader
relationship, 10–12, 26–28, 29–30,
260–61 (*see also* Serial reading, act
of); disadvantages of, 14–15, 16, 18–
25, 36, 38–39, 89, 110–11, 124, 130,
137–38, 141–43, 146–48, 186–87,
213, 248, 250–51, 261; kinds of, 5–
7, 8–9, 16–18, 182–85. *See also
under* Eliot, George, *and other Victorian authors*
Serial reading, act of: metaphors of,
240–41, 243; as process, 14, 28,
138–40, 146–47, 194–95, 196–97,
239–41, 299n. 2, 311n. 31, 312n. 33,
321n. 1; reader entanglement, 147–
48, 189–90, 210, 240, 246–47, 254–
59, 321n. 3; reader resistance, 255–
59, 321–22n. 4; readers as coauthors,
20–21, 26–28, 89, 194, 198, 244–46,
245–47, 255–59, 260–62, 322–23n.
8, 323n. 9; and the visual arts, 145,
243–44; volume reading vs., 11, 73,
74, 97–99, 137–38, 141, 142–43,
146–47, 224, 238–39, 243, 253–54,
260–61, 322n. 7. *See also* Eliot,
George; *and individual novels*
Serial reading, contemporary contexts,

STUDIES IN VICTORIAN LIFE AND LITERATURE

Richard D. Altick, Editor

The Presence of the Present:
Topics of the Day in the Victorian Novel
Richard D. Altick

The Imagined World of Charles Dickens
Mildred Newcomb

A World of Possibilities:
Romantic Irony in Victorian Literature
Clyde de L. Ryals

The Night Side of Dickens:
Cannibalism, Passion, Necessity
Harry Stone

Carlyle and the Search for Authority
Chris R. Vanden Bossche